THE WORLD'S CLASSICS

ALTON LOCKE, TAILOR AND POET.

AN AUTOBIOGRAPHY

CHARLE'S KINGSLEY (1819–75) was born at Holne, Devonshire, the son of an Anglican clergyman. He studied at King's College, London and at Cambridge, and himself took orders, becoming a rector of Eversley, Hampshire, in 1844 and holding the living until his death. He also became canon of Chester and later of Westminster. He returned to Cambridge as Regius Professor of Modern History in 1860. Influenced by the writings of Thomas Carlyle, and by his friendships with F. D. Maurice and Sidney Godolphin Osborne – 'S.G.O.', who wrote a long series of articles in *The Times* about social problems – he took a keen interest in the living and working conditions that led to Chartism. This is reflected in his first two novels, *Yeast* (1848) and *Alton Locke* (1850). A prolific writer with wide interests, he published a number of pamphlets and reviews, as well as poetry, lectures, and collections of sermons. His other novels include *Hypatia* (1853) and *Westward Ho!* (1855), and he wrote some very successful books for young readers, of which *The Heroes* (1856) and *The Water Babies* (1863) are the best known. An enthusiastic natural historian, he corresponded with Philip Gosse and Darwin about scientific matters. His controversy with J. H. Newman led to the latter's *Apologia pro Vita sua* (1864).

ELIZABETH CRIPPS is a senior lecturer at the Chelmer-Essex Institute of Higher Education, and also a tutor-counsellor for the Open University. She has published several articles on nineteenth-century children's literature.

THE WORLD'S CLASSICS

CHARLES KINGSLEY

Alton Locke

Tailor and Poet

An Autobiography

Edited by
ELIZABETH A. CRIPPS

Oxford   New York

OXFORD UNIVERSITY PRESS

Oxford University Press, Walton Street, Oxford OX2 6DP

Oxford New York Toronto
Delhi Bombay Calcutta Madras Karachi
Petaling Jaya Singapore Hong Kong Tokyo
Nairobi Dar es Salaam Cape Town
Melbourne Auckland
and associated companies in
Beirut Berlin Ibadan Nicosia

Oxford is a trade mark of Oxford University Press

Introduction, Notes, Bibliography, and Chronology
© *Elizabeth A. Cripps 1983*

This edition first published as a World's Classics paperback 1983
Reprinted 1987

British Library Cataloguing in Publication Data
Kingsley, Charles, 1819–1875
Alton Locke, tailor and poet.—(The World's classics)
I. Title II. Cripps, Elizabeth A.
823'.8[F] PR4844.A/
ISBN 0–19–281633–0

Library of Congress Cataloging in Publication Data
Kingsley, Charles, 1819–1875.
Alton Locke, tailor and poet.
(The World's classics)
Bibliography: p. 000
I. Cripps, Elizabeth A. II. Title.
PR4842.A4 1983 823'.8 83–4251
ISBN 0–19–281633–0 (pbk.)

Set by New Western Printing Ltd
Printed in Great Britain by
Hazell Watson & Viney Limited
Aylesbury, Bucks

CONTENTS

Introduction   vii

Note on the Text   xxi

Select Bibliography   xxiii

A Chronology of Charles Kingsley   xxvi

ALTON LOCKE, TAILOR AND POET   I

Explanatory Notes   391

ACKNOWLEDGEMENTS

I AM pleased to acknowledge the help and encouragement of Dr. M. D. Slater, of Birkbeck College, University of London, and of my husband, R. F. Cripps.

INTRODUCTION

'I MADE £150 by *Alton Locke*, and never lost a farthing; and I got, not in spite of, but by the rows, a name and a standing with many a one who would never have heard of me otherwise,'[1] wrote Charles Kingsley to his friend the author Thomas Hughes, a few years after the novel's first appearance. It was, in fact, the publication of *Alton Locke* in 1850 which established Kingsley as a well-known and controversial figure, an image he never entirely lost.

His first novel, *Yeast: a Problem*, serialized in *Fraser's Magazine* from July–December 1848, had already created a stir. It had been written, according to the Preface to the first edition, to 'call the attention of wiser and better men than I am to the questions which are now agitating the minds of the rising generation, and to the absolute necessity of solving them at once and earnestly'. His targets had been the game laws and the distress of the agricultural poor which, as rector of the country parish of Eversley in Hampshire, he had had the opportunity of observing at first hand.

The year 1848 had been an active one for him, and in the winter and the following spring a new novel had begun to take shape from the crowded experiences. It had been called at first 'The Autobiography of a Cockney Poet', and had again dealt with contemporary problems, in particular with Chartism. The novel was finally called *Alton Locke, Tailor and Poet. An Autobiography*.

In 1848, a year notable for revolutionary disturbances in all the countries of western Europe, England had not escaped tensions and the greatest of these had resulted from the gathering strength of the Chartist Movement. The Movement had begun in the 1830s, chiefly as a result of the changes brought about by the Industrial Revolution. The Reformed Parliament

[1] *Charles Kingsley. His Letters and Memories of his Life.* Ed. by his wife, London, 1877, I, p. 277.

of 1833 declined to extend the franchise and in the following year passed the hated Poor Law Amendment Act, which had the effect of forcing those seeking relief into workhouses. Discontent led to the issuing of a 'People's Charter' in the spring of 1838: this was a draft of a Bill to be presented to the House of Commons, containing provisions later famous as the 'six points', of which extension of the franchise to all male adults was the chief. The ten following years saw the growth of support for the Charter and fears that a 'Physical Force' group, led by Feargus O'Connor, a radical Irish MP, might incite the people to revolution. At some of the meetings of this group, red caps of liberty were worn, pistols carried, and banners held high with such exhortations as 'he that hath no sword, let him sell his garment and buy one'. There was talk of a general strike, and some Chartist leaders were given long terms of imprisonment. News that a third National Petition was to be presented by the Chartists to the Commons on 10 April filled many with alarm. A bill making it punishable by transportation to intend to intimidate Parliament by the use of force quickly reached a second reading, and elaborate military and para-military preparations were made, the military forces being put under the command of the Duke of Wellington. The event was an anticlimax. Persistent rain discouraged supporters, and uncertainty amongst the Chartist leaders led to the petition being taken ingloriously to the House in three hackney carriages. Instead of the boasted six million signatures, there were fewer than two million. The petition was rejected, and the subsequent discovery by the police of stores of crude weapons concealed about London contributed to a general loss of credit by the Chartists. The movement came to an end after a few more years, although all but one of the provisions of the Charter became law eventually.

Kingsley had reason to know about the defeat of the Chartists more intimately than the average middle-class gentleman who read apprehensively of their doings in the newspapers, since he had made a special journey from Eversley to London on the morning of the demonstration, and had remained for four days. He had stayed up nearly all that night writing political placards for public display, and two days later had joined with the theologian F. D. Maurice and others in founding a new periodical *The People's Friend* or *Politics for the People*. And on the following Sunday, he had preached to his congregation at Eversley about the Chartist disturbance.

This sudden whole-hearted involvement may seem a little unexpected, but Kingsley's concern with public disorder and the reasons for it had begun as early as 1831. He spoke of this in a lecture at Bristol, some years later. His pupil, John Martineau, also recalled Kingsley's reminiscences of how, as a schoolboy in Bristol, he had been shocked by the mob plundering, drinking and setting fire to property, while the cavalry waited for the terrified mayor to give the order to attack.[2] A similar scene occurs in *Alton Locke* (ch. XXVIII), where starving and enraged farm labourers loot and burn a farm and are then charged by the yeomanry.

While he was preparing to write *Yeast* in 1848, Kingsley had tried to go beyond gathering facts and observing from the detached position in which his profession and social class had placed him. He had wanted to know what it was like to be a working man, and so had become acquainted with Thomas Cooper, a self-educated shoemaker and poet and sometime active Chartist. Cooper's career to some extent parallels that of Kingsley's hero, Alton.[3] But about the time of the composition of *Alton Locke* Kingsley also got to know two other working men well. The first was Walter Cooper, Chartist and tailor. Kingsley sought his help with details of the tailoring trade for the novel. The second was Gerald Massey, 'our Chartist poet', as F. D. Maurice called him, self-educated son of poor parents, who had edited and written most of a working men's journal, the *Spirit of Freedom*. All three men probably helped Kingsley's understanding of a particular type of working man: intellectual, with literary aspirations and strongly-held political views.

At the end of 1849 another matter claimed his attention. The *Morning Chronicle*, in the course of a series of articles on 'London Labour and the London Poor', written by Henry

[2] *Letters and Memories*, I, pp. 22, 307–8.

[3] See L. Cazamian, *Kingsley et Thomas Cooper – étude sur une source d'Alton Locke*, Paris, 1903, and Cooper's autobiography, *The Life of Thomas Cooper*, Leicester University Press, 1971.

Mayhew, drew public attention to the terrible working conditions of the tailors and needlewomen. Kingsley's immediate response was the publication of a pamphlet called *Cheap Clothes and Nasty* under the pseudonym he used for his articles in *Politics for the People*, Parson Lot, adopted after he found himself in a minority of one during an earnest discussion amongst friends and said he felt much as Lot must have felt when he seemed 'as one that mocked' to his close companions. It set out the grim facts of the 'dishonourable' trade which it was the fate of most London tailors to be engaged in, facts he made use of to considerable effect in the novel. The solution was proposed of formation of co-operative associations by the workmen, and Kingsley and his friends actually sponsored such associations.

Kingsley was not alone in trying to increase public awareness of these acute social problems through writing novels. As government reports of official Commissions of Enquiry into a number of agricultural and industrial problems appeared during the 1830s and '40s, a growing number of writers produced literary counterparts. Dickens dealt in *Oliver Twist* (1837-8) with the indigent poor, faced with the workhouse; Frances Trollope in *Michael Armstrong* (1840) with bad urban labour relations; and Charlotte Elizabeth Tonna in *Helen Fleetwood* (1841) with the sufferings of the rural poor flocking to work in the new industrial towns. Disraeli had broadened the investigation to encompass the divide between the rich and the poor in *Sybil, or the Two Nations* (1845). Three years later Mrs. Gaskell's *Mary Barton* repeated this theme, referring significantly to the parable of Dives and Lazarus. In this novel a factory-hand murders the young son of his employer as a reprisal in an industrial dispute. Later, in *North and South* (1854), Mrs. Gaskell returned to the theme of rich and poor, master and man, attempting a more balanced presentation, and in the same year Dickens's *Hard Times* grew out of his investigation (for an article in *Household Words*) of the claims of the cotton workers involved in a strike and lock-out at Preston. Many of these novels touched on the plight of working women, especially in the clothing trade. Thomas Hood's 'Song of the Shirt', printed in the Christmas number of *Punch*, 1843, awakened the public conscience to the near-destitution of thousands of these women; this theme, especially their vulnerability to abuse and corruption, is echoed both in *Mary Barton* and Mrs. Gaskell's *Ruth* (1853), as well as in *Cheap Clothes and Nasty*, and in *Alton Locke*. At the same time the Brontës wrote on another aspect of the exploitation of women in their graphic representations of the life of the governess in *Jane Eyre* (1847), *Agnes Grey* (1847), and *Villette* (1853). Several writers besides Kingsley depicted violent outbreaks, threatening revolution, from Dickens in *Barnaby Rudge* (1841), to George Eliot in *Felix Holt, the Radical* (1866).

By the end of the 1840s, then, the scope of the novel had been greatly enlarged. As the reviewer of *Alton Locke* in *Fraser's Magazine* commented:

Fiction, no longer limiting her range to the domesticities, boldly invades those realms of politics and economy, upon the confines of which she has hitherto stopped short with hesitating tread and averted eyes. It is growing up into a kind of ambition amongst authors of all creeds, colours and capabilities, to write books 'with a purpose in them'.[4]

This enlarged potential of the novel was made use of by writers up until the end of the century and beyond – Charles Reade (1814–84), Mark Rutherford (1831–1913), George Gissing (1857–1903) and Israel Zangwill (1864–1926), treating much the same areas. All were concerned with the immediate plight of workers in a newly industrialized society and, more broadly, with the whole quality of their lives; in short, with what was known at the time as the 'Condition of England' question.

When *Alton Locke* was completed, in the spring of 1850, there was some difficulty in finding a publisher. J. Parker & Son, who had published both Kingsley's play *The Saint's Tragedy* and *Yeast*, thought they had suffered in reputation from the latter, and refused the new book. Macmillan & Co. also hesitated to accept it, perhaps anxious about the effect on their recently-established business in Cambridge of a novel which contained an attack on the University. Kingsley then offered it to Chapman & Hall, introduced to them by Carlyle

[4] *Fraser's Magazine*, XLII, November 1850, p. 574.

who had welcomed the prospect of 'a new explosion, or salvo of red-hot shot against the Devil's Dung-heap!'[5] It came out anonymously in August 1850, and went through three editions in two years.

The reception by the critics was mixed. There was still at that time a general feeling that fiction was meant to be mainly entertaining, and that a novel-with-a-purpose was a trap for the unsuspecting:

To open a book under the expectation of deriving from it a certain sort of pleasure, with, perhaps a few wholesome truths scattered amongst the leaves, and to find ourselves entrapped into an essay upon labour and capital, is by no means agreeable.[6]

Others objected more to what they took the purpose to be than to the fact that there was a political or social purpose at all. The most extreme reaction came from J. W. Croker (remembered today for his attack on Keats's *Endymion*) in the influential *Quarterly Review*.[7] Here *Alton Locke* in company with *Yeast*, a pamphlet by Maurice, and other writings found itself reviewed under the title 'Revolutionary Literature'. In the guise of Christian charity and sympathy for the poor, said Croker, two clergymen of the Church of England (whom he then named) are promulgating subversive and inflammatory ideas, and it is clear that they are Socialists, perhaps even Communists. Kingsley was probably more embarrassed than gratified by praise from *The Northern Star*, the old Chartist weekly, for the book's 'admirable exposition of the rotteness [*sic*] of our political and social system...It is...one of the finest, deepest and most eloquent invectives against society ever issued from the press'.[8] By contrast, an article in the *Revue des Deux Mondes*,[9] entitled 'Socialism and Democratic Literature in England', praised the novel for its scrupulous fairness in comparison with contemporary French fiction of a Socialist and

[5] *Letters and Memories*, I, p. 234.
[6] *Fraser's Magazine*, XLII, November 1850, p. 575.
[7] *The Quarterly Review*, LXXXIX, June–Sept. 1851, pp. 520–43.
[8] *The Northern Star*, 7 September 1850, p. 3.
[9] *Revue des Deux Mondes*. Nouvelle Période, lre Série, X May 1851, pp. 429–58.

revolutionary slant, calling it 'une enquête extra-parlementaire'. Most reviewers agreed that Kingsley's sympathetic involvement with his material made the book compelling reading, and praised his vivid realization of scene and incident, but for the hostile reviewers its good qualities only made the book more dangerous.

In the Cambridge part of the novel, Kingsley had an under-graduate oarsman refer to a rival eight as 'that dxxxd Jesus', a phrase fastened on by Croker, who called it an 'outrage'. This part of the novel, which is strongly critical of the Univer-sity, was later to prove something of an embarrassment to Kingsley after he had accepted in 1860 an invitation to become Regius Professor of Modern History at Cambridge. The Royal Commission of Enquiry into the state of the universities of 1850 had led to wide-ranging reforms being effected, and by 1862 much had improved, and Kingsley himself had become much more Establishment-minded. He revised the novel in this year, carefully writing out passages likely to give offence. Macmillan's advertisement for the edition included an extract from the new Preface written by Kingsley, addressed, 'To the Udergraduates of Cambridge': 'I have rewritten all that relates to Cambridge; while I have altered hardly one word in the book beside.'[10] Kingsley's remarks in the Preface make his motives apparent; he welcomes the changes and, convinced that the circumstances of undergraduate life which he had described as typical of the 1840s, the period of the novel's action, have ceased to exist, he does not wish to present a misleading picture. The tone of much of the Preface indicates how much he has become an upholder of what he once attacked.

Whatever the moral implications of his decision to revise the Cambridge part of the novel, on literary grounds it is to be regretted. Kingsley relied on his own memories of under-graduate life from 1838 to 1842, and there is plenty of in-dependent evidence to suggest that the Cambridge of the 1840s as it might have appeared to a young radical tailor is indeed the Cambridge of the 1850 edition of *Alton Locke*. At that date the statutes of the colleges were much as they had been since the Middle Ages, and most students studied only classics, with

[10] *The Publishers' Circular*, XXV, p. 186.

elementary mathematics and divinity. Many of George Locke's complaints about the system were true, too, for example that 'any man who wanted to get on, was forced to have a private tutor, besides his college one' (ch. XIII) and that the dons were keen to preserve the status quo for 'they get their living by it, and their livings, too, and their bishopricks, now and then' (ch. XIII). A historian of early Victorian Cambridge notes that three-quarters of the honours students as late as 1850 engaged private tutors during the greater part of their residence and that this was necessary, as college tutors were too few to meet their needs.[11] Kingsley himself, ironically, was to serve in this capacity when he was invited to be history tutor to the Prince of Wales. The idle dons who 'grew fat on port wine' (ch. XIII) are reflected in the diary kept by the University Registrar, Joseph Romilly. He records that eight Fellows of Trinity drank nine bottles of port in one evening, adding tersely – 'they drank like fishes!'[12] The rowdy behaviour of the undergraduates in the novel was also characteristic of mid-nineteenth century Cambridge. Drunkenness was common: Romilly noted in his diary for 23 January 1846: 'Today a Queen's man...paid me his fees: he was very drunk (reeling and stammering), and offered me sixpence.'[13] Numerous scenes of noise and barracking by students, especially outside the Senate House, have been recorded. Barnwell was still a haunt of prostitutes, as it had been all through the eighteenth century.

The result of the revisions is that Alton's prosperous cousin George's long and cynical analysis of the evils of the system is replaced by a discussion of the Tractarians, or High Church movement. The lively supper-party is cut; and we are no longer given Alton's critical observations on the undergraduates he saw during his stay. All of these omissions weaken the picture of university life, and remove from the text much of the exuberance and energy.

Kingsley's solutions of the major social and political problems raised in the novel are of not much more than historical interest

[11] D. A. Winstanley, *Early Victorian Cambridge*, London, 1940, pp. 410–11.
[12] Quoted by Winstanley, ibid., p. 397.
[13] Quoted by Winstanley, ibid., p. 417.

today, and were thought to be impractical and idealistic even in his own day. But his presentation of these problems does interest. His sympathy with the poor and the oppressed commands respect. Many of the questions he explores are still with us.

One such question is the fear and distrust which exist between social classes; and the choice of a hero who is both poet and working man allows its expression to be at once passionate and articulate. Alton Locke is one of a number of dissatisfied working-class heroes who began to invade the novel about the middle of the nineteenth century – others include John Barton in Mrs. Gaskell's *Mary Barton*, Stephen Blackpool in *Hard Times* and George Eliot's Felix Holt. In creating Alton Kingsley faced the difficulty of every author who sets out to write a novel with a working-class protagonist: how is he to tell his story in such a way as to hold the readers' attention and yet be realistic? Some of the reviewers complained that Alton was remarkably unrepresentative of his class in possessing such accomplishments as reading Latin and writing good prose, and in his whole manner of thinking. Yet Kingsley had deliberately created a spokesman who would be acceptable both to readers with a background like his own and also to working men. In addition, Kingsley distrusted realism as an end in itself in fiction. When Macmillan's suggested to him in 1857 that he try his hand at a novel of ordinary life, he replied:

The fault of the usual common life novels is...the insipid respectability (utterly untrue to life) of their personages...Let me go on, doing what I have always done, from *Yeast* and *Alton Locke* till now; showing how much of the heroical and tragical element, supposed to be dead, buried and white-washed over, survives in modern society, ready to reassert itself for evil and for good the moment a great cause or a great sorrow appears.[14]

Alton is certainly more disinterested and idealistic than an ordinary working man. Perhaps it is in his passionate resentment that he and the rest of his class are denied an education that he is most sympathetic and recognizable as a socially

[14] C. L. Graves, *The Life and Letters of Alexander Macmillan*, London, 1910, p. 93.

wronged and ambitious artisan, predecessor of Hardy's Jude, as well as of heroes of Gissing and Wells.

Like Wells, Kingsley has a habit of breaking into the narrative to give his opinion of a wide variety of matters; and both thought the opinions very important. 'Art', Kingsley wrote to George Brimley, 'ought to mean the art of pleasing and instructing, and, believe me, these passages in which the author speaks in his own person do so',[15] a statement very close to Wells's remark 'in some cases the whole art and delight of a novel may lie in the author's personal interventions'.[16] These authorial opinions are, in Kingsley's case, part of an intellectual exuberance which bursts out in attacks on anything from man-servants and Sabbatarianism to various Nonconformist sects in the church. This often results in lively prose, as in the witty parodies of O'Connor's rhetoric (ch. XX) and of Emerson's style and opinions in Mr. Windrush's speech (ch. XXII). One problem, however, for today's reader is that the text contains many references which can only be fully understood with the help of explanatory notes. On the other hand, an attraction of the novel is that these allusions and asides afford many fascinating glimpses of the contemporary scene.

The novel has a further period interest in its graphic and panoramic picture of Victorian England – the sweatshops of Bermondsey; the elegant drawing-rooms of the leisured classes; half-starved farm-workers in frozen fields; literary hacks in the dingy offices of political journals; Cambridge undergraduates. Frederic Harrison, one of the first to assess Kingsley's achieve-ments as a novelist after his death,[17] commented on how well he caught the spirit of his times, partly through the force of such 'scene painting'. Many of his descriptions have the merits of a good sketch, clearly and boldly drawn from life; with others, there is some heightening of effect.

Of the characters, Alton's mentor, Sandy Mackaye, by general agreement has proved the most memorable. His vitality is partly

[15] *Letters and Memories*, II, p. 40.
[16] See 'The Contemporary Novel' in *Henry James and H. G. Wells*, eds. L. Edel and G. N. Ray, London, 1958, p. 141.
[17] 'Charles Kingsley's Place in Literature', in *Studies in Early Victorian Literature*, London, 1895.

due to his resemblance to Thomas Carlyle. In common with others of his generation, Kingsley had found in Carlyle's writings a source of inspiration, especially at a time of religious doubt during his undergraduate days, and when later at Eversley he had turned to them again for their consideration of social questions. Sandy Mackaye has many of Carlyle's personal characteristics of appearance and manner; he thinks like him and echoes his phrasing as well as his sentiments. But Carlyle evidently did not recognize the likeness when he eventually read the book and praised 'the rugged old hero...a wonderfully splendid and coherent piece of Scotch bravura'.[18] Mackaye attracts interest beyond his role in the novel for his humanity and sympathy with the misery of others, and also for his sharp, uncompromisingly frank rebukes. An authoritative moral voice but no zealot he recognizes that men must make their mistakes but he never finds any satisfaction in seeing them proved wrong. With his insistence that 'naething was safe but gude Scots parrich and Athol brose' (whisky and honey), and his northern characteristics of habit and speech he is, as Carlyle remarked, entertaining in his exaggerated Scottishness; yet, paradoxically, he seems more lifelike than some of the other more realistically-drawn characters.

Perhaps this is because Kingsley's characters tend to be diagrammatic – there to illustrate a point. George Locke is endowed with every conceivable piece of good fortune: good looks, wealth, a place at Trinity (where he strokes the first eight and gets a double first), success in the courtship of Lillian, the Dean's daughter, and preferment in his chosen profession, the Church. Yet even he isn't altogether unbelievable. Such high-spirited and shamelessly cynical remarks as 'you know it isn't one out of ten [clergymen] who's ever entered a school, or a cottage even, except to light his cigar, before he goes into the church' (ch. XXIV) contrast amusingly with Alton's earnest expression of the working man's 'high idea of what a clergyman should be'. The encounters between the two cousins have a fierce animation which was perhaps a product of Kingsley's own preoccupations. Very probably he is drawing on his own inner debate about how far he was sacrificing his prospects to

[18] *Letters and Memories*, I, pp. 244–5.

his ideals by becoming involved in politics and in Christian Socialism.

For many of the minor characters, Kingsley with a few bold strokes sketches in caricatures who make his point with vigour. Skill in the art of 'fictional cartooning' has very appropriately been ascribed to him.[19] The Cockney tailors, the grim Mr. Wigginton, the rowdy, good-hearted medical students are crudely drawn but full of life and energy. They have their counterparts in the drawings of Hogarth, Cruikshank, and Rowlandson.

The Dean is much more subtly drawn, and is clearly the product of personal and shrewd observation. Kingsley showed characteristic boldness in depicting a type of senior churchman not uncommon at the time: one who saw no incongruity in devoting his time and talents to the pursuit of natural science in the study, while in the cathedral the service was an 'irreverent gabble', sparsely attended. The Dean's querulous complaints about Professor Brown, a rival scientist, also illustrate the dissensions in academic life and its occasional pettiness.

Among the women, Lillian is a conventional portrait of a shallow beauty, and is contrasted with her cousin Eleanor, an intellectual woman who is also strongly passionate. Her interest in the young poet is ambiguous: he at one time feels it vanity to think her jealous, yet she chooses to describe him as 'my servant...by the laws of chivalry', (ch. XL). This ambiguity keeps the reader in suspense as to the outcome of the courtship of Lillian. Alton's mother's attitude to her son is also ambiguous, but in her case the dictates of a harsh religious faith inhibit her affection. This is a powerful and consistent character study, which nevertheless acts as another shaft of criticism directed against those religious sects of which Kingsley disapproved.

The end of the novel is experimental and strange. The chapter 'Dreamland', (ch. XXXVI) is remarkable, like Tennyson's *In Memoriam*, for the use made of pre-Darwinian evolutionary ideas. Kingsley corresponded at various times with a number of eminent scientists on both sides of the evolutionary dispute: Philip Gosse, for example, Sir Charles Lyell, Thomas Huxley,

[19] See Thomas Byrom's Introduction to the Everyman edition of the novel, 1970.

and Darwin himself, and it is clear that he had a considerable knowledge of some of the theories preceding the publication of *On the Origin of Species* in 1859. In the chapter, the evolution of man from primitive life-forms is traced through a number of stages, and his achievement of a final state of moral and social perfection is prophesied. In his youth Kingsley experienced hallucinations and visionary dreams, some of which provided the material for an early poem 'Hypotheses Hypochondriacae'.[20] The vast landscapes and sensations of space and time in the poem anticipate this chapter. It is possible also to detect a similarity of style and mood in these passages and the opium dreams of De Quincey, as described in *Confessions of an English Opium Eater* (1822). In each case, the dreamer is shown in a state of fear and isolation; often he is an object of persecution and endures physical torment. In both writers the style of these passages is rhythmic, incantatory:

And I was a remora, weak and helpless, till I could attach myself to some living thing; and then I had power to stop the largest ship. And Lillian was a flying-fish, and skimmed over the crests of the waves on gauzy wings. And my cousin was a huge shark, rushing after her, greedy and open-mouthed. (ch. XXXVI)

I was stared at, hooted at, grinned at, chattered at, by monkeys, by paroquets, by cockatoos, I ran into pagodas; and was fixed, for centuries, at the summit, or in some secret rooms; I was an idol; I was the priest; I was worshipped; I was sacrificed.[21]

When defending the chapter against the criticisms of his friends, Kingsley wrote that 'those dreams come in for the very purpose of taking the story off the ground of the actual into the deeper and wider one of the ideal'.[22] He was referring to the social and prophetic elements in it, and without doubt these were most important to him. But the chapter seems to have meaning of a different kind. Kingsley is able to convey obliquely through the allegory Alton's feelings about his rivalry

[20] *Letters and Memories*, I, pp. 31–2.
[21] De Quincey's *Confessions of an English Opium Eater*, ed. A. Hayter, London, 1971, p. 109.
[22] Quoted in the Prefatory Memoir by Thomas Hughes prefixed to the 1876 edition of *Alton Locke*.

with George, and his struggle against the physical sensations of animal strength and destructiveness; Kingsley could hardly, at that time, have described these directly. In this symbolic representation of frustration, defeat, inadequacy, isolation, a struggle to control violent elements in the personality, there is no doubt a reflection of Kingsley's own anxieties and emotional involvement. The myth itself perhaps fails to convince: the evolution of civilized man and the Christian Socialist ideal is diminished by the drama of Alton's personal struggle with his adversary.

The conclusion of the novel has been generally considered to be the least successful part. Eleanor's long sermonizing speeches are outside the natural development of the narrative and read like part of a tract on good Christian living, and Alton becomes docile and unquestioning. He does not become altogether implausible, however: religious conversion does imply an attitude of acceptance; and it is not improbable that a disillusioned young man should become passive under the influence of a new faith. The conclusion, though, cannot be defended against the charge of anticlimax. Readers must find Alton and Crossthwaite unconvincing as champions of the Chartist Cause, since they are prevented from taking any further active part by a period of exile, and by Alton's death.

Frederic Harrison wrote of Kingsley as 'splendidly defiant of all the conventions of literature and all the ten commandments of British society in 1849'.[23] The defiance can still be felt in this work of a young enthusiastic author, caught up in the issues of his time, and writing about them with energy and confidence. It is undoubtedly part of its charm today, as it was one of the reasons for its great impact in 1850.

[23] Harrison, op. cit., pp. 191–2.

NOTE ON THE TEXT

NEITHER the manuscript materials of *Alton Locke, Tailor and Poet. An Autobiography*, nor the fair copy made by Kingsley's wife for the publisher, seems to have survived. The novel was published as an anonymous work in two volumes in August 1850 by Chapman & Hall. A second edition, corrected by the author, appeared in 1851, and a third in September 1852; the latter was in one volume, and the anonymity of the author was dropped. A Cheap Edition (dated 1856) followed in December 1855, and at that time Kingsley sold the copyright to Chapman's. The proof sheets of these early editions were apparently destroyed by fire at Chapman & Hall's premises during the Second World War. The text of these editions was superseded by that of the Revised edition of 1862, published by Macmillan's. Kingsley rewrote part of the novel after he became Professor of Modern History at Cambridge, and the change in attitude which brought this about can be traced in the two prefaces he wrote: 'Preface Addressed to the Working Men of Great Britain' (1856) and 'Preface to the Undergraduates of Cambridge' (1862) (see Introduction above).

The present text is essentially a corrected version of the first edition – Kingsley himself was probably responsible for many of the corrections. The textual revisions made before 1862 are of three kinds: corrections of errors, the introduction of fresh dialect forms, and minor changes of wording. Some of the first are of particular interest: 'Preparing for Oxford and the Church' (ch. II) and 'One cousin an Oxford undergraduate' (ch. II) were corrected 'Cambridge', showing that Kingsley did not intend originally to write about his own university. The second group of revisions has been adopted because a letter of Kingsley's to Daniel Macmillan – 'May I put your brother in mind of his kind promise to look at the *Scotch* in the proofs for me, & see that it is "gude Dawric"?' – shows that he was aiming at verisimilitude. The Cheap Edition of 1856 introduced a considerable body of corruptions, which of course have been excluded.

House style has been adopted in the case of quotation marks, dashes, and asterisks, but in general the punctuation of the first edition has been retained. The original spelling has also been retained, but has been regularized when there are inconsistencies within the text.

Asterisks throughout the text refer to the present editor's notes at the end of the volume. Double asterisks indicate Kingsley's own occasional footnotes.

SELECT BIBLIOGRAPHY

(The place of publication of the works cited is London, unless otherwise stated.)

EDITIONS OF 'ALTON LOCKE': The original text of *Alton Locke, Tailor and Poet. An Autobiography* was reprinted three times by Chapman & Hall, in 1851, 1852, and 1856 (the Cheap Edition), and a Continental edition was published in Leipzig in 1857. It was revised and partly rewritten for a new edition, published by Macmillan's in 1862, and went through numerous reprints in this form in the latter years of the nineteenth century and the first decade of the twentieth. The revised text was reprinted by Cassell in paperback (1967, with an introduction by David Lodge), and by Dent in the Everyman series (1970, with an introduction by Thomas Byrom).

COLLECTED EDITIONS: *The Works of Charles Kingsley*, 28 vols., Macmillan, 1880–5; *The Pocket Edition of Charles Kingsley's Works*, 11 vols., Macmillan, 1895; *The Life and Works of Charles Kingsley*, 19 vols., Macmillan, 1901–3.

BIBLIOGRAPHY: James Forster, *A Bibliographical Catalogue of Macmillan & Co's. Publications from 1843 to 1889*, Macmillan, 1891; *The Cambridge History of English Literature*. eds. A. Ward and A. R. Waller, vol. VIII, Cambridge, 1907–27; Michael Sadleir in *Excursions in Victorian Bibliography*, Chaundy & Cox, 1922, and *Nineteenth-Century Fiction. A Bibliographical Record Based on his own Collection*, London and Los Angeles, 1951; M. L. Parrish and B. K. Mann, *Charles Kingsley and Thomas Hughes. First editions...in the Library at Dormy House*, Constable, 1936; in M. F. Thorp, *Charles Kingsley, 1819–75*, Princeton U.P., 1937; also in *Victorian Fiction. A Guide to Research*, ed. Lionel Stevenson, Cambridge, Mass., 1964, and *The New CBEL*, ed. G. Watson, vol. III, Cambridge, 1969–77.

BIOGRAPHY: The standard nineteenth-century biography is *Charles Kingsley. His Letters and Memories of his Life*, ed. by his wife, Frances E. Kingsley, 2 vols., C. Kegan Paul, 1877, (abridged rev. ed. 1879). There are also vivid contemporary sketches of Kingsley in Thomas Hughes's Prefatory Memoir to the 1876 edition of *Alton Locke*, in C. Kegan Paul's *Biographical Sketches*, Kegan Paul, 1833, in *Selected Letters of Malcolm Kingsley Macmillan*, Macmillan, 1893, and in F. M. Müller's *Auld Lang Syne*, Longmans, 1898.

There have been a number of twentieth-century biographies: S. E. Baldwin, *Charles Kingsley*, Ithaca, 1934; M. F. Thorp, *Charles Kingsley, 1819–75*, Princeton U.P.; G. Kendall, *Charles Kingsley and his Ideas*, Hutchinson, 1947; Una Pope-Hennessy, *Canon Charles Kingsley, a Biography*, Chatto & Windus, 1948; R. B. Martin, *The Dust of Combat. A Life of Charles Kingsley*, Faber, 1959; Susan Chitty, *The Beast and the Monk. A Life of Charles Kingsley*, Hodder & Stoughton, 1975, using new manuscript sources; B. Colloms, *Charles Kingsley: the Lion of Eversley*, Constable and Barnes & Noble, London and New York, 1975.

CRITICAL STUDIES: The only contemporary review of *Alton Locke* to have been reprinted seems to be W. R. Greg's in *Essays on Political and Social Science, contributed chiefly to 'The Edinburgh Review'*, vol. I, Longmans, 1853. The earliest important assessments of Kingsley's achievement as a novelist are to be found in Leslie Stephen, *Hours in a Library*, vol. III, Smith Elder, 1879, and F. Harrison, 'Charles Kingsley's Place in Literature', reprinted in *Studies in Early Victorian Fiction*, Edward Arnold, 1895. C. W. Stubbs, *Charles Kingsley and the Christian Social Movement*, Blackie & Sons, 1899, was the first to consider the social and political aspects of Kingsley's work, followed by C. E. Vulliamy, *Charles Kingsley and Christian Socialism*, Fabian Society Publications, 1914, and W. H. Brown, *Charles Kingsley: the work and influence of Parson Lot*, Co-operative Union Publications, Manchester, 1924. L. Cazamian's *Le Roman Social en Angleterre, 1830–1850*, Paris, 1903, (English translation 1973) is a well-known general study and

E. Baker, *The History of the English Novel*, vol. VIII, H. F. & G. Witherby, 1924–39, discusses Kingsley's romanticism.

Criticism since the 1930s has been fairly sparse, the novels being considered in biographies of Kingsley, in histories of the novel, and also in general works of a sociological character, for example there is some discussion of them in T. Christensen, *Origin and History of Christian Socialism, 1848–54*, Aarhus, 1962 and more recently there have been two intensive critical studies: one of the early works, M. Reboul, *Charles Kingsley – la Formation d'une Personalité et son affirmation Littéraire, 1819–1850*, University of Poitiers, Paris, 1973, and one from a Christian Socialist point of view, A. J. Hartley, *The Novels of Charles Kingsley. A Christian Social Interpretation*, Hour Glass Press, Folkestone, 1977. There is some comment on *Alton Locke* in two works which consider Kingsley as a writer of fantasy, C. Manlove, *Modern Fantasy: Five Studies*, C.U.P., 1975 and S. Prickett, *Victorian Fantasy*, Harvester Press, 1979. There is also a chapter on *Alton Locke* in C. Dawson, *Victorian Noon. English Literature in 1850*, Baltimore, 1979, and there are many references to the novel in S. M. Smith, *The Other Nation. The Poor in English Novels of the 1840's and 1850's*, Clarendon Press, Oxford, 1980.

A CHRONOLOGY OF
CHARLES KINGSLEY

1819   12 June: Born at Holne, Devonshire

1831   Attends Clifton School, Bristol. Witnesses the Bristol riots

1832–6 Attends Helston grammar school, Cornwall

1836   Father appointed vicar of St. Luke's, Chelsea

1836–7 Attends King's College, London, as a day student

1838–41 At Magdalene College, Cambridge

1842   July: Ordained. Becomes curate of Eversley, Hampshire

1844   10 Jan.: Marries Frances Eliza Grenfell. Appointed rector
        of Eversley

1848   *The Saint's Tragedy* published. Goes to London on occa-
        sion of presentation of Chartist petition to Parliament
        (10 April). *Politics for the People*, a weekly journal,
        started (11 April). Preaches at Eversley on the Chartist
        riots (16 April). Rejected by authorities of King's College,
        London, when proposed as a lecturer. July–Dec.: *Yeast:
        a Problem* serialized in *Fraser's Magazine*

1849   *Twenty-five Village Sermons* published. Oct.–Dec.: Works
        to subdue cholera outbreak in London

1850   Jan.: *Cheap Clothes and Nasty*, a pamphlet attacking
        abuses in the tailoring trade, published under pseudonym
        'Parson Lot'. Aug.: *Alton Locke, Tailor and Poet. An
        Autobiography*, 2 vols., published anonymously. Nov.:
        Helps to start new periodical *Christian Socialist, A
        Journal of Association*

1851   May: *Yeast: a Problem*, published anonymously. Preaches
        on 'The Message of the Church to Labouring Men' at
        St. John's, Fitzroy Square (22 June), and is subsequently
        forbidden by the Bishop of London to preach in the
        diocese. Visits Germany

1852   Jan.: *Hypatia: or, New Foes with an Old Face* begins in
            *Fraser's Magazine. Phaethon; or, Loose Thoughts for
            Loose Thinkers* published. *Sermons on National Sub-
            jects*, 1st Series, published

1853   April: *Hypatia: or, New Foes with an Old Face*, 2 vols.,
            published. Feb.: Part of deputation to Lord Palmerston
            on matters concerning sanitary reform. Mar.: Outbreak
            of Crimean War. *Alexandria and her Schools, Four
            Lectures delivered at the Philosophical Institution, Edin-
            burgh* published. *Sermons on National Subjects*, 2nd
            Series, 2 vols., published. *Who causes Pestilence? Four
            Sermons* published

1855   *Westward Ho! or, the Voyage and Adventures of Sir
            Amyas Leigh*, 3 vols., published. *Glaucus; or the Wonders
            of the Shore* published. *Sermons for the Times* published

1856   Jan.: *The Heroes: or Greek Fairy Tales for my Children*
            published

1857   *Two Years Ago. A Novel*, 3 vols., published

1858   *Andromeda and other Poems* published

1859   May: Appointed Chaplain-in-Ordinary to the Queen. *The
            Good News of God — Sermons*, and *Miscellanies*, re-
            printed chiefly from 'Fraser's Magazine' and 'The North
            British Review'*, 2 vols., published

1860   May: Appointed Regius Professor of Modern History at
            Cambridge

1861   Feb.: Becomes tutor in history to the Prince of Wales at
            Cambridge. *Town and Country Sermons* published

1862   Aug.–Dec.: *The Water Babies: a Fairy Tale for a Land-
            Baby*, serialized in *Macmillan's Magazine*; revised edition
            of *Alton Locke* published

1863   *The Water Babies: a Fairy Tale for a Land-Baby*, and
            The Gospel of the Pentateuch, a set of Parish Sermons
            published

1864   Chimney Sweepers' Act passed, owing partly to the
            impact on public opinion of *The Water Babies*. Engages
            in controversy with John Henry Newman and publishes
            What, then, does Dr. Newman Mean? in reply to New-
            man's pamphlet *Mr. Kingsley and Dr. Newman: a
            Correspondence on the question whether Dr. Newman*

teaches that truth is no Virtue. The Roman and the Teuton. A Series of Lectures delivered before the University of Cambridge published

1865   Jan.–Dec.: *Hereward the Wake, the Last of the English* serialized in *Good Words*, and *David. Four Sermons Delivered Before the University of Cambridge* published

1866   Joins the supporters of Edward John Eyre, ex-governor of Jamaica, who had crushed an insurrection there. *Hereward the Wake, the Last of the English*, 2 vols., published

1867   *Three Lectures delivered at the Royal Institute on the Ancien Régime, as it Existed on the Continent before the French Revolution*, and *The Water of Life, and Other Sermons* published

1868   *The Hermits*, 3 pts., and *Discipline, and other Sermons* published

1869   April: Resigns his chair at Cambridge. Aug.: Appointed Canon of Chester. Dec.: Visits the West Indies

1870   *Madame How and Lady Why, or First Lessons in Earth Lore for Children* published

1871   *At Last: a Christmas in the West Indies* published

1872   *Town Geology* and *Poems: collected edition* published

1873   March: Appointed Canon of Westminster. *Plays and Puritans, and Other Historical Essays*, and *Prose Idylls, New and Old* published

1874   Jan.–Aug.: Visits North America. *Health and Education*, and *Westminster Sermons* published

1875   *Lectures delivered in America* published. 23 Jan.: Dies; buried in Eversley Churchyard

ALTON LOCKE

TAILOR AND POET

AN AUTOBIOGRAPHY

CONTENTS

I	A POET'S CHILDHOOD	5
II	THE TAILORS' WORKROOM	20
III	SANDY MACKAYE	34
IV	TAILORS AND SOLDIERS	42
V	THE SCEPTIC'S MOTHER	53
VI	THE DULWICH GALLERY	62
VII	FIRST LOVE	75
VIII	LIGHT IN A DARK PLACE	84
IX	POETRY AND POETS	94
X	HOW FOLKS TURN CHARTISTS	100
XI	'THE YARD WHERE THE GENTLEMEN LIVE'	114
XII	CAMBRIDGE	124
XIII	THE LOST IDOL FOUND	133
XIV	A CATHEDRAL TOWN	156
XV	THE MAN OF SCIENCE	164
XVI	CULTIVATED WOMEN	169
XVII	SERMONS IN STONES	172
XVIII	MY FALL	178
XIX	SHORT AND SAD	185
XX	PEGASUS IN HARNESS	187
XXI	THE SWEATER'S DEN	196
XXII	AN EMERSONIAN SERMON	206
XXIII	THE FREEDOM OF THE PRESS	215

CONTENTS

XXIV	THE TOWNSMAN'S SERMON TO THE GOWNSMAN	221
XXV	A TRUE NOBLEMAN	231
XXVI	THE TRIUMPHANT AUTHOR	236
XXVII	THE PLUSH BREECHES TRAGEDY	243
XXVIII	THE MEN WHO ARE EATEN	254
XXIX	THE TRIAL	273
XXX	PRISON THOUGHTS	282
XXXI	THE NEW CHURCH	292
XXXII	THE TOWER OF BABEL	296
XXXIII	A PATRIOT'S REWARD	304
XXXIV	THE TENTH OF APRIL	319
XXXV	THE LOWEST DEEP	325
XXXVI	DREAM LAND	334
XXXVII	THE TRUE DEMAGOGUE	353
XXXVII	MIRACLES AND SCIENCE	365
XXXIX	NEMESIS	372
XL	PRIESTS AND PEOPLE	377
XLI	FREEDOM, EQUALITY, AND BROTHERHOOD	385

CHAPTER I

A POET'S CHILDHOOD

I AM a Cockney among Cockneys. Italy and the Tropics, the
Highlands and Devonshire, I know only in dreams. Even the
Surrey hills, of whose loveliness I have heard so much, are to
me a distant fairy-land, whose gleaming ridges I am worthy
only to behold afar. With the exception of two journeys, never
to be forgotten, my knowledge of England is bounded by the
horizon which encircles Richmond hill.

My earliest recollections are of a suburban street; of its jumble
of little shops and little terraces, each exhibiting some fresh
variety of capricious ugliness; the little scraps of garden before
the doors, with their dusty, stunted lilacs and balsam poplars,
were my only forests; my only wild animals, the dingy, merry
sparrows, who quarrelled fearlessly on my window-sill, ignorant
of trap or gun. From my earliest childhood, through long
nights of sleepless pain, as the midnight brightened into dawn,
and the glaring lamps grew pale, I used to listen, with a pleasant
awe, to the ceaseless roll of the market-waggons, bringing up
to the great city the treasures of the gay green country, the land
of fruits and flowers, for which I have yearned all my life in
vain. They seemed to my boyish fancy mysterious messengers
from another world: the silent, lonely night, in which they were
the only moving things, added to the wonder. I used to get out
of bed to gaze at them, and envy the coarse men and sluttish
women who attended them, their labour among verdant plants
and rich brown mould, on breezy slopes, under God's own clear
sky. I fancied that they learnt what I knew I should have
learnt there; I knew not then that 'the eye only sees that
which it brings with it the power of seeing.'* When will
their eyes be opened? When will priests go forth into the
highways and the hedges, and preach to the ploughman and
the gipsy the blessed news, that there too, in every thicket
and fallow field, is the house of God, – there, too, the gate of
Heaven?

I do not complain that I am a Cockney. That, too, is God's

gift. He made me one, that I might learn to feel for poor
wretches who sit stifled in reeking garrets and workrooms,
drinking in disease with every breath, – bound in their prison-
house of brick and iron, with their own funeral pall hanging
over them, in that canopy of fog and poisonous smoke, from
their cradle to their grave. I have drunk of the cup of which
they drink. And so I have learnt – if, indeed, I have learnt –
to be a poet – a poet of the people. That honour, surely, was
worth buying with asthma, and rickets, and consumption, and
weakness, and – worst of all to me – with ugliness. It was God's
purpose about me; and, therefore, all circumstances combined
to imprison me in London. I used once, when I worshipped
circumstance, to fancy it my curse, Fate's injustice to me, which
kept me from developing my genius, and asserting my rank
among poets. I longed to escape to glorious Italy, or some other
southern climate, where natural beauty would have become the
very element which I breathed; and yet, what would have come
of that? Should I not, as nobler spirits than I have done, have
idled away my life in Elysian dreams, singing out like a bird
into the air, inarticulate, purposeless, for mere joy and fullness
of heart; and taking no share in the terrible questionings, the
terrible strugglings of this great, awful, blessed time – feeling
no more the pulse of the great heart of England stirring me?
I used, as I said, to call it the curse of circumstance that I was
a sickly, decrepit Cockney. My mother used to tell me that it
was the cross which God had given me to bear. I know now
that she was right there. She used to say that my disease was
God's will. I do not think, though, that she spoke right there
also. I think that it was the will of the world and of the devil,
of man's avarice and laziness and ignorance. And so would my
readers, perhaps, had they seen the shop in the city where I was
born and nursed, with its little garrets reeking with human
breath, its kitchens and areas with noisome sewers. A sanitary
reformer would not be long in guessing the cause of my unhealthiness. He would not rebuke me – nor would she, sweet
soul! now that she is at rest in bliss – for my wild longings to
escape, for my envying the very flies and sparrows their wings
that I might flee miles away into the country, and breathe the
air of heaven once, and die. I have had my wish. I have made

two journeys far away into the country, and they have been enough for me.

My mother was a widow. My father, whom I cannot recollect, was a small retail tradesman in the city. He was unfortunate; and when he died, my mother came down, and lived penuriously enough, I knew not how till I grew older, down in that same suburban street. She had been brought up an Independent.* After my father's death she became a Baptist,* from conscientious scruples. She considered the Baptists, as I do, as the only sect who thoroughly embody the Calvinistic doctrines. She held it, as I do, an absurd and impious thing for those who believe mankind to be children of the devil till they have been consciously 'converted', to baptise unconscious infants and give them the sign of God's mercy on the mere chance of that mercy being intended for them. When God had proved, by converting them, that they were not reprobate and doomed to hell by His absolute and eternal will, then, and not till then, dare man baptise them into His name. She dared not palm a presumptuous fiction on herself, and call it 'charity'.* So, though we had both been christened during my father's lifetime, she purposed to have us rebaptised, if ever that happened – which, in her sense of the word, never happened, I am afraid, to me.

She gloried in her dissent; for she was sprung from old Puritan blood, which had flowed again and again beneath the knife of Star-Chamber butchers,* and on the battle-fields of Naseby and Sedgemoor.* And on winter evenings she used to sit with her Bible on her knee, while I and my little sister Susan stood beside her and listened to the stories of Gideon and Barak, and Samson and Jephthah,* till her eye kindled up, and her thoughts passed forth from that old Hebrew time home into those English times which she fancied, and not untruly, like them. And we used to shudder, and yet listen with a strange fascination, as she told us how her ancestor called his seven sons off their small Cambridge farm, and horsed and armed them himself to follow behind Cromwell, and smite kings and prelates with 'the sword of the Lord and of Gideon'.* Whether she were right or wrong, what is it to me? What is it now to her, thank God? But those stories, and the strict, stern Puritan education, learnt from the Independents and not the Baptists, which accompanied them, had their effect on me, for good and ill.

My mother moved by rule and method; by God's law, as she considered, and that only. She seldom smiled. Her word was absolute. She never commanded twice, without punishing. And yet there were abysses of unspoken tenderness in her, as well as clear, sound, womanly sense and insight. But she thought herself as much bound to keep down all tenderness as if she had been some ascetic of the middle ages – so do extremes meet! It was 'carnal', she considered. She had as yet no right to have any 'spiritual affection' for us. We were still 'children of wrath and of the devil',* – not yet 'convinced of sin', 'converted, born again'. She had no more spiritual bond with us, she thought, than she had with a heathen or a Papist. She dared not even pray for our conversion, earnestly as she prayed on every other subject. For though the majority of her sect would have done so, her clear logical sense would yield to no such tender inconsistency. Had it not been decided from all eternity? We were elect, or we were reprobate. Could her prayers alter that? If He had chosen us, He would call us in His own good time: and, if not,——. Only, again and again, as I afterwards discovered from a journal of hers, she used to beseech God with agonized tears to set her mind at rest by revealing to her His will towards us. For that comfort she could at least rationally pray. But she received no answer. Poor, beloved mother! If thou couldst not read the answer, written in every flower and every sunbeam, written in the very fact of our existence here at all, what answer would have sufficed thee?

And yet, with all this, she kept the strictest watch over our morality. Fear, of course, was the only motive she employed; for how could our still carnal understandings be affected with love to God? And love to herself was too paltry and temporary to be urged by one who knew that her life was uncertain, and who was always trying to go down to the deepest eternal ground and reason of everything, and take her stand upon that. So our god, or gods rather, till we were twelve years old, were hell, the rod, the ten commandments, and public opinion. Yet under them, not they, but something deeper far, both in her and us, preserved us pure. Call it natural character, conformation of the spirit, – conformation of the brain, if you like, if you are a scientific man and a phrenologist.* I never yet could dissect and map out my own being, or my neighbour's, as you analysts do. To me, I myself, ay, and each person round me, seem one inexplicable whole; to take away a single faculty whereof, is to destroy the harmony, the meaning, the life of all the rest. That there is a duality in us – a lifelong battle between flesh and spirit – we all, alas! know well enough; but which is flesh and which is spirit, what philosophers in these days can tell us? Still less had we two found out any such duality or discord in ourselves; for we were gentle and obedient children. The pleasures of the world did not tempt us. We did not know of their existence; and no foundlings educated in a nunnery ever grew up in more virginal and spotless innocence – if ignorance be such – than did Susan and I.

The narrowness of my sphere of observation only concentrated the faculty into greater strength. The few natural objects which I met – and they, of course, constituted my whole outer world (for art and poetry were tabooed both by my rank and my mother's sectarianism, and the study of human beings only develops itself as the boy grows into the man) – these few natural objects, I say, I studied with intense keenness. I knew every leaf and flower in the little front garden; every cabbage and rhubarb-plant in Battersea-fields* was wonderful and beautiful to me. Clouds and water I learnt to delight in, from my occasional lingerings on Battersea-bridge, and yearning westward looks toward the sun setting above rich meadows and wooded gardens, to me a forbidden El Dorado.

I brought home wild-flowers and chance beetles and butterflies, and pored over them, not in the spirit of a naturalist, but of a poet. They were to me God's angels, shining in coats of mail and fairy masquerading dresses. I envied them their beauty, their freedom. At last I made up my mind, in the simple tenderness of a child's conscience, that it was wrong to rob them of the liberty for which I pined, – to take them away from the beautiful broad country whither I longed to follow them; and I used to keep them a day or two, and then, regretfully, carry them back, and set them loose on the first opportunity, with many compunctions of heart, when, as generally happened, they had been starved to death in the meantime.

They were my only recreations after the hours of the small day-school at the neighbouring chapel, where I learnt to read, write, and sum; except, now and then, a London walk, with my mother holding my hand tight the whole way. She would have hoodwinked me, stopped my ears with cotton, and led me in a string, – kind, careful soul! – if it had been reasonably safe on a crowded pavement, so fearful was she lest I should be polluted by some chance sight or sound of the Babylon which she feared and hated – almost as much as she did the Bishops.

The only books which I knew were the Pilgrim's Progress and the Bible. The former was my Shakespeare, my Dante, my Vedas,* by which I explained every fact and phenomenon of life. London was the City of Destruction, from which I was to flee; I was Christian; the Wicket of the Way of Life I had strangely identified with the turnpike at Battersea-bridge end; and the rising ground of Mortlake and Wimbledon was the Land of Beulah – the Enchanted Mountains of the Shepherds. If I could once get there, I was saved: – a carnal view, perhaps, and a childish one; but there was a dim meaning and human reality in it nevertheless.

As for the Bible, I knew nothing of it really, beyond the Old Testament. Indeed, the life of Christ had little chance of becoming interesting to me. My mother had given me formally to understand that it spoke of matters too deep for me; that, 'till converted, the natural man could not understand the things of God': and I obtained little more explanation of it from the two unintelligible, dreary sermons to which I listened every dreary Sunday, in terror lest a chance shuffle of my feet, or a hint of drowsiness, – the natural result of the stifling gallery and glaring windows and gaslights, – should bring down a lecture and a punishment when I returned home. Oh, those 'sabbaths'! – days, not of rest, but utter weariness, when the beetles and the flowers were put by, and there was nothing to fill up the long vacuity but books of which I could not understand a word; when play, laughter, or even a stare out of window at the sinful, merry, sabbath-breaking promenaders, were all forbidden, as if the commandment had run, 'In it thou shalt take no manner of amusement, thou, nor thy son, nor thy daughter.' By what strange ascetic perversion has *that* got to mean 'keeping holy the sabbath-day'?

Yet there was an hour's relief in the evening, when either my mother told us Old Testament stories, or some preacher or two came in to supper after meeting; and I used to sit in the corner and listen to their talk; not that I understood a word, but the mere struggle to understand – the mere watching my mother's earnest face – my pride in the reverent flattery with which the worthy men addressed her as 'a mother in Israel',* were enough to fill up the blank for me till bed-time.

Of 'vital Christianity'* I heard much; but, with all my efforts, could find out nothing. Indeed, it did not seem interesting enough to tempt me to find out much. It seemed a set of doctrines, believing in which was to have a magical effect on people, by saving them from the everlasting torture due to sins and temptations which I had never felt. Now and then, believing, in obedience to my mother's assurances, and the solemn prayers of the ministers about me, that I was a child of hell, and a lost and miserable sinner, I used to have accesses of terror, and fancy that I should surely wake next morning in everlasting flames. Once I put my finger a moment into the fire, as certain Papists, and Protestants too, have done, not only to themselves, but to their disciples, to see if it would be so very dreadfully painful; with what conclusions the reader may judge.... Still, I could not keep up the excitement. Why should I? – The fear of pain is not the fear of sin, that I know of; and, indeed, the thing was unreal altogether in my case, and my heart, my common-sense rebelled against it again and again; till at last I got a terrible whipping for taking my little sister's part, and saying that if she was to die, – so gentle, and obedient, and affectionate as she was, – God would be very unjust in sending her to hell-fire, and that I was quite certain He would do no such thing – unless He were the Devil: an opinion which I have since seen no reason to change. The confusion between the King of Hell and the King of Heaven has cleared up, thank God, since then!

So I was whipped and put to bed – the whipping altering my secret heart just about as much as the dread of hell-fire did.

I speak as a Christian man – an orthodox Churchman (if you require that shibboleth). Was I so very wrong? What was there in the idea of religion which was presented to me at home to captivate me? What was the use of a child's hearing of 'God's great love manifested in the scheme of redemption', when he heard, in the same breath, that the effects of that redemption were practically confined only to one human being out of a thousand, and that the other nine hundred and ninety-nine were lost and damned from their birth-hour to all eternity – not only by the absolute will and reprobation of God (though that infernal blasphemy I heard often enough), but also, putting that out of the question, by the mere fact of being born of Adam's race? And this to a generation to whom God's love shines out in every tree and flower and hedge-side bird; to whom the daily discoveries of science are revealing that love in every microscopic animalcule which peoples the stagnant pool! This to working men, whose craving is only for some idea which shall give equal hopes, claims, and deliverances, to all mankind alike! This to working men, who, in the smiles of their innocent children, see the heaven which they have lost – the messages of baby-cherubs, made in God's own image! This to me, to whom every butterfly, every look at my little sister, contradicted the lie! You may say that such thoughts were too deep for a child; that I am ascribing to my boyhood the scepticism of my manhood; but it is not so; and what went on in my mind goes on in the minds of thousands. It is the cause of the contempt into which not merely sectarian Protestantism, but Christianity altogether, has fallen, in the minds of the thinking workmen. Clergymen, who anathematize us for wandering into Unitarianism* – you, you have driven us thither. You must find some explanation of the facts of Christianity more in accordance with the truths which we do know, and will live and die for, or you can never hope to make us Christians; or, if we do return to the true fold, it will be as I returned, after long, miserable years of darkling error, to a higher truth than most of you have yet learned to preach.

But those old Jewish heroes did fill my whole heart and soul. I learnt from them lessons which I never wish to unlearn. Whatever else I saw about them, this I saw, – that they were patriots, deliverers from that tyranny and injustice from which the child's heart, – 'child of the devil' though you may call him, – instinctively, and, as I believe, by a divine inspiration, revolts. Moses leading his people out of Egypt; Gideon, Barak, and Samson, slaying their oppressors; David, hiding in the mountains from the tyrant, with his little band of those who had fled from the oppressions of an aristocracy of Nabals; Jehu, executing God's vengeance on the kings – they were my heroes, my models;* they mixed themselves up with the dim legends about the Reformation-martyrs, Cromwell and Hampden, Sidney and Monmouth,* which I had heard at my mother's knee. Not that the perennial oppression of the masses, in all ages and countries, had yet risen on me as an awful, torturing, fixed idea. I fancied, poor fool, that tyranny was the exception, and not the rule. But it was the mere sense of abstract pity and justice which was delighted in me. I thought that these were old fairy tales, such as never need be realised again. I learnt otherwise in after years.

I have often wondered since, why all cannot read the same lesson as I did in those old Hebrew Scriptures – that they, of all books in the world, have been wrested into proofs of the divine right of kings, the eternal necessity of slavery!* But the eye only sees what it brings with it, the power of seeing. The upper classes, from their first day at school to their last day at college, read of nothing but the glories of Salamis and Marathon,* of freedom and of the old republics. And what comes of it? No more than their tutors know will come of it, when they thrust into the boys' hands books which give the lie in every page to their own political superstitions.

But when I was just turned of thirteen, an altogether new fairy-land was opened to me by some missionary tracts and journals, which were lent to my mother by the ministers. Pacific coral islands and volcanoes, cocoanut groves and bananas, graceful savages with paint and feathers – what an El Dorado! How I devoured them and dreamt of them, and went there in fancy, and preached small sermons as I lay in bed at night to Tahitians and New Zealanders, though I confess my spiritual eyes were, just as my physical eyes would have been, far more busy with the scenery than with the souls of my

audience. However, that was the place for me, I saw clearly.
And one day, I recollect it well, in the little dingy, foul, reeking,
twelve-foot-square back-yard, where huge smoky party-walls
shut out every breath of air and almost all the light of heaven,
I had climbed up between the water-butt and the angle of the
wall for the purpose of fishing out of the dirty fluid which lay
there, crusted with soot and alive with insects, to be renewed
only three times in the seven days, some of the great larvæ and
kicking monsters which made up a large item in my list of
wonders: all of a sudden the horror of the place came over me;
those grim prison-walls above, with their canopy of lurid
smoke; the dreary, sloppy, broken pavement; the horrible
stench of the stagnant cesspools; the utter want of form, colour,
life, in the whole place, crushed me down, without my being
able to analyse my feelings as I can now; and then came over
me that dream of Pacific Islands, and the free, open sea; and
I slid down from my perch, and bursting into tears threw
myself upon my knees in the court, and prayed aloud to God to
let me be a missionary.

Half fearfully I let out my wishes to my mother when she
came home. She gave me no answer; but, as I found out afterwards, – too late, alas! for her, if not for me, – she, like Mary,
had 'laid up all these things, and treasured them in her heart.'*

You may guess then my delight when, a few days afterwards,
I heard that a real live missionary was coming to take tea with
us. A man who had actually been in New Zealand! – the
thought was rapture. I painted him to myself over and over
again; and when, after the first burst of fancy, I recollected that
he might possibly not have adopted the native costume of that
island, or, if he had, that perhaps it would look too strange for
him to wear it about London, I settled within myself that he
was to be a tall, venerable-looking man, like the portraits of old
Puritan divines which adorned our day-room; and as I had
heard that 'he was powerful in prayer', I adorned his right-
hand with that mystic weapon 'all-prayer', with which
Christian, when all other means had failed, finally vanquishes
the fiend – which instrument, in my mind, was somewhat after
the model of an infernal sort of bill or halbert – all hooks,
edges, spikes, and crescents – which I had passed, shuddering,

once, in the hand of an old suit of armour in Wardour-street.

He came – and with him the two ministers who often drank tea with my mother; both of whom, as they played some small part in the drama of my after-life, I may as well describe here. The elder was a little, sleek, silver-haired old man, with a bland, weak face, just like a white rabbit. He loved me, and I loved him too, for there were always lollipops in his pocket for me and Susan. Had his head been equal to his heart! – but what has been was to be – and the dissenting clergy, with a few noble exceptions among the Independents, are not the strong men of the day – none know that better than the workmen. The old man's name was Bowyer. The other, Mr. Wigginton, was a younger man; tall, grim, dark, bilious, with a narrow forehead, retreating suddenly from his eyebrows up to a conical peak of black hair over his ears. He preached 'higher doctrine', *i.e.*, more fatalist and antinomian* than his gentler colleague, – and, having also a stentorian voice, was much the greater favourite at the chapel. I hated him – and if any man ever deserved hatred, he did.

Well, they came. My heart was in my mouth as I opened the door to them, and sank back again to the very lowest depths of my inner man when my eyes fell on the face and figure of the missionary – a squat, red-faced, pig-eyed, low-browed man, with great soft lips that opened back to his very ears; sensuality, conceit, and cunning marked on every feature – an innate vulgarity, from which the artisan and the child recoil with an instinct as true, perhaps truer, than that of the courtier, show-ing itself in every tone and motion – I shrank into a corner, so crestfallen that I could not even exert myself to hand round the bread-and-butter, for which I got duly scolded afterwards. Oh! that man! – how he bawled and contradicted, and laid down the law, and spoke to my mother in a fondling, patron-ising way, which made me, I knew not why, boil over with jealousy and indignation. How he filled his teacup half full of the white sugar to buy which my mother had curtailed her yesterday's dinner – how he drained the few remaining drops of the three-pennyworth of cream, with which Susan was stealing off to keep it as an unexpected treat for my mother at breakfast the next morning – how he talked of the natives, not as St. Paul might of his converts, but as a planter might of his slaves; overlaying all his unintentional confessions of his own greed and prosperity, with cant, flimsy enough for even a boy to see through, while his eyes were not blinded with the superstition that a man must be pious who sufficiently interlards his speech with a jumble of old English picked out of our translation of the New Testament. Such was the man I saw. I don't deny that all are not like him. I believe there are noble men of all denominations, doing their best according to their light, all over the world; but such was the one I saw – and the men who are sent home to plead the missionary cause, whatever the men may be like who stay behind and work, are, from my small experience, too often such. It appears to me to be the rule that many of those who go abroad as missionaries, go simply because they are men of such inferior powers and attainments that if they stayed in England they would starve.

Three parts of his conversation, after all, was made up of abuse of the missionaries of the Church of England, not for doing nothing, but for being so much more successful than his own sect; – accusing them, in the same breath, of being just of the inferior type of which he was himself, and also of being mere University fine gentlemen. Really, I did not wonder, upon his own showing, at the savages preferring them to him; and I was pleased to hear the old white-headed minister gently interpose at the end of one of his tirades – 'We must not be jealous, my brother, if the Establishment has discovered what we, I hope, shall find out some day, that it is not wise to draft our missionaries from the offscouring of the ministry, and serve God with that which costs us nothing except the expense of providing for them beyond seas.'

There was somewhat of a roguish twinkle in the old man's eye as he said it, which emboldened me to whisper a question to him.

'Why is it, sir, that in old times the heathens used to crucify the missionaries and burn them, and now they give them beautiful farms, and build them houses, and carry them about on their backs?'

The old man seemed a little puzzled, and so did the company, to whom he smilingly retailed my question.

As nobody seemed inclined to offer a solution, I ventured one myself.

'Perhaps the heathens are grown better than they used to be?'

'The heart of man', answered the tall, dark minister, 'is, and ever was, equally at enmity with God.'*

'Then, perhaps', I ventured again, 'what the missionaries preach now is not quite the same as what the missionaries used to preach in St. Paul's time, and so the heathens are not so angry at it?'

My mother looked thunder at me, and so did all except my white-headed friend, who said, gently enough——

'It may be that the child's words come from God.'

Whether they did or not, the child took very good care to speak no more words till he was alone with his mother; and then finished off that disastrous evening by a punishment for the indecency of saying, before his little sister, that he thought it 'a great pity the missionaries taught black people to wear ugly coats and trousers; they must have looked so much handsomer running about with nothing on but feathers and strings of shells.'

So the missionary dream died out of me, by a foolish and illogical antipathy enough; though, after all, it was a child of my imagination only, not of my heart; and the fancy, having bred it, was able to kill it also. And David became my ideal. To be a shepherd-boy, and sit among beautiful mountains, and sing hymns of my own making, and kill lions and bears, with now and then the chance of a stray giant – what a glorious life! And if David slew giants with a sling and a stone, why should not I? – at all events, one ought to know how; so I made a sling out of an old garter and some string, and began to practise in the little back-yard. But my first shot broke a neighbour's window, value seven-pence, and the next flew back in my face, and cut my head open; so I was sent supperless to bed for a week, till the seven-pence had been duly saved out of my hungry stomach – and, on the whole, I found the hymn-writing side of David's character the more feasible; so I tried, and with much brains-beating, committed the following lines to a scrap of dirty paper. And it was strangely significant, that in this, my first attempt, there was an instinctive denial of the very doctrine of 'particular redemption', which I had been hearing all my life, and an instinctive yearning after the very Being in whom I had been told I had 'no part nor lot'* till I was 'converted'. Here they are. I am not ashamed to call them, – doggrel though they be, – an inspiration from Him of whom they speak. If not from Him, good readers, from whom?

> Jesus, He loves one and all;
> Jesus, He loves children small;
> Their souls are sitting round His feet,
> On high, before His mercy-seat.

> When on earth He walked in shame,
> Children small unto Him came;
> At His feet they knelt and prayed,
> On their heads His hands He laid.

> Came a spirit on them then,
> Greater than of mighty men;
> A spirit gentle, meek and mild,
> A spirit good for king and child.

> Oh! that spirit give to me,
> Jesus, Lord, where'er I be!
> So—*

But I did not finish them, not seeing very clearly what to do with that spirit when I obtained it; for, indeed, it seemed a much finer thing to fight material Apollyons* with material swords of iron, like my friend Christian, or to go bear and lion hunting with David, than to convert heathens by meekness – at least, if true meekness was at all like that of the missionary whom I had lately seen.

I showed the verses in secret to my little sister. My mother heard us singing them together, and extorted, grimly enough, a confession of the authorship. I expected to be punished for them (I was accustomed weekly to be punished for all sorts of deeds and words, of the harmfulness of which I had not a notion). It was, therefore, an agreeable surprise when the old minister, the next Sunday evening, patted my head, and praised me for them.

'A hopeful sign of young grace, brother,' said he to the dark tall man. 'May we behold here an infant Timothy!'*

'Bad doctrine, brother, in that first line – bad doctrine, which I am sure he did not learn from our excellent sister here. Remember, my boy, henceforth, that Jesus does *not* love one and all – not that I am angry with you. The carnal mind cannot be expected to understand divine things, any more than the beasts that perish. Nevertheless, the blessed message of the Gospel stands true, that Christ loves none but His Bride, the Church. His merits, my poor child, extend to none but the elect. Ah! my dear sister Locke, how delightful to think of the narrow way of discriminating grace! How it enhances the believer's view of his own exceeding privileges, to remember that there be few that he saved!'

I said nothing. I thought myself only too lucky to escape so well from the danger of having done anything out my own head. But somehow Susan and I never altered it when we sang it to ourselves.

*

I thought it necessary for the sake of those who might read my story, to string together these few scattered recollections of my boyhood, – to give, as it were, some sample of the cotyledon leaves of my young life-plant, and of the soil in which it took root, ere it was transplanted – but I will not forestall my sorrows. After all, they have been but types of the woes of thousands who 'die and give no sign'.* Those to whom the struggles of every, even the meanest, human being are scenes of an awful drama, every incident of which is to be noted with reverent interest, will not find them void of meaning; while the life which opens in my next chapter is, perhaps, full enough of mere dramatic interest (and whose life is not, were it but truly written?) to amuse merely as a novel. Ay, grim and real is the action and suffering which begins with my next page, – as you yourself would have found, high-born reader (if such chance to light upon this story), had you found yourself at fifteen, after a youth of convent-like seclusion, settled, apparently for life – in a tailor's workshop.

Ay – laugh! – we tailors can quote poetry as well as make your court-dresses:

You sit in a cloud and sing, like pictured angels,
And say the world runs smooth – while right below
Welters the black fermenting heap of griefs
Whereon your state is built... *

CHAPTER II

THE TAILORS' WORKROOM

HAVE you done laughing? Then I will tell you how the thing came to pass.

My father had a brother, who had steadily risen in life, in proportion as my father fell. They had both begun life in a grocer's shop. My father saved enough to marry, when of middle age, a woman of his own years, and set up a little shop, where there were far too many such already, in the hope – to him, as to the rest of the world, quite just and innocent – of drawing away as much as possible of his neighbours' custom. He failed, died – as so many small tradesmen do – of bad debts and a broken heart, and left us beggars. His brother, more prudent, had in the meantime, risen to be foreman; then he married, on the strength of his handsome person, his master's blooming widow; and rose and rose, year by year, till, at the time of which I speak, he was owner of a first-rate grocery establishment in the city, and a pleasant villa near Herne Hill, and had a son, a year or two older than myself, at King's College, preparing for Cambridge and the Church – that being now-a-days the approved method of converting a tradesman's son into a gentleman, – whereof let artisans, and gentlemen also, take note.

My aristocratic readers – if I ever get any, which I pray God I may – may be surprised at so great an inequality of fortune between two cousins; but the thing is common in our class. In the higher ranks, a difference in income implies none in education or manners, and the poor 'gentleman' is a fit companion for dukes and princes – thanks to the old usages of Norman chivalry, which after all were a democratic protest against the sovereignty, if not of rank, at least of money.

The knight, however penniless, was the prince's equal, even his superior, from whose hands he must receive knighthood; and the 'squire of low degree', who honourably earned his spurs, rose also into that guild, whose qualifications, however barbaric, were still higher ones than any which the pocket gives. But in the commercial classes money most truly and fearfully 'makes the man'.* A difference in income, as you go lower, makes more and more difference in the supply of the common necessaries of life; and worse – in education and manners, in all which polishes the man, till you may see often, as in my case, one cousin a Cambridge undergraduate, and the other a tailor's journeyman.

My uncle one day came down to visit us, resplendent in a black velvet waistcoat, thick gold chain, and acres of shirt-front; and I and Susan were turned to feed on our own curiosity and awe in the back-yard, while he and my mother were closeted together for an hour or so in the living room. When he was gone, my mother called me in, and with eyes which would have been tearful had she allowed herself such a weakness before us, told me very solemnly and slowly, as if to impress upon me the awfulness of the matter, that I was to be sent to a tailor's work-rooms the next day.

And an awful step it was in her eyes, as she laid her hands on my head and murmured to herself, 'Behold, I send you forth as a lamb in the midst of wolves. Be ye, therefore, wise as serpents, and harmless as doves.'* And then, rising hastily to conceal her own emotion, fled upstairs, where we could hear her throw herself on her knees by the bedside, and sob piteously.

That evening was spent dolefully enough, in a sermon of warnings against all manner of sins and temptations, the very names of which I had never heard, but to which, as she informed me, I was by my fallen nature altogether prone: and right enough was she in so saying, though, as often happens, the temptations from which I was in real danger were just the ones of which she had no notion – fighting more or less extinct Satans, as Mr. Carlyle says,* and quite unconscious of the real, modern, man-devouring Satan close at her elbow.

To me, in spite of all the terror which she tried to awaken in me, the change was not unwelcome; at all events, it promised me food for my eyes and my ears, – some escape from the narrow cage in which, though I hardly dare confess it to myself, I was beginning to pine. Little I dreamt to what a darker cage I was to be translated! Not that I accuse my uncle of neglect or cruelty, though the thing was altogether of his commanding. He was as generous to us as society required him to be. We were entirely dependent on him, as my mother told me then for the first time, for support. And had he not a right to dispose of my person, having bought it by an allowance to my mother of five-and-twenty pounds a year? I did not forget that fact; the thought of my dependence on him rankled in me, till it almost bred hatred in me to a man who had certainly never done or meant anything to me but in kindness. For what could he make me but a tailor – or a shoemaker? A pale, consumptive, ricketty, weakly boy, all forehead and no muscle – have not clothes and shoes been from time immemorial the appointed work of such? The fact that that weakly frame is generally compensated by a proportionally increased activity of brain, is too unimportant to enter into the calculations of the great King Laissez-faire.* Well, my dear Society, it is you that suffer for the mistake, after all, more than we. If you do tether your cleverest artisans on tailors' shop-boards and cobblers' benches, and they – as sedentary folk will – fall a-thinking, and come to strange conclusions thereby, they really ought to be much more thankful to you than you are to them. If Thomas Cooper* had passed his first five-and-twenty years at the plough tail instead of the shoemaker's awl, many words would have been left unsaid which, once spoken, working men are not likely to forget.

With a beating heart I shambled along by my mother's side next day to Mr. Smith's shop, in a street off Piccadilly; and stood by her side, just within the door, waiting till some one would condescend to speak to us, and wondering when the time would come when I, like the gentlemen who skipped up and down the shop, should shine glorious in patent-leather boots, and a blue satin tie sprigged with gold.

Two personages, both equally magnificent, stood talking with their backs to us; and my mother, in doubt, like myself, as to which of them was the tailor, at last summoned up courage to address the wrong one, by asking if he were Mr. Smith.

The person addressed answered by a most polite smile and bow, and assured her that he had not that honour; while the other he–he'd, evidently a little flattered by the mistake, and then uttered in a tremendous voice these words——

'I have nothing for you, my good woman – go. Mr. Elliot! how did you come to allow these people to get into the establishment?'

'My name is Locke, sir, and I was to bring my son here this morning.'

'Oh – ah! – Mr. Elliot, see to these persons. As I was saying, my lard, the crimson velvet suit, about thirty-five guineas. By-the-bye, that coat ours? I thought so – idea grand and light – masses well broken – very fine chiaroscuro about the whole – an aristocratic wrinkle just above the hips – which I flatter myself no one but myself and my friend Mr. Cooke really do understand. The vapid smoothness of the door dummy, my lard, should be confined to the regions of the Strand. Mr. Elliot, where are you? Just be so good as to show his lardship that lovely new thing in drab and *bleu foncé*.* Ah! your lardship can't wait. – Now, my good woman, is this the young man?'

'Yes,' said my mother; 'and – and – God deal so with you, sir, as you deal with the widow and the orphan.'

'Oh – ah – that will depend very much, I should say, on how the widow and the orphan deal with me. Mr. Elliot, take this person into the office and transact the little formalities with her. Jones, take the young man upstairs to the workroom.'

I stumbled after Mr. Jones up a dark, narrow, iron staircase till we emerged through a trap-door into a garret at the top of the house. I recoiled with disgust at the scene before me; and here I was to work – perhaps through life! A low lean-to room, stifling me with the combined odours of human breath and perspiration, stale beer, the sweet sickly smell of gin, and the sour and hardly less disgusting one of new cloth. On the floor, thick with dust and dirt, scraps of stuff and ends of thread, sat some dozen haggard, untidy, shoeless men, with a mingled look of care and recklessness that made me shudder. The windows were tight closed to keep out the cold winter air; and the condensed breath ran in streams down the panes, chequering the dreary out-look of chimney tops and smoke. The conductor handed me over to one of the men.

'Here, Crossthwaite, take this younker and make a tailor of him. Keep him next you, and prick him up with your needle if he shirks.'

He disappeared down the trap-door, and mechanically, as if in a dream, I sat down by the man and listened to his instructions, kindly enough bestowed. But I did not remain in peace two minutes. A burst of chatter rose as the foreman vanished, and a tall, bloated, sharp-nosed young man next me bawled in my ear,——

'I say, young'un, fork out the tin* and pay your footing* at Conscrumption Hospital?'

'What do you mean?'

'Aint he just green? – Down with the stumpy* – a tizzy* for a pot of half-and-half.'*

'I never drink beer.'

'Then never do,' whispered the man at my side; 'as sure as hell's hell, it's your only chance.'

There was a fierce, deep earnestness in the tone which made me look up at the speaker, but the other instantly chimed in,—

'Oh, yer don't, don't yer, my young Father Mathy?* then yer'll soon learn it here if yer want to keep yer victuals down.'

'And I have promised to take my wages home to my mother.'

'O criminy! hark to that, my coves! here's a chap as is going to take the blunt* home to his mammy.'

'T'aint much of it the old'un 'll see,' said another. 'Ven yer pockets it at the Cock and Bottle, my kiddy, yer won't find much of it left o' Sunday mornings.'

'Don't his mother know he's out?'* asked another; 'and won't she know it——

> Ven he's sitting in his glory
> Half-price at the Victory.*

Oh! no, ve never mentions her – her name is never heard. Certainly not, by no means. Why should it?'

'Well, if yer won't stand a pot,' quoth the tall man, 'I will, that's all, and blow temperance. "A short life and a merry one," says the tailor——

> The ministers talk a great deal about port,
>   And they makes Cape wine very dear,
> But blow their hi's if ever they tries
>   To deprive a poor cove of his beer.*

Here, Sam, run to the Cock and Bottle for a pot of half-and-half to my score.'

A thin, pale lad jumped up and vanished, while my tormentor turned to me:

'I say, young'un, do you know why we're nearer heaven here than our neighbours?'

'I shouldn't have thought so,' answered I with a *naïveté* which raised a laugh, and dashed the tall man for a moment.

'Yer don't? then I'll tell yer. A cause we're a top of the house in the first place, and next place yer'll die here six months sooner nor if yer worked in the room below. Aint that logic and science, Orator?' appealing to Crossthwaite.

'Why?' asked I.

'A cause you get all the other floors' stinks up here as well as your own. Concentrated essence of man's flesh, is this here as you're a-breathing. Cellar work-room we calls Rheumatic Ward, because of the damp. Ground-floor's Fever Ward – them as don't get typhus gets dysentery, and them as don't get dysentery gets typhus – your nose 'd tell yer why if you opened the back windy. First floor's Ashmy Ward – don't you hear 'um now through the cracks in the boards, a-puffing away like a nest of young locomotives? And this here most august and upper-crust cockloft* is the Conscrumptive Hospital. First you begins to cough, then you proceeds to expectorate – spittoons, as you see, perwided free gracious for nothing – fined a kivarten* if you spits on the floor——

Then your cheeks they grows red, and your nose it grows thin,
And your bones they stick out, till they comes through your skin:

and then, when you've sufficiently covered the poor dear shivering bare backs of the hairystocracy——

> Die, die, die,
> Away you fly,
> Your soul is in the sky!*

as the hinspired Shakespeare wittily remarks.'

And the ribald lay down on his back, stretched himself out, and pretended to die in a fit of coughing, which last was, alas! no counterfeit, while poor I, shocked and bewildered, let my tears fall fast upon my knees.

'Fine him a pot!' roared one, 'for talking about kicking the bucket. He's a nice young man to keep a cove's spirits up, and talk about "a short life and a merry one". Here comes the heavy.* Hand it here to take the taste of that fellow's talk out of my mouth.'

'Well, my young'un,' recommenced my tormentor, 'and how do you like your company?'

'Leave the boy alone,' growled Crossthwaite; 'don't you see he's crying?'

'Is that anything good to eat? Give me some on it if it is – it'll save me washing my face.' And he took hold of my hair and pulled my head back.

'I'll tell you what, Jemmy Downes,' said Crossthwaite, in a voice which made him draw back, 'if you don't drop that, I'll give you such a taste of my tongue as shall turn you blue.'

'You'd better try it on then. Do – only just now – if you please.'

'Be quiet, you fool!' said another. 'You're a pretty fellow to chaff the orator. He'll slang you up the chimney afore you can get your shoes on.'

'Fine him a kivarten for quarrelling,' cried another; and the bully subsided into a minute's silence, after a *sotto voce* – 'Blow temperance, and blow all Chartists, say I!' and then delivered himself of his feelings in a doggrel song:

> Some folks leads coves a dance,
> With their pledge of temperance,
> And their plans for donkey sociation;
> And their pockets full they crams
> By their patriotic flams,*
> And then swears 'tis for the good of the nation.

But I don't care two inions
For political opinions,
While I can stand my heavy and my quartern;
For to drown dull care within,
In baccy, beer, and gin,
Is the prime of a working-tailor's fortin!

'There's common sense for yer now; hand the pot here.'

I recollect nothing more of that day, except that I bent myself to my work with assiduity enough to earn praises from Crossthwaite. It was to be done, and I did it. The only virtue I ever possessed (if virtue it be) is the power of absorbing my whole heart and mind in the pursuit of the moment, however dull or trivial, if there be good reason why it should be pursued at all.

I owe, too, an apology to my readers for introducing all this ribaldry. God knows it is as little to my taste as it can be to theirs, but the thing exists; and those who live, if not by, yet still beside such a state of things, ought to know what the men are like to whose labour, ay, life-blood, they owe their luxuries. They are 'their brothers' keepers',* let them deny it as they will. Thank God, many are finding that out; and the morals of the working-tailors, as well as of other classes of artisans, are rapidly improving: a change which has been brought about partly by the wisdom and kindness of a few master-tailors, who have built workshops fit for human beings, and have resolutely stood out against the iniquitous and destructive alterations in the system of employment.* Among them I may, and will, whether they like it or not, make honourable mention of Mr. Willis, of St. James's-street, and Mr. Stultz, of Bond-street.

But nine-tenths of the improvement has been owing, not to the masters, but to the men themselves; and who among them, my aristocratic readers, do you think, have been the great preachers and practisers of temperance, thrift, chastity, self-respect, and education? Who? – shriek not in your Belgravian saloons – the Chartists; the communist Chartists; upon whom you and your venal press heap every kind of cowardly execration and ribald slander. You have found out many things, since Peterloo;* add that fact to the number.

It may seem strange that I did not tell my mother into what

a pandemonium I had fallen, and get her to deliver me; but a delicacy, which was not all evil, kept me back. I shrank from seeming to dislike to earn my daily bread; and still more from seeming to object to what she had appointed for me. Her will had been always law; it seemed a deadly sin to dispute it. I took for granted, too, that she knew what the place was like, and that, therefore, it must be right for me. And when I came home at night, and got back to my beloved missionary stories, I gathered materials enough to occupy my thoughts during the next day's work, and make me blind and deaf to all the evil around me. My mother, poor dear creature, would have denounced my day-dreams sternly enough, had she known of their existence; but were they not holy angels from heaven? guardians sent by that Father, whom I had been taught *not* to believe in, to shield my senses from pollution?

I was ashamed, too, to mention to my mother the wickedness which I saw and heard. With the delicacy of an innocent boy, I almost imputed the very witnessing of it as a sin to myself; and soon I began to be ashamed of more than the mere sitting by and hearing. I found myself gradually learning slang-insolence, laughing at coarse jokes, taking part in angry conversations; my moral tone was gradually becoming lower; but yet the habit of prayer remained, and every night at my bedside, when I prayed to 'be converted, and made a child of God', I prayed that the same mercy might be extended to my fellow-workmen, 'if they belonged to the number of the elect.' Those prayers may have been answered in a wider and deeper sense than I then thought of.

But, altogether, I felt myself in a most distracted, rudderless state. My mother's advice I felt daily less and less inclined to ask. A gulf was opening between us; we were moving in two different worlds, and she saw it, and imputed it to me as a sin; and was the more cold to me by day, and prayed for me (as I knew afterwards) the more passionately while I slept. But help or teacher I had none. I knew not that I had a Father in heaven. How could He be my Father till I was converted? I was a child of the Devil, they told me; and now and then I felt inclined to take them at their word, and behave like one. No sympathising face looked on me out of the wide heaven – off the wide earth, none. I was all boiling with new hopes, new temptations, new passions, new sorrows, and 'I looked to the right hand and to the left, and no man cared for my soul.'*

I had felt myself from the first strangely drawn towards Crossthwaite, carefully as he seemed to avoid me, except to give me business directions in the workroom. He alone had shown me any kindness; and he, too, alone was untainted with the sin around him. Silent, moody, and pre-occupied, he was yet the king of the room. His opinion was always asked, and listened to. His eye always cowed the ribald and the blasphemer; his songs, when he rarely broke out into merriment, were always rapturously applauded. Men hated, and yet respected him. I shrank from him at first, when I heard him called a Chartist; for my dim notions of that class were, that they were a very wicked set of people, who wanted to kill all the soldiers and policemen, and respectable people, and rob all the shops of their contents. But, Chartist or none, Crossthwaite fascinated me. I often found myself neglecting my work to study his face. I liked him, too, because he was as I was – small, pale, and weakly. He might have been five-and-twenty; but his looks, like those of too many a working man, were rather those of a man of forty. Wild grey eyes gleamed out from under huge knitted brows, and a perpendicular wall of brain, too large for his puny body. He was not only, I soon discovered, a water-drinker, but a strict 'vegetarian' also; to which, perhaps, he owed a great deal of the almost preternatural clearness, volu-bility, and sensitiveness of his mind. But whether from his ascetic habits, or the unhealthiness of his trade, the marks of ill-health were upon him; and his sallow cheek, and ever-working lip, proclaimed too surely——

> The fiery soul which, working out its way,
> Fretted the pigmy body to decay;
> And o'er informed the tenement of clay.*

I longed to open my heart to him. Instinctively I felt that he was a kindred spirit. Often, turning round suddenly in the workroom, I caught him watching me with an expression which seemed to say, 'Poor boy, and art thou too one of us? Hast thou too to fight with poverty and guidelessness,

and the cravings of an unsatisfied intellect, as I have done!'
But when I tried to speak to him earnestly, his manner
was peremptory and repellent. It was well for me that so
it was – well for me, I see now, that it was not from him my
mind received the first lessons in self-development. For guides
did come to me in good time, though not such, perhaps, as
either my mother or my readers would have chosen for me.

My great desire now was to get knowledge. By getting that
I fancied, as most self-educated men are apt to do, I should
surely get wisdom. Books, I thought, would tell me all I
needed. But where to get the books? And which? I had
exhausted our small stock at home; I was sick and tired, without
knowing why, of their narrow conventional view of everything.
After all, I had been reading them all along, not for their
doctrines but for their facts, and knew not where to find more,
except in forbidden paths. I dare not ask my mother for books,
for I dare not confess to her that religious ones were just what
I did not want; and all history, poetry, science, I had been
accustomed to hear spoken of as 'carnal learning, human
philosophy', more or less diabolic and ruinous to the soul.
So, as usually happens in this life – 'By the law was the
knowledge of sin'* – and unnatural restrictions on the development of the human spirit only associated with guilt of conscience, what ought to have been an innocent and necessary
blessing.

My poor mother, not singular in her mistake, had sent me
forth, out of an unconscious paradise into the evil world,
without allowing me even the sad strength which comes from
eating of the tree of knowledge of good and evil; she expected
in me the innocence of the dove, as if that was possible on such
an earth as this, without the wisdom of the serpent to support it.
She forbade me strictly to stop and look into the windows of
print shops, and I strictly obeyed her. But she forbade me, too,
to read any book which I had not first shown her; and that
restriction, reasonable enough in the abstract, practically meant,
in the case of a poor boy like myself, reading no books at all.
And then came my first act of disobedience, the parent of many
more. Bitterly have I repented it, and bitterly been punished.
Yet, strange contradiction! I dare not wish it undone. But such

is the great law of life. Punished for our sins we surely are; and yet how often they become our blessings, teaching us that which nothing else can teach us! Nothing else? One says so. Rich parents, I suppose, say so, when they send their sons to public schools 'to learn life.' We working men have too often no other teacher than our own errors. But surely, surely, the rich ought to have been able to discover some mode of education in which knowledge may be acquired without the price of conscience. Yet they have not; and we must not complain of them for not giving such a one to the working man when they have not yet even given it to their own children.

In a street through which I used to walk homeward was an old book shop, piled and fringed outside and in with books of every age, size, and colour. And here I at last summoned courage to stop, and timidly and stealthily taking out some volume whose title attracted me, snatch hastily a few pages and hasten on, half fearful of being called on to purchase, half ashamed of a desire which I fancied every one else considered as unlawful as my mother did. Sometimes I was lucky enough to find the same volume several days running, and to take up the subject where I had left it off; and thus I contrived to hurry through a great deal of 'Childe Harold', 'Lara', and the 'Corsair' – a new world of wonders to me. They fed, those poems, both my health and my diseases; while they gave me, little of them as I could understand, a thousand new notions about scenery and man, a sense of poetic melody and luxuriance as yet utterly unknown. They chimed in with all my discontent, my melancholy, my thirst after any life of action and excitement, however frivolous, insane, or even worse. I forgot the Corsair's sinful trade in his free and daring life; rather, I honestly eliminated the bad element – in which, God knows, I took no delight – and kept the good one. However that might be, the innocent, guilty pleasure grew on me day by day. Innocent because human – guilty, because disobedient. But have I not paid the penalty?

One evening, however, I fell accidentally on a new book – 'The Life and Poems of J. Bethune'.* I opened the story of his life – became interested, absorbed – and there I stood, I know not how long, on the greasy pavement, heedless of the

passers who thrust me right and left, reading by the flaring
gas-light that sad history of labour, sorrow, and death. – How
the Highland cotter, in spite of disease, penury, starvation itself,
and the daily struggle to earn his bread by digging and ditching,
educated himself – how he toiled unceasingly with his hands –
how he wrote his poems in secret on dirty scraps of paper and
old leaves of books – how thus he wore himself out, manful and
godly, 'bating not a jot of heart or hope',* till the weak flesh
would bear no more; and the noble spirit, unrecognized by the
lord of the soil, returned to God who gave it. I seemed to see in
his history a sad presage of my own. If he, stronger, more self-
restrained, more righteous far than ever I could be, had died
thus unknown, unassisted, in the stern battle with social disadvantages, what must be my lot?

And tears of sympathy, rather than of selfish fear, fell fast
upon the book.

A harsh voice from the inner darkness of the shop startled
me.

'Hoot, laddie, ye'll better no spoil my books wi' greeting
ower them.'

I replaced the book hastily, and was hurrying on, but the
same voice called me back in a more kindly tone.

'Stop a wee, my laddie. I'm no angered wi' ye. Come in, and
we'll just ha' a bit crack thegither.'

I went in, for there was a geniality in the tone to which I was
unaccustomed, and something whispered to me the hope of an
adventure, as indeed it proved to be, if an event deserves that
name which decided the course of my whole destiny.

'What war ye greeting about, then? What was the book?'

' "Bethune's Life and Poems", sir,' I said. 'And certainly
they did affect me very much.'

'Affect ye? Ah, Johnnie Bethune, puir fellow! Ye maunna
take on about sic like laddies, or ye'll greet your e'en out o'
your head. It's mony a braw man beside Johnnie Bethune has
gane Johnnie Bethune's gate.'

Though unaccustomed to the Scotch accent, I could make
out enough of this speech to be in nowise consoled by it.
But the old man turned the conversation by asking me abruptly
my name, and trade, and family.

'Hum, hum, widow, er? puir body! work at Smith's shop, eh? Ye'll ken John Crossthwaite, then? ay? hum, hum; an' ye're desirous o' reading books, vara weel – let's see your cawpabilities.'

And he pulled me into the dim light of the little back window, shoved back his spectacles, and peering at me from underneath them, began, to my great astonishment, to feel my head all over.

'Hum, hum, a vara gude forehead – vara gude indeed. Causative organs large, perceptive ditto. Imagination super-abundant – mun be heeded. Benevolence, conscientiousness, ditto, ditto. Caution – no that large – might be developed,' with a quiet chuckle, 'under a gude Scot's education. Just turn your head into profile, laddie. Hum, hum. Back o' the head a'thegither defective. Firmness sma' – love of approbation unco big. Beware o' leeing, as ye live; ye'll need it. Philoprogenitive-ness gude. Ye'll be fond o' bairns, I'm guessing?'

'Of what?'

'Children, laddie, – children.'

'Very,' answered I, in utter dismay, at what seemed to me a magical process for getting at all my secret failings.

'Hum, hum! Amative and combative organs sma' – a general want o' healthy animalism, as my freen' Mr. Deville* wad say. And ye want to read books?'

I confessed my desire, without, alas! confessing that my mother had forbidden it.

'Vara weel; then books I'll lend ye, after I've had a crack wi' Crossthwaite aboot ye, gin I find his opinion o' ye satisfactory. Come to me the day after to-morrow. An' mind, here are my rules: – a' damage done to a book to be paid for, or na mair books lent; ye'll mind to take no books without leave; especially ye'll mind no to read in bed o' nights, – industrious folks ought to be sleepin' betimes, an' I'd no be a party to burning puir weans in their beds; and lastly, ye'll observe not to read mair than five books at once.'

I assured him that I thought such a thing impossible; but he smiled in his saturnine way, and said, –

'We'll see this day fortnight. Now, then, I've observed ye for a month past over that aristocrat Byron's poems. And I'm willing to teach the young idea how to shoot* – but no to shoot itself; so ye'll just leave alane that vinegary, soul-destroying trash,* and I'll lend ye, gin I hear a gude report of ye, "The Paradise Lost", o' John Milton – a gran' classic model; and for the doctrine o't, it's just aboot as gude as ye'll hear elsewhere the noo. So gang your gate, and tell John Crossthwaite, privately, auld Sandy Mackaye wad like to see him the morn's night.'

I went home in wonder and delight. Books! books! books! I should have my fill of them at last. And when I said my prayers at night, I thanked God for this unexpected boon; and then remembered that my mother had forbidden it. That thought checked the thanks, but not the pleasure. Oh, parents! are there not real sins enough in the world already, without your defiling it, over and above, by inventing new ones?

CHAPTER III

SANDY MACKAYE

That day fortnight came, – and the old Scotchman's words came true. Four books of his I had already, and I came in to borrow a fifth; whereon he began with a solemn chuckle:

'Eh, laddie, laddie, I've been treating ye as the grocers do their new prentices. They first gie the boys three days' free warren* among the figs and the sugar-candy, and they get scunnered* wi' sweets after that. Noo, then, my lad, ye've just been reading four books in three days – and here's a fifth. Ye'll no open this again.'

'Oh!' I cried, piteously enough, 'just let me finish what I am reading. I'm in the middle of such a wonderful account of the Hornitos of Jorullo.'*

'Hornets or wasps, a swarm o' them ye're like to have at this rate; and a very bad substitute ye'll find them for the Attic bee.* Now tak tent. I'm no in the habit of speaking without deliberation, for it saves a man a great deal of trouble in changing his mind. If ye canna traduce to me a page o' Virgil by this day three months, ye read no more o' my books.

Desultory reading is the bane o' lads. Ye maun begin with self-restraint and method, my man, gin ye intend to gie yoursel' a liberal education. So I'll just mak' you a present of an auld Latin grammar, and ye maun begin where your betters ha' begun before you.'

'But who will teach me Latin?'

'Hoot! man! who'll teach a man anything except himsel'? It's only gentlefolks and puir aristocrat bodies that go to be spoilt wi' tutors and pedagogues, cramming and loading them wi' knowledge, as ye'd load a gun, to shoot it all out again, just as it went down, in a college examination, and forget all aboot it after.'

'Ah!' I sighed, 'if I could have gone to college!'

'What for, then? My father was a Hieland farmer, and yet he was a weel learned man; and "Sandy, my lad," he used to say, "a man kens just as much as he's taught himsel', and na mair. So get wisdom; and wi' all your getting, get understanding." And so I did. And mony's the Greek exercise I've written in the cowbyres. And mony's the page o' Virgil, too, I've turned into good Dawric Scotch* to ane that's dead and gane, puir hizzie, sitting under the same plaid, with the sheep feeding round us, up among the hills, looking out ower the broad blue sea, and the wee haven wi' the fishing cobles –'

There was a long solemn pause. I cannot tell why, but I loved the man from that moment; and I thought, too, that he began to love me. Those few words seemed a proof of confidence, perhaps all the deeper, because accidental and unconscious.

I took the Virgil which he lent me, with Hamilton's literal translation between the lines,* and an old tattered Latin grammar; I felt myself quite a learned man – actually the possessor of a Latin book! I regarded as something almost miraculous the opening of this new field for my ambition. Not that I was consciously, much less selfishly, ambitous. I had no idea as yet to be anything but a tailor to the end; to make clothes – perhaps in a less infernal atmosphere – but still to make clothes, and live thereby. I did not suspect that I possessed powers above the mass. My intense longing after knowledge had been to me like a girl's first love – a thing to be concealed from every eye – to be looked at askance, even by myself, delicious as it was, with holy shame and trembling. And thus it was not cowardice merely, but natural modesty, which put me on a hundred plans of concealing my studies from my mother, and even from my sister.

I slept in a little lean-to garret at the back of the house, some ten feet long by six wide. I could just stand upright against the inner wall, while the roof on the other side ran down to the floor. There was no fireplace in it, or any means of ventilation. No wonder I coughed all night accordingly, and woke about two every morning with choking throat and aching head. My mother often said that the room was 'too small for a Christian to sleep in, but where could she get a better?'

Such was my only study. I could not use it as such, however, at night without discovery; for my mother carefully looked in every evening, to see that my candle was out. But when my kind cough woke me, I rose, and creeping like a mouse about the room – for my mother and sister slept in the next chamber, and every sound was audible through the narrow partition – I drew my darling books out from under a board of the floor, one end of which I had gradually loosened at odd minutes, and with them a rushlight, earned by running on messages, or by taking bits of work home, and finishing them for my fellows.

No wonder that with this scanty rest, and this complicated exertion of hands, eyes, and brain, followed by the long dreary day's work of the shop, my health began to fail; my eyes grew weaker and weaker; my cough became more acute; my appetite failed me daily. My mother noticed the change, and questioned me about it, affectionately enough. But I durst not, alas! tell the truth. It was not one offence, but the arrears of months of disobedience which I should have had to confess; and so arose infinite false excuses, and petty prevarications, which embittered and clogged still more my already overtasked spirit. About my own ailments – formidable as I believe they were – I never had a moment's anxiety. The expectation of early death was as unnatural to me as it is, I suspect, to almost all. I die? Had I not hopes, plans, desires, infinite? Could I die while they were unfulfilled? Even now, I do not believe I shall die yet. I will not believe it – but let that pass.

Yes, let that pass. Perhaps I have lived long enough – longer than many a grey-headed man.

> There is a race of mortals who become
> Old in their youth, and die ere middle age.*

And might not those days of mine then have counted as months? – those days when, before starting forth to walk two miles to the shop at six o'clock in the morning, I sat some three or four hours shivering on my bed, putting myself into cramped and painful postures, not daring even to cough, lest my mother should fancy me unwell, and come in to see me, poor dear soul! – my eyes aching over the page, my feet wrapped up in the bedclothes, to keep them from the miserable pain of the cold; longing, watching, dawn after dawn, for the kind summer mornings, when I should need no candlelight. Look at the picture awhile, ye comfortable folks, who take down from your shelves what books you like best at the moment, and then lie back, amid prints and statuettes, to grow wise in an easy chair, with a blazing fire and a camphine lamp. The lower classes uneducated! Perhaps you would be so too, if learning cost you the privation which it costs some of them.

But this concealment could not last. My only wonder is, that I continued to get whole months of undiscovered study. One morning, about four o'clock, as might have been expected, my mother heard me stirring, came in, and found me sitting cross-legged on my bed, stitching away, indeed, with all my might, but with a Virgil open before me.

She glanced at the book, clutched it with one hand and my arm with the other, and sternly asked,

'Where did you get this heathen stuff?'

A lie rose to my lips; but I had been so gradually entangled in the loathed meshes of a system of concealment, and consequent prevarication, that I felt as if one direct falsehood would ruin for ever my fast-failing self-respect, and I told her the whole truth. She took the book and left the room. It was Saturday morning, and I spent two miserable days, for she never spoke a word to me till the two ministers had made their appearance, and drank their tea on Sunday evening; then at last she opened –

'And now, Mr. Wigginton, what account have you of this Mr. Mackaye, who has seduced my unhappy boy from the paths of obedience?'

'I am sorry to say, madam,' answered the dark man, with a solemn snuffle, 'that he proves to be a most objectionable and altogether unregenerate character. He is, as I am informed, neither more or less than a Chartist and an open blasphemer.'

'He is not!' I interrupted, angrily. 'He has told me more about God, and given me better advice, than any human being, except my mother.'

'Ah! madam, so thinks the unconverted heart, ignorant that the god of the Deist* is not the God of the Bible – a consuming fire to all but His beloved elect; the god of the Deist, unhappy youth, is a mere self-invented, all-indulgent phantom – a will-o'-the-wisp, deluding the unwary, as he has deluded you, into the slough of carnal reason and shameful profligacy.'

'Do you mean to call me a profligate?' I retorted fiercely, for my blood was up, and I felt I was fighting for all which I prized in the world: 'if you do, you lie. Ask my mother when I ever disobeyed her before? I have never touched a drop of anything stronger than water; I have slaved over-hours to pay for my own candle, I have – I have no sins to accuse myself of, and neither you nor any other person know of any. Do you call me a profligate because I wish to educate myself and rise in life?'

'Ah!' groaned my poor mother to herself, 'still unconvinced of sin!'

'The old Adam, my dear madam, you see – standing, as he always does, on his own filthy rags of works, while all the imaginations of his heart are only evil continually. Listen to me, poor sinner –'

'I will not listen to you,' I cried, the accumulated disgust of years bursting out once and for all, 'for I hate and despise you, eating my poor mother here out of house and home. You are one of those who creep into widows' houses, and for pretence make long prayers.* You, sir, I will hear,' I went on, turning to the dear old man who had sat by shaking his white locks with a sad and puzzled air, 'for I love you.'

'My dear sister, Locke,' he began, 'I really think sometimes – that is, a-hem – with your leave, brother – I am almost disposed – but I should wish to defer to your superior zeal – yet, at the same time, perhaps, the desire for information, however carnal in itself, may be an instrument in the Lord's hands – you know what I mean. I always thought him a gracious youth, madam, didn't you? And perhaps – I only observe it in passing – the Lord's people among the dissenting connexions are apt to undervalue human learning as a means – of course, I mean only as a means. It is not generally known, I believe, that our revered Puritan patriarchs, Howe and Baxter, Owen* and many more, were not altogether unacquainted with heathen authors; nay, that they may have been called absolutely learned men. And some of our leading ministers are inclined – no doubt they will be led rightly in so important a matter – to follow the example of the Independents in educating their young ministers, and turning Satan's weapons of heathen mythology against himself, as St. Paul is said to have done. My dear boy, what books have you now got by you of Mr. Mackaye's?'

'Milton's Poems and a Latin Virgil.'

'Ah!' groaned the dark man; 'will poetry, will Latin save an immortal soul?'

'I'll tell you what, sir; you say yourself that it depends on God's absolute counsel whether I am saved or not. So, if I am elect, I shall be saved whatever I do; and if I am not, I shall be damned whatever I do; and in the meantime you had better mind your own business, and let me do the best I can for this life, as the next is all settled for me.'

This flippant, but after all not unreasonable speech, seemed to silence the man; and I took the opportunity of running upstairs and bringing down my Milton. The old man was speaking as I re-entered.

'And you know, my dear madam, Mr. Milton was a true converted man, and a Puritan.'

'He was Oliver Cromwell's secretary,' I added.

'Did he teach you to disobey your mother?' asked my mother.

I did not answer; and the old man, after turning over a few leaves, as if he knew the book well, looked up.

'I think, madam, you might let the youth keep these books,

if he will promise, as I am sure he will, to see no more of Mr. Mackaye.'

I was ready to burst out crying, but I made up my mind and answered,

'I must see him once again, or he will think me so ungrateful. He is the best friend that I ever had, except you, mother. Besides, I do not know if he will lend me any, after this.'

My mother looked at the old minister, and then gave a sullen assent. 'Promise me only to see him once – but I cannot trust you. You have deceived me once, Alton, and you may again!'

'I shall not, I shall not,' I answered proudly. 'You do not know me' – and I spoke true.

'You do not know yourself, my poor dear foolish child!' she replied – and that was true too.

'And now, dear friends,' said the dark man,' let us join in offering up a few words of special intercession.'

We all knelt down, and I soon discovered that by the special intercession was meant a string of bitter and groundless slanders against poor me, twisted into the form of a prayer for my conversion, 'if it were God's will.' To which I responded with a closing 'Amen', for which I was sorry afterwards, when I recollected that it was said in merely insolent mockery. But the little faith I had was breaking up fast – not altogether, surely, by my own fault.**

At all events, from that day I was emancipated from modern Puritanism. The ministers both avoided all serious conversation

---

** The portraits of the minister and the missionary are surely exceptions to their class, rather than the average. The Baptists have had their Andrew Fuller and Robert Hall, and among missionaries Dr. Carey,* and noble spirits in plenty. But such men as those who excited Alton Locke's disgust are to be met with, in every sect; in the Church of England, and in the Church of Rome. And it is a real and fearful scandal to the young, to see such men listened to as God's messengers, in spite of their utter want of any manhood or virtue, simply because they are 'orthodox', each according to the shibboleths of his hearers, and possess that vulpine 'discretion of dulness', whose miraculous might Dean Swift sets forth in his "Essay on the Fates of Clergymen".* Such men do exist, and prosper; and as long as they are allowed to do so, Alton Locke will meet them, and be scandalised by them – ED.*

with me; and my mother did the same; while with a strength of mind, rare among women, she never alluded to the scene of that Sunday evening. It was a rule with her never to recur to what was once done and settled. What was to be, might be prayed over. But it was to be endured in silence; yet wider and wider ever from that time opened the gulf between us.

I went trembling the next afternoon to Mackaye and told my story. He first scolded me severely for disobeying my mother. 'He that begins o' that gate, laddie, ends by disobeying God and his ain conscience. Gin ye're to be a scholar, God will make you one – and if not, ye'll no mak' yoursel' ane in spite o' Him and His commandments.' And then he filled his pipe and chuckled away in silence; at last, he exploded in a horse-laugh.

'So ye gied the ministers a bit o' yer mind? "The deil's amang the tailors" in gude earnest, as the sang says.* There's Johnnie Crossthwaite kicked the papist priest out o' his house yestreen; puir ministers, it's ill times wi' them! They gang about keckling and screighing after the working men, like a hen that's hatched ducklings, when she sees them tak' the water. Little Dunkeld's coming to London sune, I'm thinking.

> Hech! sic a parish, a parish, a parish;
> Hech! sic a parish as little Dunkeld,
> They hae stickit* the minister, hanged the precentor,
> Dung down the steeple, and drucken the bell.*

'But may I keep the books a little while, Mr. Mackaye?'

'Keep them till ye die, gin ye will. What is the worth o' them to me? What is the worth o' anything to me, puir auld deevil, that ha' no half-a-dizen years to live, at the furthest. God bless ye, my bairn; gang hame, and mind your mither, or it's little gude books 'll do ye.'

CHAPTER IV

TAILORS AND SOLDIERS

I WAS now thrown again utterly on my own resources. I read and re-read Milton's 'Poems' and Virgil's 'Æneid' for six more months at every spare moment; thus spending over them, I suppose, all in all, far more time than most gentlemen have done. I found, too, in the last volume of Milton a few of his select prose works: the 'Areopagitica', the 'Defence of the English People', and one or two more, in which I gradually began to take an interest; and, little of them as I could comprehend, I was awed by their tremendous depth and power, as well as excited by the utterly new trains of thought into which they led me. Terrible was the amount of bodily fatigue which I had to undergo in reading at every spare moment, while walking to and fro from my work, while sitting up, often from midnight till dawn, stitching away to pay for the tallow-candle which I burnt, till I had to resort to all sorts of uncomfortable contrivances for keeping myself awake, even at the expense of bodily pain – Heaven forbid that I should weary my readers by describing them! Young men of the upper classes, to whom study – pursue it as intensely as you will – is but the business of the day, and every spare moment relaxation; little you guess the frightful drudgery undergone by a man of the people who has vowed to educate himself, – to live at once two lives, each as severe as the whole of yours, – to bring to the self-imposed toil of intellectual improvement, a body and brain already worn out by a day of toilsome manual labour. I did it. God forbid, though, that I should take credit to myself for it. Hundreds more have done it, with still fewer advantages than mine. Hundreds more, an ever-increasing army of martyrs, are doing it at this moment: of some of them, too, perhaps you may hear hereafter.

I had read through Milton, as I said, again and again; I had got out of him all that my youth and my unregulated mind enabled me to get. I had devoured, too, not without profit, a large old edition of 'Fox's Martyrs',* which the venerable minister lent me, and now I was hungering again for fresh food, and again at a loss where to find it.

I was hungering, too, for more than information – for a friend. Since my intercourse with Sandy Mackaye had been stopped, six months had passed without my once opening my lips to any human being upon the subjects with which my mind was haunted day and night. I wanted to know more about poetry, history, politics, philosophy – all things in heaven and earth. But, above all, I wanted a faithful and sympathising ear into which to pour all my doubts, discontents, and aspirations. My sister Susan, who was one year younger than myself, was growing into a slender, pretty, hectic girl of sixteen. But she was altogether a devout Puritan. She had just gone through the process of conviction of sin and conversion; and being looked upon at the chapel as an especially gracious professor, was either unable or unwilling to think or speak on any subject, except on those to which I felt a growing distaste. She had shrunk from me, too, very much, since my ferocious attack that Sunday evening on the dark minister, who was her special favourite. I remarked it, and it was a fresh cause of unhappiness and perplexity.

At last I made up my mind, come what would, to force myself upon Crossthwaite. He was the only man whom I knew who seemed able to help me; and his very reserve had invested him with a mystery, which served to heighten my imagination of his powers. I waylaid him one day coming out of the workroom to go home, and plunged at once desperately into the matter.

'Mr. Crossthwaite, I want to speak to you. I want to ask you to advise me.'

'I have known that a long time.'

'Then why did you never say a kind word to me?'

'Because I was waiting to see whether you were worth saying a kind word to. It was but the other day, remember, you were a bit of a boy. Now, I think, I may trust you with a thing or two. Besides, I wanted to see whether you trusted me enough to ask me. Now you've broke the ice at last, in with you, head and ears, and see what you can fish out.'

'I am very unhappy——'

'That's no new disorder that I know of.'

'No; but I think the reason I am unhappy is a strange one; at least, I never read of but one person else in the same way. I want to educate myself, and I can't.'

'You must have read precious little then, if you think yourself in a strange way. Bless the boy's heart! And what the dickens do you want to be educating yourself for, pray?'

This was said in a tone of good-humoured banter, which gave me courage. He offered to walk homewards with me; and, as I shambled along by his side, I told him all my story and all my griefs.

I never shall forget that walk. Every house, tree, turning, which we passed that day on our way, is indissolubly connected in my mind with some strange new thought which arose in me just at each spot; and recurs, so are the mind and the senses connected, as surely as I repass it.

I had been telling him about Sandy Mackaye. He confessed to an acquaintance with him; but in a reserved and mysterious way, which only heightened my curiosity.

We were going through the Horse Guards, and I could not help lingering to look with wistful admiration on the huge mustachoed war-machines* who sauntered about the courtyard.

A tall and handsome officer, blazing in scarlet and gold, cantered in on a superb horse, and, dismounting, threw the reins to a dragoon as grand and gaudy as himself. Did I envy him? Well – I was but seventeen. And there is something noble to the mind, as well as to the eye, in the great, strong man, who can fight – a completeness, a self-restraint, a terrible sleeping power in him. As Mr. Carlyle says, 'A soldier, after all, is one of the few remaining realities of the age. All other professions almost promise one thing, and perform – alas! what? But this man promises to fight, and does it; and, if he be told, will veritably take out a long sword and kill me.'*

So thought my companion, though the mood in which he viewed the fact was somewhat different from my own.

'Come on,' he said, peevishly clutching me by the arm; 'what do you want dawdling? Are you a nursery-maid, that you must stare at those red-coated butchers?' And a deep curse followed.

'What harm have they done you?'

'I should think I owed them turn enough.'

'What?'

'They cut my father down at Sheffield, – perhaps with the very swords he helped to make, – because he would not sit still and starve, and see us starving round him, while those who fattened on the sweat of his brow, and on those lungs of his, which the sword-grinding dust was eating out day by day, were wantoning on venison and champagne. That's the harm they've done me, my chap!'

'Poor fellows! – they only did as they were ordered, I suppose.'

'And what business have they to let themselves be ordered? What right, I say – what right has any free, reasonable soul on earth, to sell himself for a shilling a-day to murder any man, right or wrong – even his own brother or his own father – just because such a whiskered, profligate jackanapes as that officer, without learning, without any god except his own looking-glass and his opera-dancer – a fellow who, just because he is born a gentleman, is set to command grey-headed men before he can command his own meanest passions. Good heavens! that the lives of free men should be entrusted to such a stuffed cockatoo; and that free men should be such traitors to their country, traitors to their own flesh and blood, as to sell themselves, for a shilling a-day and the smirks of the nursery-maids, to do that fellow's bidding!'

'What are you a-grumbling about here, my man? – gotten the cholera?' asked one of the dragoons, a huge, stupid-looking lad.

'About you, you young long-legged cut-throat,' answered Crossthwaite, 'and all your crew of traitors.'

'Help, help, coomrades o' mine!' quoth the dragoon, bursting with laughter; 'I'm gaun be moorthered wi' a little booy that's gane mad, and toorned Chartist.'

I dragged Crossthwaite off; for what was jest to the soldiers I saw, by his face, was fierce enough earnest to him. We walked on a little, in silence.

'Now,' I said, 'that was a good-natured fellow enough, though he was a soldier. You and he might have cracked many a joke together, if you did but understand each other; – and he was a countryman of yours, too.'

'I may crack something else besides jokes with him some day,' answered he, moodily.

''Pon my word, you must take care how you do it. He is as big as four of us.'

'That vile aristocrat, the old Italian poet – what's his name? – Ariosto – ay! – he knew which quarter the wind was making for, when he said that fire-arms would be the end of all your old knights* and gentlemen in armour, that hewed down unarmed innocents as if they had been sheep. Gunpowder is your true leveller – dash physical strength! A boy's a man with a musket in his hand, my chap!'

'God forbid,' I said, 'that I should ever be made a man of in that way, or you either. I do not think we are quite big enough to make fighters; and if we were, what have we got to fight about?'

'Big enough to make fighters?' said he, half to himself; 'or strong enough, perhaps? – or clever enough? – and yet Alexander was a little man, and the Petit Caporal, and Nelson, and Cæsar, too; and so was Saul of Tarsus, and weakly he was into the bargain. Æsop was a dwarf, and so was Attila; Shakespeare was lame; Alfred, a rickety weakling; Byron, club-footed; – so much for body versus spirit – brute force versus genius – genius.'

I looked at him; his eyes glared like two balls of fire. Suddenly he turned to me.

'Locke, my boy, I've made an ass of myself, and got into a rage, and broken a good old resolution of mine, and a promise that I made to my dear little woman – bless her! – and said things to you that you ought to know nothing of for this long time; but those red-coats always put me beside myself. God forgive me!' And he held out his hand to me cordially.

'I can quite understand your feeling deeply on one point,' I said, as I took it, 'after the sad story you told me; – but why so bitter on all? What is there so very wrong about things, that we must begin fighting about it?'

'Bless your heart, poor innocent! What is wrong? – what is not wrong? Wasn't there enough in that talk with Mackaye, that you told me of just now, to show anybody that, who can tell a hawk from a handsaw?'

'Was it wrong in him to give himself such trouble about the education of a poor young fellow, who has no tie on him, who can never repay him?'

'No; that's just like him. He feels for the people, for he has been one of us. He worked in a printing-office himself many a year, and he knows the heart of the working man. But he didn't tell you the whole truth about education. He daren't tell you. No one who has money dare speak out his heart; – not that he has much certainly; but, the cunning old Scot that he is, he lives by the present system of things, and he won't speak ill of the bridge which carries him over – till the time comes.'

I could not understand whither all this tended, and walked on, silent and somewhat angry, at hearing the least slight cast on Mackaye.

'Don't you see, stupid?' he broke out at last. 'What did he say to you about gentlemen being crammed by tutors and professors? Have not you as good a right to them as any gentleman?'

'But he told me they were no use – that every man must educate himself.'

'Oh! all very fine to tell you the grapes are sour, when you can't reach them. Bah, lad! Can't you see what comes of education? – that any dolt, provided he be a gentleman, can be doctored up at school and college, enough to make him play his part decently – his mighty part of ruling us, and riding over our heads, and picking our pockets, as parson, doctor, lawyer, member of parliament – while we – you now, for instance – cleverer than ninety-nine gentlemen out of a hundred, if you had one-tenth the trouble taken with you that is taken with every pig-headed son of an aristocrat –'

'Am I clever?' asked I, in honest surprise.

'What! haven't you found that out yet? Don't try to put that on me. Don't a girl know when she's pretty, without asking her neighbours?'

'Really, I never thought about it.'

'More simpleton you. Old Mackaye has, at all events; though, canny Scotchman that he is, he'll never say a word to you about it, yet he makes no secret of it to other people. I heard him the other day telling some of our friends that you were a thorough young genius.'

I blushed scarlet, between pleasure and a new feeling; was it ambition?

'Why, hav'n't you a right to aspire to a college education as any do-nothing canon there at the abbey, lad?'

'I don't know that I have a right to anything.'

'What, not become what Nature intended you to become? What has she given you brains for, but to be educated and used? Oh! I heard a fine lecture upon that at our club the other night. There was a man there – a gentleman, too, but a thorough-going people's man, I can tell you, Mr. O'Flynn.* What an orator that man is to be sure! The Irish Æschines,* I hear they call him in Conciliation Hall.* Isn't he the man to pitch into the Mammonites? "Gentlemen and ladies", says he, "how long will a diabolic society" – no, an effete society it was – "how long will an effete, emasculate, and effeminate society, in the diabolic selfishness of its eclecticism, refuse to acknowledge what my immortal countryman, Burke, calls the 'Dei voluntatem in rebus revelatam'* – the revelation of Nature's will in the phenomena of matter? The cerebration of each is the prophetic sacrament of the yet undeveloped possibilities of his mentation. The form of the brain alone, and not the possession of the vile gauds of wealth and rank, constitute man's only right to education – to the glories of art and science. Those beaming eyes and roseate lips beneath me proclaim a bevy of undeveloped Aspasias,* of embryo Cleopatras, destined by Nature, and only restrained by man's injustice, from ruling the world by their beauty's eloquence. Those massive and beetling brows, gleaming with the lambent flames of patriotic ardour – what is needed to unfold them into a race of Shakespeares and of Gracchi,* ready to proclaim with sword and lyre the divine harmonies of liberty, equality, and fraternity, before a quailing universe?" '

'It sounds very grand,' replied I, meekly; 'and I should like very much certainly to have a good education. But I can't see whose injustice keeps me out of one if I can't afford to pay for it.'

'Whose? Why, the parsons' to be sure. They've got the monopoly of education in England, and they get their bread by it at their public schools and universities; and of course it's their interest to keep up the price of their commodity, and let no man have a taste of it who can't pay down handsomely. And so those aristocrats of college dons go on rolling in riches, and fellowships, and scholarships, that were bequeathed by the people's friends in old times, just to educate poor scholars like you and me, and give us our rights as free men.'

'But I thought the clergy were doing so much to educate the poor. At least, I hear all the dissenting ministers grumbling at their continual interference.'

'Ay, educating them to make them slaves and bigots. They don't teach them what they teach their own sons. Look at the miserable smattering of general information – just enough to serve as sauce for their great first and last lesson of "Obey the powers that be" – whatever they be; leave us alone in our comforts, and starve patiently; do, like good boys, for it's God's will. And then, if a boy does show talent in school, do they help him up in life? Not they; when he has just learnt enough to whet his appetite for more, they turn him adrift again, to sink and drudge – to do his duty, as they call it, in that state of life to which society and the devil have called him.'

'But there are innumerable stories of great Englishmen who have risen from the lowest ranks.'

'Ay; but where are the stories of those who have not risen – of all the noble geniuses who have ended in desperation, drunkenness, starvation, suicide, because no one would take the trouble of lifting them up, and enabling them to walk in the path which nature had marked out for them? Dead men tell no tales; and this old whited sepulchre, society, aint going to turn informer against itself.'

'I trust and hope,' I said, sadly, 'that if God intends me to rise, He will open the way for me; perhaps the very struggles and sorrows of a poor genius may teach him more than ever wealth and prosperity could.'

'True, Alton, my boy! and that's my only comfort. It does make men of us, this bitter battle of life. We working men, when we do come out of the furnace, come out, not tinsel and papier maché, like those fops of red-tape statesmen, but steel and granite, Alton, my boy – that has been seven times tried in the fire: and woe to the papier maché gentleman that runs against us! But,' he went on, sadly, 'for one who comes safe through the furnace, there are a hundred who crack in the burning. You are a young bear, my lad, with all your sorrows before you; and you'll find that a working man's training is like the Red Indian children's. The few who are strong enough to stand it grow up warriors; but all those who are not fire-and-water-proof by nature – just die, Alton, my lad, and the tribe thinks itself well rid of them.'

So that conversation ended. But it had implanted in my bosom a new seed of mingled good and evil, which was destined to bear fruit, precious perhaps as well as bitter. God knows it has hung on the tree long enough. Sour and harsh from the first, it has been many a year in ripening. But the sweetness of the apple, the potency of the grape, as the chemists tell us, are born out of acidity – a developed sourness. Will it be so with my thoughts? Dare I assert, as I sit writing here, with the wild waters slipping past the cabin windows, backwards and backwards ever, every plunge of the vessel one forward leap from the old world – worn-out world I had almost called it, of sham civilisation and real penury – dare I hope ever to return and triumph? Shall I, after all, lay my bones among my own people, and hear the voices of freemen whisper in my dying ears?

Silence, dreaming heart! Sufficient for the day is the evil thereof* – and the good thereof also. Would that I had known that before! Above all, that I had known it on that night, when first the burning thought arose in my heart, that I was unjustly used; that society had not given me my rights. It came to me as a revelation, celestial-infernal, full of glorious hopes of the possible future in store for me through the perfect development of all my faculties; and full, too, of fierce present rage, wounded vanity, bitter grudgings against those more favoured than myself, which grew in time almost to cursing against the God who had made me a poor untutored working man, and seemed to have given me genius only to keep me in a Tantalus'-hell of unsatisfied thirst.

Ay, respectable gentlemen and ladies, I will confess all to

you – you shall have, if you enjoy it, a fresh opportunity for indulging that supreme pleasure which the press daily affords you of insulting the classes whose powers most of you know as little as you do their sufferings. Yes; the Chartist poet is vain, conceited, ambitious, uneducated, shallow, inexperienced, envious, ferocious, scurrilous, seditious, traitorous. – Is your charitable vocabulary exhausted? Then ask yourselves, how often have you yourself honestly resisted and conquered the temptation to any one of these sins, when it has come across you just once in a way, and not as they came to me, as they come to thousands of the working men, daily and hourly, 'till their torments do, by length of time, become their elements'?* What, are we covetous, too? Yes! And if those who have, like you, still covet more, what wonder if those who have nothing, covet something? Profligate too? Well, though that imputation as a generality is utterly calumnious, though your amount of respectable animal enjoyment per annum is a hundred times as great as that of the most self-indulgent artisan, yet, if you had ever felt what it is to want, not only every luxury of the senses, but even bread to eat, you would think more mercifully of the man who makes up by rare excesses, and those only of the limited kinds possible to him, for long intervals of dull privation, and says in his madness, 'Let us eat and drink, for to-morrow we die!' We have our sins, and you have yours. Ours may be the more gross and barbaric, but yours are none the less damnable; perhaps all the more so, for being the sleek, subtle, respectable, religious sins they are. You are frantic enough if our part of the press* calls you hard names, but you cannot see that your part of the press repays it back to us with interest. *We* see those insults, and feel them bitterly enough; and do not forget them, alas! soon enough, while they pass unheeded by your delicate eyes as trivial truisms. Horrible, unprincipled, villainous, seditious, frantic, blasphemous, are epithets, of course, when applied to – to how large a portion of the English people, you will some day discover to your astonishment. When will that day come, and how? In thunder, and storm, and garments rolled in blood? Or like the dew on the mown grass, and the clear shining of the sunlight after April rain?

Yes, it was true. Society had not given me my rights. And

woe unto the man on whom that idea, true or false, rises lurid, filling all his thoughts with stifling glare, as of the pit itself. Be it true, be it false, it is equally a woe to believe it; to have to live on a negation; to have to worship for our only idea, as hundreds of thousands of us have this day, the hatred of the things which are. Ay, though one of us here and there may die in faith, in sight of the promised land, yet is it not hard, when looking from the top of Pisgah* into 'the good time coming',* to watch the years slipping away one by one, and death crawling nearer and nearer, and the people wearying themselves in the fire for very vanity, and Jordan not yet passed, the promised land not yet entered? while our little children die around us, like lambs beneath the knife, of cholera and typhus and consumption, and all the diseases which the good time can and will prevent; which, as science has proved, and you the rich confess, might be prevented at once, if you dared to bring in one bold and comprehensive measure, and not sacrifice yearly the lives of thousands to the idol of vested interests and a majority in the House. Is it not hard to men who smart beneath such things to help crying aloud – 'Thou cursed Moloch-Mammon,* take my life if thou wilt; let me die in the wilderness, for I have deserved it; but these little ones in mines and factories,* in typhus-cellars, and Tooting pandemoniums,* what have they done? If not in their fathers' cause, yet still in theirs, were it so great a sin to die upon a barricade?'

Or after all, my working brothers, is it true of our promised land, even as of that Jewish one of old, that the *priests'* feet must first cross the mystic stream into the good land and large which God has prepared for us?

Is it so indeed? Then in the name of the Lord of Hosts, ye priests of His, why will ye not awake, and arise, and go over Jordan,* that the people of the Lord may follow you?

CHAPTER V

THE SCEPTIC'S MOTHER

MY readers will perceive, from what I have detailed, that I was not likely to get any very positive ground of comfort from Crossthwaite; and from within myself there was daily less and less hope of any. Daily the struggle became more intolerable between my duty to my mother and my duty to myself – that inward thirst for mental self-improvement, which, without any clear consciousness of its sanctity or inspiration, I felt, and could not help feeling, that I *must* follow. No doubt it was very self-willed and ambitious of me to do that which rich men's sons are flogged for not doing, and rewarded with all manner of prizes, scholarships, fellowships, for doing. But the nineteenth year is a time of life at which self-will is apt to exhibit itself in other people besides tailors; and those religious persons who think it no sin to drive their sons on through classics and mathematics, in hopes of gaining them a station in life, ought not to be very hard upon me for driving myself on through the same path without any such selfish hope of gain – though perhaps the very fact of my having no wish or expectation of such advantage will constitute in their eyes my sin and folly, and prove that I was following the dictates merely of a carnal lust, and not of a proper worldly prudence. I really do not wish to be flippant or sneering. I have seen the evil of it as much as any man, in myself and in my own class. But there are excuses for such a fault in the working man. It does sour and madden him to be called presumptuous and ambitious for the very same aspirations which are lauded up to the skies in the sons of the rich – unless, indeed, he will do one little thing, and so make his peace with society. If he will desert his own class; if he will try to become a sham gentleman, a parasite, and, if he can, a Mammonite, the world will compliment him on his noble desire to 'rise in life'. He will have won his spurs, and be admitted into that exclusive pale of knighthood, beyond which it is a sin to carry arms even in self-defence. But if the working genius dares to be true to his own class – to stay among them –

to regenerate them – to defend them – to devote his talents to those among whom God placed him and brought him up – then he is the demagogue, the incendiary, the fanatic, the dreamer. So you would have the monopoly of talent, too, exclusive worldlings? And yet you pretend to believe in the miracle of Pentecost, and the religion that was taught by the carpenter's Son, and preached across the world by fishermen!

I was several times minded to argue the question out with my mother, and assert for myself the same independence of soul which I was now earning for my body by my wages. Once I had resolved to speak to her that very evening; but, strangely enough, happening to open the Bible, which, alas! I did seldom at that time, my eye fell upon the chapter where Jesus, after having justified to His parents His absence in the Temple, while hearing the doctors and asking them questions, yet went down with them to Nazareth after all, and was subject unto them.* The story struck me vividly as a symbol of my own duties. But on reading further, I found more than one passage which seemed to me to convey a directly opposite lesson, where His mother and His brethren, fancying Him mad, attempted to interfere with His labours, and asserting their family rights as reasons for retaining Him, met with a peremptory rebuff.* I puzzled my head for some time to find out which of the two cases was the more applicable to my state of self-development. The notion of asking for teaching from on high on such a point had never crossed me. Indeed, if it had, I did not believe sufficiently either in the story or in the doctrines connected with it, to have tried such a resource. And so, as may be supposed, my growing self-conceit decided for me that the latter course was the fitting one.

And yet I had not energy to carry it out. I was getting so worn out in body and mind from continual study and labour, stinted food and want of sleep, that I could not face the thought of an explosion, such as I knew must ensue, and I lingered on in the same unhappy state, becoming more and more morose in manner to my mother, while I was as assiduous as ever in all filial duties. But I had no pleasure in home. She seldom spoke to me. Indeed, there was no common topic about which we could speak. Besides, ever since that fatal Sunday evening, I saw that she suspected me and watched me. I had good reason to believe that she set spies upon my conduct. Poor dear mother! God forbid that I should accuse thee for a single care of thine, for a single suspicion even, prompted as they all were by a mother's anxious love. I would never have committed these things to paper, hadst thou not been far beyond the reach or hearing of them; and only now, in hopes that they may serve as a warning, in some degree to mothers, but ten times more to children. For I sinned against thee, deeply and shamefully, in thought and deed, while thou didst never sin against me; though all thy caution did but hasten the fatal explosion which came, and perhaps must have come, under some form or other, in any case.

I had been detained one night in the shop till late; and on my return my mother demanded, in a severe tone, the reason of my stay; and on my telling her, answered as severely that she did not believe me; that she had too much reason to suspect that I had been with bad companions.

'Who dared to put such a thought into your head?'

She 'would not give up her authorities, but she had too much reason to believe them.'

Again I demanded the name of my slanderer, and was refused it. And then I burst out, for the first time in my life, into a real fit of rage with her. I cannot tell how I dared to say what I did, but I was weak, nervous, irritable – my brain excited beyond all natural tension. Above all, I felt that she was unjust to me; and my good conscience, as well as my pride, rebelled.

'You have never trusted me,' I cried; 'you have watched me——'

'Did you not deceive me once already?'

'And if I did,' I answered, more and more excited, 'have I not slaved for you, stinted myself of clothes to pay your rent? Have I not run to and fro for you like a slave, while I knew all the time you did not respect me or trust me? If you had only treated me as a child and an idiot, I could have borne it. But you have been thinking of me all the while as an incarnate fiend – dead in trespasses and sins – a child of wrath and the devil. What right have you to be astonished if I should do my father's works?'*

'You may be ignorant of vital religion,' she answered; 'and you may insult me. But if you make a mock of God's word, you leave my house. If you can laugh at religion, you can deceive me.'

The pent-up scepticism of years burst forth.

'Mother,' I said, 'don't talk to me about religion, and election, and conversion and all that – I don't believe one word of it. Nobody does, except good kind people – (like you, alas! I was going to say, but the devil stopped the words at my lips) – who must needs have some reason to account for their goodness. That Bowyer – he's a soft heart by nature, and as he is, so he does – religion has had nothing to do with that, any more than it has with that black-faced, canting scoundrel who has been telling you lies about me. Much his heart is changed. He carries sneak and slanderer written in his face – and sneak and slanderer he will be, elect or none. Religion? Nobody believes in it. The rich don't; or they wouldn't fill their churches up with pews, and shut the poor out, all the time they are calling them brothers. They believe the gospel? Then why do they leave the men who make their clothes to starve in such hells on earth as our workroom? No more do the tradespeople believe in it; or they wouldn't go home from sermon to sand the sugar, and put sloe-leaves in the tea, and send out lying puffs of their vamped-up goods, and grind the last farthing out of the poor creatures who rent their wretched stinking houses. And as for the workmen – they laugh at it all, I can tell you. Much good religion is doing for them! You may see it's fit only for women and children – for go where you will, church or chapel, you see hardly anything but bonnets and babies! I don't believe a word of it, – once and for all. I'm old enough to think for myself, and a free-thinker I will be, and believe nothing but what I know and understand.'

I had hardly spoken the words, when I would have given worlds to recal them – but it was to be – and it was.

Sternly she looked at me full in the face, till my eyes dropped before her gaze. Then she spoke steadily and slowly:

'Leave this house this moment. You are no son of mine henceforward. Do you think I will have my daughter polluted by the company of an infidel and a blasphemer?'

'I will go,' I answered fiercely; 'I can get my own living at all events!' And before I had time to think, I had rushed upstairs, packed up my bundle, not forgetting the precious books, and was on my way through the frosty echoing streets under the cold glare of the winter's moon.

I had gone perhaps half a mile, when the thought of home rushed over me – the little room where I had spent my life – the scene of all my childish joys and sorrows – which I should never see again, for I felt that my departure was for ever. Then I longed to see my mother once again – not to speak to her – for I was at once too proud and too cowardly to do that – but to have a look at her through the window. One look – for all the while, though I was boiling over with rage and indignation, I felt that it was all on the surface – that in the depths of our hearts I loved her and she loved me. And yet I wished to be angry, wished to hate her. Strange contradiction of the flesh and spirit!

Hastily and silently I retraced my steps to the house. The gate was padlocked. I cautiously stole over the palings to the window – the shutter was closed and fast. I longed to knock – I lifted my hand to the door, and dare not; indeed, I knew that it was useless, in my dread of my mother's habit of stern determination. That room – that mother I never saw again. I turned away; sickened at heart, I was clambering back again, looking behind me towards the window, when I felt a strong grip on my collar, and turning round, had a policeman's lantern flashed in my face.

'Hullo, young 'un, and what do you want here?' with a strong emphasis, after the fashion of policemen, on all his pronouns.

'Hush! or you'll alarm my mother!'

'Oh! eh! Forgot the latch-key, you sucking Don Juan, that's it, is it? Late home from the Victory?'

I told him simply how the case stood, and entreated him to get me a night's lodging, assuring him that my mother would not admit me, or I ask to be admitted.

The policeman seemed puzzled, but after scratching his hat in lieu of his head for some seconds, replied,

'This here is the dodge – you goes outside and lies down on

the kerb-stone; whereby I spies you a-sleeping in the streets, contrary to act o' parliament; whereby it is my duty to take you to the station-house; whereby you gets a night's lodging free gracious for nothing, and company perwided by her Majesty.'

'Oh, not to the station-house!' I cried, in shame and terror.

'Werry well; then you must keep moving all night continually, whereby you avoids the hact; or else you goes to a twopenny-rope shop and gets a lie down. And your bundle you'd best leave at my house. Twopenny-rope society aint particular. I'm going off my beat; you walk home with me and leave your traps. Everybody knows me – Costello, V 21, that's my number.'

So on I went with the kind-hearted man, who preached solemnly to me all the way on the fifth commandment. But I heard very little of it; for before I had proceeded a quarter of a mile, a deadly faintness and dizziness came over me, I staggered, and fell against the railings.

'And have you been a-drinking arter all?'

'I never——a drop in my life——nothing but bread-and-water this fortnight.'

And it was true. I had been paying for my own food, and had stinted myself to such an extent, that between starvation, want of sleep, and over-exertion, I was worn to a shadow, and the last drop had filled the cup; the evening's scene and its consequences had been too much for me, and in the middle of an attempt to explain matters to the policeman, I dropped on the pavement, bruising my face heavily.

He picked me up, put me under one arm and my bundle under the other, and was proceeding on his march, when three men came rollicking up.

'Hullo, Poleax – Costello – What's that? Work for us? A demp unpleasant body?'*

'Oh, Mr. Bromley, sir! Hope you're well, sir! Werry rum go this here, sir! I finds this cove in the streets. He says his mother turned him out o' doors. He seems very fair spoken, and very bad in he's head, and very bad in he's chest, and very bad in he's legs, he does. And I can't come to no conclusions respecting my conduct in this here case, nohow!'

'Memorialise the Health of Towns Commission,'* suggested one.

'Bleed him in the great toe,' said the second.

'Put a blister* on the back of his left eye-ball,' said a third.

'Case of male * * *,' observed the first. 'Rj. Aquæ pumpis puræ quantum suff. Applicatur exterò pro re natâ.* J. Bromley, M.D., and don't he wish he may get through!'

'Tip us your daddle,* my boy,' said the second speaker. 'I'll tell you what, Bromley, this fellow's very bad. He's got no more pulse than the Pimlico sewer. Run him into the next pot'us. Here – you lay hold of him, Bromley – that last round with the cabman nearly put my humerus out.'

The huge, burly, pea-jacketed medical student – for such I saw at once he was – laid hold of me on the right tenderly enough, and walked me off between him and the policeman.

I fell again into a faintness, from which I was awakened by being shoved through the folding-doors of a gin shop, into a glare of light and hubbub of blackguardism, and placed on a settle, while my conductor called out—

'Pots round, Mary, and a go of brandy hot with,* for the patient. Here, young 'un; toss it off, it'll make your hair grow.'

I feebly answered that I never had drunk anything stronger than water.

'High time to begin, then; no wonder you're so ill. Well, if you won't, I'll make you——'

And taking my head under his arm, he seized me by the nose, while another poured the liquor down my throat – and certainly it revived me at once.

A drunken drab pulled another drunken drab off the settle to make room for the 'poor young man'; and I sat there with a confused notion that something strange and dreadful had happened to me, while the party drained their respective quarts of porter, and talked over the last boat-race with the Leander.*

'Now then, gen'l'men,' said the policeman, 'if you think he's recovered, we'll take him home to his mother; she ought for to take him in, surely.'

'Yes, if she has as much heart in her as a dried walnut.'

But I resisted stoutly; though I longed to vindicate my mother's affection, yet I could not face her. I entreated to be taken to the station-house; threatened, in my desperation, to break the bar glasses, which, like Doll Tearsheet's abuse, only elicited from the policeman a solemn 'Very well';* and, under the unwonted excitement of the brandy, struggled so fiercely, and talked so incoherently, that the medical students interfered.

'We shall have this fellow in phrenitis, or laryngitis, or dothen-enteritis, or some other itis, before long, if he's aggravated.'

'And whichever it is, it'll kill him. He has no more stamina left than a yard of pump water.'

'I should consider him chargeable to the parish,' suggested the bar-keeper.'

'Exactually so, my Solomon of licensed victuallers. Get a workhouse order for him, Costello.'

'And I should consider, also, sir,' said the licensed victualler, with increased importance, 'having been a guardian myself, and knowing the hact, as the parish couldn't refuse, because they're in power to recover all hexpenses out of his mother.'*

'To be sure; it's all the unnatural old witch's fault.'

'No, it is not,' said I, faintly.

'Wait till your opinion's asked, young 'un. Go kick up the authorities, policeman.'

'Now, I'll just tell you how that'll work, gemmen,' answered the policeman, solemnly. 'I goes to the overseer – werry good sort o' man – but he's in bed. I knocks for half an hour. He puts he's nightcap out o' windy, and sends me to the relieving officer. Werry good sort of man he, too; but he's in bed. I knocks for another half hour. He puts he's nightcap out o' windy – sends me to the medical officer for a certificate. Medical officer's gone to a midwifery case. I hunts him for an hour or so. He's got hold of a babby with three heads, or summat else; and two more women a-calling out for him like blazes. "He'll come to-morrow morning." Now, I just axes your opinion of that there most procrastinationest go.'

The big student, having cursed the parochial authorities in general, offered to pay for my night's lodging at the public-house. The good man of the house demurred at first, but relented on being reminded of the value of a medical student's custom; whereon, without more ado, two of the rough diamonds took me between them, carried me upstairs, undressed me, and put me into bed, as tenderly as if they had been women.

'He'll have the tantrums before morning, I'm afraid,' said one.

'Very likely to turn to typhus,' said the other.

'Well, I suppose – it's a horrid bore, but

> What must be must; man is but dust,
> If you can't get crumb, you must eat crust.

Send me up a go of hot with, and I'll sit up with him till he's asleep, dead, or better.'

'Well, then, I'll stay too; we may just as well make a night of it here as well as anywhere else.'

And he pulled a short black pipe out of his pocket, and sat down to meditate with his feet on the hobs of the empty grate; the other man went down for the liquor; while I, between the brandy and exhaustion, fell fast asleep, and never stirred till I woke the next morning with a racking headache, and saw the big student standing by my bedside, having, as I afterwards heard, sat by me till four in the morning.

'Hullo, young 'un, come to your senses? Headache, eh? slightly comato-crapulose?* We'll give you some soda and salvolatile, and I'll pay for your breakfast.'

And so he did, and when he was joined by his companions on their way to St. George's,* they were very anxious, having heard my story, to force a few shillings on me 'for luck', which, I need not say, I peremptorily refused, assuring them that I could and would get my own living, and never take a farthing from any man.

'That's a plucky dog, though he's a tailor,' I heard them say, as, after overwhelming them with thanks, and vowing, amid shouts of laughter, to repay them every farthing I had cost them, I took my way, sick and stunned, towards my dear old Sandy Mackaye's street.

Rough diamonds indeed! I have never met you again, but I have not forgotten you. Your early life may be a coarse, too often a profligate one – but you know the people, and the people know you: and your tenderness and care, bestowed without hope of repayment, cheers daily many a poor soul in hospital wards and fever-cellars – to meet its reward some day at the people's hands. You belong to us at heart, as the Paris barricades can tell. Alas! for the society which stifles in after-life too many of your better feelings, by making you mere flunkeys and parasites, dependent for your livelihood on the caprices and luxuries of the rich.

CHAPTER VI

THE DULWICH GALLERY

SANDY MACKAYE received me in a characteristic way – growled at me for half an hour for quarrelling with my mother, and when I was at my wit's end, suddenly offered me a bed in his house and the use of his little sitting-room – and, bliss too great to hope! of his books also; and when I talked of payment, told me to hold my tongue and mind my own business. So I settled myself at once; and that very evening he installed himself as my private tutor, took down a Latin book, and set me to work on it.

'An' mind ye, laddie,' said he, half in jest and half in earnest, 'gin I find ye playing truant, and reading a' sorts o' nonsense instead of minding the scholastic methods and proprieties, I'll just bring ye in a bill at the year's end o' twa guineas a week for lodgings and tuition, and tak the law o' ye; so mind and read what I tell ye. Do ye comprehend noo?'

I did comprehend, and obeyed him, determining to repay him some day – and somehow – how I did not very clearly see. Thus I put myself more or less into the old man's power; foolishly enough the wise world will say. But I had no suspicion in my character; and I could not look at those keen grey eyes, when, after staring into vacancy during some long preachment, they suddenly flashed round at me, and through me, full of fun and quaint thought, and kindly earnestness, and fancy that man less honest than his face seemed to proclaim him.

By-the-bye, I have as yet given no description of the old eccentric's abode – an unpardonable omission, I suppose, in these days of Dutch painting and Boz.* But the omission was correct, both historically and artistically, for I had as yet only gone to him for books, books, nothing but books; and I had been blind to everything in his shop but that fairy-land of shelves, filled, in my simple fancy, with inexhaustible treasures, wonder-working, omnipotent, as the magic seal of Solomon.*

It was not till I had been settled and at work for several nights in his sanctum, behind the shop, that I began to become conscious what a strange den that sanctum was.

It was so dark, that without a gas-light no one but he could see to read there, except on very sunny days. Not only were the shelves which covered every inch of wall crammed with books and pamphlets, but the little window was blocked up with them, the floor was piled with bundles of them, in some places three feet deep, apparently in the wildest confusion – though there was some mysterious order in them which he understood, and symbolised, I suppose, by the various strange and ludicrous nick-names on their tickets – for he never was at fault a moment if a customer asked for a book, though it were buried deep in the chaotic stratum. Out of this book alluvium a hole seemed to have been dug near the fireplace, just big enough to hold his arm-chair and a table, book-strewn like everything else, and garnished with odds and ends of MSS., and a snuffer-tray containing scraps of half-smoked tobacco, 'pipe-dottles', as he called them, which were carefully resmoked over and over again, till nothing but ash was left. His whole culinary utensils – for he cooked as well as ate in this strange hole – were an old rusty kettle, which stood on one hob, and a blue plate which, when washed, stood on the other. A barrel of true Aberdeen meal peered out of a corner, half buried in books, and 'a keg o' whusky, the gift o' freens', peeped in like case out of another.

This was his only food. 'It was a' poison', he used to say, 'in London. Bread full o' alum and bones, and sic filth – meat over-driven till it was a' braxy – water sopped wi' dead men's juice. Naething was safe but gude Scots' parritch and Athol brose.'* He carried his water-horror so far as to walk some quarter of a mile every morning to fill his kettle at a favourite pump. 'Was he a cannibal, to drink out o' that pump hard-by, right under the kirkyard?' But it was little he either ate or drank – he seemed to live upon tobacco. From four in the morning till twelve at night, the pipe never left his lips, except when he went into the outer shop. 'It promoted meditation, and drove awa' the lusts o' the flesh. Ech! it was worthy o' that auld tyrant Jamie, to write his counter-blast to the poor man's freen! The hypocrite! to gang preaching the virtues o' evil-savoured smoke "ad dæmones abigendos"* – and then rail again tobacco, as if it was no as gude for the purpose as auld rags and horn shavings!'

Sandy Mackaye had a great fancy for political caricatures, rows of which, there being no room for them on the walls, hung on strings from the ceiling – like clothes hung out to dry – and among them dangled various books to which he had taken an antipathy, principally High Tory and Benthamite,* crucified, impaled through their covers, and suspended in all sorts of torturing attitudes. Among them, right over the table, figured a copy of Icon Basilike,* dressed up in a paper shirt, all drawn over with figures of flames and devils, and surmounted by a peaked paper cap, like a victim at an *auto-da-fé*. And in the midst of all this chaos grinned from the chimney-piece, among pipes and pens, pinches of salt and scraps of butter, a tall cast of Michael Angelo's well known skinless model* – his pristine white defaced by a cap of soot upon the top of his scalpless skull, and every muscle and tendon thrown into horrible relief by the dirt which had lodged among the cracks. There it stood, pointing with its ghastly arm towards the door, and holding on its wrist a label with the following inscription:

> Here stand I, the working man,
> Get more off me if you can.

I questioned Mackaye one evening about those hanged and crucified books, and asked him if he ever sold any of them.

'Ou, ay,' he said; 'if folks are fools enough to ask for them, I'll just answer a fool according to his folly.'

'But,' I said, 'Mr. Mackaye, do you think it right to sell books of the very opinions of which you disapprove so much?'

'Hoot, laddie, it's just a spoiling o' the Egyptians; so mind yer book, and dinna tak in hand cases o' conscience for ither folk. Ye'll ha' wark eneugh wi' yer ain before ye're dune.'

And he folded round his knees his Joseph's coat, as he called it, an old dressing-gown with one plaid sleeve, and one blue one, red shawl skirts, and a black broadcloth back, not to mention innumerable patches of every imaginable stuff and colour, filled his pipe, and buried his nose in 'Harrington's Oceana'.* He read at least twelve hours every day of his life, and that exclusively old history and politics, though his favourite books were Thomas Carlyle's works. Two or three evenings in the week, when he had seen me safe settled at my studies, he used to disappear mysteriously for several hours, and it was some time before I found out, by a chance expression, that he was attending some meeting or committee of working men. I begged him to take me there with him. But I was stopped by a laconic answer.

'When ye're ready.'

'And when shall I be ready, Mr. Mackaye?'

'Read yer book till I tell ye.'

And he twisted himself into his best coat, which had once been black, squeezed on his little Scottish cap, and went out.

*

I now found myself, as the reader may suppose, in an element far more congenial to my literary tastes, and which compelled far less privation of sleep and food in order to find time and means for reading; and my health began to mend from the very first day. But the thought of my mother haunted me; and Mackaye seemed in no hurry to let me escape from it, for he insisted on my writing to her in a penitent strain, informing her of my whereabouts, and offering to return home if she should wish it. With feelings strangely mingled between the desire of seeing her again and the dread of returning to the old drudgery of surveillance, I sent the letter, and waited a whole week without any answer. At last, one evening, when I returned from work, Sandy seemed in a state of unusual exhilaration. He looked at me again and again, winking and chuckling to himself in a way which showed me that his good spirits had something to do with my concerns; but he did not open on the subject till I had settled to my evening's reading. Then, having brewed himself an unusually strong mug of whisky-toddy, and brought out with great ceremony a clean pipe, he commenced.

'Alton, laddie, I've been fiechting Philistines for ye the day.'

'Ah! have you heard from my mother?'

'I wadna say that exactly; but there's been a gran baillie body* wi' me that calls himsel your uncle, and a braw young callant, a bairn o' his, I'm thinking.'

'Ah! that's my cousin George; and tell me – do tell me, what you said to them.'

'Ou – that'll be mair concern o' mine than o' yourn. But ye're no going back to your mither.'

My heart leapt up with – joy; there is no denying it – and then I burst into tears.

'And she won't see me? Has she really cast me off?'

'Why, that'll be verra much as ye prosper, I'm thinking. Ye're an unaccreedited hero, the noo, as Thomas Carlyle has it.* "But gin ye do weel by yoursel", saith the Psalmist, "ye'll find a' men speak well o' ye"* – if ye gang their gate. But ye're to gang to see your uncle at his shop o' Monday next, at one o'clock. Now stint your greeting, and read awa'.'

On the next Monday I took a holiday, the first in which I had ever indulged myself; and having spent a good hour in scrubbing away at my best shoes and Sunday suit, started, in fear and trembling, for my uncle's 'establishment'.

I was agreeably surprised, on being shown into the little back office at the back of the shop, to meet with a tolerably gracious reception from the good-natured Mammonite. He did not shake hands with me, it is true; – was I not a poor relation? But he told me to sit down, commended me for the excellent character which he had of me both from my master and Mackaye, and then entered on the subject of my literary tastes. He heard I was a precious clever fellow. No wonder, I came of a clever stock; his poor dear brother had plenty of brains for everything but business. 'And you see, my boy' (with a glance at the big ledgers and busy shop without), 'I knew a thing or two in my time, or I should not have been here. But without capital, *I* think brains a curse. Still we must make the best of a bad matter; and if you are inclined to help to raise the family name – not that I think much of book writers myself – poor starving devils, half of them – but still people do talk about them – and a man might get a snug thing as newspaper editor, with interest; or clerk to something or other – always some new company in the wind now – and I should have no objection, if you seemed likely to do us credit, to speak a word for you. I've none of your mother's confounded puritanical notions, I can tell you; and, what's more, I have, thank Heaven, as fine a city connexion as any man. But you must mind and make yourself a good accountant – learn double entry on the Italian method – that's a good practical study; and if that old Sawney* is soft enough to teach you other things gratis, he may as well teach you that too. I'll bet he knows something about it – the old Scotch fox. There now – that'll do – there's five shillings for you – mind you don't lose them – and if I hear a good account of you, why, perhaps – but there's no use making promises.'

At this moment a tall, handsome young man, whom I did not at first recognise as my cousin George, swung into the office, and shook me cordially by the hand.

'Hullo, Alton, how are you? Why, I hear you're coming out as a regular genius – breaking out in a new place, upon my honour! Have you done with him, governor?'

'Well, I think I have. I wish you'd have a talk with him, my boy. I'm sorry I can't see more of him, but I have to meet a party on business at the West-end at two, and Alderman Tumbril and family dine with us this evening, don't they? I think our small table will be full.'

'Of course it will. Come along with me, and we'll have a chat in some quiet out-of-the-way place. This city is really so noisy that you can't hear your own ears, as our dean says in lecture.'

So he carried me off, down back streets and alleys, a little puzzled at the extreme cordiality of his manner. Perhaps it sprung, as I learned afterwards to suspect, from his consistent and perpetual habit of ingratiating himself with every one whom he approached. He never cut a chimney-sweep if he knew him. And he found it pay. The children of this world are in their generation wiser than the children of light.*

Perhaps it sprung also, as I began to suspect in the first

hundred yards of our walk, from the desire of showing off before me the university clothes, manners, and gossip, which he had just brought back with him from Cambridge.

I had not seen him more than three or four times in my life before, and then he appeared to me merely a tall, handsome, conceited, slangy boy. But I now found him much improved – in all externals at least. He had made it his business, I knew, to perfect himself in all athletic pursuits which were open to a Londoner. As he told me that day – he found it pay, when one got among gentlemen. Thus he had gone up to Cambridge a capital skater, rower, pugilist – and billiard player. Whether or not that last accomplishment ought to be classed in the list of athletic sports, he contrived, by his own account, to keep it in that of paying ones. In both these branches he seemed to have had plenty of opportunities of distinguishing himself at college; and his tall, powerful figure showed the fruit of these exercises in a stately and confident, almost martial, carriage. Something jaunty, perhaps swaggering, remained still in his air and dress, which yet sat not ungracefully on him; but I could see that he had been mixing in society more polished and artificial than that to which we had either of us been accustomed, and in his smart Rochester,* well-cut trousers, and delicate French boots, he excited, I will not deny it, my boyish admiration and envy.

'Well,' he said, as soon as we were out of the shop, 'which way? Got a holiday? And how did you intend to spend it?'

'I wanted very much', I said, meekly, 'to see the pictures at the National Gallery.'

'Oh! ah! pictures don't pay; but, if you like – much better ones at Dulwich* – that's the place to go to – you can see the others any day – and at Dulwich, you know, they've got – why let me see –' And he ran over half-a-dozen outlandish names of painters, which, as I have never again met with them, I am inclined on the whole to consider as somewhat extemporaneous creations. However, I agreed to go.

'Ah! capital – very nice quiet walk, and convenient for me – very little out of my way home. I'll walk there with you.'

'One word for your neighbour and two for yourself,' thought I; but on we walked. To see good pictures had been a long-cherished hope of mine. Everything beautiful in form or colour was beginning of late to have an intense fascination for me. I had, now that I was emancipated, gradually dared to feed my greedy eyes by passing stares into the print-shop windows, and had learnt from them a thousand new notions, new emotions, new longings after beauties of Nature, which seemed destined never to be satisfied. But pictures, above all, foreign ones, had been, in my mother's eyes, Anathema Maranatha,* as vile Popish and Pagan vanities, the rags of the scarlet woman no less than the surplice itself – and now, when it came to the point, I hesitated at an act of such awful disobedience, even though unknown to her. My cousin, however, laughed down my scruples, told me I was out of leading-strings now, and, which was true enough, that it was 'a * * * deal better to amuse oneself in picture galleries without leave, than live a life of sneaking and lying under petticoat government, as all home-birds were sure to do in the long run.' And so I went on, while my cousin kept up a running fire of chat the whole way, inter-mixing shrewd, bold observations upon every woman who passed, with sneers at the fellows of the college to which we were going – their idleness and luxury – the large grammar-school which they were bound by their charter to keep up, and did not – and hints about private interest in high quarters, through which their wealthy uselessness had been politely overlooked, when all similar institutions in the kingdom were subject to the searching examination of a government com-mission.* Then there were stories of boat-races and gay noble-men, breakfast parties, and lectures on Greek plays, flavoured with a spice of Cambridge slang, all equally new to me – glimpses into a world of wonders, which made me feel, as I shambled along at his side, trying to keep step with his strides, more weakly and awkward and ignorant than ever.

We entered the gallery. I was in a fever of expectation.

The rich sombre light of the rooms, the rich heavy warmth of the stove-heated air, the brilliant and varied colouring and gilded frames which embroidered the walls, the hushed earnest-ness of a few artists who were copying, and the few visitors who were lounging from picture to picture, struck me at once with mysterious awe. But my attention was in a moment concentrated on one figure opposite to me at the furthest end. I hurried straight towards it. When I had got half-way up the gallery I looked round for my cousin. He had turned aside to some picture of a Venus which caught my eye also, but which, I remember now, only raised in me then a shudder and a blush, and a fancy that the clergymen must be really as bad as my mother had taught me to believe, if they could allow in their galleries pictures of undressed women. I have learnt to view such things differently now, thank God. I have learnt that to the pure all things are pure. I have learnt the meaning of that great saying – the foundation of all art, as well as all modesty, all love, which tells us how 'the man and his wife were both naked, and not ashamed'.* But this book is the history of my mental growth; and my mistakes as well as my discoveries are steps in that development, and may bear a lesson in them.

How I have rambled! But as that day was the turning point of my whole short life, I may be excused for lingering upon every feature of it.

Timidly, but eagerly, I went up to the picture, and stood entranced before it. It was Guido's St. Sebastian.* All the world knows the picture, and all the world knows, too, the defects of the master, though in this instance he seems to have risen above himself, by a sudden inspiration, into that true naturalness, which is the highest expression of the Spiritual. But the very defects of the picture, its exaggeration, its theatricality, were especially calculated to catch the eye of a boy awaking out of the narrow dulness of Puritanism. The breadth and vastness of light and shade upon those manly limbs, so grand and yet so delicate, standing out against the background of lurid night, the helplessness of the bound arms, the arrow quivering in the shrinking side, the upturned brow, the eyes in whose dark depths enthusiastic faith seemed conquering agony and shame, the parted lips, which seemed to ask, like those martyrs in the Revelations, reproachful, half-resigned, 'O Lord how long?'*— Gazing at that picture since, I have understood how the idolatry of painted saints could arise in the minds even of the most educated, who were not disciplined by that stern regard for fact which is – or ought to be – the strength of Englishmen. I have understood the heart of that Italian girl, whom some such picture of St. Sebastian, perhaps this very one, excited, as the

Venus of Praxiteles the Grecian boy, to hopeless love, madness, and death.* Then I had never heard of St. Sebastian. I did not dream of any connexion between that, or indeed any picture, and Christianity; and yet, as I stood before it, I seemed to be face to face with the ghosts of my old Puritan forefathers, to see the spirit which supported them on pillories and scaffolds – the spirit of that true St. Margaret, the Scottish maiden whom Claverhouse and his soldiers chained to a post on the sea-sands to die by inches in the rising tide, till the sound of her hymns was slowly drowned in the dash of the hungry leaping waves.* My heart swelled within me, my eyes seemed bursting from my head with the intensity of my gaze, and great tears, I knew not why, rolled slowly down my face.

A woman's voice close to me, gentle yet of deeper tone than most, woke me from my trance.

'You seem to be deeply interested in that picture?'

I looked round, yet not at the speaker. My eyes, before they could meet hers, were caught by an apparition the most beautiful I had ever yet beheld. And what – what – have I seen equal to her since? Strange, that I should love to talk of her. Strange, that I fret at myself now because I cannot set down on paper line by line, and hue by hue, that wonderful loveliness of which—— But no matter. Had I but such an imagination as Petrarch, or rather, perhaps, had I his deliberate cold self-consciousness, what volumes of similes and conceits I might pour out, connecting that peerless face and figure with all lovely things which heaven and earth contain. As it is, because I cannot say all, I will say nothing, but repeat to the end again and again, Beautiful, beautiful, beautiful, beyond all statue, picture, or poet's dream. Seventeen – slight but rounded, a masque* and features delicate and regular, as if fresh from the chisel of Praxiteles* – I must try to describe after all, you see – a skin of alabaster (privet-flowers, Horace and Ariosto would have said, more true to Nature),* stained with the faintest flush; auburn hair, with that peculiar crisped wave seen in the old Italian pictures, and the warm, dark hazel eyes which so often accompany it; lips like a thread of vermilion, somewhat too thin, perhaps – but I thought little of that then; with such perfect finish and grace in every line and hue of her features and her dress, down to the little fingers and nails which showed through her thin gloves, that she seemed to my fancy fresh from the innermost chamber of some enchanted palace, 'where no air of heaven could visit her cheek too roughly.'* I dropped my eyes, quite dazzled. The question was repeated by a lady who stood with her, whose face I remarked then – as I did to the last, alas! – too little; dazzled at the first by outward beauty, perhaps because so utterly unaccustomed to it.

'It is indeed a wonderful picture,' I said, timidly. 'May I ask what is the subject of it?'

'Oh! don't you know?' said the young beauty, with a smile that thrilled through me. 'It is St. Sebastian.'

'I – I am very much ashamed,' I answered, colouring up, 'but I do not know who St. Sebastian was. Was he a Popish saint?'

A tall, stately old man, who stood with the two ladies, laughed kindly. 'No, not till they made him one against his will; and at the same time, by putting him into the mill which grinds old folks young again, converted him from a grizzled old Roman tribune into the young Apollo of Popery.'

'You will puzzle your hearer, my dear uncle,' said the same deep-toned woman's voice which had first spoken to me. 'As you volunteered the Saint's name, Lillian, you shall also tell his history.'

Simply and shortly, with just feeling enough to send through me a fresh thrill of delighted interest, without trenching the least on the most stately reserve, she told me the well-known history of the saint's martyrdom.

If I seem minute in my description, let those who read my story remember that such courteous dignity, however natural, I am bound to believe, it is to them, was to me an utterly new excellence in human nature. All my mother's Spartan nobleness of manner seemed unexpectedly combined with all my little sister's careless ease.

'What a beautiful poem the story would make!' said I, as soon as I recovered my thoughts.

'Well spoken, young man,' answered the old gentleman. 'Let us hope that your seeing a subject for a good poem will be the first step towards your writing one.'

As he spoke, he bent on me two clear eyes, full of kindliness, mingled with practised discernment. I saw that he was evidently a clergyman; but what his tight silk stockings and peculiar hat denoted I did not know. There was about him the air of a man accustomed equally to thought, to men, and to power. And I remarked somewhat maliciously, that my cousin, who had strutted up towards us on seeing me talking to two ladies, the instant he caught sight of those black silk stockings and that strange hat, fell suddenly in countenance, and sidling off somewhat meekly into the background, became absorbed in the examination of a Holy Family.

I answered something humbly, I forget what, which led to a conversation. They questioned me as to my name, my mother, my business, my studies; while I revelled in the delight of stolen glances at my newfound Venus Victrix,* who was as forward as any of them in her questions and her interest. Perhaps she enjoyed, at least she could not help seeing, the admiration for herself which I took no pains to conceal. At last the old man cut the conversation short by a quiet 'Good morning, sir,' which astonished me. I had never heard voices whose tone was so courteous and yet so chillingly peremptory. As they turned away, he repeated to himself once or twice, as if to fix them in his mind, my name and my master's, and awoke in me, perhaps too thoughtlessly, a tumult of vague hopes. Once and again the beauty and her companion looked back towards me, and seemed talking of me, and my face was burning scarlet, when my cousin swung up in his hard, off-hand way.

'By Jove, Alton, my boy! you're a knowing fellow. I congratulate you! At your years, indeed! to rise a dean and two beauties at the first throw, and hook them fast!'

'A dean!' I said, in some trepidation.

'Ay, a live dean – didn't you see the cloven foot sticking out from under his shoe-buckle? What news for your mother! What will the ghosts of your grandfathers to the seventh generation say to this, Alton? Colloquing in Pagan picture-galleries with shovel-hatted Philistines! And that's not the worst, Alton,' he ran on. 'Those daughters of Moab – those daughters of Moab——'*

'Hold your tongue,' I said, almost crying with vexation.

'Look there, if you want to save your good-temper. There, she is looking back again – not at poor me, though. What a lovely girl she is! – and a real lady – *l'air noble* – the rael genuine grit, as Sam Slick says,* and no mistake. By Jove, what a face! what hands! what feet! what a figure – in spite of crinolines and all abominations! And didn't she know it? And didn't she know that you knew it too?' And he ran on, descanting coarsely on beauties which I dared not even have profaned by naming, in a way that made me, I knew not why, mad with jealousy and indignation. She seemed mine alone in all the world. What right had any other human being, above all, he, to dare to mention her? I turned again to my St. Sebastian. That movement only brought on me a fresh volley of banter.

'Oh, that's the dodge, is it, to catch intellectual fine ladies? – to fall into an extatic attitude before a picture – But then we must have Alton's genius, you know, to find out which the fine pictures are. I must read up that subject, by-the-bye. It might be a paying one among the dons. For the present, here goes in for an attitude. Will this do, Alton?' And he arranged himself admiringly before the picture in an attitude so absurd and yet so graceful, that I did not know whether to laugh at him or hate him.

'At all events,' he added, dryly, 'it will be as good as playing the evangelical at Carus's tea-parties,* or taking the sacrament regularly for fear one's testimonials should be refused.' And then he looked at me, and through me, in his intense, confident way, to see that his hasty words had not injured him with me. He used to meet one's eye as boldly as any man I ever saw; but it was not the simple gaze of honesty and innocence, but an imperious, searching look, as if defying scrutiny. His was a true mesmeric eye, if ever there was one. No wonder it worked the miracles it did.

'Come along,' he said, suddenly seizing my arm. 'Don't you see they're leaving? Out of the gallery after them, and get a good look at the carriage and the arms upon it. I saw one standing there as we came in. It may pay us – you, that is – to know it again.'

We went out, I holding him back, I knew not why, and

arrived at the outer gate just in time to see them enter the carriage and drive off. I gazed to the last, but did not stir.

'Good boy,' he said; 'knowing still. If you had bowed, or showed the least sign of recognition, you would have broken the spell.'

But I hardly heard what he said, and stood gazing stupidly after the carriage as it disappeared. I did not know then what had happened to me. I know now, alas! too well.

CHAPTER VII

FIRST LOVE

TRULY I said, I did not know what had happened to me. I did not attempt to analyse the intense, overpowering instinct which from that moment made the lovely vision I had seen the lodestar of all my thoughts. Even now, I can see nothing in those feelings of mine but simple admiration – idolatry if you will – of physical beauty. Doubtless there was more – doubtless – I had seen pretty faces before, and knew that they were pretty, but they had passed from my retina, like the prints of beauties which I saw in the shop windows, without exciting a thought – even a conscious emotion of complacency. But this face did not pass away. Day and night I saw it, just as I had seen it in the gallery. The same playful smile – the same glance alternately turned to me, and the glowing picture above her head – and that was all I saw or felt. No child ever nestled upon its mother's shoulder with feelings more celestially pure than those with which I counted over day and night each separate lineament of that exceeding loveliness. Romantic? extravagant? Yes; if the world be right in calling a passion romantic just in proportion as it is not merely hopeless, but pure and unselfish, drawing its delicious power from no hope or faintest desire of enjoyment, but merely from simple delight in its object – then my passion was most romantic. I never thought of disparity in rank. Why should I? That could not blind the eyes of my imagination. She was beautiful, and that was all, and all in all, to me; and had our stations been exchanged, or more than exchanged; had I been King Cophetua,* and she the beggar-maid, I should have gloried in her just as much.

Beloved sleepless hours, which I spent in picturing that scene to myself, with all the brilliance of fresh recollection! Beloved hours! how soon you passed away! Soon – soon my imagination began to fade; the traces of her features on my mind's eye became confused and dim; and then came over me the fierce desire to see her again, that I might renew the freshness of that charming image. Thereon grew up an agony of longing – an agony of weeks, and months, and years. Where could I find that face again? was my ruling thought from morning until eve. I knew that it was hopeless to look for her at the gallery where I had first seen her. My only hope was, that at some place of public resort at the West-end I might catch, if but for a moment, an inspiring glance of that radiant countenance. I lingered round the Burton Arch;* and Hyde Park Gate – but in vain. I peered into every carriage, every bonnet that passed me in the thorough-fares – in vain. I stood patiently at the doors of exhibitions, and concerts, and playhouses, to be shoved back by policemen, and insulted by footmen – but in vain. Then I tried the fashionable churches, one by one; and sat in the free seats, to listen to prayers and sermons, not a word of which, alas! I cared to understand, with my eyes searching carefully every pew and gallery, face by face; always fancying, in self-torturing wayward-ness, that she might be just in the part of the gallery which I could not see. Oh! miserable days of hope deferred, making the heart sick!* Miserable gnawing of disappointment with which I returned at nightfall, to force myself down to my books! Equally miserable rack of hope on which my nerves were stretched every morning when I rose, counting the hours till my day's work should be over, and my mad search begin again! At last 'my torment did by length of time become my element.' I returned steadily as ever to the studies which I had at first neglected, much to Mackaye's wonder and disgust; and the vain hunt after that face became a part of my daily task, to be got through with the same dull, sullen effort, with which all I did was now transacted.

Mackaye, I suppose, at first, attributed my absences, and idleness to my having got into bad company. But it was some weeks before he gently enough told me his suspicions, and they were answered by a burst of tears, and a passionate denial, which set them at rest for ever. But I had not courage to tell him what was the matter with me. A sacred modesty, as well as a sense of the impossibility of explaining my emotions, held me back. I had a half-dread, too, to confess the whole truth, of his ridiculing a fancy, to say the least, so utterly impracticable; and my only confidant was a picture in the National Gallery, in one of the faces of which I had discovered some likeness to my Venus; and there I used to go and stand at spare half hours, and feel the happier for staring and staring, and whispering to the dead canvas the extravagances of my idolatry.

But soon the bitter draught of disappointment began to breed harsher thoughts in me. Those fine gentlemen who rode past me in the park, who rolled by in carriages, sitting face to face with ladies, as richly dressed, if not as beautiful, as she was – they could see her when they liked – why not I? What right had their eyes to a feast denied to mine? They, too, who did not appreciate, adore that beauty as I did – for who could worship her like me? At least they had not suffered for her as I had done; they had not stood in rain and frost, fatigue and blank despair – watching – watching – month after month; and I was making coats for them! The very garment I was stitching at, might, in a day's time, be in her presence – touching her dress; and its wearer bowing, and smiling, and whispering – he had not bought that bliss by watching in the rain. It made me mad to think of it.

I will say no more about it. That is a period of my life on which I cannot even now look back without a shudder.

At last, after perhaps a year or more, I summoned up courage to tell my story to Sandy Mackaye, and burst out with complaints more pardonable, perhaps, than reasonable.

'Why have I not as good a right to speak to her, to move in the same society in which she moves, as any of the fops of the day? Is it because these aristocrats are more intellectual than I? I should not fear to measure brains against most of them now; and give me the opportunities which they have, and I would die if I did not outstrip them. Why have I not those opportunities? Is that fault of others to be visited on me? Is it because they are more refined than I? What right have they, if this said refinement be so necessary a qualification, a difference so deep – that without it, there is to be an everlasting gulf between man and man – what right have they to refuse to let me share in it, to give me the opportunity of acquiring it?'

'Wad ye ha' them set up a dancing academy for working men, wi' "manners tocht here to the lower classes"? They'll no break up their ain monopoly; trust them for it! Na: if ye want to get amang them, I'll tell ye the way o't. Write a book o' poems, and ca' it "A Voice fra' the Goose, by a Working Tailor" – and then – why, after a dizen years or so of starving and scribbling for your bread, ye'll ha' a chance o' finding yersel a lion, and a flunkey,* and a licker o' trenchers – ane that jokes for his dinner, and sells his soul for a fine leddy's smile – till ye presume to think they're in earnest, and fancy yersel a man o' the same blude as they, and fa' in love wi' one of them – and then they'll teach you your level, and send ye off to gauge whusky like Burns,* or leave ye to die in a ditch as they did wi' puir Thom.'*

'Let me die, anywhere or anyhow, if I can but be near her – see her—'

'Married to anither body? – and nursing anither body's bairns? Ah boy, boy – do ye think that was what ye were made for; to please yersel wi' a woman's smiles, or e'en a woman's kisses – or to please yersel at all? How do ye expect ever to be happy, or strong, or a man at a', as long as ye go on looking to enjoy yersel – yersel? I ha' tried it. Mony was the year I looked for nought but my ain pleasure, and got it too, when it was a'

> Sandy Mackaye, bonny Sandy Mackaye,
> There he sits singing the lang simmer's day;
> Lassies gae to him,
> And kiss him, and woo him—
> Na bird is sa merry as Sandy Mackaye.

An' muckle good cam' o't. Ye may fancy I'm talking like a sour, disappointed auld carle. But I tell ye nay. I've got that's worth living for, though I am downhearted at times, and fancy a's wrong, and there's na hope for us on earth, we be a' sic liars – a' liars, I think; "a universal liars-rock substrawtum", as Mr.

Carlyle says.* I'm a great liar often mysel, specially when I'm
praying. Do ye think I'd live on here in this meeserable crankit
auld bane-barrel of a body, if it was not for The Cause, and for
the puir young fellows that come in to me whiles to get some
book-learning about the gran' auld Roman times, when folks
didna care for themselves, but for the nation, and a man
counted wife and bairns and money as dross and dung, in
comparison with the great Roman city, that was the mither of
them a', and wad last on, free and glorious, after they and their
bairns were a' dead thegither? Hoot man! If I had na The
Cause to care for and to work for, whether I ever see it
triumphant on earth or no – I'd just tak the cauld-water-cure off
Waterloo Bridge,* and mak' mysel a case for the Humane
Society.'*

'And what is The Cause?' I asked.

'Wud I tell ye? We want no ready-made freens o' The Cause.
I dinna hauld wi' thae French indoctrinating pedants,* that
look to stick free opinions into a man as ye'd stick pins into a
pincushion, to fa' out again the first shake. Na – The Cause
must find a man, and tak hauld o' him, willy-nilly, and grow up
in him like an inspiration, till he can see nocht but in the light
o't. Puir bairn!' he went on, looking with a half-sad, half-comic
face at me – 'puir bairn – like a young bear, wi' a' your sorrows
before ye! This time seven years ye'll ha' no need to come
speering and questioning what The Cause is, and the Gran
Cause, and the Only Cause worth working for on the earth o'
God. And noo gang your gate, and mak' fine feathers for foul
birds. I'm gaun whar ye'll be ganging too, before long.'

As I went sadly out of the shop, he called me back.

'Stay a wee, bairn; there's the Roman History* for ye. There
ye'll read what The Cause is, and how they that seek their ain
are no worthy thereof.'

I took the book, and found in the legends of Brutus, and
Cocles, and Scævola, and the retreat to the Mons Sacer, and
the Gladiator's war,* what The Cause was, and forgot awhile
in those tales of antique heroism and patriotic self-sacrifice my
own selfish longings and sorrows.

*

But, after all, the very advice which was meant to cure me of those selfish longings, only tended, by diverting me from my living outward idol, to turn my thoughts more than ever inward, and tempt them to feed on their own substance. I passed whole days on the workroom floor in brooding silence – my mind peopled with an incoherent rabble of phantasms patched up from every object of which I had ever read. I could not control my day-dreams; they swept me away with them over sea and land, and into the bowels of the earth. My soul escaped on every side from my civilized dungeon of brick and mortar, into the great free world from which my body was debarred. Now I was the corsair* in the pride of freedom on the dark blue sea. Now I wandered in fairy caverns among the bones of primæval monsters. I fought at the side of Leonidas,* and the Maccabee who stabbed the Sultan's elephant,* and saw him crushed beneath its falling bulk. Now I was a hunter in tropic forests – I heard the parrots scream, and saw the humming-birds flit on from gorgeous flower to flower. Gradually I took a voluntary pleasure in calling up these images, and working out their details into words with all the accuracy and care for which my small knowledge gave me materials. And as the self-indulgent habit grew on me, I began to live two lives – one mechanical and outward, one inward and imaginative. The thread passed through my fingers without my knowing it; I did my work as a machine might do it. The dingy stifling room, the wan faces of my companions, the scanty meals which I snatched, I saw dimly, as in a dream. The tropics, and Greece, the imaginary battles which I fought, the phantoms into whose mouths I put my thoughts, were real and true to me. They met me when I woke – they floated along beside me as I walked to work – they acted their fantastic dramas before me through the sleepless hours of night. Gradually certain faces among them became familiar – certain personages grew into coherence, as embodiments of those few types of character which had struck me the most, and played an analogous part in every fresh fantasia. Sandy Mackaye's face figured incongruously enough as Leonidas, Brutus, a Pilgrim Father; and gradually, in spite of myself, and the fear with which I looked on the recurrence of that dream, Lillian's figure

re-entered my fairy-land. I saved her from a hundred dangers;
I followed her through dragon-guarded caverns and the cor-
ridors of magic castles; I walked by her side through the forests
of the Amazon...

And now I began to crave for some means of expressing these
fancies to myself. While they were mere thoughts, parts of me,
they were unsatisfactory, however delicious. I longed to put
them outside me, that I might look at them and talk to them as
permanent independent things. First I tried to sketch them on
the whitewashed walls of my garret, on scraps of paper begged
from Mackaye, or picked up in the workroom. But from my
ignorance of any rules of drawing, they were utterly devoid of
beauty, and only excited my disgust. Besides, I had thoughts
as well as objects to express – thoughts strange, sad, wild, about
my own feelings, my own destiny, and drawing could not speak
them for me.

Then I turned instinctively to poetry: with its rules I was
getting rapidly conversant. The mere desire of imitation urged
me on, and when I tried, the grace of rhyme and metre covered
a thousand defects. I tell my story, not as I saw it then, but as
I see it now. A long and lonely voyage, with its monotonous
days and sleepless nights – its sickness and heart-loneliness, has
given me opportunities for analysing my past history which
were impossible then, amid the ceaseless in-rush of new images,
the ceaseless ferment of their re-combination, in which my life
was passed from sixteen to twenty-five. The poet, I suppose,
must be a seer as long as he is a worker, and a seer only. He has
no time to philosophise – to 'think about thinking', as Goethe,
I have somewhere read, says that he never could do. It is too
often only in sickness and prostration and sheer despair, that
the fierce voracity and swift digestion of his soul can cease, and
give him time to know himself and God's dealings with him;
and for that reason it is good for him, too, to have been afflicted.

I do not write all this to boast of it; I am ready to bear sneers
at my romance – my day-dreams – my unpractical habits of
mind, for I know that I deserve them. But such was the
appointed growth of my uneducated mind; no more unhealthy
a growth, if I am to believe books, than that of many a
carefully trained one. High-born geniuses, they tell me, have

their idle visions as well as we working men; and Oxford has seen
of late years as wild Icarias conceived as ever were fathered by
a red Republic.* For, indeed, we have the same flesh and blood,
the same God to teach us, the same devil to mislead us, whether
we choose to believe it or not. But there were excuses for me.
We Londoners are not accustomed from our youth to the poems
of a great democratic genius, as the Scotchmen are to their
glorious Burns. We have no chance of such an early acquaintance with poetic art as that which enabled John Bethune,* one
of the great unrepresented – the starving Scotch day-labourer,
breaking stones upon the parish roads, to write at the age of
seventeen such words as these:

> Hail, hallow'd evening! sacred hour to me!
> Thy clouds of grey, thy vocal melody,
> Thy dreamy silence oft to me have brought
> A sweet exchange from toil to peaceful thought.
> Ye purple heavens! how often has my eye,
> Wearied with its long gaze on drudgery,
> Look'd up and found refreshment in the hues
> That gild thy vest with colouring profuse!
>
> O, evening grey! how oft have I admired
> Thy airy tapestry, whose radiance fired
> The glowing minstrels of the olden time,
> Until their very souls flow'd forth in rhyme.
> And I have listened, till my spirit grew
> Familiar with their deathless strains, and drew
> From the same source some portion of the glow
> Which fill'd their spirits, when from earth below
> They scann'd thy golden imagery. And I
> Have consecrated *thee*, bright evening sky
> My fount of inspiration: and I fling
> My spirit on thy clouds – an offering
> To the great Deity of dying day,
> Who hath transfused o'er thee his purple ray.

*

After all, our dreams do little harm to the rich. Those who
consider Chartism as synonymous with devil-worship, should
bless and encourage them, for the very reason for which we
working men ought to dread them; for, quickened into prurient

activity by the low, novel-mongering press, they help to enervate
and besot all but the noblest minds among us. Here and there
a Thomas Cooper, sitting in Stafford gaol, after a youth spent
in cobbling shoes, vents his treasures of classic and historic
learning in a 'Purgatory of Suicides';* or a Prince* becomes
the poet of the poor, no less for having fed his boyish fancy
with 'The Arabian Nights' and 'The Pilgrim's Progress'. But,
with the most of us, sedentary and monotonous occupations, as
has long been known, create of themselves a morbidly-meditative
and fantastic turn of mind. And what else, in Heaven's name,
ye fine gentlemen – what else can a working man do with his
imagination, but dream? What else will you let him do with it,
oh ye education-pedants, who fancy that you can teach the
masses as you would drill soldiers, every soul alike,* though
you will not bestir yourselves to do even that? Are there no
differences of rank – God's rank, not man's – among us?
You have discovered, since your school-boy days, the fallacy of
the old nomenclature which civilly classed us all together as
'the snobs', 'the blackguards'; which even – so strong is habit –
tempted Burke himself to talk of us as 'the swinish multitude'.*
You are finding yourselves wrong there. A few more years'
experience, not in mis-educating the poor, but in watching the
poor really educate themselves, may teach you that we are not
all by nature dolts and idiots; that there are differences of brain
among us, just as great as there is between you; that there are
those among us whose education ought not to end, and will not
end, with the putting off of the parish cap and breeches; whom
it is cruelty, as well as folly, to toss back into the hell of mere
manual drudgery, as soon as you have – if, indeed, you have
been even so bountiful as that – excited in them a new thirst of
the intellect and imagination. If you provide that craving with
no wholesome food, you at least have no right to blame it if it
shall gorge itself with poison.

Dare for once to do a strange thing, and let yourself be
laughed at; go to a workman's meeting – a Chartist meeting,
if you will; and look honestly at the faces and brows of those
so-called incendiaries, whom your venal caricaturists have
taught you to believe a mixture of cur-dog and baboon – we,
for our part, shall not be ashamed to show foreheads* against

your laughing House of Commons – and then say, what employment can those men find in the soulless routine of mechanical labour for the mass of brain which they almost universally possess? They must either dream or agitate; perhaps they are now learning how to do both to some purpose.

But I have found, by sad experience, that there is little use in declamation. I had much better simply tell my story, and leave my readers to judge of the facts, if, indeed, they will be so far courteous as to believe them.

CHAPTER VIII

LIGHT IN A DARK PLACE

So I made my first attempt at poetry – need I say that my subject was the beautiful Lillian? And need I say, too, that I was as utterly disgusted at my attempt to express her in words, as I had been at my trial with the pencil? It chanced also, that after hammering out half-a-dozen verses, I met with Mr. Tennyson's poems; and the unequalled sketches of women that I found there,* while they had, with the rest of the book, a new and abiding influence on my mind, were quite enough to show me my own fatal incompetency in that line. I threw my verses away, never to resume them. Perhaps I proved thereby the depth of my affection. Our mightiest feelings are always those which remain most unspoken. The most intense lovers and the greatest poets have generally, I think, written very little personal love-poetry, while they have shown in fictitious characters a knowledge of the passion too painfully intimate to be spoken of in the first person.

But to escape from my own thoughts, I could not help writing something; and to escape from my own private sorrows, writing on some matter with which I had no personal concern. And so, after much casting about for subjects, Childe Harold and the old missionary records contrived to celebrate a spiritual wedding in my brain, of which anomalous marriage came a proportionately anomalous offspring.

My hero was not to be a pirate, but a pious sea-rover, who,

with a crew of saints, or at least uncommonly fine fellows, who could be very manly and jolly, and yet all be good Christians, of a somewhat vague and latitudinarian cast of doctrine (for my own was becoming rapidly so), set forth under the red-cross flag to colonise and convert one of my old paradises, a South Sea Island.

I forget most of the lines – they were probably great trash, but I hugged them to my bosom as a young mother does her first child.

> 'Twas sunset in the lone Pacific world,
> The rich gleams fading in the western sky;
> Within the still Lagoon the sails were furled,
> The red-cross flag alone was flaunting high.
> Before them was the low and palm-fringed shore,
> Behind, the outer ocean's baffled roar.

After which valiant plunge in medias res, came a great lump of description, after the manner of youths – of the island, and the white houses, and the banana groves, and above all, the single volcano towering over the whole, which

> Shaking a sinful isle with thundering shocks,
> Reproved the worshippers of stones and stocks.

Then how a line of foam appears on the Lagoon, which is supposed at first to be a shoal of fish, but turns out to be a troop of naked island beauties, swimming out to the ship. The decent missionaries were certainly guiltless of putting that into my head, whether they ever saw it or not – a great many things happening in the South Seas of which they find it convenient to say nothing. I think I picked it up from Wallis, or Cook,* or some other plain-spoken voyager.

The crew gaze in pardonable admiration, but the hero, in a long speech, reproves them for their light-mindedness, reminds them of their sacred mission, and informs them that,

> The soldiers of the cross should turn their eyes
> From carnal lusts and heathen vanities;

beyond which indisputable assertion I never got; for this being about the fiftieth stanza, I stopped to take breath a little; and reading and re-reading, patching and touching continually, grew so accustomed to my bantling's face, that, like a mother, I could not tell whether it was handsome or hideous, sense or nonsense. I have since found out that the true plan, for myself at least, is to write off as much as possible at a time, and then lay it by and forget it for weeks – if I can, for months. After that, on returning to it, the mind regards it as something altogether strange and new, and can, or rather ought to, judge of it as it would of the work of another pen.

But really, between conceit and disgust, fancying myself one day a great new poet, and the next a mere twaddler, I got so puzzled and anxious, that I determined to pluck up courage, go to Mackaye, and ask him to solve the problem for me.

'Hech, sirs, poetry! I've been expecting it. I suppose it's the appointed gate o' a workman's intellectual life – that same lust o' versification. Aweel, aweel – let's hear.'

Blushing and trembling, I read my verses aloud in as resonant and magniloquent a voice as I could command. I thought Mackaye's upper lip would never stop lengthening, or his lower lip protruding. He chuckled intensely at the unfortunate rhyme 'shocks' and 'stocks'. Indeed, it kept him in chuckling matter for a whole month afterwards; but when I had got to the shoal of naked girls, he could bear no more, and burst out—

'What the deevil! is there no harlotry and idolatry here in England, that ye maun gang speering after it in the Cannibal Islands? Are ye gaun to be like they puir aristocrat bodies, that wad suner hear an Italian dog howl, than an English nightingale sing, and winna harken to Mr. John Thomas till he calls himself Giovanni Thomasino; or do ye tak yoursel for a singing-bird, to go all your days tweedledumdeeing out into the lift,* just for the lust o' hearing your ain clan clatter? Will ye be a man or a lintie?* Coral Islands? Pacific? What do ye ken anent Pacifics? Are ye a cockney or a Cannibal Islander? Dinna stand there, ye gowk, as fusionless as a docken,* but tell me that. Whaur de ye live?'

'What do you mean, Mr. Mackaye!' asked I, with a doleful and disappointed visage.

'Mean – why, if God had meant ye to write anent Pacifics, He'd ha put ye there – and because He means ye to write aboot London town, He's put ye there – and gien ye an unco sharp taste o' the ways o't; and I'll gie ye anither. Come along wi' me.'

And he seized me by the arm, and hardly giving me time to put on my hat, marched me out into the streets, and away through Clare Market to St. Giles's*

It was a foul, chilly, foggy Saturday night. From the butchers' and greengrocers' shops the gas-lights flared and flickered, wild and ghastly, over haggard groups of slip-shod dirty women, bargaining for scraps of stale meat and frostbitten vegetables, wrangling about short weight and bad quality. Fish-stalls and fruit-stalls lined the edge of the greasy pavement, sending up odours as foul as the language of sellers and buyers. Blood and sewer-water crawled from under doors and out of spouts, and reeked down the gutters among offal, animal and vegetable, in every stage of putrefaction. Foul vapours rose from cowsheds and slaughter-houses, and the doorways of undrained alleys, where the inhabitants carried the filth out on their shoes from the back-yard into the court, and from the court up into the main street; while above, hanging like cliffs over the streets – those narrow, brawling torrents of filth, and poverty, and sin – the houses with their teeming load of life were piled up into the dingy choking night. A ghastly, deafening, sickening sight it was. Go, scented Belgravian! and see what London is! and then go to the library which God has given thee* – one often fears in vain – and see what science says this London might be!

'Ay,' he muttered to himself, as he strode along, 'sing awa; get yoursel wi' child wi' pretty fancies and gran' words, like the rest of the poets, and gang to hell for it.'

'To hell, Mr. Mackaye?'

'Ay, to a verra real hell, Alton Locke, laddie – a warse ane than ony fiends' kitchen, or subterranean Smithfield that ye'll hear o' in the pulpits – the hell on earth o' being a flunkey, and a humbug, and a useless peacock, wasting God's gifts on your ain lusts and pleasures – and kenning it – and not being able to get oot o'it, for the chains o' vanity and self-indulgence. I've warned ye. Now look there——'

He stopped suddenly before the entrance of a miserable alley—

'Look! there's not a soul down that yard but's either beggar, drunkard, thief, or warse. Write anent that! Say how ye saw the mouth o' hell, and the two pillars thereof at the entry – the pawnbroker's shop o' one side and the gin palace at the other – twa monstrous deevils, eating up men, and women, and bairns, body and soul. Look at the jaws o' the monsters, how they open and open, and swallow in anither victim and anither. Write anent that.'

'What jaws, Mr. Mackaye!'

'They faulding-doors o' the gin shop, goose. Are na they a mair damnable man-devouring idol than ony red-hot statue o' Moloch, or wicker Gogmagog, wherein thae auld Britons burnt their prisoners?* Look at thae bare-footed, bare-backed hizzies, with their arms roun' the men's necks, and their mouths full o' vitriol and beastly words! Look at that Irishwoman pouring the gin down the babbie's throat! Look at that raff o' a boy gaun out o' the pawnshop, where he's been pledging the handkerchief he stole the morning, into the gin shop, to buy beer poisoned wi' grains o' paradise, and cocculus indicus, and saut,* and a' damnable, maddening, thirst-breeding, lust-breeding drugs! Look at that girl that went in wi' a shawl on her back and cam' out wi'out ane! Drunkards frae the breast! – harlots frae the cradle! – damned before they're born! John Calvin had an inkling o' the truth there, I'm a'most driven to think, wi' his reprobation deevil's doctrines!'

'Well – but – Mr. Mackaye, I know nothing about these poor creatures.'

'Then ye ought. What do ye ken anent the Pacific? Which is maist to your business? – thae bare-backed hizzies that play the harlot o' the other side o' the warld, or these – these thousands o' bare-backed hizzies that play the harlot o' your ain side – made out o' your ain flesh and blude? You a poet! True poetry, like true charity, my laddie, begins at hame. If ye'll be a poet at a', ye maun be a cockney poet; and while the cockneys be what they be, ye maun write, like Jeremiah of old, o' lamentation and mourning and woe, for the sins o' your people. Gin ye want to learn the spirit o' a people's poet, down wi' your Bible and read thae auld Hebrew prophets; gin ye wad learn the style, read your Burns frae morning till night; and gin ye'd learn the matter, just gang after your nose, and keep your eyes open, and ye'll no miss it.'

'But all this is so – so unpoetical.'

'Hech! Is there no the heeven above them there, and the hell beneath them? and God frowning, and the deevil grinning? No poetry there! Is no the verra idea of the classic tragedy defined to be, man conquered by circumstance? Canna ye see it there? And the verra idea of the modern tragedy, man conquering circumstance? – and I'll show ye that, too – in mony a garret where no eye but the gude God's enters, to see the patience, and the fortitude, and the self-sacrifice, and the luve stronger than death, that's shining in thae dark places o' the earth. Come wi' me, and see.'

We went on through a back street or two, and then into a huge, miserable house, which, a hundred years ago, perhaps, had witnessed the luxury, and rung to the laughter of some one great fashionable family, alone there in their glory. Now every room of it held its family, or its group of families – a phalanstery of all the fiends; – its grand staircase, with the carved ballustrades rotting and crumbling away piecemeal, converted into a common sewer for all its inmates. Up stair after stair we went, while wails of children, and curses of men, steamed out upon the hot stifling rush of air from every doorway, till, at the topmost story, we knocked at a garret door. We entered. Bare it was of furniture, comfortless, and freezing cold; but, with the exception of the plaster dropping from the roof, and the broken windows patched with rags and paper, there was a scrupulous neatness about the whole, which contrasted strangely with the filth and slovenliness outside. There was no bed in the room – no table. On a broken chair by the chimney sat a miserable old woman, fancying that she was warming her hands over embers which had long been cold, shaking her head, and muttering to herself with palsied lips about the guardians and the workhouse; while upon a few rags on the floor lay a girl, ugly, small-pox-marked, hollow-eyed, emaciated, her only bedclothes the skirt of a large handsome new riding-habit, at which two other girls, wan and tawdry, were stitching busily, as they sat right and left of her on the floor. The old woman took no notice of us as we entered; but one of the girls looked up, and, with a pleased gesture of recognition, put her finger up to her lips, and whispered, 'Ellen's asleep.'

'I'm not asleep, dears,' answered a faint, unearthly voice; 'I was only praying. Is that Mr. Mackaye?'

'Ay, my lasses; but ha' ye gotten na fire the nicht?'

'No,' said one of them bitterly, 'we've earned no fire to-night, by fair trade or foul either.'

The sick girl tried to raise herself up and speak, but was stopped by a frightful fit of coughing and expectoration, as painful, apparently, to the sufferer as it was, I confess, disgusting even to me.

I saw Mackaye slip something into the hand of one of the girls, and whisper, 'A half-hundred of coals', to which she replied with an eager look of gratitude that I never can forget, and hurried out. Then the sufferer, as if taking advantage of her absence, began to speak quickly and eagerly.

'Oh, Mr. Mackaye – dear, kind Mr. Mackaye – do speak to her; and do speak to poor Lizzy here! I'm not afraid to say it before her, because she's more gentle like, and hasn't learnt to say bad words yet – but do speak to them, and tell them not to go the bad way, like all the rest. Tell them it'll never prosper. I know it is want that drives them to it, as it drives all of us – but tell them it's best to starve and die honest girls, than to go about with the shame and the curse of God on their hearts, for the sake of keeping this poor, miserable, vile body together a few short years more in this world o' sorrow. Do tell them, Mr. Mackaye.'

'I'm thinking,' said he, with the tears running down his old, withered face, 'ye'll mak a better preacher at that text than I shall, Ellen.'

'Oh, no, no; who am I, to speak to them? – it's no merit o' mine, Mr. Mackaye, that the Lord's kept me pure through it all. I should have been just as bad as any of them, if the Lord had not kept me out of temptation in His great mercy, by making me the poor, ill-favoured creature I am. From that time I was burnt when I was a child, and had the small-pox afterwards, oh! how sinful I was, and repined and rebelled against the Lord! And now I see it was all His blessed mercy to keep me out of evil, pure and unspotted for my dear Jesus, when He comes to take me to himself. I saw Him last night, Mr. Mackaye, as plain as I see you now, all in a flame of beautiful white fire, smiling at me so sweetly; and He showed me the wounds in His hands and His feet, and He said, 'Ellen, my own child, those that suffer with me here, they shall be glorified with me hereafter, for I'm coming very soon to take you home.'

Sandy shook his head at all this with a strange expression of face, as if he sympathised and yet disagreed, respected and yet smiled at the shape which her religious ideas had assumed; and I remarked in the mean time that the poor girl's neck and arm were all scarred and distorted, apparently from the effects of a burn.

'Ah,' said Sandy, at length, 'I tauld ye ye were the better preacher of the two; ye've mair comfort to gie Sandy than he has to gie the like o' ye. But how is the wound in your back the day?'

Oh, it was wonderfully better! the doctor had come and given her such blessed ease with a great thick leather he had put under it, and then she did not feel the boards through so much. 'But oh, Mr. Mackaye, I'm so afraid it will make me live longer to keep me away from my dear Saviour. And there's one thing, too, that's breaking my heart, and makes me long to die this very minute, even if I didn't go to Heaven at all, Mr. Mackaye.' (And she burst out crying, and between her sobs it came out, as well as I could gather, that her notion was, that her illness was the cause of keeping the girls in '*the bad way*', as she called it.) 'For Lizzy here, I did hope that she had repented of it after all my talking to her; but since I've been so bad, and the girls have had to keep me most o' the time, she's gone out of nights just as bad as ever.'

Lizzy had hid her face in her hands the greater part of this speech. Now she looked up passionately, almost fiercely—

'Repent – I have repented – I repent of it every hour – I hate myself, and hate all the world because of it; but I must – I must; I cannot see her starve, and I cannot starve myself. When she first fell sick she kept on as long as she could, doing what she could, and then between us we only earned three shillings-a-week, and there was ever so much to take off for fire, and twopence for thread, and fivepence for candles; and then we were always getting fined, because they never gave us out the work till too late on purpose, and then they lowered prices

again; and now Ellen can't work at all, and there's four of us
with the old lady, to keep off two's work that couldn't keep
themselves alone.'

'Doesn't the parish allow the old lady anything?' I ventured
to ask.

'They used to allow half-a-crown for a bit; and the doctor
ordered Ellen things from the parish, but it isn't half of 'em
she ever got; and when the meat came, it was half times not fit
to eat, and when it was her stomach turned against it. If she
was a lady she'd be cockered up with all sorts of soups and
jellies, and nice things, just the minute she fancied 'em, and lie
on a water bed instead of the bare floor – and so she ought; but
where's the parish 'll do that? And the hospital wouldn't take
her in because she was incurable; and, besides, the old 'un
wouldn't let her go – nor into the union neither. When she's in
a good-humour like, she'll sit by her by the hour, holding her
hand and kissing of it, and nursing of it, for all the world like
a doll. But she won't hear of the workhouse; so now, these last
three weeks, they takes off all her pay, because they says she
must go into the house, and not kill her daughter by keeping
her out – as if they warn't a-killing her themselves.'

'No workhouse – no workhouse!' said the old woman,
turning round suddenly, in a clear, lofty voice. 'No workhouse,
sir, for an officer's daughter.'

And she relapsed into her stupor.

At that moment the other girl entered with the coals – but
without staying to light the fire, ran up to Ellen with some
trumpery dainty she had bought, and tried to persuade her to eat
it.

'We have been telling Mr. Mackaye everything,' said poor
Lizzy.

'A pleasant story, isn't it? Oh! if that fine lady, as we're
making that riding-habit for, would just spare only half the
money that goes in dressing her up to ride in the park, to send
us out to the colonies,* wouldn't I be an honest girl there? –
Maybe an honest man's wife! Oh! my God! wouldn't I slave
my fingers to the bone for him! Wouldn't I mend my life then!
I couldn't help it – it would be like getting into heaven out of
hell. But now – we must – we must – I tell you. I shall go mad

soon, I think, or take to drink. When I passed the gin shop down there just now, I had to run like mad for fear I should go in – and if I once took to that – Now then to work again. Make up the fire, Mrs. * * *, please do.'

And she sat down and began stitching frantically at the riding-habit, from which the other girl had hardly lifted her hands or eyes for a moment during our visit.

We made a motion as if to go.

'God bless you,' said Ellen; 'come again soon, dear Mr. Mackaye.'

'Good-bye!' said the elder girl, 'and good night to you. Night and day's all the same here – we must have this home by seven o'clock to-morrow morning. My lady's going to ride early they say, whoever she may be, and we must just sit up all night. It's often we haven't had our clothes off for a week together, from four in the morning till two the next morning sometimes – stitch, stitch, stitch. – Somebody's wrote a song about that* – I'll learn to sing it – it'll sound fitting-like, up here.'

'Better sing hymns,' said Ellen.

'Hymns for * * *?' answered the other, and then burst out into that peculiar wild, ringing, fiendish laugh – has my reader never heard it?

I pulled out the two or three shillings which I possessed, and tried to make the girls take them, for the sake of poor Ellen.

'No; you're a working man, and we won't feed on you – you'll want it some day – all the trade's going the same way as we, as fast as ever it can!'

Sandy and I went down the stairs.

'Poetic element? Yon lassie, rejoicing in her disfigurement and not her beauty, like the nuns of Peterborough in auld time, – is there no poetry there? That puir lassie, dying on the bare boards and seeing her Saviour in her dreams, is there na poetry there, callant? That auld body owre the fire, wi' her 'an officer's dochter', is there na poetry there? That ither, prostituting hersel to buy food for her freen – is there na poetry there? – tragedy—

> With hues as when some mighty painter dips
> His pen in dyes of earthquake and eclipse.*

Ay, Shelley's gran'; always gran'; but Fact is grander – God and Satan are grander. All around ye, in every gin shop and coster-monger's cellar, are God and Satan at death grips; every garret is a haill Paradise Lost or Paradise Regained: and will ye think it beneath ye to be the 'People's Poet''?'

CHAPTER IX

POETRY AND POETS

In the history of individuals, as well as in that of nations, there is often a period of sudden blossoming – a short luxuriant summer, not without its tornadoes and thunder-glooms, in which all the buried seeds of past observation leap forth together into life, and form, and beauty. And such with me were the two years that followed. I thought – I talked poetry to myself all day long. I wrote nightly on my return from work. I am astonished, on looking back, at the variety and quantity of my productions during that short time. My subjects were inten-tionally and professedly cockney ones. I had taken Mackaye at his word. I had made up my mind, that if I had any poetic power, I must do my duty therewith in that station of life to which it had pleased God to call me, and look at everything simply and faithfully as a London artisan. To this, I suppose, is to be attributed the little geniality and originality for which the public have kindly praised my verses; – a geniality which sprung, not from the atmosphere whence I drew, but from the honesty and single-mindedness with which, I hope, I laboured. Not from the atmosphere, indeed – that was ungenial enough; crime and poverty, all-devouring competition, and hopeless struggles against Mammon and Moloch, amid the roar of wheels, the ceaseless stream of pale, hard faces, intent on gain, or brooding over woe; amid endless prison-walls of brick, beneath a lurid, crushing sky of smoke and mist. It was a dark, noisy, thunderous element, that London life; a troubled sea that cannot rest, casting up mire and dirt; resonant of the clanking of chains, the grinding of remorseless machinery, the wail of lost spirits from the pit. And it did its work upon me; it gave a gloomy colouring, a glare as of some Dantean 'Inferno', to all my utterances. It did not excite me, or make me fierce – I was too much inured to it – but it crushed and saddened me; it deepened in me that peculiar melancholy of intellectual youth, which Mr. Carlyle has christened for ever by one of his immortal nicknames, 'Werterism';* I battened on my own melancholy. I believed, I loved to believe, that every face I immortal nicknames, 'Werterism';* I battened on my own and was I so far wrong? Was I so far wrong either in the gloomy tone of my own poetry? Should not a London poet's work just now be to cry, like the Jew of old,* about the walls of Jerusalem – 'Woe, woe to this city!' Is this a time to listen to the voices of singing men and singing women? or to cry, 'Oh! that my head were a fountain of tears, that I might weep for the sins of my people'? Is it not noteworthy, also, that it is in this vein that the London poets have always been greatest? Which of poor Hood's lyrics have an equal chance of immortality with 'The Song of the Shirt', and 'The Bridge of Sighs', rising, as they do, right out of the depths of that Inferno, sublime from their very simplicity? Which of Charles Mackay's lyrics can compare for a moment with the Æschylean grandeur, the terrible rhythmic lilt of his 'Cholera Chaunt'*—

> Dense on the stream the vapours lay,
> Thick as wool on the cold highway;
> Spungy and dim each lonely lamp,
> Shone o'er the streets so dull and damp;
> The moonbeams could not pierce the cloud
> That swathed the city like a shroud;
> There stood three shapes on the bridge alone,
> Three figures by the coping-stone;
> Gaunt and tall and undefined,
> Spectres built of mist and wind.
>
> I see his foot-marks east and west –
> I hear his tread in the silence fall –
> He shall not sleep, he shall not rest –
> He comes to aid us one and all.
> Were men as wise as men might be,
> They would not work for you, for me,
> For him that cometh over the sea;

But they will not hear the warning voice:
The Cholera comes, – Rejoice! rejoice!
He shall be lord of the swarming town!
And mow them down, and mow them down!

Not that I neglected, on the other hand, every means of extending the wanderings of my spirit into sunnier and more verdant pathways. If I had to tell the gay ones above of the gloom around me, I had also to go forth into the sunshine to bring home if it were but a wild-flower garland to those that sat in darkness and the shadow of death. That was all that I could offer them. The reader shall judge, when he has read this book throughout, whether I did not at last find for them something better than even all the beauties of nature.

But it was on canvas, and not among realities, that I had to choose my garlands; and therefore the picture galleries became more than ever my favourite – haunt, I was going to say; but, alas! it was not six times a-year that I got access to them. Still, when once every May I found myself, by dint of a hard-saved shilling, actually within the walls of that to me enchanted palace, the Royal Academy Exhibition – Oh, ye rich! who gaze round you at will upon your prints and pictures, if hunger is, as they say, a better sauce than any Ude invents,* and fasting itself may become the handmaid of luxury, you should spend, as I did perforce, weeks and months shut out from every glimpse of Nature, if you would taste her beauties, even on canvas, with perfect relish and childish self-abandonment. How I loved and blest those painters! how I thanked Creswick for every transparent, shade-chequered pool; Fielding, for every rain-clad down; Cooper, for every knot of quiet cattle beneath the cool, grey willows; Stanfield, for every snowy peak, and sheet of foam-fringed sapphire* – each and every one of them a leaf out of the magic book which else was ever closed to me. Again, I say, how I loved and blest those painters! On the other hand, I was not neglecting to read as well as to write poetry; and, to speak first of the highest, I know no book, always excepting Milton, which at once so quickened and exalted my poetical view of man and his history, as that great prose poem, the single epic of modern days, Thomas Carlyle's 'French Revolution'. Of the general effect which his works had on me,

I shall say nothing: it was the same as they have had, thank God, on thousands of my class and of every other. But that book above all first recalled me to the overwhelming and yet ennobling knowledge that there was such a thing as Duty; first taught me to see in history not the mere farce-tragedy of man's crimes and follies, but the dealings of a righteous Ruler of the universe, whose ways are in the great deep, and whom the sins and errors, as well as the virtues and discoveries of man, must obey and justify.*

Then, in a happy day, I fell on Alfred Tennyson's poetry, and found there, astonished and delighted, the embodiment of thoughts about the earth around me which I had concealed, because I fancied them peculiar to myself. Why is it that the latest poet has generally the greatest influence over the minds of the young? Surely not for the mere charm of novelty? The reason is, that he, living amid the same hopes, the same temptations, the same sphere of observation as they, gives utterance and outward form to the very questions which, vague and wordless, have been exercising their hearts. And what endeared Tennyson especially to me, the working man, was, as I afterwards discovered, the altogether democratic tendency of his poems. True, all great poets are by their office democrats; seers of man only as man; singers of the joys, the sorrows, the aspirations common to all humanity; but in Alfred Tennyson there is an element especially democratic, truly levelling; not his political opinions, about which I know nothing, and care less, but his handling of the trivial every-day sights and sounds of nature. Brought up, as I understand, in a part of England* which possesses not much of the picturesque, and nothing of that which the vulgar call sublime, he has learnt to see that in all nature, in the hedgerow and the sandbank, as well as in the alp peak and the ocean waste, is a world of true sublimity, – a minute infinite, – an ever-fertile garden of poetic images, the roots of which are in the unfathomable and the eternal, as truly as any phenomenon which astonishes and awes the eye. The descriptions of the desolate pools and creeks where the dying swans floated, the hint of the silvery marsh mosses by Mariana's moat,* came to me like revelations. I always knew there was something beautiful, wonderful, sublime in those flowery dykes of Battersea-fields; in the long gravelly sweeps of that lone tidal shore; and here was a man who had put them into words for me! This is what I call democratic art – the revelation of the poetry which lies in common things. And surely all the age is tending in that direction: in Landseer and his dogs* – in Fielding and his downs,* with a host of noble fellow-artists – and in all authors who have really seized the nation's mind, from Crabbe and Burns and Wordsworth to Hood and Dickens, the great tide sets ever onward, outward, towards that which is common to the many, not that which is exclusive to the few – towards the likeness of Him who causes His rain to fall on the just and on the unjust, and His sun to shine on the evil and the good; who knoweth the cattle upon a thousand hills, and all the beasts of the field are in His sight.

Well – I must return to my story. And here some one may ask me, 'But did you not find this true spiritual democracy, this universal knowledge and sympathy, in Shakespeare above all other poets?' It may be my shame to have to confess it; but though I find it now, I did not then. I do not think, however, my case is singular: from what I can ascertain, there is even with regularly educated minds a period of life at which that great writer is not appreciated, just on account of his very greatness; on account of the deep and large experience which the true understanding of his plays requires – experience of man, of history, of art, and above all of those sorrows whereby, as Hezekiah says, and as I have learnt almost too well – 'whereby men live, and in all which is the life of the spirit.'* At seventeen, indeed, I had devoured Shakespeare, though merely for the food to my fancy which his plots and incidents supplied, for the gorgeous colouring of his scenery; but at the period of which I am now writing, I had exhausted that source of mere pleasure; I was craving for more explicit and dogmatic teaching than any which he seemed to supply; and for three years, strange as it may appear, I hardly ever looked into his pages. Under what circumstances I afterwards recurred to his exhaustless treasures, my readers shall in due time be told.

So I worked away manfully with such tools and stock as I possessed, and of course produced, at first, like all young writers, some sufficiently servile imitations of my favourite poets.

'Ugh!' said Sandy, 'wha wants mongrels atween Burns and Tennyson? A gude stock baith, but gin ye'd cross the breed ye maun unite the spirits, and no the manners, o' the men. Why maun ilk a one the noo steal his neebor's barnacles* before he glints out o' windows? Mak a style for yoursel, laddie; ye're na mair Scots' hind than ye are Lincolnshire laird; sae gang yer ain gate and leave them to gang theirs; and just mak a gran, brode, simple Saxon style for yoursel.'

'But how can I, till I know what sort of a style it ought to be?'

'O! but yon's amazing like Tom Sheridan's answer to his father.* "Tom", says the auld man, "I'm thinking ye maun tak a wife." "Vera weel, father", says the puir skellum; "and wha's wife shall I tak?" Wha's style shall I tak? say all the callants the noo. Mak a style as ye would mak a wife, by marrying her a' to yoursel; and ye'll nae mair ken what's your style till it's made, than ye'll ken what your wife's like till she's been mony a year by your ingle.'

'My dear Mackaye,' I said, 'you have the most unmerciful way of raising difficulties, and then leaving poor fellows to lay the ghost for themselves.'

'Hech, then, I'm a'thegither a negative teacher, as they ca' it in the new lallans.* I'll gang out o' my gate to tell a man his kye are laired,* but I'm no obligated thereby to pu' them out for him. After a', nae man is rid o' a difficulty till he's conquered it single-handed for himsel: besides, I'm nae poet, mair's the gude hap for you.'

'Why then?'

'Och, och! they're puir, feckless, crabbit, unpractical bodies, they poets: but if it's your doom, ye maun dree it; and I'm sair afeard ye ha' gotten the disease o' genius, mair's the pity, and maun write, I suppose, willy-nilly. Some's folks booels are that made o' catgut, that they canna stir without chirrupping and screeking.'

However, æstro percitus,* I wrote on; and in about two years and a half had got together 'Songs of the Highways' enough to fill a small octavo volume, the circumstances of whose birth shall be given hereafter. Whether I ever attained to anything like an original style, readers must judge for themselves – the readers of the said volume I mean, for I have inserted none of those poems in this my autobiography; first, because it seems too like puffing my own works; and next, because I do not want to injure the as yet not over great sale of the same. But, if any one's curiosity is so far excited that he wishes to see what I have accomplished, the best advice which I can give him is, to go forth and buy all the working men's poetry which has appeared during the last twenty years, without favour or exception; among which he must needs, of course, find mine, and also, I am happy to say, a great deal which is much better and more instructive than mine.

CHAPTER X

HOW FOLKS TURN CHARTISTS

THOSE who read my story only for amusement, I advise to skip this chapter. Those, on the other hand, who really wish to ascertain what working men actually do suffer – to see whether their political discontent has not its roots, not merely in fanciful ambition, but in misery and slavery most real and agonizing – those in whose eyes the accounts of a system, or rather barbaric absence of all system, which involves starvation, nakedness, prostitution, and long imprisonment in dungeons worse than the cells of the Inquisition, will be invested with something at least of tragic interest, may, I hope, think it worth their while to learn how the clothes which they wear are made, and listen to a few occasional statistics, which, though they may seem to the wealthy mere lists of dull figures, are to the workmen symbols of terrible physical realities – of hunger, degradation, and despair.**

** Facts still worse than those which Mr. Locke's story contains have been made public by the *Morning Chronicle* in a series of noble letters on 'Labour and the Poor',* which we entreat all Christian people to 'read, mark, learn, and inwardly digest'. 'That will be better for them', as Mahomet, in similar cases, used to say.*

Well: one day our employer died. He had been one of the old sort of fashionable West-end tailors in the fast decreasing honourable trade;* keeping a modest shop, hardly to be distinguished from a dwelling-house, except by his name on the window blinds. He paid good prices for work, though not as good, of course, as he had given twenty years before, and prided himself upon having all his work done at home. His workrooms, as I have said, were no elysiums; but still, as good, alas! as those of three tailors out of four. He was proud, luxurious, foppish; but he was honest and kindly enough, and did many a generous thing by men who had been long in his employ. At all events, his journeymen could live on what he paid them.

But his son, succeeding to the business, determined like Rehoboam of old, to go a-head with the times.* Fired with the great spirit of the nineteenth century – at least with that one which is vulgarly considered its especial glory – he resolved to make haste to be rich. His father had made money very slowly of late; while dozens, who had begun business long after him, had now retired to luxurious ease and suburban villas. Why should he remain in the minority? Why should he not get rich as fast as he could? Why should he stick to the old, slow-going, honourable trade? Out of some four hundred and fifty West-end tailors, there were not one hundred left who were old-fashioned and stupid enough to go on keeping down their own profits by having all their work done at home and at first-hand. Ridiculous scruples! The government knew none such.* Were not the army clothes, the post-office clothes, the policemen's clothes, furnished by contractors and sweaters,* who hired the work at low prices, and let it out again to journeymen at still lower ones? Why should he pay his men two shillings where the government paid them one? Were there not cheap houses even at the West-end, which had saved several thousands a year merely by reducing their workmen's wages? And if the workmen chose to take lower wages, he was not bound actually to make them a present of more than they asked for! They would go to the cheapest market for anything they wanted, and so must he. Besides, wages had really been quite exorbitant. Half his men threw each of them as much money away in gin and beer yearly, as would pay two workmen at a cheap house. Why was he to be robbing his family of comforts to pay for their extravagance? And charging his customers, too, unnecessarily high prices – it was really robbing the public!

Such, I suppose, were some of the arguments which led to an official announcement, one Saturday night, that our young employer intended to enlarge his establishment, for the purpose of commencing business in the 'show trade'; and that emulous of Messrs. Aaron, Levi, and the rest of that class, magnificent alterations were to take place in the premises, to make room for which our workrooms were to be demolished, and that for that reason – for, of course, it was only for that reason – all work would in future be given out, to be made up at the men's own homes.

Our employer's arguments, if they were such as I suppose, were reasonable enough according to the present code of commercial morality. But strange to say, the auditory, insensible to the delight with which the public would view the splendid architectural improvements – with taste too grovelling to appreciate the glories of plate-glass shop fronts and brass scroll work – too selfish to rejoice, for its own sake, in the beauty of arabesques and chandeliers, which though they never might behold, the astonished public would – with souls too niggardly to leap for joy at the thought that gents would henceforth buy the registered guanaco vest, and the patent elastic omni-seasonum paletot* half-a-crown cheaper than ever – or that needy noblemen would pay three pound-ten, instead of five pounds, for their footmen's liveries – received the news, clod-hearted as they were, in sullen silence, and actually, when they got into the street, broke out into murmurs, perhaps into execrations.

'Silence!' said Crossthwaite; 'walls have ears. Come down to the nearest house of call, and talk it out like men, instead of grumbling in the street, like fish-fags.'

So down we went. Crossthwaite, taking my arm, strode on in moody silence – once muttering to himself bitterly—

'Oh, yes; all right and natural! What can the little sharks do but follow the big ones?'

We took a room, and Crossthwaite coolly saw us all in; and locking the door, stood with his back against it.

'Now then, mind, "One and all", as the Cornishmen say,* and no peaching. If any man is scoundrel enough to carry tales, I'll——'

'Do what?' asked Jemmy Downes, who had settled himself on the table with a pipe and a pot of porter. 'You aint the King of the Cannibal Islands,* as I know of, to cut a cove's head off?'

'No; but if a poor man's prayer can bring God's curse down upon a traitor's head – it may stay on his rascally shoulders till it rots.'

'If ifs and ans were pots and pans. – Look at Shechem Isaacs, that sold penknives in the street six months ago, now a-riding in his own carriage, all along of turning sweater. If God's curse is like that – I'll be happy to take any man's share of it.'

Some new idea seemed twinkling in the fellow's cunning bloated face as he spoke. I, and others also, shuddered at his words; but we all forgot them a moment afterwards, as Crossthwaite began to speak.

'We were all bound to expect this. Every working tailor must come to this at last, on the present system; and we are only lucky in having been spared so long. You all know where this will end – in the same misery as fifteen thousand out of twenty thousand of our class are enduring now. We shall become the slaves, often the bodily prisoners, of Jews, middlemen, and sweaters,* who draw their livelihood out of our starvation. We shall have to face, as the rest have, ever decreasing prices of labour, ever increasing profits made out of that labour by the contractors who will employ us – arbitrary fines, inflicted at the caprice of hirelings – the competition of women, and children, and starving Irish – our hours of work will increase one-third, our actual pay decrease to less than one-half; and in all this we shall have no hope, no chance of improvement in wages, but ever more penury, slavery, misery, as we are pressed on by those who are sucked by fifties – almost by hundreds – yearly, out of the honourable trade in which we were brought up, into the infernal system of contract work, which is devouring our trade and many others, body and soul. Our wives will be forced to sit up night and day to help us – our children must labour from the cradle without chance of going to school, hardly of breathing the fresh air of Heaven, – our boys, as they grow up, must turn beggars or paupers – our daughters, as thousands do, must eke out their miserable earnings by prostitution. And after all, a whole family will not gain what one of us had been doing, as yet, single-handed. You know there will be no hope for us. There is no use appealing to government or parliament. I don't want to talk politics here. I shall keep them for another place. But you can recollect as well as I can, when a deputation of us went up to a member of parliament* – one that was reputed a philosopher, and a political economist, and a liberal – and set before him the ever-increasing penury and misery of our trade and of those connected with it; you recollect his answer – that, however glad he would be to help us, it was impossible – he could not alter the laws of nature – that wages were regulated by the amount of competition among the men themselves, and that it was no business of government, or any one else, to interfere in contracts between the employer and employed, that those things regulated themselves by the laws of political economy, which it was madness and suicide to oppose. He may have been a wise man. I only know that he was a rich one. Every one speaks well of the bridge which carries him over. Every one fancies the laws which fill his pockets to be God's laws. But I say this. If neither government nor members of parliament can help us, we must help ourselves. Help yourselves and Heaven will help you. Combination among ourselves is the only chance. One thing we can do – sit still.'

'And starve!' said some one.

'Yes, and starve! Better starve than sin. I say, it is a sin to give in to this system. It is a sin to add our weight to the crowd of artisans who are now choking and strangling each other to death, as the prisoners did in the black hole of Calcutta.* Let those who will, turn beasts of prey, and feed upon their fellows; but let us at least keep ourselves pure. It may be the law of political civilisation, the law of nature, that the rich should eat up the poor, and the poor eat up each other. Then I here rise up and curse that law, that civilisation, that nature. Either I will destroy them, or they shall destroy me. As a slave, as an increased burden on my fellow-sufferers, I will not live. So help me God! I will take no work home to my house; and I call upon every one here to combine, and to sign a protest to that effect.'

'What's the use of that, my good Mr. Crossthwaite?' interrupted some one, querulously. 'Don't you know what come of the strike a few years ago, when this piece-work and sweating first came in? The masters made fine promises, and never kept 'em; and the men who stood out had their places filled up with poor devils who were glad enough to take the work at any price – just as ours will be. There's no use kicking against the pricks. All the rest have come to it, and so must we. We must live somehow, and half a loaf is better than no bread; and even that half-loaf will go into other men's mouths, if we don't snap at it at once. Besides, we can't force others to strike. We may strike and starve ourselves, but what's the use of a dozen striking out of twenty thousand?'

'Will you sign the protest, gentlemen, or not?' asked Crossthwaite, in a determined voice.

Some half-dozen said they would, if the others would.

'And the others won't. Well, after all, one man must take the responsibility, and I am that man. I will sign the protest by myself. I will sweep a crossing – I will turn cress-gatherer, rag-picker;* I will starve piecemeal, and see my wife starve with me; but do the wrong thing I will not! The Cause wants martyrs. If I must be one, I must.'

All this while my mind had been undergoing a strange perturbation. The notion of escaping that infernal work-room and the company I met there – of taking my work home, and thereby, as I hoped, gaining more time for study – at least, having my books on the spot ready at every odd moment, was most enticing. I had hailed the proposed change as a blessing to me, till I heard Crossthwaite's arguments: not that I had not known the facts before, but it had never struck me till then that it was a real sin against my class to make myself a party in the system by which they were allowing themselves (under temptation enough, God knows) to be enslaved. But now I looked with horror on the gulf of penury before me, into the vortex of which not only I, but my whole trade, seemed irresistibly sucked. I thought with shame and remorse of the few shillings which I had earned at various times by taking piece-work home, to buy my candles for study. I whispered my doubts to Crossthwaite, as he sat, pale and determined, watching the excited and querulous discussions among the other work-men.

'What? So you expect to have time to read? Study, after sixteen hours a-day stitching? Study, when you cannot earn money enough to keep you from wasting and shrinking away day by day? Study, with your heart full of shame and indigna-tion, fresh from daily insult and injustice? Study, with the black cloud of despair and penury in front of you? Little time, or heart, or strength, will you have to study, when you are making the same coats you make now, at half the price.'

I put my name down beneath Crossthwaite's on the paper which he handed me, and went out with him.

'Ay,' he muttered to himself, 'be slaves – what you are worthy to be, that you will be! You dare not combine – you dare not starve – you dare not die – and therefore you dare not be free! Oh! for six hundred men like Barbaroux's Marseillois – "who knew how to die!" '*

'Surely, Crossthwaite, if matters were properly represented to the government, they would not, for their own existence sake, to put conscience out of the question, allow such a system to continue growing.'

'Government – government? You a tailor, and not know that government are the very authors of this system? Not to know that they first set the example, by getting the army and navy clothes made by contractors, and taking the lowest tenders? Not to know that the police clothes, the postmen's clothes, the convicts' clothes, are all contracted for on the same infernal plan, by sweaters, and sweaters' sweaters, and sweaters' sweaters' sweaters, till government work is just the very last, lowest resource to which a poor starved-out wretch betakes himself to keep body and soul together? Why, the government prices, in almost every department, are half, and less than half, the very lowest living price. I tell you, the careless iniquity of government about these things will come out some day. It will be known, the whole abomination, and future generations will class it with the tyrannies of the Roman emperors and the Norman barons. Why, it's a fact, that the colonels of the regiments – noblemen, most of them – make their own vile profit out of us tailors* – out of the pauperism of the men, the slavery of the children, the prostitution of the women. They get so much a uniform allowed them by government to clothe the men with; and then – then, they let out the jobs to the contractors at less than half what government give them, and pocket the difference. And then you talk of appealing to government!'

'Upon my word,' I said, bitterly, 'we tailors seem to owe the army a double grudge. They not only keep under other artisans, but they help to starve us first, and then shoot us, if we complain too loudly.'

'Oh, ho! your blood's getting up, is it? Then you're in the humour to be told what you have been hankering to know so long – where Mackaye and I go at night. We'll strike while the iron's hot, and go down to the Chartist meeting at * * *.'

'Pardon me, my dear fellow,' I said. 'I cannot bear the thought of being mixed up in conspiracy – perhaps, in revolt and bloodshed. Not that I am afraid. Heaven knows, I am not. But I am too much harassed, miserable, already. I see too much wretchedness around me, to lend my aid in increasing the sum of suffering, by a single atom, among rich and poor, even by righteous vengeance.'

'Conspiracy? Bloodshed? What has that to do with the Charter? It suits the venal Mammonite press well enough to jumble them together, and cry "Murder, rape, and robbery", whenever the six points* are mentioned; but they know, and any man of common sense ought to know, that the Charter is just as much an open political question as the Reform Bill, and ten times as much as Magna Charta was, when it got passed. What have the six points, right or wrong, to do with the question whether they can be obtained by moral force, and the pressure of opinion alone, or require what we call ulterior measures* to get them carried? Come along!'

So with him I went that night.

*

'Well, Alton! where was the treason and murder? Your nose must have been a sharp one, to smell out any there. Did you hear anything that astonished your weak mind so very exceedingly, after all?'

'The only thing that did astonish me, was to hear men of my own class – and lower still, perhaps, some of them – speak with such fluency and eloquence. Such a fund of information – such excellent English – where did they get it all?'

'From the God who knows nothing about ranks. They're the unknown great – the unaccredited heroes, as Master Thomas Carlyle would say, whom the flunkeys aloft have not acknowledged yet – though they'll be forced to, some day, with a vengeance. Are you convinced, once for all?'

'I really do not understand political questions, Crossthwaite.'

'Does it want so very much wisdom to understand the rights and the wrongs of all that? Are the people represented? Are you represented? Do you feel like a man that's got any one to fight your battle in parliament, my young friend, eh?'

'I'm sure I don't know——'

'Why, what in the name of common sense – what interest or feeling of yours or mine, or any man's you ever spoke to, except the shopkeeper, do Alderman A*** or Lord C*** D*** represent? They represent property – and we have none. They represent rank – we have none. Vested interests – we have none. Large capitals – those are just what crush us. Irresponsibility of employers, slavery of the employed, competition among masters, competition among workmen, that is the system they represent – they preach it – they glory in it. – Why, it is the very ogre that is eating us all up. They are chosen by the few, they represent the few, and they make laws for the many – and yet you don't know whether or not the people are represented!'

We were passing by the door of the Victoria Theatre; it was just half-price time* – and the beggary and rascality of London were pouring in to their low amusement, from the neighbouring gin palaces and thieves' cellars. A herd of ragged boys, vomiting forth slang, filth, and blasphemy, pushed past us, compelling us to take good care of our pockets.

'Look there! look at the amusements, the training, the civilisation, which the government permits to the children of the people! – These licensed pits of darkness, traps of temptation, profligacy, and ruin, triumphantly yawning night after night – and then tell me that the people who see their children thus kidnapped into hell, are represented by a government who licenses such things!'

'Would a change in the franchise cure that?'

'Household suffrage mightn't – but give us the Charter, and we'll see about it! Give us the Charter, and we'll send workmen into parliament that shall soon find out whether something better can't be put in the way of the ten thousand boys and girls in London who live by theft and prostitution, than the tender mercies of the Victoria – a pretty name! They say the Queen's a good woman – and I don't doubt it. I wonder often if she knows what her precious namesake here is like?'

'But, really, I cannot see how a mere change in representation can cure such things as that.'

'Why, didn't they tell us, before the Reform Bill, that extension of the suffrage was to cure everything? And how can you have too much of a good thing? We've only taken them at their word, we Chartists. Haven't all politicians been preaching for years that England's national greatness was all owing to her political institutions – to Magna Charta, and the Bill of Rights,* and representative parliaments, and all that? It was but the other day I got hold of some Tory paper, that talked about the English constitution, and the balance of queen, lords, and commons, as the "Talismanic Palladium"* of the country. 'Gad, we'll see if a move onward in the same line won't better the matter. If the balance of classes is such a blessed thing, the sooner we get the balance equal, the better; for it's rather lopsided just now, no one can deny. So, representative institutions are the talismanic palladium of the nation, are they? The palladium of the classes that have them, I dare say; and that's the very best reason why the classes that haven't got 'em should look out for the same palladium for themselves. What's sauce for the gander is sauce for the goose, isn't it? We'll try – we'll see whether the talisman they talk of has lost its power all of a sudden since '32 – whether we can't rub the magic ring a little for ourselves, and call up genii to help us out of the mire, as the shopkeepers and the gentlemen have done.'

*

From that night I was a Chartist, heart and soul – and so were a million and a half more of the best artisans in England – at least, I had no reason to be ashamed of my company. Yes; I too, like Crossthwaite, took the upper classes at their word; bowed down to the idol of political institutions, and pinned my hopes of salvation on 'the possession of one-tenthousandth part of a talker in the national palaver'.* True, I desired the Charter, at first (as I do, indeed, at this moment), as a means to glorious ends – not only because it would give a chance of elevation, a a free sphere of action, to lowly worth and talent; but because it was the path to reforms, – social, legal, sanatory, educational, – to which the veriest Tory – certainly not the great and good Lord Ashley* – would not object. But soon, with me, and I am afraid with many, many more, the means became, by the frailty of poor human nature, an end, an idol in itself. I had so made up my mind that it was the only method of getting what I wanted, that I neglected, alas! but too often, to try the methods which lay already by me. 'If we had but the Charter' – was the excuse for a thousand lazinesses, procrastinations. 'If we had but the Charter' – I should be good, and free, and happy. Fool that I was! It was within, rather than without, that I needed reform.

And so I began to look on man (and too many of us, I am afraid, are doing so) as the creature and puppet of circumstances – of the particular outward system, social or political, in which he happens to find himself. An abominable heresy, no doubt; but, somehow, it appears to me just the same as Benthamites, and economists, and high-churchmen, too, for that matter, have been preaching for the last twenty years with great applause from their respective parties. One set informs the world that it is to be regenerated by cheap bread,* free trade, and that peculiar form of the 'freedom of industry'* which, in plain language, signifies 'the despotism of capital'; and which, whatever it means, is merely some outward system, circumstance, or 'dodge', *about* man, and not *in* him. Another party's nostrum is more churches, more schools, more clergymen* – excellent things in their way – better even than cheap bread, or free trade, provided only that they are excellent – that the churches, schools, clergymen, are good ones. But the party of whom I am speaking seem to us workmen to consider the quality quite a secondary consideration, compared with the quantity. They expect the world to be regenerated, not by becoming more a Church – none would gladlier help them in bringing that about than the Chartists themselves, paradoxical as it may seem – but by being dosed somewhat more with a certain 'Church system', circumstance, or 'dodge'. For my part, I seem to have learnt that the only thing to regenerate the world is not more of any system, good or bad, but simply more of the Spirit of God.

About the supposed omnipotence of the Charter I have found out my mistake. I believe no more in 'Morison's-Pill-remedies', as Thomas Carlyle calls them.* Talismans are worthless. The age of spirit-compelling spells, whether of parchment or carbuncle,* is past – if, indeed, it ever existed. The Charter will no more make men good, than political economy, or the observance of the Church Calendar – a fact which we working men, I really believe, have, under the pressure of wholesome defeat and God-sent affliction, found out sooner than our more 'enlightened' fellow-idolaters. But, at that time, as I have confessed already, we took our betters at their word, and believed in Morison's Pills. Only, as we looked at the world from among a class of facts somewhat different from theirs, we differed from them proportionably as to our notions of the proper ingredients in the said Pill.

*

But what became of our protest?

It was received – and disregarded. As for turning us off, we had, *de facto*, like Coriolanus banished the Romans, turned our master off.* All the other hands, some forty in number, submitted and took the yoke upon them, and went down into the house of bondage, knowing whither they went. Every man of them is now a beggar, compared with what he was then. Many are dead in the prime of life of consumption, bad food and lodging, and the peculiar diseases of our trade. Some have not been heard of lately – we fancy them imprisoned in some sweaters' dens – but thereby hangs a tale, whereof more hereafter.

But it was singular, that every one of the six who had merely professed their conditional readiness to sign the protest, were contumeliously discharged the next day, without any reason being assigned. It was evident that there had been a traitor at the meeting; and every one suspected Jemmy Downes, especially as he fell into the new system with suspiciously strange alacrity. But it was as impossible to prove the offence against him as to punish him for it. Of that wretched man, too, and his subsequent career, I shall have somewhat to say hereafter. Verily, there is a God who judgeth the earth!

But now behold me and my now intimate and beloved friend, Crossthwaite, with nothing to do – a gentlemanlike occupation; but, unfortunately, in our class, involving starvation. What was to be done? We applied for work at several 'honourable shops'; but at all we received the same answer. Their trade was decreasing – the public ran daily more and more to the cheap show shops – and they themselves were forced, in order to compete with these latter, to put more and more of their work out at contract prices. *Facilis descensus Averni!** Having once been hustled out of the serried crowd of competing workmen, it was impossible to force our way in again. So, a week or ten days past, our little stocks of money were exhausted. I was downhearted at once; but Crossthwaite bore up gaily enough.

'Katie and I can pick a crust together without snarling over it. And, thank God, I have no children, and never intend to have, if I can keep true to myself, till the good times come.'

'Oh! Crossthwaite, are not children a blessing?'

'Would they be a blessing to me now? No, my lad. – Let those bring slaves into the world who will! I will never beget children to swell the numbers of those who are trampling each other down in the struggle for daily bread, to minister in ever deepening poverty and misery to the rich man's luxury – perhaps his lust.'

'Then you believe in the Malthusian doctrines?'*

'I believe them to be an infernal lie, Alton Locke; though good and wise people like Miss Martineau* may sometimes be deluded into preaching them. I believe there's room on English soil for twice the number there is now; and when we get the

Charter we'll prove it; we'll show that God meant living human heads and hands to be blessings and not curses, tools and not burdens. But in such times as these, let those who have wives be as though they had none – as St. Paul said,* when he told his people under the Roman emperor to be above begetting slaves and martyrs. A man of the people should keep himself as free from incumbrances as he can just now. He will find it all the more easy to dare and suffer for the people, when their turn comes——'

And he set his teeth firmly, almost savagely.

'I think I can earn a few shillings, now and then, by writing for a paper I know of. If that won't do, I must take up agitating for a trade, and live by spouting, as many a Tory member as well as Radical ones do. A man may do worse, for he may do nothing. At all events, my only chance now is to help on the Charter; for the sooner it comes the better for me. And if I die – why, the little woman won't be long in coming after me, I know that well; and there's a tough business got well over for both of us!'

'Hech,' said Sandy,

> To every man
> Death comes but once a life –*

as my countryman, Mr. Macaulay, says, in thae gran' Roman ballants o' his. But for ye, Alton, laddie, ye're owre young to start off in the People's Church Meelitant, sae just bide wi' me, and the barrel o' meal in the corner there winna waste, – nae mair than it did wi' the widow o' Zareptha;* a tale which coincides sae weel wi' the everlasting righteousnesses, that I'm at times no inclined to consider it a' thegither mythical.'

But I, with thankfulness which vented itself through my eyes, finding my lips alone too narrow for it, refused to eat the bread of idleness.

'Aweel, then, ye'll just mind the shop, and dust the books whiles; I'm getting auld and stiff, and ha' need o' help i' the business.'

'No,' I said; 'you say so out of kindness; but if you can afford no greater comforts than these, you cannot afford to keep me in addition to yourself.'

Hech, then! How do ye ken that the auld Scot eats a' he makes? I was na born the spending side o' Tweed, my man. But gin ye daur, why dinna ye pack up your duds, and the poems wi' them, and gang till your cousin i' the university? he'll surely put you in the way o' publishing them. He's bound to it by blude; and there's na shame in asking him to help you towards reaping the fruits o' your ain labours. A few punds on a bond for repayment when the edition was sauld, noo, – I'd do that for mysel; but I'm thinking ye'd better try to get a list o' subscribers. Dinna mind your independence; it's but spoiling the Egyptians, ye ken; and thae bit ballants will be their money's worth, I'll warrant, and tell them a wheen facts they're no that well acquentit wi'. Hech? Johnnie, my Chartist?'

'Why not go to my uncle?'

'Puir sugar-and-spice-selling baillie bodie! is there aught in his ledger about poetry, and the incommensurable value o' the products o' genius? Gang till the young scholar: he's a canny one, too, and he'll ken it to be worth his while to fash himsel a wee anent it.'

So I packed up my little bundle, and lay awake all that night in a fever of expectation about the as yet unknown world of green fields and woods through which my road to Cambridge lay.

CHAPTER XI

'THE YARD WHERE THE GENTLEMEN LIVE'

I MAY be forgiven, surely, if I run somewhat into detail about this my first visit to the country.

I had, as I have said before, literally never been farther a-field than Fulham or Battersea Rise. One Sunday evening, indeed, I had got as far as Wandsworth Common; but it was March, and, to my extreme disappointment, the heath was not in flower.

But, usually, my Sundays had been spent entirely in study; which to me was rest, so worn out were both my body and my mind with the incessant drudgery of my trade, and the slender fare to which I restricted myself. Since I had lodged with Mackaye, certainly, my food had been better. I had not required to stint my appetite for money wherewith to buy candles, ink, and pens. My wages, too, had increased with my years, and altogether I found myself gaining in strength, though I had no notion how much I possessed till I set forth on this walk to Cambridge.

It was a glorious morning at the end of May; and when I escaped from the pall of smoke which hung over the city, I found the sky a sheet of cloudless blue. How I watched for the ending of the rows of houses, which lined the road for miles – the great roots of London, running far out into the country, up which poured past me an endless stream of food, and merchandise, and human beings – the sap of the huge metropolitan life-tree! How each turn of the road opened a fresh line of terraces or villas, till hope deferred made the heart sick, and the country seemed – like the place where the rainbow touches the ground, or the El Dorado of Raleigh's Guiana settlers* – always a little farther off! How, between gaps in the houses right and left, I caught tantalizing glimpses of green fields, shut from me by dull lines of high-spiked palings! How I peeped through gates and over fences at trim lawns and gardens, and longed to stay, and admire, and speculate on the names of the strange plants and gaudy flowers; and then hurried on, always expecting to find something still finer a-head – something really worth stopping to look at – till the houses thickened again into a street, and I found myself, to my disappointment, in the midst of a town! And then more villas and palings; and then a village; – when would they stop, those endless houses?

At last they did stop. Gradually the people whom I passed began to look more and more rural, and more toil-worn and ill-fed. The houses ended, cattle yards and farm buildings appeared; and right and left, far away, spread the low rolling sheet of green meadows and corn fields. Oh, the joy! The lawns with their high elms and firs, the green hedgerows, the delicate hue and scent of the fresh clover fields, the steep clay banks where I stopped to pick nosegays of wild flowers, and became again a child, – and then recollected my mother, and a walk with her on the river bank towards the Red House.* I hurried on again, but could not be unhappy, while my eyes ranged free, for the first time in my life, over the chequered squares of cultivation, over glittering brooks, and hills quivering in the green haze, while above hung the skylarks, pouring out their souls in melody. And then, as the sun grew hot, and the larks dropped one by one into the growing corn, the new delight of the blessed silence! I listened to the stillness; for noise had been my native element; I had become in London quite unconscious of the ceaseless roar of the human sea, casting up mire and dirt. And now, for the first time in my life, the crushing, confusing hubbub had flowed away, and left my brain calm and free. How I felt at that moment a capability of clear, bright meditation, which was as new to me, as I believe it would have been to most Londoners in my position. I cannot help fancying that our unnatural atmosphere of excitement, physical as well as moral, is to blame for very much of the working men's restlessness and fierceness. As it was, I felt that every step forward, every breath of fresh air, gave me new life. I had gone fifteen miles before I recollected, that for the first time for many months, I had not coughed since I rose.

So on I went, down the broad, bright road, which seemed to beckon me forward into the unknown expanses of human life.

The world was all before me, where to choose,*

and I saw it both with my eyes and my imagination, in the temper of a boy broke loose from school. My heart kept holiday. I loved and blessed the birds which flitted past me, and the cows which lay dreaming on the sward. I recollect stopping with delight at a picturesque descent into the road, to watch a nursery garden, full of roses of every shade, from brilliant yellow to darkest purple; and as I wondered at the innumerable variety of beauties which man's art had developed from a few poor and wild species, it seemed to me the most delightful life on earth, to follow in such a place the primæval trade of gardener Adam; to study the secrets of the flower world, the laws of soil and climate; to create new species, and gloat over the living fruit of one's own science and perseverance. And then I recollected the tailor's shop, and the Charter, and the starvation, and the oppression, which I had left behind, and ashamed of my own selfishness, went hurrying on again.

At last I came to a wood – the first real wood that I had ever seen; not a mere party of stately park trees growing out of smooth turf, but a real wild copse; tangled branches and grey stems fallen across each other; deep, ragged underwood of shrubs, and great ferns like princes' feathers, and gay beds of flowers, blue and pink and yellow, with butterflies flitting about them, and trailers that climbed and dangled from bough to bough – a poor, commonplace bit of copse, I dare say, in the world's eyes, but to me a fairy wilderness of beautiful forms, mysterious gleams and shadows, teeming with manifold life. As I stood looking wistfully over the gate, alternately at the inviting vista of the green embroidered path, and then at the grim notice over my head, 'All trespassers prosecuted', a young man came up the ride, dressed in velveteen jacket and leather gaiters, sufficiently bedrabbled with mud. A fishing-rod and basket bespoke him some sort of destroyer, and I saw in a moment that he was 'a gentleman'. After all, there is such a thing as looking like a gentleman. There are men whose class no dirt or rags could hide, any more than they could Ulysses.* I have seen such men in plenty among workmen, too; but, on the whole, the gentlemen – by whom I do not mean just now the rich – have the superiority in that point. But not, please God, for ever. Give us the same air, water, exercise, education, good society, and you will see whether this 'haggardness', this 'coarseness', &c., &c., for the list is too long to specify, be an accident, or a property, of the man of the people.

'May I go into your wood?' asked I at a venture, curiosity conquering pride.

'Well! what do you want there, my good fellow?'

'To see what a wood is like – I never was in one in my life.'

'Humph! well – you may go in for that, and welcome. Never was in a wood in his life! – poor devil!'

'Thank you!' quoth I. And I slowly clambered over the gate. He put his hand carelessly on the top rail, vaulted over it like a deer, and then turned to stare at me.

'Hullo! I say – I forgot – don't go far in, or ramble up and down, or you'll disturb the pheasants.'

I thanked him again for what license he had given me – went in, and lay down by the path-side.

Here, I suppose, by the rules of modern art, a picturesque

description of the said wood should follow; but I am the most
incompetent person in the world to write it. And, indeed, the
whole scene was so novel to me, that I had no time to analyse;
I could only enjoy. I recollect lying on my face and fingering
over the delicately cut leaves of the weeds, and wondering
whether the people who lived in the country thought them as
wonderful and beautiful as I did; – and then I recollected the
thousands whom I had left behind, who, like me, had never
seen the green face of God's earth; and the answer of the poor
gamin in St. Giles's, who, when he was asked what the country
was, answered, *'the yard where the gentlemen live when they
go out of town'** – significant that, and pathetic; – then I
wondered whether the time would ever come when society
would be far enough advanced to open to even such as he a
glimpse, if it were only once a year, of the fresh, clean face of
God's earth; – and then I became aware of a soft mysterious
hum, above me and around me, and turned on my back
to look whence it proceeded, and saw the leaves, gold –
green and transparent in the sunlight, quivering against
the deep heights of the empyrean blue; and hanging in the
sunbeams that pierced the foliage, a thousand insects, like
specks of fire, that poised themselves motionless on thrilling
wings, and darted away, and returned to hang motionless
again; – and I wondered what they eat, and whether they
thought about anything, and whether they enjoyed the sunlight; – and then that brought back to me the times when I used
to lie dreaming in my crib on summer mornings, and watched
the flies dancing reels between me and the ceilings; – and that
again brought the thought of Susan and my mother; and I
prayed for them – not sadly – I could not be sad there; and
prayed that we might all meet again some day and live happily
together; perhaps in the country, where I could write poems in
peace; and then, by degrees, my sentences and thoughts grew
incoherent, and in happy, stupid animal comfort, I faded away
into a heavy sleep, which lasted an hour or more, till I was
awakened by the efforts of certain enterprising great black and
red ants, who were trying to found a small Algeria in my left
ear.

I rose and left the wood, and a gate or two on, stopped again to look at the same sportsman fishing in a clear silver brook. I could not help admiring with a sort of childish wonder the graceful and practised aim with which he directed his tiny bait, and called up mysterious dimples on the surface, which in a moment increased to splashings and strugglings of a great fish, compelled, as if by some invisible spell, to follow the point of the bending rod till he lay panting on the bank. I confess, in spite of all my class prejudices against 'game-preserving aristocrats', I almost envied the man; at least I seemed to understand a little of the universally attractive charms which those same outwardly contemptible field sports possess; the fresh air, fresh fields and copses, fresh running brooks; the exercise, the simple freedom, the excitement just sufficient to keep alive expectation and banish thought. – After all, his trout produced much the same mood in him as my turnpike road did in me. And perhaps the man did not go fishing or shooting every day. The laws prevented him from shooting, at least, all the year round; so sometimes there might be something in which he made himself of use. An honest, jolly face too he had – not without thought and strength in it. 'Well, it is a strange world,' said I to myself, 'where those who can, need not; and those who cannot, must!'

Then he came close to the gate, and I left it just in time to see a little group arrive at it – a woman of his own rank, young, pretty, and simply dressed, with a little boy, decked out as a Highlander, on a shaggy Shetland pony, which his mother, as I guessed her to be, was leading. And then they all met, and the little fellow held up a basket of provisions to his father, who kissed him across the gate, and hung his creel of fish behind the saddle, and patted the mother's shoulder, as she looked up lovingly and laughingly in his face. Altogether, a joyous, genial bit of – Nature? Yes, Nature. Shall I grudge simple happiness to the few, because it is as yet, alas! impossible for the many?

And yet the whole scene contrasted so painfully with me – with my past, my future, my dreams, my wrongs, that I could not look at it; and with a swelling heart I moved on – all the faster because I saw they were looking at me and talking of me, and the fair wife threw after me a wistful, pitying glance, which I was afraid might develop itself into some offer of food or money – a thing which I scorned and dreaded, because it involved the trouble of a refusal.

Then, as I walked on once more, my heart smote me. If they had wished to be kind, why had I grudged them the opportunity of a good deed? At all events, I might have asked their advice. In a natural and harmonious state, when society really means brotherhood, a man could go up to any stranger, to give and receive, if not succour, yet still experience and wisdom: and was I not bound to tell them what I knew? was sure that they did not know? Was I not bound to preach the cause of my class wherever I went? Here were kindly people who, for aught I knew, would do right the moment they were told where it was wanted; if there was an accursed artificial gulf between their class and mine, had I any right to complain of it, as long as I helped to keep it up by my false pride and surly reserve? No! I would speak my mind henceforth – I would testify of what I saw and knew of the wrongs, if not of the rights, of the artisan, before whomsoever I might come. Oh! valiant conclusion of half an hour's self-tormenting scruples! How I kept it, remains to be shown.

I really fear that I am getting somewhat trivial and prolix: but there was hardly an incident in my two days' tramp which did not give me some small fresh insight into the *terra incognita* of the country; and there may be those among my readers, to whom it is not uninteresting to look, for once, at even the smallest objects with a cockney workman's eyes.

Well, I trudged on – and the shadows lengthened, and I grew footsore and tired; but every step was new, and won me forward with fresh excitements for my curiosity.

At one village I met a crowd of little, noisy, happy boys and girls pouring out of a smart new Gothic school-house. I could not resist the temptation of snatching a glance through the open door. I saw on the walls maps, music, charts, and pictures. How I envied those little urchins! A solemn, sturdy elder, in a white cravat, evidently the parson of the parish, was patting children's heads, taking down names, and laying down the law to a shrewd, prim young schoolmaster.

Presently, as I went up the village, the clergyman strode past me, brandishing a thick stick and humming a chant, and joined a motherly-looking wife, who, basket on arm, was popping in and out of the cottages, looking alternately serious and funny, cross and kindly – I suppose, according to the sayings and doings of the folks within.

'Come,' I thought, 'this looks like work at least.' And as I went out of the village, I accosted a labourer, who was trudging my way, fork on shoulder, and asked him if that was the parson and his wife?

I was surprised at the difficulty with which I got into conversation with the man; at his stupidity, feigned or real, I could not tell which; at the dogged, suspicious reserve with which he eyed me, and asked me whether I was 'one of they parts?' and whether I was a Londoner, and what I wanted on the tramp, and so on, before he seemed to think it safe to answer a single question. He seemed, like almost every labourer I ever met, to have something on his mind; to live in a state of perpetual fear and concealment. When, however, he found I was both a cockney and a passer-by, he began to grow more communicative, and told me, 'Ees – that were the parson, sure enough.'

'And what sort of man was he?'

'Oh! he was a main kind man to the poor; leastwise in the matter of visiting 'em, and praying with 'em, and getting 'em to put into clubs, and such like;* and his lady too. Not that there was any fault to find with the man about money – but 'twasn't to be expected of him.'

'Why, was he not rich?'

'Oh, rich enough to the likes of us. But his own tithes here arn't more than a thirty pounds we hears tell; and if he'd hadn't summat of his own, he couldn't do not nothing by the poor; as it be, he pays for that ere school all to his own pocket, next part. All the rest o' the tithes goes to some great lord or other – they say he draws a matter of a thousand a-year out of the parish, and not a foot ever he sot into it; and that's the way with a main lot o' parishes, up and down.'

This was quite a new fact to me. 'And what sort of folks were the parsons all round?'

'Oh, some of all sorts, good and bad. About six and half a-dozen. There's two or three nice young gentlemen come'd

round here now, but they're all what's-'em-a-call-it? – some
sort o' papishes;* – leastwise, they has prayers in the church
every day, and doesn't preach the Gospel, no how, I hears by
my wife, and she knows all about it, along of going to meeting.
Then there's one over thereaway, as had to leave his living –
he knows why. He got safe over seas. If he had been a poor
man, he'd a been in * * * gaol, safe enough, and soon enough.
Then there's two or three as goes a-hunting – not as I sees no
harm in that; if a man's got plenty of money, he ought to enjoy
himself, in course: but still he can't be here and there too, to
once. Then there's two or three as is bad in their healths, or
thinks themselves so – or else has livings summer' else; and they
lives summer' or others, and has curates. Main busy chaps is
they curates, always, and wonderful hands to preach; but then,
just as they gets a little knowing like at it, and folks gets to like
'em, and run to hear 'em, off they pops to summat better; and
in course they're right to do so; and so we country-folks get
nought but the young colts, afore they're broke, you see.'

'And what sort of a preacher was his parson?'

'Oh, he preached very good Gospel. Not that he went very
often hisself, acause he couldn't make out the meaning of it;
he preached too high, like. But his wife said it was uncommon
good Gospel; and surely when he come to visit a body, and
talked plain English, like, not sermon-ways, he was a very
pleasant man to heer, and his lady uncommon kind to nurse
folk. They sot up with me and my wife, they two did, two
whole nights, when we was in the fever, afore the officer could
get us a nurse.'

'Well,' said I, 'there are some good parsons left.'

'Oh, yes; there's some very good ones – each one after his
own way; and there'd be more on 'em, if they did but know
how bad we labourers was off. Why bless ye, I mind when they
was very different. A new parson is a mighty change for the
better, mostwise, we finds. Why, when I was a boy, we never
had no schooling. And now mine goes and learns singing and
jobrafy, and ciphering, and sich like. Not that I sees no good in
it. We was a sight better off in the old times, when there weren't
no schooling. Schooling harn't made wages rise, nor preaching
neither.'

'But surely,' I said, 'all this religious knowledge ought to give you comfort, even if you are badly off.'

'Oh! religion's all very well for them as has time for it; and a very good thing – we ought all to mind our latter end. But I don't see how a man can hear sermons with an empty belly; and there's so much to fret a man, now, and he's so cruel tired coming home o' nights, he can't nowise go to pray a lot, as gentlefolks does.'

'But are you so ill off?'

'Oh! he'd had a good harvesting enough; but then he owed all that for he's rent; and he's club-money wasn't paid up, nor he's shop. And then, with he's wages—' (I forget the sum – under ten shillings), 'how could a man keep his mouth full, when he had five children? And then, folks is so unmarciful – I'll just tell you what they says to me, now, last time I was over at the board——'

And thereon he rambled off into a long jumble of medical-officers, and relieving-officers, and Farmer This, and Squire That, which indicated a mind as ill-educated as discontented. He cursed, or rather grumbled at – for he had not spirit, it seemed, to curse anything – the New Poor Law; because it 'ate up the poor, flesh and bone'; – bemoaned the 'Old Law', when 'the Vestry was forced to give a man whatsomdever he axed for, and if they didn't he'd go to the magistrates and make 'em, and so sure as a man got a fresh child, he went and got another loaf allowed him next vestry, like a Christian';* – and so turned through a gate, and set to work forking up some weeds on a fallow, leaving me many new thoughts to digest.

That night, I got to some town or other, and there found a night's lodging, good enough for a walking traveller.

CHAPTER XII

CAMBRIDGE

WHEN I started again next morning, I found myself so stiff and footsore, that I could hardly put one leg before the other, much less walk upright. I was really quite in despair, before the end of the first mile; for I had no money to pay for a lift on the coach, and I knew, besides, that they would not be passing that way for several hours to come. So, with aching back and knees, I made shift to limp along, bent almost double, and ended by sitting down for a couple of hours, and looking about me, in a country which would have seemed dreary enough, I suppose, to any one but a freshly-liberated captive, such as I was. At last I got up and limped on, stiffer than ever from my rest, when a gig drove past me towards Cambridge, drawn by a stout cob, and driven by a tall, fat, jolly-looking farmer, who stared at me as he passed, went on, looked back, slackened his pace, looked back again, and at last came to a dead stop, and hailed me in a broad nasal dialect—

'Whor be ganging, then, bor?'

'To Cambridge.'

'Thew'st na git there that gate. Be'est thee honest man?'

'I hope so,' said I, somewhat indignantly.

'What's trade?'

'A tailor,' I said.

'Tailor! – guide us! Tailor a-tramp? Barn't accoostomed to tramp, then?'

'I never was out of London before,' said I, meekly; for I was too worn-out to be cross – lengthy and impertinent as this cross-examination seemed.

'Oi'll gie thee lift; dee yow joomp in. Gae on, powney! Tailor, then! Oh! ah! tailor,' saith he.

I obeyed most thankfully, and sat crouched together, looking up out of the corner of my eyes at the huge tower of broad-cloth by my side, and comparing the two red shoulders of mutton which held the reins, with my own wasted, white, woman-like fingers.

I found the old gentleman most inquisitive. He drew out of me all my story – questioned me about the way 'Lunnon folks' lived, and whether they got any shooting or 'pattening' – whereby I found he meant skating – and broke in, every now and then, with ejaculations of childish wonder, and clumsy sympathy, on my accounts of London labour and London misery.

'Oh, father, father! – I wonders they bears it. Us'n in the fens wouldn't stand that likes. They'd roit, and roit, and roit, and tak' oot the dook-gunes to un – they would, as they did five-and-twenty year agone.* Never to goo ayond the housen! – never to goo ayond the housen! Kill me in a three months, that would – bor', then!'

'Are you a farmer?' I asked, at last, thinking that my turn for questioning was come.

'I bean't varmer; I be yooman born. Never paid rent in moy life, nor never wool. I farms my own land, and my vathers avore me, this ever so mony hoondred year. I've got the swoord of 'em to home, and the helmet that they fut with into the wars, then when they chopped off the king's head – what was the name of um?'

'Charles the First?'

'Ees – that's the booy. We was Parliament side – true Britons all we was, down into the fens, and Oliver Cromwell, as dug Botsham lode, to the head of us.* You coom down to Metholl,* and I'll shaw ye a country. I'll shaw 'ee some'at like bullocks to call, and some'at like a field o' beans – I wool, – none 'o this here darned ups and downs o' hills' (though the country through which we drove was flat enough, I should have thought, to please any one), 'to shake a body's victuals out of his inwards – all so flat as a barn's floor, for vorty mile on end – there's the country to live in! – and vour sons – or was vour on 'em – every one on 'em fifteen stone in his shoes, to patten* again' any man from Whit'sea Mere to Denver Sluice,* for twenty pounds o' gold; and there's the money to lay down, and let the man as dare cover it, down with his money, and on wi' his pattens, thirteen-inch runners, down the wind, again' ether a one o' the bairns!'

And he jingled in his pocket a heavy bag of gold, and

winked, and chuckled, and then suddenly checking himself, repeated in a sad, dubious tone, two or three times, 'vour on 'em there was – vour on 'em there was'; and relieved his feelings, by springing the pony into a canter till he came to a public house, where he pulled up, called for a pot of hot ale, and insisted on treating me. I assured him that I never drank fermented liquors.

'Aw? Eh? How can yow do that then? Die o' cowd i' the fen, that gate, yow would. Love ye then! they as dinnot tak' spirits down thor, tak' their pennord o' elevation, then – women-folk especial.'

'What's elevation?'

'Oh! ho! ho! – yow goo into druggist's shop o' market-day, into Cambridge, and you'll see the little boxes, doozens and doozens, a' ready on the counter; and never a ven-man's wife goo by, but what calls in for her pennord o' elevation, to last her out the week. Oh! ho! ho! Well, it keeps women-folk quiet, it do; and it's mortal good agin ago pains.'

'But what is it?'

'Opium, bor' alive, opium!'

'But doesn't it ruin their health? I should think it the very worst sort of drunkenness.'

'Ow, well, yow moi say that – mak'th 'em cruel thin then, it do; but what can bodies do i' th' ago? Bot it's a bad thing, it is. Harken yow to me. Did'st ever know one called Porter, to yowr trade?'

I thought a little, and recollected a man of that name, who had worked with us a year or two before – a great friend of a certain scatter-brained Irish lad, brother of Crossthwaite's wife.

'Well, I did once, but I have lost sight of him twelve months, or more.'

The old man faced sharp round on me, swinging the little gig almost over, and then twisted himself back again, and put on a true farmer-like look of dogged, stolid reserve. We rolled on a few minutes in silence.

'Dee yow consider, now, that a mon mought be lost, like, into Lunnon?'

'How lost?'

'Why, yow told o' they sweaters – dee yow think a mon

might get in wi' one o' they, and they that mought be looking vor un not to vind un?'

'I do, indeed. There was a friend of that man Porter got turned away from our shop, because he wouldn't pay some tyrannical fine for being saucy, as they called it, to the shopman; and he went to a sweater's – and then to another; and his friends have been tracking him up and down this six months, and can hear no news of him.'

'Aw! guide us! And what'n, think yow, be gone wi' un?'

'I am afraid he has got into one of those dens, and has pawned his clothes, as dozens of them do, for food, and so can't get out.'

'Pawned his clothes for victuals! To think o' that, noo! But if he had work, can't he get victuals?'

'Oh!' I said, 'there's many a man who, after working seventeen or eighteen hours a-day, Sundays and all, without even time to take off his clothes, finds himself brought in in debt to his tyrant at the week's end. And if he gets no work, the villain won't let him leave the house; he has to stay there starving, on the chance of an hour's job. I tell you, I've known half-a-dozen men imprisoned in that way, in a little dungeon of a garret, where they had hardly room to stand upright, and only just space to sit and work between their beds, without breathing the fresh air, or seeing God's sun, for months together, with no victuals but a few slices of bread-and-butter, and a little slop of tea, twice a-day, till they were starved to the very bone.'

'Oh, my God! my God!' said the old man, in a voice which had a deeper tone of feeling than mere sympathy with others' sorrow was likely to have produced. There was evidently something behind all these inquiries of his. I longed to ask him if his name, too, was not Porter.

'Aw yow knawn Billy Porter? What was a like? Tell me, now – what was a like, in the Lord's name! what was a like unto?'

'Very tall and bony,' I answered.

'Ah! sax feet, and more? and a yard across? – but a was starved, a was a' thin, though, maybe, when yow sawn un? – and beautiful fine hair, hadn't a, like a lass's?'

'The man I knew had red hair,' quoth I.

'Ow, ay, an' that it wor, red as a rising sun, and the curls of un like gowlden guineas! And thou knew'st Billy Porter! To think o' that, noo—'

Another long silence.

'Could you find un, dee yow think, noo, into Lunnon? Suppose, now, there was a mon 'ud gie – may be five pund – ten pund – twenty pund, by * * * – twenty pund down, for to ha' him brocht home safe and soun' – Could yow do't, bor'? I zay, could yow do't?'

'I could do it as well without the money as with, if I could do it at all. But have you no guess as to where he is?'

He shook his head sadly.

'We – that's to zay, they as wants un – hav'n't heerd tell of un vor this three year – three year coom Whitsuntide as ever was—' And he wiped his eyes with his cuff.

'If you will tell me all about him, and where he was last heard of, I will do all I can to find him.'

'Will ye, noo? will ye? The Lord bless ye for zaying that.' – And he grasped my hand in his great iron fist, and fairly burst out crying.

'Was he a relation of yours?' I asked, gently.

'My bairn – my bairn – my eldest bairn. Dinnot yow ax me no moor – dinnot then, bor'. Gie on yow powney, and yow goo leuk vor un.'

Another long silence.

'I've a been to Lunnon, looking vor un.'

Another silence.

'I went up and down, up and down, day and night, day and night, to all pot-houses as I could zee; vor, says I, he was a'ways a main chap to drink, he was. Oh, deery me! and I never cot zight on un – and noo I be most spent, I be' —

And he pulled up at another public-house, and tried this time a glass of brandy. He stopped, I really think, at every inn between that place and Cambridge, and at each tried some fresh compound; but his head seemed, from habit, utterly fire-proof.

At last, we neared Cambridge, and began to pass groups of gay horsemen, and then those strange caps and gowns – ugly and unmeaning remnant of obsolete fashion.

The old man insisted on driving me up to the gate of Trinity, and there dropped me, after I had given him my address, entreating me to 'vind the bairn, and coom to zee him down to Metholl. But dinnot goo ax for Farmer Porter – they's all Porters there away. Yow ax for Wooden-house Bob – that's me; and if I barn't to home, ax for Mucky Billy – that's my brawther – we're all gotten our names down to ven; and if he barn't to home, yow ax for Frog-hall — that's where my sister do live; and they'll all veed ye, and lodge ye, and welcome ye. We be all like one, doon in the ven; and do ye, do ye vind my bairn!' And he trundled on, down the narrow street.

I was soon directed, by various smart-looking servants, to my cousin's rooms; and after a few mistakes, and wandering up and down noble courts and cloisters, swarming with gay young men, whose jaunty air and dress seemed strangely out of keeping with the stern antique solemnity of the Gothic build-ings around, espied my cousin's name over a door; and, uncertain how he might receive me, I gave a gentle, half-apologetic knock, which was answered by a loud 'Come in!' and I entered on a scene, even more incongruous than anything I had seen outside.

'If we can only keep away from that d * * * d Jesus as far as the corner, I don't care.'

'If we don't run into that first Trinity* before the willows, I shall care with a vengeance.'

'If we don't, it's a pity,' said my cousin. 'Wadham ran up by the side of that first Trinity yesterday, and he said that they were as well gruelled as so many posters,* before they got to the stile.'

This unintelligible, and, to my inexperienced ears, blasphem-ous conversation, proceeded from half-a-dozen powerful young men, in low-crowned sailor's hats and flannel trousers, some in shooting-jackets, some smoking cigars, some beating up eggs in sherry; while my cousin, dressed like 'a fancy waterman',* sat on the back of a sofa, puffing away at a huge meerschaum.

'Alton! why, what wind on earth has blown you here?'

By the tone, the words seemed rather an inquiry as to what wind would be kind enough to blow me back again. But he recovered his self-possession in a moment.

'Delighted to see you! Where's your portmanteau? Oh – left it at the Bull! Ah! I see. Very well, we'll send the gyp for it in a minute, and order some luncheon. We're just going down to the boat-race. Sorry I can't stop, but we shall all be fined – not a moment to lose. I'll send you in luncheon as I go through the butteries; then, perhaps, you'd like to come down and see the race. Ask the gyp* to tell you the way. Now, then, follow your noble captain, gentlemen – to glory and a supper.' And he bustled out with his crew.

While I was staring about the room, at the jumble of Greek books, boxing-gloves, and luscious prints of pretty women, a shrewd-faced, smart man entered, much better dressed than myself.

'What would you like, sir? Ox-tail soup, sir, or gravy-soup, sir? Stilton cheese, sir, or Cheshire, sir? Old Stilton, sir, just now.'

Fearing lest many words might betray my rank – and, strange to say, though I should not have been afraid of confessing myself an artisan before the 'gentlemen' who had just left the room, I was ashamed to have my low estate discovered, and talked over with his compeers, by the flunkey who waited on them – I answered, 'Anything – I really don't care', in as aristocratic and off-hand a tone as I could assume.

'Porter or ale, sir?'

'Water,' without a 'thank you', I am ashamed to say, for I was not at that time quite sure whether it was well-bred to be civil to servants.

The man vanished, and re-appeared with a savoury luncheon, silver forks, snowy napkins, smart plates – I felt really quite a gentleman.

He gave me full directions as to my 'way to the boats, sir'; and I started out much refreshed; passed through back streets, dingy, dirty, and profligate-looking enough; out upon wide meadows, fringed with enormous elms; across a ferry, through a pleasant village, with its old grey church and spire; by the side of a sluggish river, alive with wherries; along a towing-path swarming with bold, bedizened women, who jested with the rowers, – of their profession, alas! there could be no doubt. I had walked down some mile or so, and just as I heard a cannon, as I thought, fire at some distance, and wondered at its meaning, I came to a sudden bend of the river, with a church-tower hanging over the stream on the opposite bank, a knot of tall poplars, weeping willows, rich lawns, sloping down to the water's side, gay with bonnets and shawls; while, along the edge of the stream, light, gaudily-painted boats apparently waited for the race, — altogether the most brilliant and graceful group of scenery which I had beheld in my little travels. I stopped to gaze; and among the ladies on the lawn opposite, caught sight of a figure – my heart leapt into my mouth! Was it she at last? It was too far to distinguish features; the dress was altogether different – but was it not she? I saw her move across the lawn, and take the arm of a tall, venerable-looking man; and his dress was the same as that of the Dean, at the Dulwich Gallery – was it? was it not? To have found her, and a river between us! It was ludicrously miserable – miserably ludicrous. Oh, that accursed river, which debarred me from certainty, from bliss! I would have plunged across – but there were three objections – first, that I could not swim; next, what could I do when I had crossed? and thirdly, it might not be she after all.

And yet I was certain – instinctively certain – that it was she, the idol of my imagination for years. If I could not see her features under that little white bonnet, I could imagine them there; they flashed up in my memory as fresh as ever. Did she remember my features, as I did hers? Would she know me again? Had she ever even thought of me, from that day to this? Fool! But there I stood, fascinated, gazing across the river, heedless of the racing-boats, and the crowd, and the roar that was rushing up to me at the rate of ten miles an hour, and in a moment more, had caught me, and swept me away with it, whether I would or not, along the towing-path, by the side of the foremost boats.

Oh, the Babel of horse and foot, young and old! the cheering, and the exhorting, and the objurgations of number this, and number that! and the yelling of the most sacred names, inter-mingled too often with oaths. – And yet, after a few moments, I ceased to wonder either at the Cambridge passion for boat-racing, or at the excitement of the spectators. *'Honi soit qui mal y pense.'* It was a noble sport – a sight such as could only be seen in England – some hundred of young men, who might, if they had chosen, been lounging effeminately about the streets, subjecting themselves voluntarily to that intense exertion, for the mere pleasure of toil. The true English stuff came out there; I felt that, in spite of all my prejudices – the stuff which has held Gibraltar* and conquered at Waterloo – which has created a Birmingham and a Manchester, and colonised every quarter of the globe – that grim, earnest, stubborn energy, which, since the days of the old Romans, the English possess alone of all the nations of the earth. I was as proud of the gallant young fellows, as if they had been my brothers – of their courage and endurance (for one could see that it was no child's-play, from the pale faces, and panting lips), their strength and activity, so fierce and yet so cultivated, smooth, harmonious, as oar kept time with oar, and every back rose and fell in concert – and felt my soul stirred up to a sort of sweet madness, not merely by the shouts and cheers of the mob around me, but by the loud, fierce pulse of the rowlocks, the swift whispering rush of the long, snake-like eight oars, the swirl and gurgle of the water in their wake, the grim, breathless silence of the straining rowers. My blood boiled over, and fierce tears swelled into my eyes; for I, too, was a man, and an Englishman; and when I caught sight of my cousin, pulling stroke to the second boat in the long line, with set teeth and flashing eyes, the great muscles on his bare arms springing up into knots at every rapid stroke, I ran and shouted among the maddest and the foremost.

But I soon tired, and, footsore as I was, began to find my strength fail me. I tried to drop behind, but found it impossible in the press. At last, quite out of breath, I stopped; and instantly received a heavy blow from behind, which threw me on my face. I looked up, and saw a huge long-legged grey horse, with his knees upon my back, in the act of falling over me. His rider, a little ferret-visaged boy, dressed in sporting style, threw himself back in the saddle, and recovered the horse in an instant, with a curse at me, as I rolled down the steep bank into the river, among the laughter and shouts of the women, who seemed to think it quite a grand act on the part of the horse-man.

'Well saved, upon my word, my lord!' shouted out a rider beside him.

'Confound the snob!* – I'm glad he got his ducking.

What do the fellows want here, getting in a gentleman's way?'

'For shame, Swindon! the man is hurt,' said another rider, a very tall and handsome man, who pulled up his horse, and, letting the crowd pass, sprang off to my assistance.

'Leave him alone, Lord Lynedale,' said one of the women; 'let him go home and ask his mammy to hang him out to dry.'

'Why do you bother yourself with such muffs?' &c. &c. &c.

But I had scrambled out, and stood there dripping, and shaking with rage and pain.

'I hope you are not much hurt, my man?' asked the nobleman, in a truly gentlemanlike, because truly gentle, voice, and he pulled out half-a-crown, and offered it to me, saying, 'I am quite ashamed to see one of my own rank behave in a way so unworthy of it.'

But I, in my shame and passion, thrust back at once the coin and the civility.

'I want neither you nor your money,' said I, limping off down the bank. 'It serves me right, for getting among you cursed aristocrats.'

How the nobleman took my answer I did not stay to see, for I was glad to escape the jeers of the bystanding blackguards, male and female, by scrambling over the fences, and making my way across the fields back to Cambridge.

CHAPTER XIII

THE LOST IDOL FOUND

ON my return, I found my cousin already at home, in high spirits at having, as he informed me, 'bumped the first Trinity.' I excused myself for my dripping state, simply by saying that I had slipped into the river. To tell him the whole of the story, while the insult still rankled fresh in me, was really too disagreeable both to my memory and my pride.

Then came the question, 'What had brought me to Cambridge?' I told him all, and he seemed honestly to sympathise with my misfortunes.

'Never mind; we'll make it all right somehow. Those poems of yours – you must let me have them and look over them; and I dare say I shall persuade the governor to do something with them. After all, it's no loss for you; you couldn't have gone on tailoring – much too sharp a fellow for that; – you ought to be at college, if one could only get you there. These sizarships, now, were meant for just such cases as yours – clever fellows who could not afford to educate themselves; but, like everything in the university, the people for whom they are meant never get them. Do you know what the golden canon is, Alton, for understanding all university questions?'

'No.'

'Then I'll tell you. That the employment of any money whatsoever, for any purpose whatsoever, is a certain sign that it was originally meant for some purpose totally different.'

'What do you mean?' I asked.

'Oh! you shall stay here with me a few days, and you'll soon find out. Hush! now; don't come the independent dodge. One cousin may visit another, I hope, without contracting obligations, and all that. I'll find you a bedroom out of college, and you'll live in my rooms all day, and I'll show you a thing or two. How do you like the university?'

'The buildings,' I said, 'strike me as very noble and reverent.'

'They are the only noble and reverent things you'll find here, I can tell you. It's a system of humbug, from one end to the other. But the Dons get their living by it, and their livings too, and their bishopricks, now and then; and I intend to do the same, if I have a chance. Do at Rome as Rome does.' And he lighted his pipe, and winked knowingly at me.

I mentioned the profane use of sacred names, which had so disgusted me at the boat-race. He laughed.

'Ah! my dear fellow, it's a very fair specimen of Cambridge – shows what's the matter with us all – putting new wine into old bottles, and into young bottles, too, as you'll see at my supper party to-night.'

'Really,' I said, 'I am not fit for presentation at any such aristocratic amusements.'

'Oh! I'll lend you clothes till your own are dried; and as for behaviour, hold your tongue, and don't put your knife in your mouth, are quite rules enough to get any man mistaken for a gentleman here.' And he laughed again in his peculiar sneering way.

'By-the-bye, don't get drunk; for in vino veritas. You know what that means.'

'So well,' I answered, 'that I never intend to touch a drop of fermented liquor.'

'Capital rule for a poor man. I've got a strong head, luckily. If I hadn't, I should keep sober on principle. It's great fun to have a man taking you into his confidence after the second bottle; and then to see the funk he's in next day, when he recollects he's shown you more of his hand than is good for his own game.'

All this sickened me; and I tried to turn the conversation, by asking him what he meant by new wine in old bottles.

'Can't you see? The whole is monastic – dress, unmarried fellows, the very names of the colleges. I dare say it did very well for the poor scholars in the middle ages, who, three-fourths of them, turned either monks or priests; but it won't do for the young gentlemen of the nineteenth century. Those very names of colleges are of a piece with the rest. The colleges were dedicated to various sacred personages and saints, to secure their interest in heaven for the prosperity of the college; but who believes in all that now? And therefore the names remain only to be desecrated. The men can't help it. They must call the colleges by their names.'

'Why don't they alter the names?' I said.

'Because, my dear fellow, they are afraid to alter anything, for fear of bringing the whole rotten old house down about their ears. They say themselves, that the slightest innovation will be a precedent for destroying the whole system, bit by bit. Why should they be afraid of that, if they did not know that the whole system would not bear canvassing an instant? That's why they retain statutes that can't be observed; because they know, if they once began altering the statutes the least, the world would find out how they have themselves been breaking the statutes. That's why they keep up the farce of swearing to the Thirty-Nine Articles,* and all that; just because they know, if they attempted to alter the letter of the old forms, it would come out, that half the young men of the university don't believe three words of them at heart. They know the majority of us are at heart neither churchmen nor Christians, not even decently moral: but the one thing they are afraid of is scandal. So they connive at the young men's ill-doings; they take no real steps to put down profligacy; and, in the mean time, they just keep up the forms of Church of Englandism, and pray devoutly that the whole humbug may last out their time. There isn't one Don in a hundred who has any personal influence over the gownsmen. A man may live here from the time he's a fresh-man, to the time he's taken his degree, without ever being spoken to as if he had a soul to be saved; unless he happens to be one of the Simeonite party,* and they are getting fewer and fewer every year; and in ten years more there won't be one of them left, at the present rate. Besides, they have no influence over the rest of the undergraduates. They are very good, excellent fellows in their way, I do believe; but they are not generally men of talent; and they keep entirely to themselves; and know nothing, and care nothing, for the questions of the day.'

And so he rambled on, complaining and sneering, till supper time; when we went out and lounged about the venerable cloisters, while the room was being cleared and the cloth laid.

To describe a Cambridge supper party among gay young men is a business as little suited to my taste as to my powers. The higher classes ought to know pretty well what such things are like; and the working men are not altogether ignorant, seeing that Peter Priggins* and other university men have been turning Alma Mater's shame to as lucrative account in their fictions, as the Irish scribblers* have that of their mother country. But I must say, that I was utterly disgusted; and when, after the removal of the eatables, the whole party, twelve or fourteen in number, set to work to drink hard and deliberately at milk punch, and bishop, and copus, and grog, and I know not what other inventions of bacchanalian luxury, and to sing, one after another, songs of the most brutal indecency, I was glad to escape into the cool night air, and under pretence of going home, wander up and down the King's Parade, and watch the tall gables of King's College Chapel, and the classic front of the senate-house, and the stately tower of St. Mary's, as they stood, stern and silent, bathed in the still glory of the moonshine, and seeming to watch, with a steadfast sadness, the scene of frivolity and sin, pharisaism, formalism, hypocrisy, and idleness, below.

Noble buildings! and noble institutions! given freely to the people, by those who loved the people, and the Saviour who died for them. They gave us what they had, those mediæval founders: whatsoever narrowness of mind or superstition defiled their gift was not their fault, but the fault of their whole age. The best they knew they imparted freely, and God will reward them for it. To monopolise those institutions for the rich, as is done now, is to violate both the spirit and the letter of the foundations; to restrict their studies to the limits of middle-age Romanism,** their conditions of admission to those fixed at the Reformation, is but a shade less wrongful. The letter is kept – the spirit is thrown away. You refuse to admit any who are not members of the Church of England;* – say, rather, any who will not sign the dogmas of the Church of England, whether they believe a word of them or not. Useless formalism! which lets through the reckless, the profligate, the ignorant, the hypocritical; and only excludes the honest and the conscientious, and the mass of the intellectual working men. And whose fault is it that THEY are not members of the Church of England? Whose fault is it, I ask? Your predecessors neglected the lower orders, till they have ceased to reverence either you or your doctrines; – you confess that, among yourselves, freely enough. You throw the blame of the present wide-spread dislike to the Church of England on her sins during 'the godless eighteenth century'. Be it so. Why are those sins to be visited on us? Why are we to be shut out from the universities, which were founded for us, because you have let us grow up, by millions, heathens and infidels, as you call us? Take away your subterfuge! It is not

** This, like the rest of Mr. Locke's Cambridge reminiscences, may appear to many exaggerated and unfair. But he seems to be speaking of both universities, and at a time when they had not even commenced the process of reformation. We fear, however, that in spite of many noble exceptions, his picture of Cambridge represents, if not the whole truth, still the impression which she leaves on the minds of too many, strangers and, alas! students also. – ED.

merely because we are bad churchmen that you exclude us, else
you would be crowding your colleges, now, with the talented
poor of the agricultural districts, who, as you say, remain faithful to the church of their fathers. But are there six labourers'
sons educating in the universities at this moment? No! The real
reason for our exclusion, churchmen or not, is because we are
poor – because we cannot pay your exorbitant fees, often, as in
the case of bachelors of arts, exacted for tuition which is never
given, and residence which is not permitted – because we could
not support the extravagance which you not only permit, but
encourage, because, by your own unblushing confession, it
insures the university 'the support of the aristocracy'.

'But, on religious points, at least, you must abide by the
statutes of the university.'

Strange argument, truly, to be urged literally by English
Protestants in possession of Roman Catholic bequests! If that be
true in the letter, as well as in the spirit, you should have given
place long ago to the Dominicans and the Franciscans. In the
spirit it is true, and the Reformers acted on it when they rightly
converted the universities to the uses of the new faith. They
carried out the spirit of the founders' statutes by making the
universities as good as they could be, and letting them share in
the new light of the Elizabethan age. But was the sum of
knowledge, human and divine, perfected at the Reformation?
Who gave the Reformers, or you, who call yourselves their
representatives, a right to say to the mind of man, and to the
teaching of God's Spirit, 'Hitherto, and no farther!' Society
and mankind, the children of the Supreme, will not stop
growing for your dogmas – much less for your vested interests;
and the righteous law of mingled development and renovation,
applied in the sixteenth century, must be re-applied in the
nineteenth; while the spirits of the founders, now purged from
the superstitions and ignorances of their age, shall smile from
heaven, and say, 'So would we have had it, if we had lived in
the great nineteenth century, into which it has been your
privilege to be born.'

But such thoughts soon passed away. The image which I had
seen that afternoon upon the river-banks, had awakened imperiously the frantic longings of past years; and now it re-ascended

its ancient throne, and tyrannously drove forth every other object, to keep me alone with its own tantalizing and torturing beauty. I did not think about her – No; I only stupidly and steadfastly stared at her with my whole soul and imagination, through that long sleepless night; and in spite of the fatigue of my journey, and the stiffness proceeding from my fall and wetting, I lay tossing till the early sun poured into my bedroom window. Then I arose, dressed myself, and went out to wander up and down the streets, gazing at one splendid building after another, till I found the gates of King's College open. I entered eagerly, through a porch which, to my untutored taste, seemed gorgeous enough to form the entrance to a fairy palace, and stood in the quadrangle, rivetted to the spot by the magnificence of the huge chapel on the right.

If I had admired it the night before, I felt inclined to worship it this morning, as I saw the lofty buttresses and spires, fretted with all their gorgeous carving, and 'storied windows richly dight',* sleeping in the glare of the newly risen sun, and throwing their long shadows due westward down the sloping lawn, and across the river which dimpled and gleamed below, till it was lost among the towering masses of crisp elms and rose-garlanded chestnuts in the rich gardens beyond.

Was I delighted? Yes – and yet no. There is a painful feeling in seeing anything magnificent which one cannot understand. And perhaps it was a morbid sensitiveness, but the feeling was strong upon me that I was an interloper there – out of harmony with the scene and the system which had created it; that I might be an object of unpleasant curiosity, perhaps of scorn (for I had not forgotten the nobleman at the boat-race), amid those monuments of learned luxury. Perhaps, on the other hand, it was only from the instinct which makes us seek for solitude under the pressure of intense emotions, when we have neither language to express them to ourselves, nor loved one in whose silent eyes we may read kindred feelings – a sympathy which wants no words. Whatever the cause was, when a party of men, in their caps and gowns, approached me down the dark avenue which led into the country, I was glad to shrink for concealment behind the weeping-willow at the foot of the bridge, and slink off unobserved to breakfast with my cousin.

We had just finished breakfast, my cousin was lighting his meerschaum, when a tall figure passed the window, and the taller of the noblemen, whom I had seen at the boat-race, entered the room with a packet of papers in his hand.

'Here, Locule mi! my pocket-book – or rather, to stretch a bad pun till it bursts, my pocket-dictionary. I require the aid of your benevolently-squandered talents for the correction of these proofs. I am, as usual, both idle and busy this morning; so draw pen, and set to work for me.'

'I am exceedingly sorry, my lord,' answered George, in his most obsequious tone, 'but I must work this morning with all my might. Last night, recollect, was given to triumph, Bacchus, and idleness.'

'Then find some one who will do them for me, my Ulysses polumechane, polutrope, panurge.'*

'I shall be most happy (with a half-frown and a wince) to play Panurge to your lordship's Pantagruel,* on board the new yacht.'

'Oh, I am perfect in that character, I suppose? And is she, after all, like Pantagruel's ship, to be loaded with hemp?* Well, we must try two or three milder cargoes first. But come, find me some starving genius – some græculus esuriens*——'

'Who will ascend to the heaven of your lordship's eloquence for the bidding?'

'Five shillings a sheet – there will be about two of them, I think, in the pamphlet.'

'May I take the liberty of recommending my cousin here?'

'Your cousin?' And he turned to me, who had been examining with a sad and envious eye the contents of the bookshelves. Our eyes met, and first a faint blush, and then a smile of recognition, passed over his magnificent countenance.

'I think I had – I am ashamed that I cannot say the pleasure, of meeting him at the boat-race yesterday.'

My cousin looked inquiringly and vexed at us both. The nobleman smiled.

'Oh, the shame was ours, not his.'

'I cannot think', I answered, 'that you have any reasons to remember with shame your own kindness and courtesy. As for me,' I went on bitterly, 'I suppose a poor journeyman tailor, who ventures to look on at the sports of gentlemen, only deserves to be ridden over.'

'Sir,' he said, looking at me with a severe and searching glance, 'your bitterness is pardonable – but not your sneer. You do not yourself think what you say, and you ought to know that I think it still less than yourself. If you intend your irony to be useful, you should keep it till you can use it courageously against the true offenders.'

I looked up at him fiercely enough, but the placid smile which had returned to his face disarmed me.

'Your class,' he went on, 'blind yourselves and our class as much by wholesale denunciations of us, as we, alas! who should know better, do by wholesale denunciations of you. As you grow older, you will learn that there are exceptions to every rule.'

'And yet the exception proves the rule.'

'Most painfully true, sir. But that argument is two-edged. For instance, am I to consider it the exception or the rule, when I am told, that you, a journeyman tailor, are able to correct these proofs for me?'

'Nearer the rule, I think, than you yet fancy.'

'You speak out boldly and well; but how can you judge what I may please to fancy? At all events, I will make trial of you. There are the proofs. Bring them to me by four o'clock this afternoon, and if they are well done, I will pay you more than I should to the average hack-writer, for you will deserve more.'

I took the proofs; he turned to go, and by a side-look at George beckoned him out of the room. I heard a whispering in the passage; and I do not deny that my heart beat high with new hopes, as I caught unwillingly the words—

'Such a forehead! – such an eye! – such a contour of feature as that! – Locule mi – that boy ought not to be mending trousers.'

My cousin returned, half laughing, half angry.

'Alton, you fool, why did you let out that you were a snip?'

'I am not ashamed of my trade.'

'I am, then. However, you've done with it now; and if you can't come the gentleman, you may as well come the rising genius. The self-educated dodge pays well just now; and after all, you've hooked his lordship – thank me for that. But you'll never hold him, you impudent dog, if you pull so hard on him' – He went on, putting his hands into his coat-tail pockets, and sticking himself in front of the fire, like the Delphic Pythoness upon the sacred tripod,* in hopes, I suppose, of some oracular afflatus – 'You will never hold him, I say, if you pull so hard on him. You ought to "My lord" him for months yet, at least. You know, my good fellow, you must take every possible care to pick up what good-breeding you can, if I take the trouble to put you in the way of good society, and tell you where my private birds'-nests are, like the green schoolboy some poet or other talks of.'

'He is no lord of mine,' I answered, 'in any sense of the word, and therefore I shall not call him so.'

'Upon my honour! here is a young gentleman who intends to rise in the world, and then commences by trying to walk through the first post he meets! Noodle! can't you do like me, and get out of the carts' way when they come by? If you intend to go ahead, you must just dodge in and out, like a dog at a fair. "She stoops to conquer" is my motto, and a precious good one too.'

'I have no wish to conquer Lord Lynedale, and so I shall not stoop to him.'

'I have, then; and to very good purpose, too. I am his whetstone, for polishing up that classical wit of his on, till he carries it into Parliament to astonish the country squires. He fancies himself a second Goethe; I hav'n't forgot his hitting at me, before a large supper party, with a certain epigram of that old turkey-cock's* about the whale having his unmentionable parasite – and the great man likewise. Whale, indeed! I bide my time, Alton, my boy – I bide my time; and then let your grand aristocrat look out! If he does not find the supposed whale-unmentionable a good stout holding harpoon, with a tough line to it, and a long one, it's a pity, Alton, my boy!'

And he burst into a coarse laugh, tossed himself down on the sofa, and re-lighted his meerschaum.

'He seemed to me,' I answered, 'to have a peculiar courtesy and liberality of mind towards those below him in rank.'

'Oh! he had, had he? Now, I'll just put you up to a dodge.

He intends to come the Mirabeau – fancies his mantle has fallen on him – prays before the fellow's bust, I believe, if one knew the truth, for a double portion of his spirit; and therefore it is a part of his game to ingratiate himself with all pot-boy-dom, while at heart he is as proud, exclusive an aristocrat, as ever wore nobleman's hat.* At all events, you may get something out of him, if you play your cards well – or, rather, help me to play mine; for I consider him as my property, and you only as my aide-de-camp.'

'I shall play no one's cards,' I answered, sulkily. 'I am doing work fairly, and shall be fairly paid for it, and keep my own independence.'

'Independence! hey-day! Have you forgotten that, after all, you are my – guest, to call it by the mildest term?'

'Do you upbraid me with that?' I said, starting up. 'Do you expect me to live on your charity, on condition of doing your dirty work? You do not know me, sir. I leave your roof this instant!'

'You do not!' answered he, laughing loudly, as he sprang over the sofa, and set his back against the door. 'Come, come, you Will o' the Wisp, as full of flights, and fancies, and vagaries, as a sick old maid! Can't you see which side your bread is buttered? Sit down, I say! Don't you know that I'm as good-natured a fellow as ever lived, although I do parade a little Gil Blas morality* now and then, just for fun's sake? Do you think I should be so open with it, if I meant anything very diabolic? There – sit down, and don't go into King Cambyses' vein, or Queen Hecuba's tears, either,* which you seem inclined to do.'

'I know you have been very generous to me,' said I, penitently, 'but a kindness becomes none when you are upbraided with it.'

'So say the copybooks – I deny it. At all events, I'll say no more; – and you shall sit down there, and write as still as a mouse, till two, while I tackle this never-to-be-enough-by-unhappy-third-years'-men-execrated Griffin's Optics.'*

*

At four that afternoon, I knocked, proofs in hand, at the door of Lord Lynedale's rooms in the King's Parade. The door was opened by a little elderly groom, grey-coated, grey-gaitered, grey-haired, grey-visaged. He had the look of a respectable old family retainer, and his exquisitely neat groom's dress gave him a sort of interest in my eyes. Class costumes, relics though they are of feudalism, carry a charm with them. They are symbolic, definitive; they bestow a personality on the wearer; which satisfies the mind, by enabling it instantly to classify him, to connect him with a thousand stories and associations; and to my young mind, the wiry, shrewd, honest, grim old serving-man seemed the incarnation of all the wonders of Newmarket, and the hunting-kennel, and the steeple-chase, of which I had read, with alternate admiration and contempt, in the newspapers.

From between his legs peeped out a mass of shaggy grizzled hair, containing a Skye-terrier's eyes, and a long snout, which, by its twisting and sniffing, seemed investigating whether my trousers came within the biting degree of shabbiness.

'And what do you want here, young man?'

'I was bidden by Lord Lynedale to come here at four with these papers.'

'Oh, yes! very likely! that's an old story; and to be paid money, I guess?'

'And to be paid money.'

'Not a doubt on't. Then you must wait a little longer, like the rest of you bloodsuckers. Go back, and tell your master that he needn't send your sort here any more, with his post obits,* and post mortems, and the like devilry. The old earl's good to last these three months more, the Lord be praised. Therefore, come, sir – you go back to your master, and take him my compliments, and * * *.'

'I have no master,' quoth I, puzzled, but half laughing; for I liked the old fellow's iron honest visage.

'No master, eh? then darned if you shall come in. Comes on your own account, eh? Got a little bit of paper for his lordship in that bundle?'

'I told you already that I had,' said I, peevishly.

'Werry good; but you didn't tell me whether they come from the bayleaves or not.'

'Nonsense! Take the papers in yourself, if you like.'

'Oh, you young wagabond! Do you take me for Judas Iscariot? And what do you expect – to set a man on serving a writ on a man's own master? Wait a bit, till I gets the hors'up, that's all, and I'll show you what's what.'

If I could not understand him, the dog did; for he ran instantly at my legs, secured a large piece of my best trousers, and was returning for a second, if I had not, literally, in my perplexity, thrust the clean proofs into his mouth, which he worried and shook, as if they had been the grandfather of all white mice. At this moment, the inner door opened, and Lord Lynedale appeared. There was an explanation, and a laugh, in which I could not but join, in spite of the torn trousers, at the expense of the groom. The old man retired, mingling his growls with those of the terrier, and evidently quite disappointed at my not being a dun – an honest, douce barn-door fowl, and not *fera naturæ*,* and fair game for his sporting propensities.

Lord Lynedale took me into the inner room, and bade me sit down while he examined the proofs. I looked round the low-wainscotted apartment, with its narrow mullioned windows, in extreme curiosity. What a real nobleman's abode could be like, was naturally worth examining, to one who had, all his life, heard of the aristocracy as of some mythic Titans – whether fiends or gods, being yet a doubtful point – altogether enshrined on 'cloudy Olympus', invisible to mortal ken. The shelves were gay with Morocco, Russia leather, and gilding – not much used, as I thought, till my eye caught one of the gorgeously-bound volumes lying on the table in a loose cover of polished leather – a refinement of which poor I should never have dreamt. The walls were covered with prints, which soon turned my eyes from everything else, to range delighted over Landseers, Turners, Roberts's Eastern sketches,* the ancient Italian masters; and I recognised, with a sort of friendly affection, an old print of my favourite St. Sebastian, in the Dulwich Gallery. It brought back to my mind a thousand dreams, and a thousand sorrows. Would those dreams be ever realised? Might this new acquaintance possibly open some pathway towards their fulfilment? – some vista towards the attainment of a station where they would, at least, be less chimerical? – And at that thought, my heart beat loud with hope. The room was choked up with chairs and tables, of all sorts of strange shapes and problematical uses. The floor was strewed with skins of bear, deer, and seal. In a corner lay hunting-whips and fishing-rods, foils, boxing-gloves, and gun-cases; while over the chimney-piece, an array of rich Turkish pipes, all amber and enamel, contrasted curiously with quaint old swords and daggers – bronze classic casts, upon gothic oak brackets, and fantastic scraps of continental carving. On the centre-table, too, reigned the same rich profusion, or, if you will, confusion – MSS., 'Notes in Egypt',* 'Goethe's Walverwandschaften',* 'Murray's hand-books',* and 'Plato's Republic'. What was there not there? And I chuckled inwardly, to see how *Bell's Life in London* and the *Ecclesiologist* had, between them, got down 'McCulloch on Taxation',* and were sitting, arm-in-arm, triumphantly astride of him. Everything in the room, even to the fragrant flowers in a German glass, spoke of a travelled and cultivated luxury – manifold tastes and powers of self-enjoyment and self-improvement, which Heaven forgive me if I envied, as I looked upon them. If I, now, had had one-twentieth part of those books, prints, that experience of life, not to mention that physical strength and beauty, which stood towering there before the fire – so simple – so utterly unconscious of the innate nobleness and grace which shone out from every motion of those stately limbs and features – all the delicacy which blood can give, combined, as one does sometimes see, with the broad strength of the proletarian – so different from poor me! – and so different too, as I recollected with perhaps a savage pleasure, from the miserable, stunted specimen of over-bred imbecility which had ridden over me the day before! A strange question that of birth! and one in which the philosopher, in spite of himself, must come to democratic conclusions. For, after all, the physical and intellectual superiority of the high-born is only preserved, as it was in the old Norman times, by the continual practical abnegation of the very caste-lie on which they pride themselves – by continual renovation of their race, by intermarriage with the ranks below them. The blood of Odin flowed in the veins of Norman William; true – and so did the tanner's of Falaise!*

At last he looked up, and spoke courteously—

'I'm afraid I have kept you long; but now, here is for your corrections, which are capital. I have really to thank you for a lesson in writing English.' And he put a sovereign into my hand.

'I am very sorry,' said I, 'but I have no change.'

'Never mind that. Your work is well worth the money.'

'But,' I said, 'you agreed with me for five shillings a sheet, and—— I do not wish to be rude, but I cannot accept your kindness. We working men make a rule of abiding by our wages, and taking nothing which looks like——'

'Well, well – and a very good rule it is. I suppose, then, I must find out some way for you to earn more. Good-afternoon.' And he motioned me out of the room, followed me downstairs, and turned off towards the College Gardens.

I wandered up and down, feeding my greedy eyes, till I found myself again upon the bridge where I had stood that morning, gazing with admiration and astonishment at a scene which I have often expected to see painted or described, and which, nevertheless, in spite of its unique magnificence, seems strangely overlooked by those who cater for the public taste, with pen and pencil. The vista of bridges, one after another, spanning the stream; the long line of great monastic palaces, all unlike, and yet all in harmony, sloping down to the stream, with their trim lawns and ivied-walls, their towers and buttresses; and opposite them, the range of rich gardens and noble timber-trees, dimly seen through which, at the end of the gorgeous river avenue, towered the lofty buildings of St. John's. The whole scene, under the glow of a rich May afternoon, seemed to me a fragment out of the 'Arabian Nights' or Spenser's 'Fairy Queen'. I leaned upon the parapet, and gazed, and gazed, so absorbed in wonder and enjoyment, that I was quite unconscious, for some time, that Lord Lynedale was standing by my side, engaged in the same employment. He was not alone. Hanging on his arm was a lady, whose face, it seemed to me, I ought to know. It certainly was one not to be easily forgotten. She was beautiful, but with the face and figure rather of a Juno than a Venus – dark, imperious, restless – the lips almost too firmly set, the brow almost too massive and projecting – a queen, rather to be feared than loved – but a queen still, as truly royal as the man into whose face she was looking up with eager admiration and delight, as he pointed out to her eloquently the several beauties of the landscape. Her dress was as plain as that of any quaker; but the grace of its arrangement, of every line and fold, was enough, without the help of the heavy gold bracelet on her wrist, to proclaim her a fine lady; by which term, I wish to express the result of that perfect education in taste and manner, down to every gesture, which Heaven forbid that I, professing to be a poet, should undervalue. It is beautiful; and therefore I welcome it, in the name of the Author of all beauty. I value it so highly, that I would fain see it extend, not merely from Belgravia to the tradesman's villa, but thence, as I believe it one day will, to the labourer's hovel, and the needlewoman's garret.

Half in bashfulness, half in the pride which shrinks from anything like intrusion, I was moving away; but the nobleman, recognising me with a smile and a nod, made some observation on the beauty of the scene before us. Before I could answer, however, I saw that his companion's eyes were fixed intently on my face.

'Is this,' she said to Lord Lynedale, 'the young person of whom you were speaking to me just now? I fancy that I recollect him, though, I dare say, he has forgotten me.'

If I had forgotten the face, that voice, so peculiarly rich, deep, and marked in its pronunciation of every syllable, recalled her instantly to my mind. It was the dark lady of the Dulwich Gallery!

'I met you, I think,' I said, 'at the picture-gallery at Dulwich, and you were kind enough, and——and some persons who were with you, to talk to me about a picture there.'

'Yes; Guido's St. Sebastian. You seemed fond of reading, then. I am glad to see you at college.'

I explained, that I was not at college. That led to fresh gentle questions on her part, till I had given her all the leading points of my history. There was nothing in it of which I ought to have been ashamed.

She seemed to become more and more interested in my story, and her companion also.

'And have you tried to write? I recollect my uncle advising you to try a poem on St. Sebastian. It was spoken, perhaps, in jest; but it will not, I hope, have been labour lost, if you have taken it in earnest.'

'Yes – I have written on that and on other subjects, during the last few years.'

'Then, you must let us see them, if you have them with you. I think my uncle, Arthur, might like to look over them; and if they were fit for publication, he might be able to do something towards it.'

'At all events,' said Lord Lynedale, 'a self-educated author is always interesting. Bring any of your poems, that you have with you, to the Eagle this afternoon, and leave them there for Dean Winnstay; and to-morrow morning, if you have nothing better to do, call there between ten and eleven o'clock.'

He wrote me down the dean's address, and nodding a civil good morning, turned away with his queenly companion, while I stood gazing after him, wondering whether all noblemen and high-born ladies were like them in person and in spirit – a question, which, in spite of many noble exceptions, some of them well known and appreciated by the working men, I am afraid must be answered in the negative.

I took my MSS. to the Eagle, and wandered out once more, instinctively, among those same magnificent trees at the back of the colleges, to enjoy the pleasing torment of expectation. 'My uncle!' was he the same old man whom I had seen at the gallery; and if so, was Lillian with him? Delicious hope! And yet, what if she was with him – what to me? But yet I sat silent, dreaming, all the evening, and hurried early to bed – not to sleep, but to lie and dream on and on, and rise almost before light, eat no breakfast, and pace up and down, waiting impatiently for the hour at which I was to find out whether my dream was true.

And it was true! The first object I saw, when I entered the room, was Lillian, looking more beautiful than ever. The child of sixteen had blossomed into the woman of twenty. The ivory and vermilion of the complexion had toned down together into still richer hues. The dark hazel eyes shone with a more liquid lustre. The figure had become more rounded, without losing a line of that fairy lightness, with which her light morning-dress, with its delicate French semitones of colour, gay and yet not gaudy, seemed to harmonize. The little plump jewelled hands – the transparent chestnut hair, banded round the beautiful oval masque – the tiny feet, which, as Suckling has it,

> Underneath her petticoat
> Like little mice peeped in and out –*

I could have fallen down, fool that I was! and worshipped—— what? I could not tell then, for I cannot tell even now.

The dean smiled recognition, bade me sit down, and disposed my papers, meditatively, on his knee. I obeyed him, trembling, choking – my eyes devouring my idol – forgetting why I had come – seeing nothing but her – listening for nothing but the opening of those lips. I believe the dean was some sentences deep in his oration, before I became conscious thereof.

'——And I think I may tell you, at once, that I have been very much surprised and gratified with them. They evince, on the whole, a far greater acquaintance with the English classic models, and with the laws of rhyme and melody, than could have been expected from a young man of your class – *macte virtute puer.** Have you read any Latin?'

'A little.' And I went on staring at Lillian, who looked up, furtively, from her work, every now and then, to steal a glance at me, and set my poor heart thumping still more fiercely against my side.

'Very good; you will have the less trouble, then, in the preparation for college. You will find out for yourself, of course, the immense disadvantages of self-education. The fact is, my dear lord' (turning to Lord Lynedale), 'it is only useful as an indication of a capability of being educated by others. One never opens a book written by working men, without shuddering at a hundred faults of style. However, there are some very tolerable attempts among these – especially the imitations of Milton's 'Comus'.

Poor I had by no means intended them as imitations; but such, no doubt, they were.

'I am sorry to see that Shelley has had so much influence on your writing. He is a guide as irregular in taste, as unorthodox in doctrine; though there are some pretty things in him now and then. And you have caught his melody tolerably here, now——'

'Oh, that is such a sweet thing!' said Lillian. 'Do you know, I read it over and over last night, and took it upstairs with me. How very fond of beautiful things you must be, Mr. Locke, to be able to describe so passionately the longing after them.'

That voice once more! It intoxicated me, so that I hardly knew what I stammered out – something about working men having very few opportunities of indulging the taste for – I forget what. I believe I was on the point of running off into some absurd compliment, but I caught the dark lady's warning eye on me.

'Ah, yes! I forgot. I dare say it must be a very stupid life. So little opportunity, as he says. What a pity he is a tailor, papa! Such an unimaginative employment! How delightful it would be to send him to college, and make him a clergyman!'

Fool that I was! I fancied – what did I not fancy? Never seeing how that very '*he*' bespoke the indifference – the gulf between us. I was not a man – an equal; but a thing – a subject, who was to be talked over, and examined, and made into something like themselves, of their supreme and undeserved benevolence.

'Gently, gently, fair lady! We must not be as headlong as some people would kindly wish to be. If this young man really has a proper desire to rise into a higher station, and I find him a fit object to be assisted in that praiseworthy ambition, why, I think he ought to go to some training college; St. Mark's,* I should say, on the whole, might, by its strong Church principles, give the best antidote to any little remaining taint of sans-culottism. You understand me, my lord? And, then, if he distinguished himself there, it would be time to think of getting him a sizarship.'

'Poor Pegasus in harness!' half smiled, half sighed, the dark lady.

'Just the sort of youth,' whispered Lord Lynedale, loud enough for me to hear, 'to take out with us to the Mediterranean, as secretary – s'il y avait là de la morale, of course –'

Yes – and of course, too, the tailor's boy was not expected to understand French. But the most absurd thing was, how every-body, except perhaps the dark lady, seemed to take for granted that I felt myself exceedingly honoured, and must consider it, as a matter of course, the greatest possible stretch of kindness thus to talk me over, and settle everything for me, as if I was not a living soul, but a plant in a pot. Perhaps they were not unsupported by experience. I suppose too many of us would have thought it so; there are flunkeys in all ranks, and to spare. Perhaps the true absurdity was the way in which I sat, demented, inarticulate, staring at Lillian, and only caring for any word which seemed to augur a chance of seeing her again; instead of saying, as I felt, that I had no wish whatever to rise above my station; no intention whatever of being sent to training-schools or colleges, or anywhere else at the expense of other people. And therefore it was that I submitted blindly, when the dean, who looked as kind, and was really, I believe, as kind as ever was human being, turned to me with a solemn authoritative voice—

'Well, my young friend, I must say that I am, on the whole, very much pleased with your performance. It corroborates, my dear lord, the assertion, for which I have been so often ridiculed, that there are many real men, capable of higher things, scattered up and down among the masses. Attend to me, sir!' (a hint which I suspect I very much wanted). 'Now, recollect; if it should be hereafter in our power to assist your prospects in life, you must give up, once and for all, the bitter tone against the higher classes, which I am sorry to see in your MSS. As you know more of the world, you will find that the poor are not by any means as ill-used as they are taught, in these days, to believe. The rich have their sorrows too – no one knows it better than I' (and he played pensively with his gold pencil case) – 'and good and evil are pretty equally distributed among all ranks, by a just and merciful God. I advise you most earnestly, as you value your future success in life, to give up reading those unprincipled authors, whose aim is to excite the evil passions of the multitude; and to shut your ears betimes to the extravagant calumnies of demagogues, who make tools of enthusiastic and imaginative minds, for their own selfish aggrandisement. Avoid politics; the workman has no more to do with them than the clergyman. We are told, on divine authority, to fear God and the king, and meddle not with those who are given to change. Rather put before yourself the example of such a man as the excellent Dr. Brown, one of the richest and most respected men of the university, with whom I hope to have the pleasure of dining this evening – and yet that man actually, for several years of his life, worked at a carpenter's bench!'

I too had something to say about all that. I too knew something about demagogues and working men: but the sight of Lillian made me a coward; and I only sat silent as the thought flashed across me, half ludicrous, half painful, by its contrast, of another who once worked at a carpenter's bench, and fulfilled his mission – not by an old age of wealth, respectability, and port wine; but on the cross of Calvary. After all, the worthy old gentleman gave me no time to answer.

'Next – I think of showing these MSS. to my publisher, to get his opinion as to whether they are worth printing just now. Not that I wish you to build much on the chance. It is not necessary that you should be a poet. I should prefer mathematics for you, as a methodic discipline of the intellect. Most active minds write poetry, at a certain age – I wrote a good deal, I recollect, myself. But that is no reason for publishing. This haste to rush into print is one of the bad signs of the times – a symptom of the unhealthy activity which was first called out by the French revolution. In the Elizabethan age, every decently-educated gentleman was able, as a matter of course, to indite a sonnet to his mistress's eyebrow, or an epigram on his enemy; and yet he never dreamt of printing them. One of the few rational things I have met with, Eleanor, in the works of your very objectionable pet Mr. Carlyle – though indeed his style is too intolerable to have allowed me to read much – is the remark that "speech is silver" – "silvern" he calls it pedantically – "while silence is golden".'*

At this point of the sermon, Lillian fled from the room, to my extreme disgust. But still the old man prosed—

'I think, therefore, that you had better stay with your cousin for the next week. I hear from Lord Lynedale, that he is a very studious, moral, rising young man; and I only hope that you

will follow his good example. At the end of the week I shall
return home, and then I shall be glad to see more of you at my
house at D***, about *** miles from this place. Good
morning.'

I went, in rapture at the last announcement – and yet my
conscience smote me. I had not stood up for the working men.
I had heard them calumniated, and held my tongue – but I was
to see Lillian. I had let the dean fancy I was willing to become a
pensioner on his bounty – that I was a member of the Church
of England, and willing to go to a Church Training School –
but I was to see Lillian. I had lowered myself in my own eyes –
but I had seen Lillian. Perhaps I exaggerated my own offences:
however that may be, love soon silenced conscience, and I
almost danced into my cousin's rooms on my return.

*

That week passed rapidly and happily. I was half amused
with the change in my cousin's demeanour. I had evidently
risen immensely in his eyes; and I could not help applying,
in my heart, to him, Mr. Carlyle's dictum about the valet
species* – how they never honour the unaccredited hero, having
no eye to find him out till properly accredited, and counter-
signed, and accoutred with full uniform and diploma by that
great God, Public Opinion. I saw through the motive of his
new-fledged respect for me – and yet I encouraged it; for it
flattered my vanity. The world must forgive me. It was something for the poor tailor to find himself somewhat appreciated
at last, even outwardly. And besides, this said respect took a
form which was very tempting to me now – though the week
before it was just the one which I should have repelled with
scorn. George became very anxious to lend me money, to order
me clothes at his own tailor's, and set me up in various little
toilet refinements, that I might make a respectable appearance
at the dean's. I knew that he consulted rather the honour of
the family, than my good; but I did not know that his aim was
also to get me into his power; and I refused more and more
weakly at each fresh offer, and at last consented, in an evil hour,
to sell my own independence, for the sake of indulging my
love-dream, and appearing to be what I was not.

I saw a good deal more of the young university men that week. I cannot say that my recollections of them were pleasant. A few of them were very bigoted Tractarians* – some of whom seemed to fancy that a dilettante admiration for crucifixes and Gothic architecture, was a form of religion, which, by its extreme perfection, made the virtues of chastity and sobriety quite unnecessary – and the rest, of a more ascetic and moral turn, seemed as narrow, bitter, flippant, and un-earnest young men as I had ever met, dealing in second-hand party statements, gathered, as I could discover, entirely from periodicals of their own party – taking pride in reading nothing but what was made for them, indulging in the most violent nicknames and railing, and escaping from anything like severe argument by a sneer or an expression of theatrical horror at so 'painful' a notion. I had good opportunities of seeing what they were really like; for my cousin seemed to take delight in tormenting them – making them contradict themselves, getting them into dilemmas, and putting them into passions, – while the whole time he professed to be of their party, as indeed he was. But his consciousness of power, and his natural craft, seemed to make him consider his own party as his private preserve for sporting over; and when he was tired with the amusement, he used to try to call me in, and set me by the ears with his guests, which he had no great trouble in doing. And then, when he saw me at all confused, or borne down by statements from authors, of whose very names I had never heard, or by expressions of horror and surprise which made me suspect that I had unconsciously committed myself to an absurdity, he used to come 'hurling into the midst of the press', like some knight at a tournament, or Socrates when he saved Alcibiades at Delium,* and, by a dexterous repartee, turn the tide of battle, and get me off safe – taking care, by-the-bye, to hint to me the obligation which he considered himself to have conferred upon me.

But the great majority of the young men whom I met were even of a lower stamp. I was utterly shocked and disappointed at the contempt and unbelief with which they seemed to regard everything beyond mere animal enjoyment, and here and there the selfish advantage of a good degree. They seemed, if one

could judge from appearances, to despise and disbelieve everything generous, enthusiastic, enlarged. Thoughtfulness was a
'bore'; – earnestness, 'romance'. Above all, they seemed to
despise the university itself. The 'Dons' were 'idle, fat old
humbugs'; chapel, 'a humbug, too'; tutors, 'humbugs' too,
who played into the tradesmen's hands, and charged men high
fees for lectures not worth attending – so that any man who
wanted to get on, was forced to have a private tutor, besides his
college one. The university-studies were 'a humbug' – no use
to man in after-life. The masters of arts were 'humbugs' too;
for 'they knew all the evils, and clamoured for reform till they
became Dons themselves; and then, as soon as they found the
old system pay, they settled down on their lees, and grew fat on
port wine, like those before them.' They seemed to consider
themselves in an atmosphere of humbug – living in a lie – out
of which lie-element those who chose were very right in making
the most, for the gaining of fame or money. And the tone
which they took about everything – the coarseness, hollowness,
Gil Blas selfishness – was just what might have been expected.
Whether they were right or wrong in their complaints, I, of
course, have no means of accurately knowing. But it did seem
strange to me, as it has to others, to find in the mouths of almost
all the gownsmen, those very same charges against the universities which, when working men dare to make them, excite
outcries of 'calumny', 'sedition', 'vulgar radicalism', 'attacks
on our time-honoured institutions', &c., &c.

CHAPTER XIV

A CATHEDRAL TOWN

At length, the wished-for day had arrived; and, with my
cousin, I was whirling along, full of hope and desire, toward
the cathedral town of D*** – through a flat fen country,
which, though I had often heard it described as ugly, struck
my imagination much. The vast height and width of the sky-
arch, as seen from those flats as from an ocean – the grey haze

shrouding the horizon of our narrow land-view, and closing us in, till we seemed to be floating through infinite space, on a little platform of earth; the rich poplar-fringed farms, with their herds of dappled oxen – the luxuriant crops of oats and beans – the tender green of the tall rape,* a plant till then unknown to me – the long, straight, silver dykes, with their gaudy carpets of strange floating water-plants, and their black banks, studded with the remains of buried forests – the innumerable draining-mills, with their creaking sails and groaning wheels – the endless rows of pollard willows, through which the breeze moaned and rung, as through the strings of some vast Æolian harp; the little island knolls in that vast sea of fen, each with its long village street, and delicately tapered spire; all this seemed to me to contain an element of new and peculiar beauty.

'Why!' exclaims the reading public, if perchance it ever sees this tale of mine, in its usual prurient longing after anything like personal gossip, or scandalous anecdote – 'why, there is no cathedral town which begins with a D! Through the fen, too! He must mean either Ely, Lincoln, or Peterborough; that's certain.' Then, at one of those places, they find there is a dean – not of the name of Winnstay, true – 'but his name begins with a W; and he has a pretty daughter – no, a niece; well, that's very near it; – it must be him. No; at another place – there is not a dean, true – but a canon, or an archdeacon – something of that kind; and he has a pretty daughter, really; and his name begins – not with W, but with Y; well, that's the last letter of Winnstay, if it is not the first: that must be the poor man! What a shame to have exposed his family secrets in that way!' And then a whole circle of myths grow up round the man's story. It is credibly ascertained that I am the man who broke into his house last year, after having made love to his housemaid, and stole his writing-desk and plate – else, why should a burglar steal family-letters, if he had not some interest in them?...And before the matter dies away, some worthy old gentleman, who has not spoken to a working man since he left his living, thirty years ago, and hates a radical as he does the Pope, receives two or three anonymous letters, condoling with him on the cruel betrayal of his confidence – base ingratitude for undeserved condescension, &c., &c.; and, perhaps, with an enclosure of good advice for his lovely daughter.

But, wherever D * * * is, we arrived there; and with a beating heart, I – and I now suspect my cousin also – walked up the sunny slopes, where the old convent had stood, now covered with walled gardens and noble timber trees, and crowned by the richly-fretted towers of the cathedral, which we had seen, for the last twenty miles, growing gradually larger and more distinct across the level flat. 'Ely?' 'No; Lincoln!' 'Oh! but really, it's just as much like Peterborough!' Never mind, my dear reader; the essence of the fact, as I think, lies not quite so much in the name of the place, as in what was done there – to which I, with all the little respect which I can muster, entreat your attention.

It is not from false shame at my necessary ignorance, but from a fear lest I should bore my readers with what seems to them trivial, that I refrain from dilating on many a thing, which struck me as curious in this my first visit to the house of an English gentleman. I must say, however, though I suppose that it will be numbered, at least, among trite remarks, if not among trivial ones, that the wealth around me certainly struck me, as it has others, as not very much in keeping with the office of one who professed to be a minister of the Gospel of Jesus of Nazareth. But I salved over that feeling, being desirous to see everything in the brightest light, with the recollection that the dean had a private fortune of his own; though it did seem, at moments, that if a man has solemnly sworn to devote himself, body and soul, to the cause of the spiritual welfare of the nation, that vow might be not unfairly construed to include his money, as well as his talents, time, and health: unless, perhaps, money is considered by spiritual persons as so worthless a thing, that it is not fit to be given to God – a notion which might seem to explain how a really pious and universally respected arch-bishop, living within a quarter of a mile of one of the worst *infernos* of destitution, disease, filth, and profligacy – can yet find it in his heart to save a hundred and twenty thousand pounds, out of church revenues, and leave it to his family;* though it will not explain how Irish bishops can reconcile it to their consciences to leave behind them, one and all, large fortunes – for I suppose from fifty to a hundred thousand pounds is something – saved from fees and tithes, taken from the pockets of a Roman Catholic population, whom they have been put there to convert to Protestantism for the last three hundred years – with what success, all the world knows. Of course, it is a most impertinent, and almost a blasphemous thing, for a working man to dare to mention such subjects. Is it not 'speaking evil of dignities'?* Strange, by-the-bye, that merely to mention facts, without note or comment, should be always called 'speaking evil'! Does not that argue ill for the facts themselves? Working men think so; but what matter what 'the swinish multitude'* think?

When I speak of wealth, I do not mean that the dean's household would have been considered by his own class at all too luxurious. He would have been said, I suppose, to live in a 'quiet, comfortable, gentlemanlike way' – 'everything very plain and very good.' It included a butler – a quiet, good-natured old man – who ushered us into our bedrooms; a footman, who opened the door – a sort of animal for which I have an extreme aversion – young, silly, conceited, over-fed, florid – who looked just the man to sell his soul for a livery, twice as much food as he needed, and the opportunity of unlimited flirtations with the maids; and a coachman, very like other coachmen, whom I saw taking a pair of handsome carriage-horses out to exercise, as we opened the gate.

The old man, silently and as a matter of course, unpacked for me my little portmanteau (lent me by my cousin), and placed my things neatly in various drawers – went down, brought up a jug of hot water, put it on the washing-table – told me that dinner was at six – that the half-hour bell rang at half-past five – and that, if I wanted anything, the footman would answer the bell (bells seeming a prominent idea in his theory of the universe) – and so left me, wondering at the strange fact that free men, with free wills, do sell themselves, by the hundred thousand, to perform menial offices for other men, not for love, but for money; becoming, to define them strictly, bell-answering animals; and are honest, happy, contented, in such a life. A man-servant, a soldier, and a Jesuit, are to me the three great wonders of humanity – three forms of moral suicide, for which I never had the slightest gleam of sympathy, or even comprehension.

*

At last we went down to dinner, after my personal adornments had been carefully superintended by my cousin, who gave me, over-and-above, various warnings and exhortations as to my behaviour; which, of course, took due effect, in making me as nervous, constrained, and affected, as possible. When I appeared in the drawing-room, I was kindly welcomed by the dean, the two ladies, and Lord Lynedale.

But as I stood fidgeting and blushing, sticking my arms, and legs, and head, into all sorts of quaint positions – trying one attiude, and thinking it looked awkward, and so exchanging it for another, more awkward still – my eye fell suddenly on a slip of paper, which had conveyed itself, I never knew how, upon the pages of the Illustrated Book of Ballads, which I was turning over:—

'Be natural, and you will be gentlemanlike. If you wish others to forget your rank, do not forget it yourself. If you wish others to remember you with pleasure, forget yourself; and be just what God has made you.'

I could not help fancying that the lesson, whether intentionally or not, was meant for me; and a passing impulse made me take up the slip, fold it together, and put it in my bosom. Perhaps it was Lillian's handwriting! I looked round at the ladies; but their faces were each buried behind a book.

We went in to dinner; and, to my delight, I sat next to my goddess, while opposite me was my cousin. Luckily, I had got some directions from him as to what to say and do, when my wonders, the servants, thrust eatables and drinkables over my shoulders.

Lillian and my cousin chatted away about church-architecture, and the restorations which were going on at the cathedral; while I, for the first-half of dinner, feasted my eyes with the sight of a beauty, in which I seemed to discover every moment some new excellence. Every time I looked up at her, my eyes dazzled, my face burnt, my heart sank, and soft thrills ran through every nerve. And yet, Heaven knows, my emotions were as pure as those of an infant. It was beauty, longed for, and found at last, which I adored as a thing not to be possessed, but worshipped. The desire, even the thought, of calling her my own, never crossed my mind. I felt that I could gladly die, if by death I could purchase the permission to watch her. I understood, then, and for ever after, the pure devotion of the old knights and troubadours of chivalry. I seemed to myself to be their brother – one of the holy guild of poet-lovers. I was a new Petrarch, basking in the light-rays of a new Laura. I gazed, and gazed, and found new life in gazing, and was content.

But my simple bliss was perfected, when she suddenly turned to me, and began asking me questions on the very points on which I was best able to answer. She talked about poetry, Tennyson and Wordsworth; asked me if I understood Browning's Sordello;* and then comforted me, after my stammering confession that I did not, by telling me she was delighted to hear that; for she did not understand it either, and it was so pleasant to have a companion in ignorance. Then she asked, if I was much struck with the buildings in Cambridge? – had they inspired me with any verses yet? – I was bound to write something about them – and so on; making the most commonplace remarks look brilliant, from the ease and liveliness with which they were spoken, and the tact with which they were made pleasant to the listener: while I wondered at myself, for enjoying from her lips the flippant, sparkling tattle, which had hitherto made young women to me objects of unspeakable dread, to be escaped by crossing the street, hiding behind doors, and rushing blindly into back-yards and coal-holes.

The ladies left the room; and I, with Lillian's face glowing bright in my imagination, as the crimson orb remains on the retina of the closed eye, after looking intently at the sun, sat listening to a pleasant discussion between the dean and the nobleman, about some country in the East, which they had both visited, and greedily devouring all the new facts which they incidentally brought forth out of the treasures of their highly-cultivated minds.

I was agreeably surprised (don't laugh, reader) to find that I was allowed to drink water; and that the other men drank not more than a glass or two of wine, after the ladies had retired. I had, somehow, got both lords and deans associated in my mind with infinite swillings of port wine, and bacchanalian orgies, and sat down, at first, in much fear and trembling, lest I should be compelled to join, under penalties of salt-and-water; but I had made up my mind, stoutly, to bear anything rather than get drunk; and so I had all the merit of a temperance-martyr, without any of its disagreeables.

'Well,' said I to myself, smiling in spirit, 'what would my Chartist friends say if they saw me here? Not even Crossthwaite himself could find a flaw in the appreciation of merit for its own sake, the courtesy and condescension – ah! but he would complain of it, simply for being condescension.' But, after all, what else could it be? Were not these men more experienced, more learned, older than myself? They were my superiors; it was in vain for me to attempt to hide it from myself. But the wonder was, that they themselves were the ones to appear utterly unconscious of it. They treated me as an equal; they welcomed me – the young viscount and the learned dean – on the broad ground of a common humanity; as I believe hundreds more of their class would do, if we did not ourselves take a pride in estranging them from us – telling them that fraternization between our classes is impossible, and then cursing them for not fraternizing with us. But of that, more hereafter.

At all events, now my bliss was perfect. No! I was wrong – a higher enjoyment than all awaited me, when, going into the drawing-room, I found Lillian singing at the piano. I had no idea that music was capable of expressing and conveying emotions so intense and ennobling. My experience was confined to street-music, and to the bawling at the chapel. And, as yet, Mr. Hullah* had not risen into a power more enviable than that of kings, and given to every workman a free entrance into the magic world of harmony and melody, where he may prove his brotherhood with Mozart and Weber, Beethoven and Mendelssohn. Great unconscious demagogue! – leader of the people, and labourer in the cause of divine equality! – thy reward is with the Father of the people!

The luscious softness of the Italian airs overcame me with a delicious enervation. Every note, every interval, each shade of expression spoke to me – I knew not what: and yet they spoke to my heart of hearts. A spirit out of the infinite heaven seemed calling to my spirit, which longed to answer – and was dumb – and could only vent itself in tears, which welled unconsciously forth, and eased my heart from the painful tension of excitement.

> Her voice is hovering o'er my soul – it lingers,
>   O'ershadowing it with soft and thrilling wings;
> The blood and life within those snowy fingers
>   Teach witchcraft to the instrumental strings.
> My brain is wild, my breath comes quick,
>   The blood is listening in my frame;
> And thronging shadows, fast and thick,
>   Fall on my overflowing eyes.
> My heart is quivering like a flame;
>   As morning-dew that in the sunbeam dies,
>   I am dissolved in these consuming ecstasies.*

The dark lady, Miss Staunton, as I ought to call her, saw my emotion, and, as I thought unkindly, checked the cause of it at once.

'Pray do not give us any more of those die-away Italian airs, Lillian. Sing something manful, German or English, or anything you like, except those sentimental wailings.'

Lillian stopped, took another book, and commenced, after a short prelude, one of my own songs. Surprise and pleasure overpowered me more utterly than the soft southern melodies had done. I was on the point of springing up and leaving the room, when my raptures were checked by our host, who turned round, and stopped short in an oration on the geology of Upper Egypt.

'What's that about brotherhood and freedom, Lillian? We don't want anything of that kind here.'

'It's only a popular London song, papa,' answered she, with an arch smile.

'Or likely to become so,' added Miss Staunton, in her marked dogmatic tone.

'I'm very sorry for London, then.' And he returned to the deserts.

CHAPTER XV

THE MAN OF SCIENCE

AFTER breakfast the next morning, Lillian retired, saying laughingly, that she must go and see after her clothing-club and her dear old women at the almshouse, which, of course, made me look on her as more an angel than ever. And while George was left with Lord Lynedale, I was summoned to a private conference with the dean, in his study.

I found him in a room lined with cabinets of curiosities, and hung all over with strange horns, bones, and slabs of fossils. But I was not allowed much time to look about me; for he commenced at once on the subject of my studies, by asking me whether I was willing to prepare myself for the university by entering on the study of mathematics?

I felt so intense a repugnance to them, that at the risk of offending him – perhaps, for aught I knew, fatally – I dared to demur. He smiled——

'I am convinced, young man, that even if you intended to follow poetry as a profession – and a very poor one you will find it – yet you will never attain to any excellence therein, without far stricter mental discipline than any to which you have been accustomed. That is why I abominate our modern poets. They talk about the glory of the poetic vocation, as if they intended to be kings and world-makers, and all the while they indulge themselves in the most loose and desultory habits of thought. Sir, if they really believed their own grandiloquent assumptions, they would feel that the responsibility of their mental training was greater, not less, than any one's else. Like the Quakers, they fancy that they honour inspiration by supposing it to be only extraordinary and paroxysmic:* the true poet, like the rational Christian, believing that inspiration is continual and orderly, that it reveals harmonious laws, not merely excites sudden emotions. You understand me?'

I did, tolerably; and subsequent conversations with him fixed the thoughts sufficiently in my mind, to make me pretty sure that I am giving a faithful verbal transcript of them.

'You must study some science. Have you read any logic?'

I mentioned Watts' 'Logic', and Locke 'On the Use of the Understanding'* – two books well known to reading artisans.

'Ah,' he said; 'such books are very well, but they are merely popular. 'Aristotle', 'Ritter on Induction', and Kant's 'Prolegomena' and 'Logic'* – when you had read them some seven or eight times over, you might consider yourself as knowing somewhat about the matter.'

'I have read a little about induction in Whately.'*

'Ah – very good book, but popular. Did you find that your method of thought received any benefit from it?'

'The truth is – I do not know whether I can quite express myself clearly – but logic, like mathematics, seems to tell me too little about things. It does not enlarge my knowledge of man or nature; and those are what I thirst for. And you must remember – I hope I am not wrong in saying it – that the case of a man of your class, who has the power of travelling, of reading what he will, and seeing what he will, is very different from that of an artisan, whose chances of observation are so sadly limited. You must forgive us, if we are unwilling to spend our time over books which tell us nothing about the great universe outside the shop-windows.'

He smiled compassionately. 'Very true, my boy. There are two branches of study, then, before you, and by either of them a competent subsistence is possible, with good interest. Philology is one. But before you could arrive at those depths in it which connect with ethnology, history, and geography, you would require a lifetime of study. There remains yet another. I see you stealing glances at those natural curiosities. In the study of them, you would find, as I believe more and more daily, a mental discipline superior even to that which language or mathematics give. If I had been blest with a son – but that is neither here nor there – it was my intention to have educated him almost entirely as a naturalist. I think I should like to try the experiment on a young man like yourself.'

Sandy Mackaye's definition of legislation for the masses, 'Fiat experimentum in corpore vili',* rose up in my thoughts, and, half unconsciously, past my lips. The good old man only smiled.

'That is not my reason, Mr. Locke. I should choose, by preference, a man of your class for experiments, not because the nature is coarser, or less precious in the scale of creation, but because I have a notion, for which, like many others, I have been very much laughed at, that you are less sophisticated, more simple and fresh from nature's laboratory, than the young persons of the upper classes, who begin from the nursery to be more or less trimmed up, and painted over by the artificial state of society – a very excellent state, mind, Mr. Locke. Civilisation is, next to Christianity of course, the highest blessing; but not so good a state for trying anthropological experiments on.'

I assured him of my great desire to be the subject of such an experiment; and was encouraged by his smile to tell him something about my intense love for natural objects, the mysterious pleasure which I had taken, from my boyhood, in trying to classify them, and my visits to the British Museum, for the purpose of getting at some general knowledge of the natural groups.

'Excellent,' he said, 'young man; the very best sign I have yet seen in you. And what have you read on these subjects?' I mentioned several books: Bingley, Bewick, 'Humboldt's Travels', 'The Voyage of the Beagles', various scattered articles in the Penny and Saturday Magazines, &c., &c.*

'Ah!' he said, 'popular – you will find, if you will allow me to give you my experience——'

I assured him that I was only too much honoured – and I truly felt so. I knew myself to be in the presence of my rightful superior – my master on that very point of education which I idolised. Every sentence which he spoke gave me fresh light on some matter or other; and I felt a worship for him, totally irrespective of any vulgar and slavish respect for his rank or wealth. The working man has no want for real reverence. Mr. Carlyle's being a 'gentleman', has not injured his influence with the people. On the contrary, it is the artisan's intense longing to find his real *lords* and guides, which makes him despise and execrate his sham ones.* Whereof let society take note.

'Then,' continued he, 'your plan is to take up some one section of the subject, and thoroughly exhaust that. Universal laws manifest themselves only by particular instances. They say, man is the microcosm, Mr. Locke; but the man of science finds every worm and beetle a microcosm in its way. It exemplifies, directly or indirectly, every physical law in the universe, though it may not be two lines long. It is not only a part, but a mirror, of the great whole. It has a definite relation to the whole world, and the whole world has a relation to it. Really, by-the-bye, I cannot give you a better instance of what I mean, than in my little diatribe on the Geryon Trifurcifer,* a small reptile which I found, some years ago, inhabiting the mud of the salt lakes of Balkhan, which fills up a long-desired link between the Chelonia and the Perenni branchiate Batrachians, and, as I think, though Professor Brown differs from me, connects both with the Herbivorous Cetacea.* – Professor Brown is an exceedingly talented man, but a little too cautious in accepting any one's theories but his own. There it is,' he said, as he drew out of a drawer a little pamphlet of some thirty pages – 'an old man's darling. I consider that book the outcome of thirteen years' labour.'

'It must be very deep,' I replied, 'to have been worth such long-continued study.'

'Oh! science is her own reward. There is hardly a great physical law which I have not brought to bear on the subject of that one small animal; and above all – what is in itself worth a life's labour – I have, I believe, discovered two entirely new laws of my own, though one of them, by-the-bye, has been broached by Professor Brown since, in his lectures. He might have mentioned my name in connexion with the subject, for I certainly imparted my ideas to him, two years at least before the delivery of those lectures of his. Professor Brown is a very great man, certainly, and a very good man, but not quite so original as is generally supposed. Still, a scientific man must expect his little disappointments and injustices. If you were behind the scenes in the scientific world, I can assure you, you would find as much party-spirit, and unfairness, and jealousy, and emulation there, as anywhere else. Human nature, human nature, everywhere!'

I said nothing, but thought the more; and took the book, promising to study it carefully.

'There is Cuvier's 'Animal Kingdom',* and a dictionary of

scientific terms to help you; and mind, it must be got up thoroughly, for I purpose to set you an examination or two in it, a few days hence. Then I shall find out whether you know what is worth all the information in the world.'

'What is that, sir?'

'The art of getting information – *artem discendi*, Mr. Locke, wherewith the world is badly provided just now, as it is over-stocked with the *artem legendi* – the knack of running the eye over books, and fancying that it understands them, because it can talk about them. You cannot play that trick with my Geryon Trifurcifer, I assure you! he is as dry and tough as his name. But, believe me, he is worth mastering, not because he is mine, but simply because he is tough.'

I promised all diligence.

'Very good. And be sure, if you intend to be a poet for these days (and I really think you have some faculty for it), you must become a scientific man. Science has made vast strides, and introduced entirely new modes of looking at nature; and poets must live up to the age. I never read a word of Goethe's verse, but I am convinced that he must be the great poet of the day; just because he is the only one who has taken the trouble to go into the details of practical science. And, in the mean time, I will give you a lesson myself. I see you are longing to know the contents of these cabinets. You shall assist me, by writing out the names of this lot of shells, just come from Australia, which I am now going to arrange.'

I set to work at once, under his directions; and passed that morning, and the two or three following, delightfully. But I question whether the good dean would have been well satisfied, had he known how all his scientific teaching confirmed my democratic opinions. The mere fact, that I could understand these things when they were set before me, as well as any one else, was to me a simple demonstration of the equality in worth, and therefore in privilege, of all classes. It may be answered, that I had no right to argue from myself to the mob; and that other working geniuses have no right to demand universal enfranchisement for their whole class, just because they, the exceptions, are fit for it. But surely it is hard to call such an error, if it be one, 'the insolent assumption of democratic conceit', &c. &c. Does it not look more like the humility of men who are unwilling to assert for themselves peculiar excellence, peculiar privileges; who, like the apostles of old, want no glory, save that which they can share with the outcast and the slave? Let society, among other matters, take note of that.

CHAPTER XVI

CULTIVATED WOMEN

I was thus brought in contact, for the first time in my life, with two exquisite specimens of cultivated womanhood; and they naturally, as the reader may well suppose, almost entirely engrossed my thoughts and interest.

Lillian, for so I must call her, became daily more and more agreeable; and tried, as I fancied, to draw me out, and show me off to the best advantage; whether from the desire of pleasing herself, or pleasing me, I know not, and do not wish to know – but the consequences to my boyish vanity were such as are more easy to imagine, than pleasant to describe. Miss Staunton, on the other hand, became, I thought more and more unpleasant; not that she ever, for a moment, outstepped the bounds of the most perfect courtesy; but her manner, which was soft to no one except to Lord Lynedale, was, when she spoke to me, especially dictatorial and abrupt. She seemed to make a point of carping at chance words of mine, and of setting me down suddenly, by breaking in with some severe, pithy observation, on conversations to which she had been listening unobserved. She seemed, too, to view with dislike anything like cordiality between me and Lillian – a dislike, which I was actually at moments vain enough (such a creature is man!) to attribute to – jealousy!!! till I began to suspect and hate her, as a proud, harsh, and exclusive aristocrat. And my suspicion and hatred received their confirmation, when, one morning, after an evening even more charming than usual, Lillian came down, reserved, peevish, all but sulky and showed that that bright heaven of sunny features had room in it for a cloud, and that an ugly one. But I, poor fool, only pitied her; made up my mind

that some one had ill-used her; and looked on her as a martyr –
perhaps to that harsh cousin of hers.

That day was taken up with writing out answers to the
dean's searching questions on his pamphlet, in which, I believe,
I acquitted myself tolerably; and he seemed far more satisfied
with my commentary, than I was with his text. He seemed to
ignore utterly anything like religion, or even the very notion of
God, in his chains of argument. Nature was spoken of as the
willer and producer of all the marvels which he describes; and
every word in the book, to my astonishment, might have been
written, just as easily, by an Atheist, as by a dignitary of the
Church of England.

I could not help, that evening, hinting this defect, as
delicately as I could, to my good host, and was somewhat
surprised to find that he did not consider it a defect at all.

'I am in nowise anxious to weaken the antithesis between
natural and revealed religion. Science may help the former, but
it has absolutely nothing to do with the latter. She stands on
her own ground, has her own laws, and is her own reward.
Christianity is a matter of faith and of the teaching of the
Church. It must not go out of its way for science, and science
must not go out of her way for it; and where they seem to
differ, it is our duty to believe that they are reconcilable by
fuller knowledge,* but not to clip truth in order to make it
match with doctrine.'

'Mr. Carlyle,' said Miss Staunton, in her abrupt way, 'can
see that the God of Nature is the God of man.'

'Nobody denies that, my dear.'

'Except in every word and action; else why do they not
write about Nature as if it was the expression of a living, loving
spirit, not merely a dead machine?'

'It may be very easy, my dear, for a Deist* like Mr. Carlyle
to see *his* God in Nature; but if he would accept the truths of
Christianity, he would find that there were deeper mysteries in
them than trees and animals can explain.'

'Pardon me, sir,' I said, 'but I think that a very large portion
of thoughtful working men agree with you, though, in their
case, that opinion has only increased their difficulties about
Christianity. They complain, that they cannot identify the God

of the Bible with the God of the world around them; and one of their great complaints against Christianity is, that it demands assent to mysteries which are independent of, and even contradictory to, the laws of Nature.'*

The old man was silent.

'Mr. Carlyle is no Deist,' said Miss Staunton; 'and I am sure, that unless the truths of Christianity contrive soon to get themselves justified by the laws of science, the higher orders will believe in them as little as Mr. Locke informs us that the working classes do.'

'You prophesy confidently, my darling.'

'Oh, Eleanor is in one of her prophetic moods to-night,' said Lillian, slyly. 'She has been foretelling me I know not what misery and misfortune, just because I choose to amuse myself in my own way.'

And she gave another sly pouting look at Eleanor, and then called me to look over some engravings, chatting over them so charmingly! – and stealing, every now and then, a pretty, saucy look at her cousin, which seemed to say, 'I shall do what I like, in spite of your predictions.'

This confirmed my suspicions that Eleanor had been trying to separate us; and the suspicion received a further corroboration, indirect, and perhaps very unfair, from the lecture which I got from my cousin after I went upstairs.

He had been flattering me very much lately about 'the impression' I was making on the family, and tormenting me by compliments on the clever way in which I 'played my cards'; and when I denied indignantly any such intention, patting me on the back, and laughing me down in a knowing way, as much as to say that he was not to be taken in by my professions of simplicity. He seemed to judge every one by himself, and to have no notion of any middle characters, between the mere green-horn and the deliberate schemer. But to-night, after commencing with the usual compliments, he went on:

'Now, first let me give you one hint, and be thankful for it. Mind your game with that Eleanor – Miss Staunton. She is a regular tyrant, I happen to know; a strong-minded woman, with a vengeance. She manages every one here; and unless you are in her good books, don't expect to keep your footing in this house, my boy. So just mind and pay her a little more attention, and Miss Lillian a little less. After all, it is worth the trouble. She is uncommonly well read; and says confounded clever things, too, when she wakes up out of the sulks; and you may pick up a wrinkle or two from her, worth pocketing. You mind what she says to you. You know she is going to be married to Lord Lyndale?'

I nodded assent.

'Well, then, if you want to hook him, you must secure her first.'

'I want to hook no one, George; I have told you that a thousand times.'

'Oh, no! certainly not – by no means! Why should you?' said the artful dodger.* And he swung, laughing, out of the room, leaving in my mind a strange suspicion, of which I was ashamed, though I could not shake it off, that he had remarked Eleanor's wish to cool my admiration for Lillian, and was willing, for some purpose of his own, to further that wish. The truth is, I had very little respect for him, or trust in him; and I was learning to look, habitually, for some selfish motive in all he said or did. Perhaps, if I had acted more boldly upon what I did see, I should not have been here now.

CHAPTER XVII

SERMON IN STONES

THE next afternoon was the last but one of my stay at D***. We were to dine late, after sunset, and, before dinner, we went into the cathedral. The choir had just finished practising. Certain exceedingly ill-looking men, whose faces bespoke principally sensuality and self-conceit, and whose function was that of praising God, on the sole qualification of good bass and tenor voices, were coming chattering through the choir gates; and behind them, a group of small boys were suddenly transforming themselves from angels into sinners, by tearing off their white surplices, and pinching and poking each other noisily as they passed us, with as little reverence as Voltaire himself could have desired.*

I had often been in the cathedral before – indeed, we attended the service daily, and I had been appalled, rather than astonished, by what I saw and heard: the unintelligible service – the irreverent gabble of the choristers and readers – the scanty congregation – the meagre portion of the vast building which seemed to be turned to any use: but never more than that evening, did I feel the desolateness, the doleful inutility, of that vast desert nave, with its aisles and transepts – built for some purpose or other now extinct. The whole place seemed to crush and sadden me; and I could not re-echo Lillian's remark—

'How those pillars, rising story above story, and those lines of pointed arches, all lead the eye heavenward! It is a beautiful notion, that about pointed architecture being symbolic of Christianity.'

'I ought to be very much ashamed of my stupidity,' I answered; 'but I cannot feel that, though I believe I ought to do so. That vast groined roof, with its enormous weight of hanging stone, seems to crush one – to bar out the free sky above. Those pointed windows, too – how gloriously the western sun is streaming through them! but their rich hues only dim and deface his light. I can feel what you say, when I look at the cathedral on the outside; there, indeed, every line sweeps the eye upward – carries it from one pinnacle to another, each with less and less standing-ground, till at the summit the building gradually vanishes in a point, and leaves the spirit to wing its way unsupported and alone into the ether. Perhaps,' I added, half bitterly, 'these cathedrals may be true symbols of the superstition which created them – on the outside, offering to enfranchise the soul and raise it up to heaven; but when the dupes had entered, giving them only a dark prison, and a crushing bondage, which neither we nor our fathers have been able to bear.'

'You may sneer at them, if you will, Mr. Locke,' said Eleanor, in her severe, abrupt way. 'The working classes would have been badly off without them. They were, in their day, the only democratic institution in the world; and the only socialist one, too. The only chance a poor man had of rising by his worth, was by coming to the monastery. And bitterly the working classes felt the want of them, when they fell. Your own Cobbett can tell you that.'*

'Ah!' said Lillian, 'how different it must have been four hundred years ago! – how solemn and picturesque those old monks must have looked, gliding about the aisles! – and how magnificent the choir must have been, before all the glass and carving, and that beautiful shrine of St. * * *, blazing with gold and jewels, were all plundered and defaced by those horrid Puritans!'

'Say, reformer-squires,' answered Eleanor; 'for it was they who did the thing; only it was found convenient, at the Restoration, to lay on the people of the seventeenth century the iniquities which the country-gentlemen committed in the sixteenth.'

'Surely,' I added, emboldened by her words, 'if the monasteries were what their admirers say, some method of restoring the good of the old system, without its evil, ought to be found; and would be found, if it were not——' I paused, recollecting whose guest I was.

'If it were not, I suppose,' said Eleanor, 'for those lazy, overfed, bigoted hypocrites, the clergy. That, I presume, is the description of them to which you have been most accustomed. Now, let me ask you one question. Do you mean to condemn, just now, the Church as it was, or the Church as it is, or the Church as it ought to be? Radicals have a habit of confusing those three questions, as they have of confusing other things when it suits them.'

'Really,' I said – for my blood was rising – 'I do think that, with the confessed enormous wealth of the clergy, the cathedral establishments especially, they might do more for the people.'

'Listen to me a little, Mr. Locke. The laity now-a-days take a pride in speaking evil of the clergy, never seeing that if they are bad, the laity have made them so. Why, what do you impute to them? Their worldliness, their being like the world, like the laity round them – like you, in short? Improve yourselves, and by so doing, if there is this sad tendency in the clergy to imitate you, you will mend them; if you do not find that after all, it is they who will have to mend you. "As with the people, so with the priest", is the everlasting law. When, fifty years ago, all classes were drunkards, from the statesman to the peasant, the clergy were drunken also, but not half as bad as the laity. Now the laity are eaten up with covetousness and ambition; and the clergy are covetous and ambitious, but not half as bad as the laity. The laity, and you working men especially, are the dupes of frothy, insincere, official rant, as Mr. Carlyle would call it,* in Parliament, on the hustings, at every debating society and Chartist meeting; and therefore the clergyman's sermons are apt to be just what people like elsewhere, and what, therefore, they suppose people will like there.'

'If, then,' I answered, 'in spite of your opinions, you confess the clergy to be so bad, why are you so angry with men of our opinions, if we do plot sometimes a little against the Church?'

'I do not think you know what my opinions are, Mr. Locke. Did you not hear me just now praising the monasteries, because they were socialist and democratic? But why is the badness of the clergy any reason for pulling down the Church? That is another of the confused irrationalities into which you all allow yourselves to fall. What do you mean by crying shame on a man for being a bad clergyman, if a good clergyman is not a good thing? If the very idea of a clergyman was abominable, as your Church-destroyers ought to say, you ought to praise a man for being a bad one, and not acting out this same abominable idea of priesthood. Your very outcry against the sins of the clergy shows that, even in your minds, a dim notion lies somewhere that a clergyman's vocation is, in itself, a divine, a holy, a beneficent one.'

'I never looked at it in that light, certainly,' said I, somewhat staggered.

'Very likely not. One word more, for I may not have another opportunity of speaking to you as I would on these matters. You working men complain of the clergy for being bigoted and obscurantist, and hating the cause of the people. Does not nine-tenths of the blame of that lie at your door? I took up, the other day, at hazard, one of your favourite liberty-preaching newspapers; and I saw books advertised in it, whose names no modest woman should ever behold; doctrines and practices advocated in it, from which all the honesty, the decency, the common human feeling which is left in the English mind, ought to revolt, and does revolt. You cannot deny it. Your class has told the world that the cause of liberty, equality, and fraternity, the cause which the working masses claim as theirs, identifies itself with blasphemy and indecency, with the tyrannous persecutions of trades-unions, with robbery, assassination, vitriol-bottles, and midnight incendiarism. And then you curse the clergy for taking you at your word! Whatsoever they do, you attack them. If they believe you, and stand up for common morality, and for the truths which they know are all-important to poor as well as rich, you call them bigots and persecutors; while if they neglect, in any way, the very Christianity for believing which you insult them, you turn round and call them hypocrites. Mark my words, Mr. Locke, till you gain the respect and confidence of the clergy, you will never rise. The day will come when you will find that the clergy are the only class who can help you. Ah, you may shake your head. I warn you of it. They were the only bulwark of the poor against the mediæval tyranny of Rank; you will find them the only bulwark against the modern tyranny of Mammon.'

I was on the point of intreating her to explain herself farther, but at that critical moment Lillian interposed.

'Now, stay your prophetic glances into the future; here comes Lynedale and papa.' And in a moment, Eleanor's whole manner and countenance altered – the petulant, wild unrest, the harsh, dictatorial tone vanished; and she turned to meet her lover, with a look of tender, satisfied devotion, which transfigured her whole face. It was most strange, the power he had over her. His presence, even at a distance, seemed to fill her whole being with rich quiet life. She watched him with folded hands, like a mystic worshipper, waiting for the afflatus of the spirit; and, suspicious and angry as I felt towards her, I could not help being drawn to her by this revelation of depths of strong healthy feeling, of which her usual manner gave so little sign.

This conversation thoroughly puzzled me; it showed me that there might be two sides to the question of the people's cause, as well as to that of others. It shook a little my faith in the infallibility of my own class, to hear such severe animadversions on them, from a person who professed herself as much a disciple of Carlyle as any working man, and who evidently had no lack, either of intellect to comprehend, or boldness to speak out, his doctrines; who could praise the old monasteries for being democratic and socialist, and spoke far more severely of the clergy than I could have done – because she did not deal merely in trite words of abuse, but showed a real analytic insight into the causes of their short-coming.

*

That same evening, the conversation happened to turn on dress, of which Miss Staunton spoke scornfully and disparagingly, as mere useless vanity and frippery – an empty substitute for real beauty of person as well as the higher beauty of mind. And I, emboldened by the courtesy with which I was always called on to take my share in everything that was said or done, ventured to object, humbly enough, to her notions.

'But is not beauty,' I said, 'in itself a good and blessed thing, softening, refining, rejoicing the eyes of all who behold?' (and my eyes, as I spoke, involuntarily rested on Lillian's face – who saw it, and blushed). 'Surely nothing which helps beauty is to be despised. And, without the charms of dress, beauty, even that of expression, does not really do itself justice. How many lovely and loveable faces there are, for instance, among the working classes, which, if they had but the advantages which ladies possess, might create delight, respect, chivalrous worship, in the beholder – but are now never appreciated, because they have not the same fair means of displaying themselves which even the savage girl of the South Sea Islands possesses!'

Lillian said it was so very true – she had really never thought of it before – and, somehow, I gained courage to go on.

'Besides, dress is a sort of sacrament, if I may use the word – a sure sign of the wearer's character; according as any one is orderly, or modest, or tasteful, or joyous, or brilliant' – and I glanced again at Lillian – 'those excellences, or the want of them, are sure to show themselves, in the colours they choose, and the cut of their garments. In the workroom, I and a friend of mine used often to amuse ourselves over the clothes we were making, by speculating from them on the sort of people the wearers were to be; and I fancy we were not often wrong.'

My cousin looked daggers at me, and for a moment I fancied I had committed a dreadful mistake in mentioning my tailor-life. So I had in his eyes, but not in those of the really well-bred persons round me.

'Oh, how very amusing it must have been! I think I shall turn milliner, Eleanor, for the fun of divining every one's little failings from their caps and gowns!'

'Go on, Mr. Locke,' said the dean, who had seemed buried in the 'Transactions of the Royal Society'. 'The fact is novel, and I am more obliged to any one who gives me that, than if he gave me a bank-note. The money gets spent and done with; but I cannot spend the fact: it remains for life as permanent capital, returning interest and compound-interest *ad infinitum*. By-the-bye, tell me about those same workshops. I have heard more about them than I like to believe true.'

And I did tell him all about them; and spoke, my blood rising as I went on, long and earnestly, perhaps eloquently. Now and then I got abashed, and tried to stop; and then the dean informed me that I was speaking well and sensibly, while Lillian entreated me to go on. She had never conceived such things possible – it was as interesting as a novel, &c., &c.; and Miss Staunton sat with compressed lips and frowning brow, apparently thinking of nothing but her book, till I felt quite angry at her apathy – for such it seemed to me to be.

CHAPTER XVIII

MY FALL

AND now the last day of our stay at D * * * had arrived, and I had as yet heard nothing of the prospects of my book; though, indeed, the company in which I had found myself had driven literary ambition, for the time being, out of my head, and bewitched me to float down the stream of daily circumstance, satisfied to snatch the enjoyment of each present moment. That morning, however, after I had fulfilled my daily task of arranging and naming objects of natural history, the dean settled himself back in his arm-chair, and bidding me sit down, evidently meditated a business-conversation.

He had heard from his publisher, and read his letter to me. 'The poems were on the whole much liked. The most satisfactory method of publishing for all parties, would be by procuring so many subscribers, each agreeing to take so many copies. In consideration of the dean's known literary judgment and great influence, the publisher would, as a private favour, not object to take the risk of any further expenses.'

So far everything sounded charming. The method was not a very independent one, but it was the only one; and I should actually have the delight of having published a volume. But, alas! 'he thought that the sale of the book might be greatly facilitated, if certain passages of a strong political tendency were omitted. He did not wish personally to object to them as statements of facts, or to the pictorial vigour with which they were expressed; but he thought that they were somewhat too strong for the present state of the public taste; and though he should be the last to allow any private considerations to influence his weak patronage of rising talent, yet, considering his present connexion, he should hardly wish to take on himself the responsibility of publishing such passages, unless with great modifications.'

'You see,' said the good old man, 'the opinion of respectable practical men, who know the world, exactly coincides with mine. I did not like to tell you that I could not help in the publication of your MSS. in their present state; but I am sure, from the modesty and gentleness which I have remarked in you, your readiness to listen to reason, and your pleasing freedom from all violence or coarseness in expressing your opinions, that you will not object to so exceedingly reasonable a request, which, after all, is only for your good. Ah! young man,' he went on, in a more feeling tone than I had yet heard from him, 'if you were once embroiled in that political world, of which you know so little, you would soon be crying like David, "Oh, that I had wings like a dove, then would I flee away and be at rest"!* Do you fancy that you can alter a fallen world? What it is, it always has been, and will be to the end. Every age has its political and social nostrums, my dear young man, and fancies them infallible; and the next generation arises to curse them as failures in practice, and superstitious in theory, and try some new nostrum of its own.'

I sighed.

'Ah! you may sigh. But we have each of us to be disenchanted of our dream. There was a time once when I talked republicanism as loudly as raw youth ever did – when I had an excuse for it, too; for when I was a boy, I saw the French Revolution; and it was no wonder if young, enthusiastic young brains were excited by all sorts of wild hopes – "perfectibility of the species", "rights of man", "universal liberty, equality, and brotherhood." – My dear sir, there is nothing new under the sun; all that, is stale and trite to a septuagenarian, who has seen where it all ends. I speak to you freely, because I am deeply interested in you. I feel that this is the important question of your life, and that you have talents, the possession of which is a heavy responsibility. Eschew politics, once and for all, as I have done. I might have been, I may tell you, a bishop at this moment, if I had condescended to meddle again in those party questions of which my youthful experience sickened me. But I knew that I should only weaken my own influence, as that most noble and excellent man, Dr. Arnold, did, by interfering in politics.* The poet, like the clergyman and the philosopher, has nothing to do with politics. Let them choose the better part, and it shall not be taken from them. The world may rave,' he continued, waxing eloquent as he approached his favourite subject – 'the world may rave, but in the study there is quiet. The world may change, Mr. Locke, and will; but "the earth abideth for ever". Solomon had seen somewhat of politics, and social improvement, and so on; and behold, then, as now, "all was vanity and vexation of spirit. That which is crooked cannot be made straight, and that which is wanting cannot be numbered. What profit hath a man of all his labour which he taketh under the sun? The thing which hath been, it is that which shall be, and there is no new thing under the sun. One generation passeth away, and another cometh; but the earth abideth for ever".* No wonder that the wisest of men took refuge from such experience, as I have tried to do, in talking of all herbs, from the cedar of Lebanon to the hyssop that groweth on the wall!*

'Ah! Mr. Locke,' he went on, in a soft, melancholy, half-abstracted tone – 'ah! Mr. Locke, I have felt deeply, and you will feel some day, the truth of Jarno's saying in 'Wilhelm Meister', when he was wandering alone in the Alps, with his geological hammer, "These rocks, at least, tell me no lies, as men do."* Ay,; there is no lie in Nature, no discord in the revelations of science, in the laws of the universe. Infinite, pure, unfallen, earth-supporting Titans, fresh as on the morning of creation, those great laws endure; your only true democrats, too – for nothing is too great or too small for them to take note of. No tiniest gnat, or speck of dust, but they feel it, guide it, and preserve it. – Hail and snow, wind and vapour, fulfilling their Maker's word; and like him, too, hiding themselves from the wise and prudent, and revealing themselves unto babes. Yes, Mr. Locke; it is the childlike, simple, patient, reverent heart, which science at once demands and cultivates. To prejudice or haste, to self-conceit or ambition, she proudly shuts her treasuries – to open them to men of humble heart, whom this world thinks simple dreamers – her Newtons, and Owens,* and Faradays. Why should you not become such a man as they? You have the talents – you have the love for nature, you seem to have the gentle and patient spirit, which, indeed, will grow up more and more in you, if you become a real student of science. Or, if you must be a poet, why not sing of Nature, and leave those to sing political squabbles, who have no eye for the beauty of her repose? How few great poets have been politicians!'

I gently suggested Milton.

'Ay! he became a great poet only when he had deserted politics, because they had deserted him. In blindness and poverty, in the utter failure of all his national theories, he wrote the works which have made him immortal. Was Shakespeare a politician? or any one of the great poets who have risen during the last thirty years? Have they not all seemed to consider it a sacred duty to keep themselves, as far as they could, out of party-strife?'

I quoted Southey, Shelley, and Burns, as instances to the

contrary; but his induction was completed already, to his own satisfaction.

'Poor dear Southey was a great verse-maker, rather than a great poet; and I always consider that his party-prejudices and party-writing narrowed and harshened a mind which ought to have been flowing forth freely and lovingly towards all forms of life. And as for Shelley and Burns, their politics dictated to them at once the worst portions of their poetry and of their practice. Shelley, what little I have read of him, only seems himself when he forgets radicalism for nature; and you would not set Burns's life or death, either, as a model for imitation in any class.* Now, do you know, I must ask you to leave me a little. I am somewhat fatigued with this long discussion' (in which, certainly, I had borne no great share); 'and I am sure, that after all I have said, you will see the propriety of acceding to the publisher's advice. Go and think over it, and let me have your answer by post-time.'

I did go and think over it – too long for my good. If I had acted on the first impulse, I should have refused, and been safe. These passages were the very pith and marrow of the poems. They were the very words which I had felt it my duty, my glory, to uter. I, who had been a working man, who had experienced all their sorrows and temptations – I, seemed called by every circumstance of my life to preach their cause, to expose their wrongs – I to quash my convictions, to stultify my book, for the sake of popularity, money, patronage! And yet – all that involved seeing more of Lillian. They were only too powerful inducements in themselves, alas! but I believe I could have resisted them tolerably, if they had not been backed by love. And so a struggle arose, which the rich reader may think a very fantastic one, though the poor man will understand it, and surely pardon it also – seeing that he himself is Man. Could I not, just once in a way, serve God and Mammon at once? – or rather, not Mammon, but Venus: a worship which looked to me, and really was in my case, purer than all the Mariolatry in Popedom. After all, the fall might not be so great as it seemed – perhaps I was not infallible on these same points. (It is wonderful how humble and self-denying one becomes when one is afraid of doing one's duty.) Perhaps the dean might be right. He had been republican himself once, certainly. The facts, indeed, which I had stated, there could be no doubt of; but I might have viewed them through a prejudiced and angry medium – I might have been not quite logical in my deductions from them – I might. In short, between 'perhapses' and 'mights', I fell – a very deep, real, damnable fall; and consented to emasculate my poems, and become a flunkey and a dastard.

I mentioned my consent that evening to the party; the dean purred content thereat. Eleanor, to my astonishment, just said, sternly and abruptly,

'Weak!' and then turned away, while Lillian began:

'Oh! what a pity! And really they were some of the prettiest verses of all! But of course my father must know best; you are quite right to be guided by him, and do whatever is proper and prudent. After all, papa, I have got the naughtiest of them all, you know, safe. Eleanor set it to music, and wrote it out in her book; and I thought it so charming that I copied it.'

What Lillian said about herself, I drank in as greedily as usual; what she said about Eleanor, fell on a heedless ear, and vanished, not to re-appear in my recollection till ——. But I must not anticipate.

So it was all settled pleasantly; and I sat up that evening, writing a bit of verse for Lillian, about the Old Cathedral, and 'Heaven-aspiring towers', and 'Aisles of cloistered shade', and all that sort of thing; which I did not believe, or care for; but I thought it would please her, and so it did; and I got golden smiles and compliments for my first, though not my last, insincere poem. I was going fast down hill, in my hurry to rise. However, as I said, it was all pleasant enough. I was to return to town, and there await the dean's orders; and, most luckily, I had received that morning from Sandy Mackaye a character-istic letter:

'Gowk, Telemachus, hearken!* Item 1. Ye're fou wi' the Circean cup,* aneath the shade o' shovel hats and steeple-houses.

'Item 2. I, cuif-Mentor* that I am, wearing out a gude pair o' gude Scots brogues, that my sister's husband's third cousin sent me a towmond* gane fra Aberdeen, rinning ower the town to a' journals, respectable and ither, anent the sellin' o' your

'Autobiography of an Engine-Boiler in the Vauxhall-road', the whilk I ha' disposit o' at the last, to O'Flynn's *Weekly Warwhoop*;* and gin ye ha' ony mair sic trash in your head, ye may get your meal whiles out o' the same kist; unless, as I sair misdoubt, ye're praying already, like Eli's bairns, "to be put into ane o' the priest's offices, that ye may eat a piece o' bread."*

'Ye'll be coming the-morrow? I'm lane without ye; though I look for ye surely to come ben wi' a gowd shoulder-knot,* and a red nose.'

This letter, though it hit me hard, and made me, I confess, a little angry at the moment with my truest friend, still offered me a means of subsistence, and enabled me to decline safely the pecuniary aid which I dreaded the dean's offering me. And yet I felt dispirited and ill at ease. My conscience would not let me enjoy the success I felt I had attained. But next morning I saw Lillian; and I forgot books, people's cause, conscience, and everything.

*

I went home by coach – a luxury on which my cousin insisted – as he did on lending me the fare; so that in all I owed him somewhat more than eleven pounds. But I was too happy to care for a fresh debt, and home I went, considering my fortune made.

My heart fell, as I stepped into the dingy little old shop. Was it the meanness of the place, after the comfort and elegance of my late abode? Was it disappointment at not finding Mackaye at home? Or was it that black-edged letter which lay waiting for me on the table? I was afraid to open it; I knew not why. I turned it over and over several times, trying to guess whose the handwriting on the cover might be; the post-mark was two days old; and at last I broke the seal.

'SIR, – This is to inform you, that your mother, Mrs. Locke, died this morning, a sensible sinner, not without assurance of her election; and that her funeral is fixed for Wednesday, the 29th instant.

The humble servant of the Lord's people,
J. WIGGINTON.'

CHAPTER XIX

SHORT AND SAD

I SHALL pass over the agonies of the next few days. There is self-exenteration enough and to spare in my story, without dilating on them. They are too sacred to publish, and too painful, alas! even to recal. I write my story, too, as a working man. Of those emotions which are common to humanity, I shall say but little – except when it is necessary to prove that the working man has feelings like the rest of his kind. But those feelings may, in this case, be supplied by the reader's own imagination. Let him represent them to himself as bitter, as remorseful as he will, he will not equal the reality. True, she had cast me off; but had I not rejoiced in that rejection which should have been my shame? True, I had fed on the hope of some day winning reconciliation, by winning fame; but before the fame had arrived, the reconciliation had become impossible. I had shrunk from going back to her, as I ought to have done, in filial humility, and, therefore, I was not allowed to go back to her in the pride of success. Heaven knows, I had not forgotten her. Night and day I had thought of her with prayers and blessings; but I had made a merit of my own love to her – my forgiveness of her, as I dared to call it. I had pampered my conceit with the notion that I was a martyr in the cause of genius and enlightenment. How hollow, windy, heartless, all that looked now. There! I will say no more. Heaven preserve any who read these pages, from such days and nights as I dragged on till that funeral, and for weeks after it was over, when I had sat once more in the little old chapel, with all the memories of my childhood crowding up, and tantalizing me with the vision of their simple peace – never, never to return! I heard my mother's dying pangs, her prayers, her doubts, her agonies, for my reprobate soul, dissected for the public good by my old enemy, Mr. Wigginton, who dragged in, among his fulsome eulogies of my mother's 'signs of grace', rejoicings that there were 'babes span-long in hell'. I saw my sister Susan, now a tall handsome woman, but become all rigid, sour, with coarse grim lips, and that crushed, self-conscious, reserved, almost dishonest look about the eyes, common to fanatics of every creed. I heard her cold farewell, as she put into my hands certain notes and diaries of my mother's, which she had bequeathed to me on her death-bed. I heard myself proclaimed inheritor of some small matters of furniture, which had belonged to her; told Susan, carelessly, to keep them for herself; and went forth, fancying that the curse of Cain was on my brow.

I took home the diary; but several days elapsed before I had courage to open it. Let the words I read there be as secret as the misery which dictated them. I had broken my mother's heart! – no! I had not! – The infernal superstition which taught her to fancy that Heaven's love was narrower than her own – that God could hate his creature, not for its sins but for the very nature which he had given it – that, that had killed her!

And I remarked, too, with a gleam of hope, that in several places where sunshine seemed ready to break through the black cloud of fanatic gloom – where she seemed inclined not merely to melt towards me (for there was, in every page, an under-current of love, deeper than death, and stronger than the grave), but also to dare to trust God on my behalf – whole lines carefully erased, page after page torn out, evidently long after the MSS. were written. I believe, to this day, that either my poor sister or her father-confessor was the perpetrator of that act. The *fraus pia** is not yet extinct; and it is as inconvenient now as it was in popish times, to tell the whole truth about saints, when they dare to say or do things which will not quite fit into the formulæ of their sect.

But what was to become of Susan? Though my uncle continued to her the allowance which he had made to my mother, yet I was her natural protector – and she was my only tie on earth. Was I to lose her, too? Might we not, after all, be happy together, in some little hole in Chelsea, like Elia and his Bridget?* That question was solved for me. She declined my offers; saying, that she could not live with any one whose religious opinions differed from her own, and that she had already engaged a room at the house of a Christian friend; and was shortly to be united to that dear man of God, Mr.

Wigginton, who was to be removed to the work of the Lord in Manchester.

I knew the scoundrel, but it would have been impossible for me to undeceive her. Perhaps he was only a scoundrel – perhaps he would not ill-treat her. And yet – my own little Susan! my playfellow! my only tie on earth! – to lose her – and not only her, but her respect, her love! – And my spirit, deep enough already, sank deeper still into sadness; and I felt myself alone on earth, and clung to Mackaye as to a father – and a father indeed that old man was to me!

CHAPTER XX

PEGASUS IN HARNESS

BUT, in sorrow or in joy, I had to earn my bread; and so, too, had Crossthwaite, poor fellow! How he contrived to feed himself and his little Katie for the next few years, is more than I can tell; at all events, he worked hard enough. He scribbled, agitated; ran from London to Manchester, and Manchester to Bradford, spouting, lecturing – sowing the east wind,* I am afraid, and little more. Whose fault was it? What could such a man do, with that fervid tongue, and heart, and brain of his, in such a station as his, such a time as this? Society had helped to make him an agitator. Society has had, more or less, to take the consequences of her own handiwork. For Crossthwaite did not speak without hearers. He could make the fierce, shrewd, artisan nature flash out into fire – not always celestial, nor always, either, infernal. So he agitated, and lived – how, I know not. That he did do so, is evident from the fact that he and Katie are at this moment playing chess in the cabin, before my eyes, and making love, all the while, as if they had not been married a week . . . Ah, well!

I, however, had to do more than get my bread; I had to pay off those fearful eleven pounds odd, which, now that all the excitement of my stay at D * * * had been so sadly quenched, lay like lead upon my memory. My list of subscribers filled slowly, and I had no power of increasing it, by any canvassing of my own. My uncle, indeed, had promised to take two copies, and my cousin one; not wishing, of course, to be so uncommercial as to run any risk, before they had seen whether my poems would succeed. But, with those exceptions, the dean had it all his own way; and he could not be expected to forego his own literary labours for my sake; so, through all that glaring summer, and sad foggy autumn, and nipping winter, I had to get my bread as I best could – by my pen. Mackaye grumbled at my writing so much, and so fast, and sneered about the *furor scribendi*.* But it was hardly fair upon me. 'My mouth craved it of me,' as Solomon says.* I had really no other means of livelihood. Even if I could have got employment as a tailor, in the honourable trade,* I loathed the business utterly – perhaps, alas! to confess the truth, I was beginning to despise it. I could bear to think of myself as a poor genius, in connexion with my new wealthy and high-bred patrons; for there was precedent for the thing. Penniless bards and squires of low degree, low-born artists, ennobled by their pictures – there was something grand in the notion of mind triumphant over the inequalities of rank, and associating with the great and wealthy, as their spiritual equal, on the mere footing of its own innate nobility; no matter to what den it might return, to convert it into a temple of the Muses, by the glorious creations of its fancy, &c. &c. But to back daily from the drawing-room and the publisher's to the goose* and shop-board, was too much for my weakness, even if it had been physically possible, as, thank Heaven, it was not.

So I became a hack writer, and sorrowfully, but deliberately, 'put my Pegasus into heavy harness', as my betters had done before me. It was miserable work, there is no denying it – only not worse than tailoring. – To try and serve God and Mammon too; to make miserable compromises daily, between the two great incompatabilities, what was true, and what would pay; to speak my mind, in fear and trembling, by hints, and halves, and quarters; to be daily hauling poor Truth just up to the top of her well, and then, frightened at my own success, let her plump down again to the bottom; to sit there, trying to teach others, while my mind was in a whirl of doubt; to feed others' intellects, while my own was hungering; to grind on in the

Philistine's mill, or occasionally make sport for them, like some weary-hearted clown grinning in a pantomime, in a 'light article', as blind as Samson, but not, alas! as strong, for indeed my Delilah of the West-end had clipped my locks, and there seemed little chance of their growing again. That face and that drawing-room flitted before me from morning till eve, and enervated and distracted my already over-wearied brain.

I had no time, besides, to concentrate my thoughts sufficiently for poetry; no time to wait for inspiration. From the moment I had swallowed my breakfast, I had to sit scribbling off my thoughts anyhow in prose; and soon my own scanty stock was exhausted, and I was forced to beg, borrow, and steal notions and facts, wherever I could get them. Oh! the misery of having to read, not what I longed to know, but what I thought would pay! – to skip page after page of interesting matter, just to pick out a single thought or sentence which could be stitched into my patchwork! – and then the still greater misery of seeing the article which I had sent to press a tolerably healthy and lusty bantling, appear in print next week, after suffering the inquisition-tortures of the editorial censorship, all maimed, and squinting, and one-sided, with the colour rubbed off its poor cheeks, and generally a villanous hang-dog look of ferocity, so different from its birth-smile that I often did not know my own child again! – and then, when I dared to remonstrate, however feebly, to be told, by way of comfort, that the public taste must be consulted! It gave me a hopeful notion of the said taste, certainly; and often and often I groaned in spirit over the temper of my own class, which not only submitted to, but demanded, such one-sided bigotry, prurience, and ferocity, from those who set up as its guides and teachers.

Mr. O'Flynn,* editor of the *Weekly Warwhoop*, whose white slave I now found myself, was, I am afraid, a pretty faithful specimen of that class, as it existed before the bitter lesson of the 10th of April brought the Chartist working men and the Chartist press to their senses. Thereon sprang up a new race of papers, whose moral tone, whatever may be thought of their political or doctrinal opinions, was certainly not inferior to that of the Whig and Tory press. The *Commonwealth*, the *Standard of Freedom*, the *Plain Speaker*,* were reprobates, if to be a

Chartist is to be a reprobate: but none except the most one-sided bigots could deny them the praise of a stern morality and a lofty earnestness, a hatred of evil and a craving after good, which would often put to shame many a paper among the oracles of Belgravia and Exeter Hall.* But those were the days of lubricity and O'Flynn. Not that the man was an unredeemed scoundrel. He was no more profligate, either in his literary or his private morals, than many a man who earns his hundreds, sometimes his thousands, a year, by prophesying smooth things to Mammon, crying in daily leaders, 'Peace! peace!' when there is no peace, and daubing the rotten walls of careless luxury and self-satisfied covetousness with the untempered mortar of party statistics and garbled foreign news – till 'the storm shall fall, and the breaking thereof cometh suddenly in an instant.'* Let those of the respectable press who are without sin, cast the first stone at the unrespectable. Many of the latter class, who have been branded as traitors and villains, were single-minded, earnest, valiant men; and, as for even O'Flynn, and those worse than him, what was really the matter with them was, that they were too honest – they spoke out too much of their whole minds. Bewildered, like Lear, amid the social storm, they had determined, like him, to become 'unsophisticated', 'to owe the worm no silk, the cat no perfume'* – seeing, indeed, that if they had, they could not have paid for them; so they tore off, of their own will, the peacock's feathers of gentility, the sheep's clothing of moderation, even the fig-leaves of decent reticence, and became just what they really were – just what hundreds more would become, who now sit in the high places of the earth, if it paid them as well to be unrespectable as it does to be respectable; if the selfishness and covetousness, bigotry and ferocity, which are in them, and more or less in every man, had happened to enlist them against existing evils, instead of for them. O'Flynn would have been gladly as respectable as they; but, in the first place, he must have starved; and in the second place, he must have lied; for he believed in his own radicalism with his whole soul. There was a ribald sincerity, a frantic courage in the man. He always spoke the truth when it suited him, and very often when it did not. He did see, which is more than all do, that oppression is oppression, and humbug, humbug. He had faced the gallows before now, without flinching. He had spouted rebellion in the Birmingham Bullring,* and elsewhere, and taken the consequences like a man; while his colleagues left their dupes to the tender mercies of broadswords and bayonets, and decamped in the disguise of sailors, old women, and dissenting preachers.* He had sat three months in Lancaster Castle, the Bastile of England, one day perhaps to fall like that Parisian one, for a libel which he never wrote, because he would not betray his cowardly contributor. He had twice pleaded his own cause, without help of attorney, and showed himself as practised in every law-quibble and practical cheat as if he had been a regularly-ordained priest of the blue-bag;* and each time, when hunted at last into a corner, had turned valiantly to bay, with wild witty Irish eloquence, 'worthy', as the press say of poor misguided Mitchell,* 'of a better cause.' Altogether, a much-enduring Ulysses, unscrupulous, tough-hided, ready to do and suffer anything fair or foul, for what he honestly believed – if a confused, virulent positiveness be worthy of the name 'belief' – to be the true and righteous cause.

Those who class all mankind compendiously and comfortably under the two exhaustive species of saints and villains, may consider such a description garbled and impossible. I have seen few men, but never yet met I among those few either perfect saint or perfect villain. I draw men as I have found them – inconsistent, piece-meal, better than their own actions, worse than their own opinions, and poor O'Flynn among the rest. Not that there were no questionable spots in the sun of his fair fame. It was whispered that he had in old times done dirty work for Dublin Castle bureaucrats – nay, that he had even, in a very hard season, written court poetry for the *Morning Post*; but all these little peccadilloes he carefully veiled in that kindly mist which hung over his youthful years. He had been a medical student, and got plucked, his foes declared, in his examination. He had set up a savings-bank, which broke. He had come over from Ireland, to agitate for 'repale' and 'rint', and, like a wise man as he was, had never gone back again. He had set up three or four papers in his time, and entered into partnership with every leading democrat in turn; but his papers failed, and he quarrelled with his partners, being addicted to profane swearing and personalities. And now at last, after Ulyssean wanderings, he had found rest in the office of the *Weekly Warwhoop*, if rest it could be called, that perennial hurricane of plotting, railing, sneering, and bombast, in which he lived, never writing a line, on principle, till he had worked himself up into a passion.

I will dwell no more on so distasteful a subject. Such leaders, let us hope, belong only to the past – to the youthful self-will and licentiousness of democracy; and as for reviling O'Flynn, or any other of his class, no man has less right than myself, I fear, to cast stones at such as they. I fell as low as almost any, beneath the besetting sins of my class; and shall I take merit to myself, because God has shown me, a little earlier perhaps than to them, somewhat more of the true duties and destinies of The Many? Oh, that they could see the depths of my affection to them! Oh! that they could see the shame and self-abasement with which, in rebuking their sins, I confess my own! If they are apt to be flippant and bitter, so was I. If they lust to destroy, without knowing what to build up instead, so did I. If they make an almighty idol of that Electoral Reform, which ought to be, and can be, only a preliminary means, and expect final deliverance from 'their twenty-thousandth part of a talker in the national palaver',* so did I. Unhealthy and noisome as was the literary atmosphere in which I now found myself, it was one to my taste. The very contrast between the peaceful, intellectual luxury which I had just witnessed, and the misery of my class and myself, quickened my delight in it. In bitterness, in sheer envy, I threw my whole soul into it, and spoke evil, and rejoiced in evil. It was so easy to find fault! It pampered my own self-conceit, my own discontent, while it saved me the trouble of inventing remedies. Yes; it was indeed easy to find fault. 'The world was all before me, where to choose.'* In such a disorganised, anomalous, grumbling, party-embittered element as this English society, and its twin pauperism and luxury, I had but to look straight before me to see my prey.

And thus I became daily more and more cynical, fierce, reckless. My mouth was filled with cursing – and too often justly. And all the while, like tens of thousands of my class, I had no man to teach me. Sheep scattered on the hills, we were, that had no shepherd. What wonder if our bones lay bleaching among rocks and quagmires, and wolves devoured the heritage of God?

Mackaye had nothing positive, after all, to advise or propound. His wisdom was one of apophthegms and maxims, utterly impractical, too often merely negative, as was his creed, which, though he refused to be classed with any sect, was really a somewhat undefined Unitarianism – or rather Islamism. He could say, with the old Moslem, 'God is great – who hath resisted his will?'* And he believed what he said, and lived manful and pure, reverent and self-denying, by that belief, as the first Moslem did. But that was not enough.

'Not enough? Merely negative?'

No – *that* was positive enough, and mighty; but I repeat it, it was not enough. He felt it so himself; for he grew daily more and more cynical, more and more hopeless about the prospects of his class and of all humanity. Why not? Poor suffering wretches! what is it to them to know that 'God is great', unless you can prove to them that God is also merciful? Did He indeed care for men at all? – was what I longed to know; was all this misery and misrule around us His will – His stern and necessary law – His lazy connivance? And were to free ourselves from it by any frantic means that came to hand? or had He ever interfered himself? Was there a chance, a hope, of his interfering now, in our own time, to take the matter into His own hand, and come out of His place to judge the earth in righteousness? That was what we wanted to know; and poor Mackaye could give no comfort there: 'God was great – the wicked would be turned into hell.' Ay – the few wilful, triumphant wicked; but the millions of suffering, starving wicked, the victims of society and circumstance – what hope for them? 'God was great.' And for the clergy, our professed and salaried teachers, all I can say is – and there are tens, perhaps hundreds of thousands of workmen who can re-echo my words – with the exception of the dean and my cousin, and one who shall be mentioned hereafter, a clergyman never spoke to me in my life.

Why should he? Was I not a Chartist and an Infidel? The truth is, the clergy are afraid of us. To read the *Dispatch*, is to be excommunicated.* Young men's classes? Honour to them, however few they are – however hampered by the restrictions of religious bigotry and political cowardice. But the working men, whether rightly or wrongly, do not trust them; they do not trust the clergy who set them on foot; they do not expect to be taught at them the things they long to know – to be taught the whole truth in them about history, politics, science, the Bible. They suspect them to be mere tubs to the whale – mere substitutes for education, slowly and late adopted, in order to stop the mouths of the importunate. They may misjudge the clergy; but whose fault is it if they do? Clergymen of England! – look at the history of your Establishment for the last fifty years, and say, what wonder is it if the artisan mistrust you? Every spiritual reform, since the time of John Wesley, has had to establish itself in the teeth of insult, calumny, and persecution. Every ecclesiastical reform comes not from within, but from without your body. Mr. Horsman,* struggling against every kind of temporising and trickery, has to do the work which bishops, by virtue of their seat in the House of Lords, ought to have been doing years ago. Everywhere we see the clergy, with a few persecuted exceptions (like Dr. Arnold),* proclaiming themselves the advocates of Toryism, the dogged opponents of our political liberty, living either by the accursed system of pew-rents, or else by one which depends on the high price of corn;* chosen exclusively from the classes who crush us down; prohibiting all free discussion on religious points; commanding us to swallow down, with faith as passive and implicit as that of a Papist, the very creeds from which their own bad example, and their scandalous neglect, have, in the last three generations, alienated us; never mixing with the thoughtful working men, except in the prison, the hospital, or in extreme old age; betraying, in every tract, in every sermon, an ignorance of the doubts, the feelings, the very language of the masses, which would be ludicrous, were it not accursed before God and man. And then will you show us a few tardy improvements here and there, and ask us, indignantly, why we distrust you? Oh! gentlemen, if you cannot see for yourselves the causes of our distrust, it is past our power to show you. We must leave it to God.

*

But to return to my own story. I had, as I said before, to live by my pen; and in that painful, confused, maimed way, I contrived to scramble on the long winter through, writing regularly for the *Weekly Warwhoop*, and sometimes getting an occasional scrap into some other cheap periodical, often on the very verge of starvation, and glad of a handful of meal from Sandy's widow's barrel. If I had had more than my share of feasting in the summer, I made the balance even, during those frosty months, by many a bitter fast.

And, here let me ask you, gentle reader, who are just now considering me ungentle, virulent, and noisy, did you ever, for one day in your whole life, literally, involuntarily, and in spite of all your endeavours, longings, and hungerings, *not get enough to eat*? If you ever have, it must have taught you several things.

But all this while, it must not be supposed that I had forgotten my promise to good Farmer Porter, to look for his missing son. And, indeed, Crossthwaite and I were already engaged in a similar search for a friend of his – the young tailor, who, as I told Porter, had been lost for several months. He was the brother of Crossthwaite's wife, a passionate, kind-hearted Irishman Mike Kelly by name, reckless and scatter-brained enough to get himself into every possible scrape, and weak enough of will never to get himself out of one. For these two, Crossthwaite and I had searched from one sweater's den to another, and searched in vain. And though the present interest and exertion kept us both from brooding over our own difficulties, yet in the long run, it tended only to embitter and infuriate our minds. The frightful scenes of hopeless misery which we witnessed – the ever widening pit of pauperism and slavery, gaping for fresh victims day by day, as they dropped out of the fast lessening 'honourable trade', into the ever-increasing miseries of sweating, piece-work, and starvation-prices; the horrible certainty that the same process which was devouring our trade, was slowly, but surely, eating up every other also; the knowledge that there was no remedy, no salvation for us in man, that political economists had declared such to be the law and constitution of society, and that our rulers had believed that message, and were determined to act upon it; –

if all these things did not go far towards maddening us, we must have been made of sterner stuff than any one who reads this book.

At last, about the middle of January, just as we had given up the search as hopeless, and poor Katie's eyes were getting red and swelled with daily weeping, a fresh spur was given to our exertions, by the sudden appearance of no less a person than the farmer himself. What ensued upon his coming, must be kept for another chapter.

CHAPTER XXI

THE SWEATER'S DEN

I WAS greedily devouring Lane's 'Arabian Nights',* which had made their first appearance in the shop that day.

Mackaye sat in his usual place, smoking a clean pipe, and assisting his meditations by certain mysterious chironomic signs;* while opposite to him was Farmer Porter – a stone or two thinner than when I had seen him last, but one stone is not much missed out of seventeen. His forehead looked smaller, and his jaws larger than ever; and his red face was sad, and furrowed with care.

Evidently, too, he was ill at ease about other matters besides his son. He was looking out of the corners of his eyes, first at the skinless cast on the chimney-piece, then at the crucified books hanging over his head, as if he considered them not altogether safe companions, and rather expected something 'uncanny' to lay hold of him from behind – a process which involved the most horrible contortions of visage, as he carefully abstained from stirring a muscle of his neck or body, but sat bolt upright, his elbows pinned to his sides, and his knees as close together as his stomach would permit, like a huge corpulent Egyptian Memnon* – the most ludicrous contrast to the little old man opposite, twisted up together in his Joseph's coat, like some wizard magician in the stories which I was reading. A curious pair of 'poles' the two made; the mesothet* whereof, by no means a *'punctum indifferens'*,* but a true connecting spiritual idea, stood on the table – in the whisky-bottle.

Farmer Porter was evidently big with some great thought, and had all a true poet's bashfulness about publishing the fruit of his creative genius. He looked round again at the skinless man, the caricatures, the books; and, as his eyes wandered from pile to pile, and shelf to shelf, his face brightened, and he seemed to gain courage.

Solemnly he put his hat on his knees, and began solemnly brushing it with his cuff. Then he saw me watching him, and stopped. Then he put his pipe solemnly on the hob, and cleared his throat for action, while I buried my face in the book.

'Them's a sight o' larned beuks, Muster Mackaye?'

'Humph!'

'Yow maun ha' got a deal o' scholarship among they, noo?'

'Humph!'

'Dee yow think, noo, yow could find of my boy out of un, by any ways o' conjuring like?'

'By what?'

'Conjuring – to strick a perpendicular,* noo, or say the Lord's Prayer backwards?'

'Wadna ye prefer a meeracle or twa?' asked Sandy, after a long pull at the whisky-toddy.

'Or a few efreets?'* added I.

'Whatsoever you likes, gentlemen. You're best judges, to be sure,' answered Farmer Porter, in an awed and helpless voice.

'Aweel – I'm no that disinclined to believe in the occult sciences. I dinna haud a'thegither wi' Salverte.* There was mair in them than Magia naturalis, I'm thinking. Mesmerism* and magic-lanterns, benj and opium,* winna explain all facts, Alton, laddie. Dootless they were an unco' barbaric an' empiric method o' expressing the gran' truth o' man's mastery ower matter. But the interpenetration o' the spiritual an' physical worlds is a gran' truth too; an' aiblins* the Deity might ha' allowed witchcraft, just to teach that to puir barbarous folk – signs and wonders, laddie, to mak' them believe in somewhat mair than the beasts that perish: an' so ghaists an' warlocks might be a necessary element o' the divine education in dark and carnal times. But I've no read o' a case in which necromancy, nor geomancy, nor coskinomancy,* nor ony ither mancy, was applied to sic a purpose as this. Unco gude they were, may be, for the discovery o' stolen spunes – but no that o' stolen tailors.'

Farmer Porter had listened to this harangue, with mouth and eyes gradually expanding between awe and the desire to comprehend; but at the last sentence his countenance fell.

'So I'm thinking, Mister Porter, that the best witch in siccan a case is ane that ye may find at the police-office.'

'Anan?'

'Thae detective police are gran' necromancers an' canny in their way: an' I just took the liberty, a week agone, to ha' a crack wi' ane o' 'em. And noo, gin ye're inclined, we'll leave the whusky awhile, an' gang up to that cave o' Trophawnius,* ca'd by the vulgar Bow-street, an' speir for tidings o' the twa lost sheep.'

So to Bow-street we went, and found our man, to whom the farmer bowed with obsequiousness most unlike his usual burly independence. He evidently half suspected him to have dealings with the world of spirits: but whether he had such or not, they had been utterly unsuccessful; and we walked back again, with the farmer between us half-blubbering—

'I tell ye, there's nothing like ganging to a wise 'ooman. Bless ye, I mind one up to Guy Hall, when I was a barn, that two Irish reapers coom down, and murthered her for the money – and if you lost aught she'd vind it, so sure as the church – and a mighty hand to cure burns; and they two villains coom back, after harvest, seventy mile to do it – and when my vather's cows was shrew-struck, she made un be draed under a brimble as growed together at the both ends, she a-praying like mad all the time; and they never got nothing but fourteen shilling and a crooked sixpence; for why, the devil carried off all the rest of her money: and I seen um both a-hanging in chains by Wisbeach river, with my own eyes. So when they Irish reapers comes into the vens, our chaps always says, "Yow goo to Guy Hall, there's yor brithren a-waitin' for yow," and that do make um joost mad loike, it do. I tell ye there's nowt like a wise 'ooman, for vinding out the likes o' this.'

At this hopeful stage of the argument I left them, to go to

the Magazine office. As I passed through Covent Garden, a pretty young woman stopped me under a gas-lamp. I was pushing on, when I saw that it was Jemmy Downes's Irish wife, and saw, too, that she did not recognise me. A sudden instinct made me stop and hear what she had to say.

'Shure then, and yer a tailor, my young man?'

'Yes,' I said, nettled a little that my late loathed profession still betrayed itself in my gait.

'From the counthry?'

I nodded, though I dared not speak a white lie to that effect. I fancied that, somehow, through her I might hear of poor Kelly and his friend Porter.

'Ye'll be wanting work thin?'

'I have no work.'

'Och then, it's I can show ye the flower o' work, I can. Bedad, there's a shop I know of where ye'll earn – bedad, if ye're the ninth part of a man, let alone a handy young fellow like the looks of you – och, ye'll earn thirty shillings the week, to the very least – an' beautiful lodgings; – och, thin, just come and see 'em – as chape as mother's milk! Come along thin – och, it's the beauty ye are – just the nate figure for a tailor.'

The fancy still possessed me; and I went with her through one dingy back street after another. She seemed to be purposely taking an indirect road, to mislead me as to my whereabouts; but after a half-hour's walking, I knew, as well as she, that we were in one of the most miserable slop-working nests of the East-end.

She stopped at a house door, and hurried me in, up to the first floor, and into a dirty, slatternly parlour, smelling infamously of gin; where the first object I beheld was Jemmy Downes, sitting before the fire, three-parts drunk, with a couple of dirty, squalling children on the hearth-rug, whom he was kicking and cuffing alternately.

'Och, thin, ye villain, bating the poor darlints whinever I lave ye a minute!' and pouring out a volley of Irish curses, she caught up the urchins, one under each arm, and kissed and hugged them till they were nearly choked. 'Och, ye plague o' my life – as drunk as a baste; an' I brought home this darlint of a young gentleman to help ye in the business.'

Downes got up, and steadying himself by the table, leered at me with lack-lustre eyes, and attempted a little ceremonious politeness. How this was to end I did not see; but I was determined to carry it through, on the chance of success, infinitely small as that might be.

'An' I've told him thirty shillings a week's the least he'll earn; and charges for board and lodging only seven shillings.'

'Thirty! – she lies; she's always a-lying; don't you mind her. Five-and-forty is the werry lowest figure. Ask my respectable and most piousest partner, Shemei Solomons. Why, blow me – it's Locke!'

'Yes, it is Locke; and surely you're my old friend, Jemmy Downes? Shake hands. What an unexpected pleasure to meet you again!'

'Werry unexpected pleasure. Tip us your daddle! De-lighted – delighted, as I was a-saying, to be of the least use to yer. Take a caulker?* Summat heavy, then? No? "Tak' a drap o' kindness yet, for auld langsyne"?'

'You forget I was always a teetotaller.'

'Ay,' with a look of unfeigned pity. 'An' you're a-going to lend us a hand? Oh, ah! perhaps you'd like to begin? Here's a most beautiful uniform, now, for a markis in her Majesty's Guards; we don't mention names – tarn't business like. P'r'aps you'd like best to work here to-night, for company – "for auld langsyne, my boys"; and I'll introduce yer to the gents upstairs to-morrow.'

'No,' I said; 'I'll go up at once, if you've no objection.'

'Och, thin, but the sheets isn't aired – no – faix; and I'm thinking the gentleman as is a-going isn't gone yet.'

But I insisted on going up at once; and, grumbling, she followed me. I stopped on the landing of the second floor, and asked which way; and seeing her in no hurry to answer, opened a door, inside which I heard the hum of many voices, saying in as sprightly a tone as I could muster, that I supposed that was the workroom.

As I had expected, a fetid, choking den, with just room enough in it for the seven or eight sallow, starved beings, who, coatless, shoeless, and ragged, sat stitching, each on his truckle-bed. I glanced round; the man whom I sought was not there.

My heart fell; why it had ever risen to such a pitch of hope I cannot tell; and half-cursing myself for a fool, in thus wildly thrusting my head into a squabble, I turned back and shut the door, saying—

'A very pleasant room, ma'am, but a leetle too crowded.'

Before she could answer, the opposite door opened; and a face appeared – unwashed, unshaven, shrunken to a skeleton. I did not recognise it at first.

'Blessed Vargen! but that wasn't your voice, Locke?'

'And who are you?'

'Tear and ages! and he don't know Mike Kelly!'

My first impulse was to catch him up in my arms, and run downstairs with him. I controlled myself, however, not knowing how far he might be in his tyrant's power. But his voluble Irish heart burst out at once—

'Oh! blessed saints, take me out o' this! – take me out, for the love of Jesus! – take me out o' this hell, or I'll go mad intirely! Och! will nobody have pity on poor sowls in purgatory – here in prison like negur slaves? We're starved to the bone, we are, and kilt intirely with cowld.'

And as he clutched my arm, with his long, skinny, trembling fingers, I saw that his hands and feet were all chapped and bleeding. Neither shoe nor stocking did he possess; his only garments were a ragged shirt and trousers; and – and, in horrible mockery of his own misery, a grand new flowered satin vest, which to-morrow was to figure in some gorgeous shop-window!

'Och! Mother of Heaven!' he went on, wildly, 'when will I get out to the fresh air? For five months I haven't seen the blessed light of sun, nor spoken to the praste, nor ate a bit o' mate, barring bread-and-butter. Shure, it's all the blessed sabbaths and saints' days I've been a-working like a haythen Jew, and niver seen the insides o' the chapel to confess my sins, and me poor sowl's lost intirely – and they've pawned the relaver** this fifteen weeks, and not a boy of us iver sot foot in the street since.'

** A coat, we understand, which is kept by the coatless wretches in these sweaters' dungeons, to be used by each of them in turn when they want to go out. – ED.

'Vot's that row?' roared at this juncture Downes's voice from below.

'Och, thin,' shrieked the woman, 'here's that thief o' the warld, Micky Kelly, slandhering o' us afore the blessed heaven, and he owing 2*l*. 14*s*. ½*d*. for his board an' lodgin', let alone pawn-tickets, and goin' to rin away, the black-hearted ongrateful sarpent!' And she began yelling indiscriminately 'Thieves!' 'Murder!' 'Blasphemy!' and such other ejaculations, which (the English ones at least) had not the slightest reference to the matter in hand.

'I'll come to him!' said Downes, with an oath, and rushed stumbling up the stairs, while the poor wretch sneaked in again, and slammed the door to. Downes battered at it, but was met with a volley of curses from the men inside; while, profiting by the Babel, I blew out the light, ran downstairs, and got safe into the street.

In two hours afterwards, Mackaye, Porter, Crossthwaite and I, were at the door, accompanied by a policeman, and a search-warrant. Porter had insisted on accompanying us. He had made up his mind that his son was at Downes's; and all representations of the smallness of his chance were fruitless. He worked himself up into a state of complete frenzy, and flourished a huge stick in a way which shocked the policeman's orderly and legal notions.

'That may do very well down in your country, sir; but you aren't a-goin' to use that there weapon here, you know, not by no hact o' Parliament as I knows on.'

'Ow, it's joost a way I ha' wi' me.' And the stick was quiet for fifty yards or so, and then recommenced smashing imaginary skulls.

'You'll do somebody a mischief, sir, with that. You'd much better a-lend it me.'

Porter tucked it under his arm for fifty yards more; and so on, till we reached Downes's house.

The policeman knocked; and the door was opened, cautiously, by an old Jew, of a most un-'Caucasian' cast of features, however 'high nosed', as Mr. Disraeli has it.*

The policeman asked to see Michael Kelly.

'Michaelsh? I do't know such namesh—' But before the

parley could go further, the farmer burst past policeman and Jew, and rushed into the passage, roaring, in a voice which made the very windows rattle,

'Billy Poorter! Billy Poorter! whor be yow? whor be yow?'

We all followed him upstairs, in time to see him charging valiantly, with his stick for a bayonet, the small person of a Jew-boy, who stood at the head of the stairs in a scientific attitude.* The young rascal planted a dozen blows in the huge carcase – he might as well have thumped the rhinoceros in the Regent's Park; the old man ran right over him, without stopping, and dashed up the stairs; at the head of which – oh, joy! – appeared a long, shrunken, red-haired figure, the tears on his dirty cheeks glittering in the candle-glare. In an instant, father and son were in each other's arms.

'Oh, my barn! my barn! my barn! my barn!' and then the old Hercules held him off at arm's length, and looked at him with a wistful face, and hugged him again with 'My barn! my barn!' He had nothing else to say. Was it not enough? And poor Kelly danced frantically around them, hurrahing; his own sorrows forgotten in his friend's deliverance.

The Jew-boy shook himself, turned, and darted downstairs past us; the policeman quietly put out his foot, tripped him headlong, and jumping down after him, extracted from his grasp a heavy pocket-book.

'Ah! my dear mothersh's dying gift! Oh, dear! oh dear! give it back to a poor orphansh!'

'Didn't I see you take it out o' the old un's pocket – you young villain?' answered the maintainer of order, as he shoved the book into his bosom, and stood with one foot on his writhing victim, a complete nineteenth-century St. Michael.*

'Let me hold him,' I said, 'while you go upstairs.'

'*You* hold a Jew-boy! – you hold a mad cat!' answered the policeman, contemptuously – and with justice – for at that moment Downes appeared on the first-floor landing, cursing and blaspheming.

'He's my 'prentice! he's my servant! I've got a bond, with his own hand to it, to serve me for three years. I'll have the law of you – I will!'

Then the meaning of the big stick came out. The old man

leapt down the stairs, and seized Downes. 'You're the tyrant as has locked my barn up here!' and a thrashing commenced, which it made my bones ache only to look at. Downes had no chance; the old man felled him on his face in a couple of blows, and taking both hands to his stick, hewed away at him as if he had been a log.

'I waint hit a's head! I waint hit a's head!' – whack, whack. 'Let me be!' – whack, whack – puff. 'It does me gude, it does me gude!' puff, puff, puff – whack. 'I've been a-bottling of it up for three years, come Whitsuntide!' – whack, whack, whack – while Mackaye and Crossthwaite stood coolly looking on, and the wife shut herself up in the side-room, and screamed murder.

The unhappy policeman stood at his wit's end, between the prisoner below, and the breach of the peace above, bellowing in vain, in the Queen's name, to us, and to the grinning tailors on the landing. At last, as Downes's life seemed in danger, he wavered; the Jew-boy seized the moment, jumped up, upsetting the constable, dashed like an eel between Crossthwaite and Mackaye, gave me a back-handed blow in passing, which I felt for a week after, and vanished through the street-door, which he locked after him.

'Very well!' said the functionary, rising solemnly, and pulling out a note-book – 'Scar under left eye, nose a little twisted to the right, bad chilblains on the hands. You'll keep till next time, young man. Now, you fat gentleman up there, have you done a-qualifying of yourself for Newgate?'

The old man had run upstairs again, and was hugging his son; but when the policeman lifted Downes, he rushed back to his victim, and begged, like a great school-boy, for leave to 'bet him joost won bit moor.'

'Let me bet un! I'll pay un; – I'll pay all as my son owes un! Marcy me! where's my pooss?' and so on raged the Babel, till we got the two poor fellows safe out of the house – we had to break open the door to do it, thanks to that imp of Israel.

'For God's sake, take us too!' almost screamed five or six other voices.

'They're all in debt – every onesh; they sha'n't go till they paysh, if there's law in England,' whined the old Jew, who had re-appeared.

'I'll pay for 'em – I'll pay every farden, if so be as they treated my boy well. Here, you, Mr. Locke, there's the ten pounds as I promised you. Why, whor is my pooss?'

The policeman solemnly handed it to him. He took it, turned it over, looked at the policeman half frightened, and pointed with his fat thumb at Mackaye.

'Well, he said as you was a conjuror – and sure he was right.'

He paid me the money. I had no mind to keep it in such company; so I got the poor fellows' pawn-tickets, and Crossthwaite and I took their things out for them. When we returned, we found them in a group in the passage, holding the door open, in their fear lest we should be locked up, or entrapped in some way. Their spirits seemed utterly broken. Some three or four went off to lodge where they could; the majority went upstairs again to work. That, even that dungeon, was their only home – their only hope, as it is of thousands of 'free' Englishmen at this moment.

We returned, and found the old man with his newfound prodigal sitting on his knee, as if he had been a baby. Sandy told me afterwards, that he had scarcely kept him from carrying the young man all the way home; he was convinced that the poor fellow was dying of starvation. I think really he was not far wrong. In the corner sat Kelly, crouched together like a baboon, blubbering, hurrahing, invoking the saints, cursing the sweaters, and blessing the present company. We were afraid, for several days, that his wits were seriously affected.

And, in his old arm-chair, pipe in mouth, sat good Sandy Mackaye, wiping his eyes with the many-coloured sleeve, and moralising to himself, *sotto voce*:

'The auld Romans made slaves o' their debitors;* sae did the Anglo-Saxons, for a' good Major Cartwright* has writ to the contrary. But I didna ken the same Christian practice was part o' the Breetish constitution. Aweel, aweel – atween Riot Acts,* Government by Commissions, and ither little extravagants and codicils o' Mammon's making, it's no that easy to ken, the day, what is the Breetish constitution, and what isn't. Tak' a drappie, Billy Porter, lad?'

'Never again so long as I live. I've learnt a lesson and a half about that, these last few months.'

'Aweel, moderation's best, but abstinence better than naething. Nae man sall deprive me o' my leeberty, but I'll tempt nae man to gie up his.' And he actually put the whisky-bottle by into the cupboard.

The old man and his son went home next day, promising me, if I would but come to see them, 'twa hundert acres o' the best partridge-shooting, and wild dooks as plenty as sparrows; and to live in clover till I bust, if I liked.' And so, as Bunyan has it,* they went on their way, and I saw them no more.

[*At this point in the first and second editions, Volume I ended.*]

CHAPTER XXII

AN EMERSONIAN SERMON

CERTAINLY, if John Crosthwaite held the victim-of-circumstance doctrine in theory, he did not allow Mike Kelly to plead it in practice, as an extenuation of his misdeeds. Very different from his Owenite 'it's-nobody's-fault' harangues* in the debating society, or his admiration for the teacher of whom my readers shall have a glimpse shortly, was his lecture that evening to the poor Irishman on "It's all your own fault." Unhappy Kelly! he sat there like a beaten cur, looking first at one of us, and then at the other, for mercy, and finding none. As soon as Crosthwaite's tongue was tired, Mackaye's began, on the sins of drunkenness, hastiness, improvidence, over-trustfulness, &c., &c., and, above all, on the cardinal offence of not having signed the protest years before, and spurned the dishonourable trade,* as we had done. Even his most potent excuse that 'a boy must live somehow', Crosthwaite treated as contemptuously as if he had been a very Leonidas,* while Mackaye chimed in with—

'An' ye a papist! ye talk o' praying to saints an' martyrs, that died in torments because they wad na do what they should na do? What ha' ye to do wi' martyrs? – a meeserable wretch that sells his soul for a mess o' pottage – four slices per diem o' thin bread and butter? Et propter veetam veevendi perdere causas!*

Dinna tell me o' your hardships – ye've had your deserts – your rights were just equivalent to your mights,* an' so ye got them.'

'Faix thin, Misther Mackaye, darlint, an' whin did I desarve to pawn me own goose* an' board, an' sit looking at the spidhers for the want o' them?'

'Pawn his ain goose? Pawn himsel! pawn his needle – gin it had been worth the pawning, they'd ha' ta'en it. An' yet there's a command in Deuteronomy,* Ye shall na tak' the millstone in pledge, for it's a man's life; nor yet keep his raiment owre night, but gie it the puir body back, that he may sleep in his ain claes, an' bless ye. O – but pawnbrokers dinna care for blessings – na marketable value in them, whatsoever.'

'And the shopkeeper,' said I, 'in the "Arabian Nights",* refuses to take the fisherman's net in pledge, because he gets his living thereby.'

'Ech! but, laddie, they were puir legal Jews, under carnal ordinances, an' daur na even tak an honest five per cent. interest for their money. An' the baker o' Bagdad, why he was a benighted heathen, ye ken, an' deceivit by that fause prophet, Mahomet, to his eternal damnation, or he wad never ha' gone aboot to fancy a fisherman was his brither.'

'Faix, an' ain't we all brothers?' asked Kelly.

'Ay, and no,' said Sandy, with an expression which would have been a smile, but for its depth of bitter earnestness; 'brithren in Christ, my laddie.'

'An' ain't that all over the same?'

'Ask the preachers. Gin they meant brothers, they'd say brothers, be sure; but because they don't mean brothers at a', they say brithren – ye'll mind, brithren – to soun' antiquate, an' professional, an' perfunctory-like, for fear it should be owre real, an' practical, an' startling, an' a' that; and then jist limit it down wi' a "in Christ", for fear o' owre wide applications, and a' that. But

> For a' that, an' a' that,
> It's comin' yet for a' that,
> When man an' man, the warld owre,
> Shall brothers be, for a' that –*

An' na brithren ony mair at a'!'

'An' didn't the blessed Jesus die for all?'

'What? for heretics, Micky?'

'Bedad thin, an' I forgot that intirely!'

'Of course you did! It's strange, laddie,' said he, turning to me, 'that that Name suld be everywhere, fra the thunderers o' Exeter Ha' to this puir feckless Paddy, the watchword o' exclusiveness. I'm thinking ye'll no find the workmen believe in 't, till somebody can fin' the plan o' making it the sign o' universal comprehension. Gin I had na seen in my youth that a brither in Christ meant less a thousandfold than a brither out o' him, I might ha' believit the noo – we'll no say what. I've an owre great organ o' marvellousness, an' o' veneration too, I'm afeard.'

'Ah,' said Crosshthwaite, 'you should come and hear Mr. Windrush* to-night, about the all-embracing benevolence of the Deity, and the abomination of limiting it by all those narrow creeds and dogmas.'

'An' wha's Meester Windrush, then?'

'Oh, he's an American; he was a Calvinist preacher originally, I believe; but, as he told us last Sunday evening, he soon cast away the worn-out vestures of an obsolete faith, which were fast becoming only crippling fetters.'

'An' ran oot sarkless on the public, eh? I'm afeard there's mony a man else that throws awa' the gude auld plaid o' Scots Puritanism, an' is unco fain to cover his nakedness wi' ony cast popinjay's feathers he can forgather wi'. Aweel, aweel – a puir priestless age it is, the noo. We'll e'en gang hear him the nicht, Alton, laddie; ye ha' na darkened the kirk door this mony a a day – nor I neither, mair by token.'

It was too true. I had utterly given up the whole problem of religion as insoluble. I believed in poetry, science, and democracy – and they were enough for me then; enough, at least, to leave a mighty hunger in my heart, I knew not for what. And as for Mackaye, though brought up, as he told me, a rigid Scotch Presbyterian, he had gradually ceased to attend the church of his fathers.

'It was no the kirk o' his fathers – the auld God-trusting kirk that Clavers* dragoonit down by burns and muirsides. It was a' gane dead an' dry; a piece of Auld-Bailey barristration anent

soul-saving dodges. What did he want wi' proofs o' the being o'
God, an' o' the doctrine o' original sin? He could see eneugh o'
them ayont the shop-door, ony tide. They made puir Rabbie
Burns an anything-arian,* wi' their blethers, an' he was near
gaun the same gate.'

And, besides, he absolutely refused to enter any place of
worship where there were pews. 'He wad na follow after a
multitude to do evil; he wad na gang before his Maker wi' a
lee in his right hand. Nae wonder folks were so afraid o' the
names o' equality an' britherhood, when they'd kicked them
out e'en o' the kirk o' God. Pious folks may ca' me a sinful
auld Atheist. They winna gang to be a harmless stage-play –
an' richt they – for fear o' countenancing the sin that's dune
there; an' I wanna gang to the kirk, for fear o' countenancing
the sin that's dune there, by putting down my hurdies on that
stool o' antichrist, a haspit pew!'*

I was, therefore, altogether surprised at the promptitude with
which he agreed to go and hear Crossthwaite's new-found
prophet. His reasons for so doing may be, I think, gathered
from the conversation towards the end of this chapter.

Well, we went; and I, for my part, was charmed with
Mr. Windrush's eloquence. His style, which was altogether
Emersonian,* quite astonished me by its alternate bursts of
what I considered brilliant declamation, and of forcible epi-
grammatic antithesis. I do not deny that I was a little startled
by some of his doctrines, and suspected that he had not seen
much, either of St. Giles's cellar or tailors' workshops either,
when he talked of sin as 'only a lower form of good. Nothing,'
he informed us, 'was produced in nature without pain and
disturbance; and what we had been taught to call sin, was, in
fact, nothing but the birth-throes attendant on the progress of
the species. – As for the devil, Novalis, indeed, had gone so far
as to suspect him to be a necessary illusion.* Novalis was a
mystic, and tainted by the old creeds. The illusion was not
necessary – it was disappearing before the fast-approaching
meridian light of philosophic religion. Like the myths of
Christianity, it had grown up in an age of superstition, when
men, blind to the wondrous order of the universe, believed that
supernatural beings, like the Homeric gods, actually interfered

in the affairs of mortals. Science had revealed the irrevocability
of the laws of nature – was man alone to be exempt from them?
No. The time would come, when it would be as obsolete an
absurdity to talk of the temptation of a fiend, as it was now to
talk of the weir-wolf, or the angel of the thundercloud. The
metaphor might remain, doubtless, as a metaphor, in the
domain of poetry, whose office was to realize, in objective
symbols, the subjective ideas of the human intellect; but philosophy, and the pure sentiment of religion, which found all
things, even God himself, in the recesses of its own enthusiastic
heart, must abjure such a notion.

*

'What!' he asked again, 'shall all nature be a harmonious
whole, reflecting, in every drop of dew which gems the footsteps
of the morning, the infinite love and wisdom of its Maker, and
man alone be excluded from his part in that concordant choir?
Yet such is the doctrine of the advocates of free-will, and of
sin – its phantom-bantling. Man disobey his Maker! disarrange
and break the golden wheels and springs of the infinite machine!
The thought were blasphemy! – impossibility! All things fulfil
their destiny; and so does man, in a higher or lower sphere of
being. Shall I punish the robber? Shall I curse the profligate?
As soon destroy the toad, because my partial taste may judge
him ugly; or doom to hell, for his carnivorous appetite, the
muscanonge* of my native lakes! Toad is not horrible to toad,
or thief to thief. Philanthropists or statesmen may environ him
with more genial circumstances, and so enable his propensities
to work more directly for the good of society; but to punish
him – to punish nature for daring to be nature! – Never! I may
thank the Upper Destinies that they have not made me as other
men are – that they have endowed me with nobler instincts, a
more delicate conformation than the thief; but I have my part
to play, and he has his. Why should we wish to be other than
the All-wise has made us?'

'Fine doctrine, that,' grumbled Sandy; 'gin ye've first made
up your mind wi' the Pharisee,* that ye *are* no like ither men.'

'Shall I pray, then? For what? I will coax none, flatter
none – not even the Supreme! I will not be absurd enough to

wish to change that order, by which sun and stars, saints and
sinners, alike fulfil their destinies. There is one comfort, my
friends; coax and flatter as we will, He will not hear us.'

'Pleasant, for puir deevils like us!' quoth Mackaye.

'What then remains? Thanks, thanks — not of words, but
of actions. Worship is a life, not a ceremony. He who
would honour the Supreme, let him cheerfully succumb to
the destiny which the Supreme has allotted, and, like the shell
or the flower — ('Or the pickpocket,' added Mackaye, almost
audibly), — 'become the happy puppet of the universal impulse.
He who would honour Christ, let him become a Christ himself!
Theodore of Mopsuestia* — born, alas! before his time — a
prophet for whom as yet no audience stood ready in the
amphitheatre of souls — "Christ!" he was wont to say; "I can
become Christ myself, if I will." Become thou Christ, my
brother! He is an idea — the idea of utter submission — abnegation
of his own fancied will before the supreme necessities. Fulfil
that idea, and thou art He! Deny thyself, and then only wilt thou
be a reality; for thou hast no self. If thou hadst a self, thou
wouldst but lie in denying it — and would The Being thank
thee for denying what He had given thee? But thou hast none!
God is circumstance, and thou His creature! Be content! Fear
not, strive not, change not, repent not! Thou art nothing!
Be nothing, and thou becomest a part of all things!'

And so Mr. Windrush ended his discourse, which Crossthwaite
had been all the while busily taking down in short-hand, for
the edification of the readers of a certain periodical, and also
for those of this my Life.

I plead guilty to having been entirely carried away by what
I heard. There was so much which was true, so much more
which seemed true, so much which it would have been convenient to believe true, and all put so eloquently and originally,
as I then considered, that, in short, I was in raptures, and so
was poor dear Crossthwaite; and as we walked home, we dinned
Mr. Windrush's praises one into each of Mackaye's ears.
The old man, however, paced on silent and meditative. At last—

'A hunder sects or so in the land o' Gret Britain; an' a
hunder or so single preachers, each man a sect of his ain! an'
this the last fashion! Last indeed! The moon of Calvinism's far

gone in the fourth quarter, when it's come to the like o' that. Truly, the soul-saving business is a'thegither fa'n to a low ebb, as Master Tummas says somewhere!'*

'Well, but,' asked Crossthwaite, 'was not that man, at least, splendid?'

'An' hoo much o' thae gran' objectives an' subjectives did ye comprehen', then, Johnnie, my man?'

'Quite enough for me,' answered John, in a somewhat nettled tone.

'An' sae did I.'

'But you ought to hear him often. You can't judge of his system from one sermon, in this way.'

'Seestem! and what's that like?'

'Why, he has a plan for uniting all sects and parties, on the one broad fundamental ground of the unity of God as revealed by science——'

'Verra like uniting o' men by just pu'ing aff their claes, and telling 'em, "There, ye're a' brithers noo, on the one broad fundamental principle o' want o' breeks."'

'Of course,' went on Crossthwaite, without taking notice of this interruption, 'he allows full liberty of conscience. All he wishes for is the emancipation of intellect. He will allow every one, he says, to realize that idea to himself, by the representations which suit him best.'

'An' so he has no objection to a wee playing at Papistry, gin a man finds it good to tickle up his soul?'

'Ay, he did speak of that – what did he call it? Oh! "one of the ways in which the Christian idea naturally embodied itself in imaginative minds!" but the higher intellects, of course, would want fewer helps of that kind. "They would see –" ay, that was it – "the pure white light of truth, without requiring those coloured refracting media."'

'That wad depend muckle on whether the light o' truth chose or not – I'm thinking. But, Johnnie, lad – guide us and save us! – whaur got ye a' these gran' outlandish words the nicht?'

'Haven't I been taking down every one of these lectures for the press?'

'The press gang to the father o't – and you too, for lending your han' in the matter – for a mair accursed aristocrat I never heerd, sin' I first ate haggis. Oh, ye gowk – ye gowk! Dinna ye see what be the upshot o' siccan doctrine? That every puir fellow as has no gret brains in his head will be left to his superstition, an' his ignorance, to fulfil the lusts o' his flesh; while the few that are geniuses, or fancy themselves sae, are to ha' the monopoly o' this private still o' philosophy – these carbonari, illuminati, vehmgericht, samothracian* mysteries o' bottled moonshine. An' when that comes to pass, I'll just gang back to my schule and my catechism, and begin again wi' "who was born o' the Virgin Mary, suffered oonder Pontius Pilate"! Hech! lads, there's no subjectives and objectives there, na beggarly, windy abstractions, but joost a plain fact, that God cam' down to look for puir bodies, instead o' leaving puir bodies to gang looking for Him. An' here's a pretty place to be left looking for Him in – between gin-shops and gutters! A pretty gospel for the publicans an' harlots, to tell 'em that if their bairns are canny eneugh, they may possibly some day be allowed to believe that there is one God, and not twa! And then, by way of practical application – "Hech! my dear, starving, simple brothers, ye manna be sae owre conscientious, and gang fashing yourselves anent being brutes an' deevils, for the gude God's made ye sae, and He's verra weel content to see ye sae, gin ye be content or no." '

'Then, do you believe in the old doctrines of Christianity?' I asked.

'Dinna speir what I believe in. I canna tell ye. I've been seventy years trying to believe in God, and to meet anither man that believed in him. So I'm just like the Quaker o' the town o' Redcross, that met by himsel every First-day in his ain hoose.'

'Well, but,' I asked again, 'is not complete freedom of thought a glorious aim – to emancipate man's noblest part – the intellect – from the trammels of custom and ignorance?'

'Intellect – intellect!' rejoined he, according to his fashion, catching one up at a word, and playing on that in order to answer, not what one said, but what one's words led to. 'I'm sick o' all the talk anent intellect I hear noo. An' what's the use o' intellect? "Aristocracy o'intellect", they cry. Curse a' aristocracies – intellectual anes, as weel as anes o' birth, or rank,

or money! What! will I ca' a man my superior, because he's
cleverer than mysel? – will I boo down to a bit o' brains, ony
mair than to a stock or a stane? Let a man prove himsel' better
than me, my laddie – honester, humbler, kinder, wi' mair
sense o' the duty o' man, an' the weakness o' man – and that
man I'll acknowledge – that man's my king, my leader, though
he war as stupid as Eppe Dalgleish, that could na count five on
her fingers, and yet keepit her drucken father by her ain hands'
labour, for twenty-three yeers.'

We could not agree to all this, but we made a rule of never
contradicting the old sage in one of his excited moods, for fear
of bringing on a week's silent fit – a state which generally
ended in his smoking himself into a bilious melancholy; but
I made up my mind to be henceforth a frequent auditor of
Mr. Windrush's oratory.

'An' sae the deevil's dead!' said Sandy, half to himself, as he
sat crooning and smoking that night over the fire. 'Gone at last,
puir fallow! – an' he sae little appreciated, too! Every gowk
laying his ain sins on Nickie's back. Puir Nickie! – verra like
that much misunderstood politeecian, Mr. John Cade, as Charles
Buller ca'd him in the Hoose o' Commons* – an' he to be dead
at last! The warld 'll seem quite unco without his auld-farrant
phizog on the streets. Aweel, aweel – aiblins he's but sham-
min.'——

> When pleasant Spring came on apace,
>   And showers began to fa',
> John Barleycorn got up again,
>   And sore surprised them a'.*

At ony rate, I'd no bury him till he began smell a wee strong,
like. It's a grewsome thing, is premature interment, Alton,
laddie!'

CHAPTER XXIII

THE FREEDOM OF THE PRESS

But all this while, my slavery to Mr. O'Flynn's party-spirit and coarseness was becoming daily more and more intolerable: an explosion was inevitable; and an explosion came.

Mr. O'Flynn found out that I had been staying at Cambridge, and at a cathedral city too; and it was quite a godsend to him to find any one who knew a word about the institutions at which he had been railing weekly for years. So nothing would serve him, but my writing a set of articles on the Universities, as a prelude to one on the Cathedral Establishments. In vain I pleaded the shortness of my stay there, and the smallness of my information.

'Och, were not abuses notorious? And couldn't I get them up out of any Radical paper – and just put in a little of my own observations, and a dashing personal cut or two, to spice the thing up, and give it an original look? and if I did not choose to write that – why,' with an enormous oath, 'I should write nothing.' So – for I was growing weaker and weaker, and indeed my hack-writing was breaking down my moral sense, as it does that of most men – I complied; and burning with vexation, feeling myself almost guilty of a breach of trust toward those from whom I had received nothing but kindness, I scribbled off my first number and sent it to the editor – to see it appear next week, three-parts rewritten, and every fact of my own furnishing twisted and misapplied, till the whole thing was as vulgar and common-place a piece of rant as ever disgraced the people's cause. And all this, in spite of a solemn promise, confirmed by a volley of oaths, that I 'should say what I liked, and speak my whole mind, as one who had seen things with his own eyes had a right to do.'

Furious, I set off to the editor; and not only my pride, but what literary conscience I had left, was stirred to the bottom by seeing myself made, whether I would or not, a blackguard and a slanderer.

As it was ordained, Mr. O'Flynn was gone out for an hour

or two; and, unable to settle down to any work till I had fought my battle with him fairly out, I wandered onward towards the West-end, staring into print-shop windows, and meditating on many things.

As it was ordained, also, I turned up Regent-street, and into Langham-place; when, at the door of All-Souls Church, behold a crowd, and a long string of carriages arriving, and all the pomp and glory of a grand wedding.

I joined the crowd from mere idleness, and somehow found myself in the first rank, just as the bride was stepping out of the carriage – it was Miss Staunton; and the old gentleman who handed her out was no other than the dean. They were, of course, far too deeply engaged to recognize insignificant little me, so that I could stare as thoroughly to my heart's content as any of the butcher-boys and nursery-maids around me.

She was closely veiled – but not too closely to prevent my seeing her magnificent lip and nostril curling with pride, resolve, rich tender passion. Her glorious black-brown hair – the true 'purple locks' which Homer so often talks of* – rolled down beneath her veil in great heavy ringlets; and with her tall and rounded figure, and step as firm and queenly as if she were going to a throne, she seemed to me the very ideal of those magnificent Eastern Zubeydehs and Nourmahals,* whom I used to dream of after reading the 'Arabian Nights'.

As they entered the door-way, almost touching me, she looked round, as if for some one. The dean whispered something in his gentle, stately way, and she answered by one of those looks so intense, and yet so bright, so full of unutterable depths of meaning and emotion, that, in spite of all my antipathy, I felt an admiration akin to awe thrill through me, and gazed after her so intently, that Lillian – Lillian herself – was at my side, and almost passed me before I was aware of it.

Yes, there she was, the foremost among a bevy of fair girls, 'herself the fairest far',* all April smiles and tears, golden curls, snowy rosebuds, and hovering clouds of lace – a fairy queen; but yet – but yet – how shallow that hazel eye, how empty of meaning those delicate features, compared with the strength and intellectual richness of the face which had preceded her!

It was too true – I had never remarked it before; but now it flashed across me like lightning – and like lightning vanished; for Lillian's eye caught mine, and there was the faintest spark of a smile of recognition, and pleased surprise, and a nod. I blushed scarlet with delight; some servant-girl or other, who stood next to me, had seen it too – quick-eyed that women are – and was looking curiously at me. I turned, I know not why, in my delicious shame, and plunged through the crowd to hide I knew not what.

I walked on – poor fool! – in an extacy; the whole world was transfigured in my eyes, and virtue and wisdom beamed from every face I passed. The omnibus-horses were racers, and the drivers – were they not my brothers of the people? The very policemen looked sprightly and philanthropic. I shook hands earnestly with the crossing-sweeper of the Regent-circus, gave him my last two-pence, and rushed on, like a young David, to exterminate that Philistine O'Flynn.

Ah well! I was a great fool, as others too have been; but yet, that little chance-meeting did really raise me. It made me sensible that I was made for better things than low abuse of the higher classes. It gave me courage to speak out, and act without fear of consequences, once at least in that confused facing-both-ways period of my life. O woman! woman! only true missionary of civilization and brotherhood, and gentle, forgiving charity; it is in thy power, and perhaps in thine only, to bind up the broken-hearted, to preach deliverance to the captives!* One real lady, who should dare to stoop, what might she not do with us – with our sisters? If——

There are hundreds, answers the reader, who do stoop. Elizabeth Fry* was a lady, well-born, rich, educated, and she has many scholars.

True, my dear readers, true – and may God bless her and her scholars. Do you think the working men forget them? But look at St. Giles's, or Spitalfields, or Shadwell, and say, is not the harvest plentiful, and the labourers, alas! few? No one asserts that nothing is done; the question is, is enough done? Does the supply of mercy meet the demand of misery? Walk into the next court and see!

*

I found Mr. O'Flynn in his sanctum, busy with paste and scissors, in the act of putting in a string of advertisements – indecent French novels, Atheistic tracts, quack medicines, and slopsellers' puffs; and commenced with as much dignity as I could muster.

'What on earth, do you mean, sir, by re-writing my article?'

'What – (in the other place) – do you mean by giving me the trouble of re-writing it? Me head's splitting now with sitting up, cutting out, and putting in. Poker o' Moses! but ye'd given it an intirely aristocratic tendency. What did ye mane' (and three or four oaths rattled out) 'by talking about the pious intentions of the original founders, and the democratic tendencies of monistic establishments?'

'I wrote it because I thought it.'

'Is that any reason ye should write it? And there was another bit, too – it made my hair stand on end when I saw it, to think how near I was sending the copy to press without looking at it – something about a French Socialist, and Church Property.'

'Oh! you mean, I suppose, the story of the French Socialist, who told me that church property was just the only property in England which he would spare, because it was the only one which had definite duties attached to it; that the real devourers of the people were not the bishops, who, however rich, were at least bound to work in return for their riches, but the landlords and millionaires, who refused to confess the duties of property, while they raved about its rights.'

'Bedad, that's it; and pretty doctrine, too!'

'But it's true: it's an entirely new, and a very striking notion, and I consider it my duty to mention it.'

'Thrue! What the devil does that matter? There's a time to speak the truth, and a time not, isn't there? It'll make a grand hit, now, in a leader upon the Irish Church question, to back the prastes against the landlords. But if I'd let that in as it stood, bedad, I'd have lost three parts of my subscribers the next week. Every soul of the Independents, let alone the Chartists, would have bid me good morning. Now do, like a good boy, give us something more the right thing next time. Draw it strong. – A good drunken supper-party and a police row; if ye

haven't seen one, get it up out of Pater Priggins – or Laver*
might do, if the other wasn't convanient. That's Dublin to be
sure, but one university's just like another. And give us a
seduction or two, and a brace of Dons carried home drunk from
Barnwell* by the Procthors.'

'Really I never saw anything of the kind; and as for profligacy
amongst the Dons, I don't believe it exists. I'll call them idle,
and bigoted, and careless of the morals of the young men,
because I know that they are so; but as for anything more,
I believe them to be as sober, respectable a set of Pharisees as
the world ever saw.'

Mr. O'Flynn was waxing warm, and the bully-vein began
fast to show itself.

'I don't care a curse, sir! My subscribers won't stand it, and
they shan't! I am a man of business, sir, and a man of the world,
sir, and faith that's more than you are, and I know what will
sell the paper, and by J——s I'll let no upstart spalpeen* dictate
to me!'

'Then I'll tell you what, sir,' quoth I, waxing warm in my
turn, 'I don't know which are the greater rogues, you or your
subscribers. You a patriot! You are a humbug. Look at those
advertisements, and deny it if you can. Crying out for education, and helping to debauch the public mind with Voltaire's
"Candide", and Eugène Sue* – swearing by Jesus, and puffing
Atheism and blasphemy – yelling at a quack government, quack
law, quack priesthoods, and then dirtying your fingers with
half-crowns for advertising Holloway's ointment, and Parr's life
pills* – shrieking about slavery of labour to capital, and inserting Moses & Son's doggrel* – ranting about searching investi-
gations and the march of knowledge, and concealing every fact
which cannot be made to pander to the passions of your dupes –
extolling the freedom of the press, and showing yourself in your
own office a tyrant and a censor of the press. You a patriot!
You the people's friend! You are doing everything in your
power to blacken the people's cause in the eyes of their enemies.
You are simply a humbug, a hypocrite, and a scoundrel; and
so I bid you good morning.'

Mr. O'Flynn had stood, during this harangue, speechless
with passion, those loose lips of his wreathing like a pair of

earthworms. It was only when I stopped that he regained his breath, and with a volley of incoherent oaths, caught up his chair and hurled it at my head. Luckily, I had seen enough of his temper already, to keep my hand on the lock of the door for the last five minutes. I darted out of the room quicker than I ever did out of one before or since. The chair took effect on the luckless door; and as I threw a flying glance behind me, I saw one leg sticking through the middle pannel, in a way that augured ill for my skull, had it been in the way of Mr. O'Flynn's fury.

I ran home to Mackaye in a state of intense self-glorification, and told him the whole story. He chuckled, he crowed, he hugged me to his bosom.

'Leeze me o' ye! but I kenned ye were o' the true Norse blude after a'!

> For a' that, an' a' that,
> A man's a man for a' that.

Oh, but I hae expeckit it this month an' mair! Oh, but I prophesied it, Johnnie!'

'Then, why in Heaven's name did you introduce me to such a scoundrel?'

'I sent ye to schule, lad, I sent ye to schule. Ye wad na be ruled by me. Ye tuk me for a puir doited* auld misanthrope; an' I thocht to gie ye the meat ye lusted after, an' fill ye wi' the fruit o' your ain desires. An' noo that ye've gane doon into the fire o' temptation, an' conquered, here's your reward standin' ready. Special prawvidences! – wha can doot them? I ha' had mony – miracles I might ca' them, to see how they cam' just when I was gaun daft wi' despair.'

And then he told me that the editor of a popular journal, of the Howitt and Eliza Cook school,* had called on me that morning, and promised me work enough, and pay enough, to meet all present difficulties.

I did indeed accept the curious coincidence, if not as a reward for an act of straightforwardness, in which I saw no merit, at least, as proof that the upper powers had not altogether forgotten me. I found both the editor and his periodical, as I should have wished them, temperate and sunny – somewhat clap-trap and sentimental, perhaps, and afraid of speaking out, as all parties are, but still willing to allow my fancy free range in light fictions, descriptions of foreign countries, scraps of showy rose-pink morality, and such like; which, though they had no more power against the raging mass of crime, misery, and discontent, around, than a peacock's feather against a three-decker, still were all genial, graceful, kindly, humanizing, and soothed my discontented and impatient heart in the work of composition.

CHAPTER XXIV

THE TOWNSMAN'S SERMON TO THE GOWN'SMAN

ONE morning in February, a few days after this explosion, I was on the point of starting to go to the dean's house about that weary list of subscribers, which seemed destined never to be filled up, when my cousin George burst in upon me. He was in the highest good spirits at having just taken a double first-class at Cambridge; and after my congratulations, sincere and hearty enough, were over, he offered to accompany me to that reverend gentleman's house.

He said, in an off-hand way, that he had no particular business there, but he thought it just as well to call on the dean and mention his success, in case the old fellow should not have heard of it.

'For you see,' he said, 'I'm a sort of *protégé*, both on my own account and on Lord Lynedale's – Ellerton, he is now – you know he's just married to the dean's niece, Miss Staunton – and Ellerton's a capital fellow – promised me a living as soon as I'm in priest's orders. So my cue is now,' he went on as we walked down the Strand together, 'to get ordained as fast as ever I can.'

'But,' I asked, 'have you read much for ordination, or seen much of what a clergyman's work should be?'

'Oh! as for that – you know it isn't one out of ten who's ever entered a school, or a cottage even, except to light his cigar, before he goes into the church: and as for the examination, that's all humbug; any man may cram it all up in a month –

and thanks to King's College, I knew all I wanted to know before I went to Cambridge. And I shall be three-and-twenty by Trinity Sunday, and then in I go, neck or nothing. Only the confounded bore is, that this Bishop of London won't give one a title – won't let any man into his diocese, who has not been ordained two years; and so I shall be shoved down into some poking little country-curacy, without a chance of making play before the world, or getting myself known at all. Horrid bore! isn't it?'

'I think,' I said, 'considering what London is just now, the bishop's regulation seems to be one of the best specimens of episcopal wisdom that I've heard of for some time.'

'Great bore for me, though, all the same; for I must make a name, I can tell you, if I intend to get on. A person must work like a horse now-a-days, to succeed at all; and Lynedale's a desperately particular fellow, with all sorts of *outré* notions about people's duties and vocations and heaven knows what.'

'Well,' I said, 'my dear cousin, and have you no high notions of a clergyman's vocation? because we – I mean the working men – have. It's just their high idea of what a clergyman should be, which makes them so furious at clergymen for being what they are.'

'It's a queer way of showing their respect to the priesthood,' he answered, 'to do all they can to exterminate it.'

'I dare say they are liable, like other men, to confound the thing with its abuses, but if they hadn't some dim notion that the thing might be made a good thing in itself, you may depend upon it they would not rave against those abuses so fiercely.' (The reader may see that I had not forgotten my conversation with Miss Staunton.) 'And,' thought I to myself, 'is it not you, and such as you, who do so incorporate the abuses into the system, that one really cannot tell which is which, and longs to shove the whole thing aside as rotten to the core, and make a trial of something new?'

'Well, but,' I said, again returning to the charge, for the subject was altogether curious and interesting to me, 'do you really believe the doctrines of the Prayer-book, George?'

'Believe them!' he answered, in a tone of astonishment, 'why not? I was brought up a Churchman, whatever my parents were; I was always intended for the ministry. I'd sign the Thirty-nine Articles now, against any man in the three kingdoms; and as for all the proofs out of Scripture and Church History, I've known them ever since I was sixteen – I'll get them all up again in a week as fresh as ever.'

'But,' I rejoined, astonished in my turn at my cousin's notion of what belief was, 'have you any personal faith? – you know what I mean – I hate using cant words – but inward experience of the truth of all these great ideas, which, true or false, you will have to preach and teach? Would you live by them, die for them, as a patriot would for his country, now?'

'My dear fellow, I don't know anything about all those Methodistical, mystical, Calvinistical, inward experiences, and all that. I'm a Churchman, remember, and a High Churchman, too; and the doctrine of the Church is, that children are regenerated in holy baptism; and there's not the least doubt, from the authority both of Scripture and the fathers, that that's the——.'

'For heaven's sake,' I said, 'no polemical discussions! Whether you're right or wrong, that's not what I'm talking about. What I want to know is this:—You are going to teach people about God and Jesus Christ. Do you delight in God? Do you love Jesus Christ? Never mind what I do, or think, or believe. What do you do, George?'

'Well, my dear fellow, if you take things in that way, you know, of course—' and he dropped his voice into that peculiar tone, by which all sects seem to think they show their reverence; while to me, as to most other working men, it never seemed anything but a symbol of the separation and discrepancy between their daily thoughts and their religious ones – 'of course, we don't any of us think of these things half enough, and I'm sure I wish I could be more earnest than I am; but I can only hope it will come in time. The Church holds that there's a grace given in ordination; and really – really, I do hope and wish to do my duty – indeed, one can't help doing it; one is so pushed on by the immense competition for preferment; an idle parson hasn't a chance now-a-days.'

'But,' I asked again, half-laughing, half-disgusted, 'do you know what your duty is?'

'Bless you, my good fellow, a man can't go wrong there. Carry out the Church-system; that's the thing – all laid down by rule and method. A man has but to work out that – and it's the only one for the lower classes, I'm convinced.'

'Strange,' I said, 'that they have from the first been so little of that opinion, but every attempt to enforce it, for the last three hundred years, has ended either in persecution or revolution.'

'Ah! that was all those vile puritans' fault. They wouldn't give the Church a chance of showing her powers.'

'What! not when she had it all her own way, during the whole eighteenth century?'

'Ah! but things are very different now. The clergy are awakened now to the real beauty of the Catholic machinery; and you have no notion how much is doing in church-building, and schools, and societies of every sort and kind. It is quite incredible what is being done now for the lower orders by the Church.'

'I believe,' I said, 'that the clergy are exceedingly improved; and I believe, too, that the men to whom they owe all their improvement, are the Wesleys, and Whitfields* – in short, the very men whom they drove one by one out of the Church, from persecution or disgust. And I do think it strange, that if so much is doing for the lower classes, the working men, who form the mass of the lower classes, are just those who scarcely feel the effects of it; while the churches seem to me filled with children, and rich and respectable, to the almost entire exclusion of the adult lower classes. A strange religion this!' I went on, 'and, to judge by its effects, a very different one from that preached in Judea eighteen hundred years ago, if we are to believe the Gospel story.'

'What on earth do you mean? Is not the Church of England the very purest form of Apostolic Christianity?'

'It may be – and so may the other sects. But, somehow, in Judea, it was the publicans and harlots who pressed into the kingdom of heaven; it was the common people who heard Christ gladly. Christianity, then, was a movement in the hearts of the lower order. But now, my dear fellow, you rich, who used to be told, in St. James's time, to weep and howl,* have turned the tables upon us poor. It is *you* who are talking, all

day long, of converting *us*. Look at any place of worship you like, orthodox and heretical. — Who fill the pews? – the outcast and the reprobate? No! – the Pharisees and the covetous, who used to deride Christ, fill His churches, and say still "This people, these masses, who know not the Gospel, are accursed."*
And the universal feeling, as far as I can judge, seems to be, not "how hardly shall they who have", but how hardly shall they who have *not*, "riches, enter into the kingdom of heaven"!*

'Upon my word,' said he, laughing, 'I did not give you credit for so much eloquence: you seem to have studied the Bible to some purpose, too. I didn't think that so much Radicalism could be squeezed out of a few texts of Scripture. It's quite a new light to me. I'll just mark that card, and play it when I get a convenient opportunity. It may be a winning one in these democratic times.'

And he did play it, as I heard hereafter; but at present he seemed to think, that the less that was said further on clerical subjects the better, and commenced quizzing the people whom we passed, humorously and neatly enough; while I walked on in silence, and thought of Mr. Bye-Ends,* in the 'Pilgrim's Progress'. And yet I believe the man was really in earnest. He was really desirous to do what was right, as far as he knew it; and all the more desirous, because he saw in the present state of society, what was right would pay him. God shall judge him, not I. Who can unravel the confusion of mingled selfishness and devotion that exists even in his own heart, much less in that of another?

The dean was not at home that day, having left town on business. George nodded familiarly to the footman who opened the door.

'You'll mind and send me word the moment your master comes home – mind, now!'

The fellow promised obedience, and we walked away.

'You seem to be very intimate here,' said I, 'with all parties?'

'Oh! footmen are useful animals – a half-sovereign now and then is not altogether thrown away upon them. But as for the higher powers, it is very easy to make oneself at home in the dean's study, but not so much so to get a footing in the drawing-room above. I suspect he keeps a precious sharp eye upon the fair Miss Lillian.'

'But,' I asked, as a jealous pang shot through my heart, 'how did you contrive to get this same footing at all? When I met you at Cambridge, you seemed already well acquainted with these people.'

'How? – how does a hound get a footing on a cold scent? By working and casting about and about, and drawing on it inch by inch, as I drew on them for years, my boy; and cold enough the scent was. You recollect that day at the Dulwich Gallery? I tried to see the arms on the carriage, but there were none; so that cock wouldn't fight.'

'The arms! I should never have thought of such a plan.'

'Dare say you wouldn't. Then I harked back to the door-keeper, while you were St. Sebastianizing. He didn't know their names, or didn't choose to show me their ticket, on which it ought to have been; so I went to one of the fellows whom I knew, and got him to find out. There comes out the value of money – for money makes acquaintances. Well, I found who they were. – Then I saw no chance of getting at them. But for the rest of that year, at Trinity, I beat every bush in the University, to find some one who knew them; and as fortune favours the brave, at last I hit off this Lord Lynedale; and he, of course, was the ace of trumps – a fine catch in himself, and a double catch, because he was going to marry the cousin. So I made a dead set at him; and tight work I had to nab him, I can tell you, for he was three or four years older than I, and had travelled a good deal, and seen life. But every man has his weak side; and I found his was a sort of a High-Church Radicalism, and that suited me well enough, for I was always a deuce of a radical myself; so I stuck to him like a leech, and stood all his temper, and his pride, and those unpractical, windy visions of his, that made a common-sense fellow like me sick to listen to; but I stood it, and here I am.'

'And what on earth induced you to stoop to all this——' meanness I was on the point of saying. 'Surely you are in no want of money – your father could buy you a good living to-morrow.'

'And he will, but not the one I want; and he could not buy me reputation, power, rank, do you see, Alton, my genius?

And what's more, he couldn't buy me a certain little tit-bit, a jewel, worth a Jew's-eye and a half, Alton, that I set my heart on from the first moment I set my eye on it.'

My heart beat fast and fierce, but he ran on—

'Do you think I'd have eaten all this dirt, if it hadn't lain in my way to her? Eat dirt! I'd drink blood, Alton – though I don't often deal in strong words – if it lay in that road. I never set my heart on the thing yet, that I didn't get it at last by fair means or foul – and I'll get her! I don't care for her money, though that's a pretty plum. – Upon my life, I don't. I worship her, limbs and eyes. – I worship the very ground she treads on. She's a duck and a darling,' said he, smacking his lips like an ogre over his prey, 'and I'll have her before I've done, so help me——'

'Whom do you mean?' I stammered out.

'Lillian! you blind beetle!'

I dropped his arm – 'Never, as I live!'

He started back, and burst into a horse laugh.

'Hullo! my eye and Betty Martin! You don't mean to say that I have the honour of finding a rival in my talented cousin?'

I made no answer.

'Come, come, my dear fellow, this is too ridiculous. You and I are very good friends, and we may help each other, if we choose, like kith and kin in this here wale. So if you're fool enough to quarrel with me, I warn you I'm not fool enough to return the compliment. Only' (lowering his voice), 'just bear one little thing in mind – that I am, unfortunately, of a some-what determined humour; and if folks will get in my way, why it's not my fault if I drive over them. You understand? Well, if you intend to be sulky, I don't. So good morning, till you feel yourself better.'

And he turned gaily down a side-street, and disappeared, looking taller, handsomer, manfuller than ever.

I returned home miserable; I now saw in my cousin, not merely a rival, but a tyrant: and I began to hate him with that bitterness which fear alone can inspire. The eleven pounds still remained unpaid. Between three and four pounds was the utmost which I had been able to hoard up that autumn, by dint of scribbling and stinting; there was no chance of profit from my book for months to come – if indeed it ever got published, which I hardly dare believe it would; and I knew him too well to doubt that neither pity nor delicacy would restrain him from using his power over me, if I dared even to seem an obstacle in his way.

I tried to write, but could not. I found it impossible to direct my thoughts, even to sit still; a vague spectre of terror and degradation crushed me. Day after day I sat over the fire, and jumped up and went into the shop, to find something which I did not want, and peep listlessly into a dozen books, one after the other, and then wandered back again to the fireside, to sit mooning and moping, staring at that horrible incubus of debt – a devil which may give mad strength to the strong, but only paralyzes the weak. And I was weak, as every poet is, more or less. There was in me, as I have somewhere read that there is in all poets, that feminine vein – a receptive as well as a creative faculty – which kept up in me a continual thirst after beauty, rest, enjoyment. And here was circumstance after circumstance goading me onward, as the gadfly did Io,* to continual wander-ings, never ceasing exertions; every hour calling on me to do, while I was only longing to be – to sit and observe, and fancy, and build freely at my own will. And then – as if this necessity of perpetual petty exertion was not in itself sufficient torment – to have that accursed debt – that knowledge that I was in a rival's power, rising up like a black wall before me, to cripple, and render hopeless, for aught I knew, the very exertions to which it compelled me! I hated the bustle – the crowds, the ceaseless roar of the street outside maddened me. I longed in vain for peace – for one day's freedom – to be one hour a shepherd-boy, and lie looking up at the blue sky, without a thought beyond the rushes I was plaiting! 'Oh, that I had wings as a dove! – then would I flee away, and be at rest!'*——

And then, more than once, or twice either, the thoughts of suicide crossed me; and I turned it over, and looked at it, and dallied with it, as a last chance in reserve. And then the thought of Lillian came, and drove away the fiend. And then the thought of my cousin came, and paralyzed me again; for it told me that one hope was impossible. And then some fresh instance of misery or oppression forced itself upon me, and made me feel the awful sacredness of my calling, as a champion of the poor, and the base cowardice of deserting them for any selfish love of rest. And then I recollected how I had betrayed my suffering brothers. – How, for the sake of vanity and patronage, I had consented to hide the truth about their rights – their wrongs. And so on, through weary weeks of moping melancholy – 'a double-minded man, unstable in all his ways'!*

At last, Mackaye, who, as I found afterwards, had been watching all along my altered mood, contrived to worm my secret out of me. I had dreaded, that whole autumn, having to tell him the truth, because I knew that his first impulse would be to pay the money instantly out of his own pocket; and my pride, as well as my sense of justice, revolted at that, and sealed my lips. But now this fresh discovery – the knowledge that it was not only in my cousin's power to crush me, but also his interest to do so – had utterly unmanned me; and, after a little innocent and fruitless prevarication, out came the truth, with tears of bitter shame.

The old man pursed up his lips, and, without answering me, opened his table drawer, and commenced fumbling among accounts and papers.

'No! no! no! best, noblest of friends! I will not burden you with the fruits of my own vanity and extravagance. I will starve, go to gaol, sooner than take your money. If you offer it me, I will leave the house, bag and baggage, this moment.' And I rose to put my threat into execution.

'I havena at present ony sic intention,' answered he, deliberately; 'seeing that there's na necessity for paying debits twice owre, when ye ha' the stampt receipt for them.' And he put into my hands, to my astonishment and rapture, a receipt in full for the money, signed by my cousin.

Not daring to believe my own eyes, I turned it over and over, looked at it, looked at him – there was nothing but clear, smiling assurance in his beloved old face, as he twinkled, and winked, and chuckled, and pulled off his spectacles, and wiped them, and put them on upside-down; and then relieved himself by rushing at his pipe, and cramming it fiercely with tobacco till he burst the bowl.

Yes, it was no dream! – the money was paid, and I was free!

The sudden relief was as intolerable as the long burden had been; and, like a prisoner suddenly loosed from off the rack, my whole spirit seemed to collapse, and I sunk with my head upon the table, too faint even for gratitude.

*

But who was my benefactor? Mackaye vouchsafed no answer, but that I 'suld ken better than he.' But when he found that I was really utterly at a loss to whom to attribute the mercy, he assured me, by way of comfort, that he was just as ignorant as myself; and at last, piecemeal, in his circumlocutory and cautious Scotch method, informed me, that some six weeks back he had received an anonymous letter, 'a'thegither o' a Belgravian cast o' phizog,' containing a bank-note for twenty pounds, and setting forth the writer's suspicions that I owed my cousin money, and their desire that Mr. Mackaye 'o' whose uprightness an' generosity they were pleased to confess themselves no that ignorant,' should write to George, ascertain the sum, and pay it without my knowledge, handing over the balance, if any, to me, when he thought fit – 'Sae there's the remnant – aucht pounds, sax shillings, an' saxpence; tippence being deduckit for expense o' twa letters, anent the same transaction.'

'But what sort of handwriting was it?' asked I, almost disregarding the welcome coin.

'Ou, then – aiblins a man's, aiblins a maid's. He was na chirographosophic himsel' – an' he had na curiosity anent ony sic passages o' aristocratic romance.'

'But what was the post-mark of the letter?'

'Why for suld I ha' speired? Gin the writers had been minded to be beknown, they'd ha' sign't their names upon the document. An' gin they didna sae intend, wad it be coorteous o' me to gang speiring an' peering ower covers an' seals?'

'But where is the cover?'

'Ou, then,' he went on, with the same provoking coolness, 'white paper's o' geyan use, in various operations o' the domestic economy. Sae I just tare it up – aiblins for pipe-lights – I canna mind at this time.'

'And why –' asked I, more vexed and disappointed than I liked to confess – 'why did you not tell me before?'

'How wad I ken that you had need o't? An' verily, I thocht it no that bad a lesson for ye, to let ye experiment a towmond mair on the precious balms that break the head* – whereby I opine the psalmist was minded to denote the delights o' spending borrowed siller.'

There was nothing more to be extracted from him; so I was fain to set to work again (a pleasant compulsion truly) with a free heart, eight pounds in my pocket, and a brainful of con- jectures. Was it the dean? Lord Lynedale? or was it – could it be – Lillian herself? That thought was so delicious, that I made up my mind, as I had free choice among half-a-dozen equally improbable fancies, to determine that the most pleasant should be the true one; and I hoarded the money, which I shrunk from spending as much as I should from selling her miniature or a lock of her beloved golden hair. They were a gift from her – a pledge – the first fruits of – I dared not confess to myself what.

Whereat the reader will smile, and say, not without reason, that I was fast fitting myself for Bedlam;* if indeed, I had not proved my fitness for it already, by paying the tailors' debts, instead of my own, with the ten pounds which Farmer Porter had given me. I am not sure that he would not be correct, but so I did, and so I suffered.

CHAPTER XXV

A TRUE NOBLEMAN

At last my list of subscribers was completed, and my poems actually in the press. Oh! the childish joy with which I fondled my first set of proofs! And how much finer the words looked in print than they ever did in manuscript! – One took in the idea of a whole page so charmingly at a glance, instead of having to feel one's way through line after line, and sentence after sentence. – There was only one drawback to my happiness – Mackaye did not seem to sympathise with it. He had never grumbled at what I considered, and still do consider, my cardinal offence, the omission of the strong political passages; he seemed, on the contrary, in his inexplicable waywardness, to be rather pleased at it than otherwise. It was my publishing at all at which he growled.

'Ech,' he said, 'owre young to marry, is owre young to write; but it's the way o' these puir distract times. Nae chick can find a grain o' corn, but oot he rins cackling wi' the shell on his head, to tell it to a' the warld, as if there was never barley grown on the face o' the earth before. I wonder whether Isaiah began to write before his beard was grown, or Dawvid either? He had mony a long year o' shepherding an' moss-trooping, an' rugging an' riving i' the wilderness, I'll warrant, afore he got thae gran' lyrics o' his oot o' him. Ye might tak' example too, gin ye were minded, by Moses, the man o' God, that was joost forty years at the learning o' the Egyptians, afore he thocht gude to come forward into public life, an' then fun', to his gran' surprise, I warrant, that he'd begun forty years too sune – an' then had forty years mair, after that, o' marching an' law-giving, an' bearing the burdens o' the people, before he turned poet.'

'Poet, sir! I never saw Moses in that light before.'

'Then ye'll just read the 90th Psalm – "the prayer o' Moses, the man o' God" – the grandest piece o' lyric, to my taste, that I ever heard o' on the face o' God's earth, an' see what a man can write that'll have the patience to wait a century or twa before he rins to the publisher's. I gie ye up fra' this moment; the letting out o' ink is like the letting out o' waters, or the eating o' opium, or the getting up at public meetings. – When a man begins he canna stop. There's nae mair enslaving lust o' the flesh under the heaven than that same *furor scribendi*, as the Latins hae it.'

But at last my poems were printed, and bound, and actually published; and I sat staring at a book of my own making, and wondering how it ever got into being! And what was more, the book 'took', and sold, and was reviewed in People's journals, and in newspapers; and Mackaye himself relaxed into a grin, when his oracle, the *Spectator*,* the only honest paper, according to him, on the face of the earth, condescended, after asserting its impartiality by two or three searching sarcasms, to dismiss me, grimly-benignant, with a paternal pat on the shoulder. Yes – I was a real live author at last, and signed myself, by special request, in the * * * Magazine, as 'the author of Songs of the Highways'. At last it struck me, and Mackaye too, who, however he hated flunkeydom, never overlooked an act of discourtesy, that it would be right for me to call upon the dean, and thank him formally for all the real kindness he had shown me. So I went to the handsome house off Harley-street, and was shown into his study, and saw my own book lying on the table; and was welcomed by the good old man, and congratulated on my success, and asked if I did not see my own wisdom in 'yielding to more experienced opinions than my own, and submitting to a censorship which, however severe it might have appeared at first, was, as the event proved, benignant both in its intentions and effects?'

And then I was asked, even I, to breakfast there the next morning. And I went, and found no one there but some scientific gentlemen, to whom I was introduced as 'the young man whose poems we were talking of last night.' And Lillian sat at the head of the table, and poured out the coffee and tea. And between extacy at seeing her, and the intense relief of not finding my dreaded and now hated cousin there, I sat in a delirium of silent joy, stealing glances at her beauty, and listening with all my ears to the conversation, which turned upon the new-married couple.

I heard endless praises, to which I could not but assent in silence, of Lord Ellerton's perfections. His very personal appearance had been enough to captivate my fancy; and then they went on to talk of his magnificent philanthropic schemes, and his deep sense of the high duties of a landlord; and how finding himself, at his father's death, the possessor of two vast but neglected estates, he had sold one in order to be able to do justice to the other, instead of laying house to house, and field to field, like most of his compeers, 'till he stood alone in the land, and there was no place left';* and how he had lowered his rents, even though it had forced him to put down the ancestral pack of hounds, and live in a corner of the old castle; and how he was draining, claying, breaking up old moorlands, and building churches, and endowing schools, and improving cottages; and how he was expelling the old ignorant bankrupt race of farmers, and advertising everywhere for men of capital,

and science, and character. who would have courage to cultivate
flax and silk, and try every species of experiment; and how he
had one scientific farmer after another, staying in his house as
a friend; and how he had numbers of his books re-bound in
plain covers, that he might lend them to every one on his
estate who wished to read them; and how he had thrown
open his picture-gallery, not only to the inhabitants of the neighbouring town, but what (strange to say) seemed to strike the
party as still more remarkable, to the labourers of his own
village; and how he was at that moment busy transforming an
old unoccupied manor-house into a great associate-farm, in
which all the labourers were to live under one roof, with a
common kitchen and dining-hall, clerks and superintendants,
whom they were to choose, subject only to his approval, and all
of them, from the least to the greatest, have their own interest
in the farm, and be paid by per-centage on the profits; and how
he had one of the first political economists of the day staying
with him, in order to work out for him tables of proportionate
remuneration, applicable to such an agricultural establishment;
and how, too, he was giving the spade-labour system a fair trial,
by laying out small cottage-farms, on rocky knolls and sides of
glens, too steep to be cultivated by the plough; and was locating
on them the most intelligent artisans whom he could draft from
the manufacturing town hard by——

And at that notion, my brain grew giddy with the hope of
seeing myself one day in one of those same cottages, tilling the
earth, under God's sky, and perhaps——and then a whole
cloud-world of love, freedom, fame, simple, graceful country
luxury steamed up across my brain, to end – not, like the man's
in the 'Arabian Nights',* in my kicking over the tray of
China, which formed the base-point of my inverted pyramid of
hope – but in my finding the contents of my plate deposited in
my lap, while I was gazing fixedly at Lillian.

I must say for myself, though, that such accidents happened
seldom; whether it was bashfulness, or the tact which generally,
I believe, accompanies a weak and nervous body, and an
active mind; or whether it was that I possessed enough relationship to the monkey-tribe to make me a first-rate mimic, I used
to get tolerably well through on these occasions, by acting on

the golden rule of never doing anything which I had not seen some one else do first – a rule which never brought me into any greater scrape than swallowing something intolerably hot, sour, and nasty (whereof I never discovered the name), because I had seen the dean do so a moment before.

But one thing struck me through the whole of this conversation – the way in which the new-married Lady Ellerton was spoken of, as aiding, encouraging, originating – a help-meet, if not an oracular guide, for her husband – in all these noble plans. She had already acquainted herself with every woman on the estate; she was the dispenser, not merely of alms, for those seemed a disagreeable necessity, from which Lord Ellerton was anxious to escape as soon as possible, but of advice, comfort, and encouragement. She not only visited the sick, and taught in the schools – avocations which, thank God, I have reason to believe are matters of course, not only in the families of clergymen, but those of most squires and noblemen, when they reside on their estates – but seemed, from the hints which I gathered, to be utterly devoted, body and soul, to the welfare of the dwellers on her husband's land.

'I had no notion,' I dared at last to remark, humbly enough, 'that Miss – Lady Ellerton cared so much for the people.'

'Really! One feels inclined sometimes to wish that she cared for anything beside them,' said Lillian, half to her father and half to me.

This gave a fresh shake to my estimate of that remarkable woman's character. But still, who could be prouder, more imperious, more abrupt in manner, harsh even to the very verge of good-breeding? (for I had learnt what good-breeding was, from the debating society as well as from the drawing-room); and, above all, had she not tried to keep me from Lillian? But these cloudy thoughts melted rapidly away in that sunny atmosphere of success and happiness, and I went home as merry as a bird, and wrote all the morning more gracefully and sportively, as I fancied, than I had ever yet done.

But my bliss did not end here. In a week or so, behold one morning a note – written, indeed, by the dean – but directed in Lillian's own hand, inviting me to come there to tea, that I might see a few of the literary characters of the day.

I covered the envelope with kisses, and thrust it next my fluttering heart. I then proudly showed the note to Mackaye. He looked pleased, yet pensive, and then broke out with a fresh adaptation of his favourite song,

——and shovel hats and a' that—
A man's a man for a' that.

'The auld gentleman is a man and a gentleman; an' has made a verra courteous, an' weel considerit move, gin ye ha' the sense to profit by it, an' no' turn it to yer ain destruction.'

'Destruction?'

'Ay – that's the word, an' nothing less, laddie!'

And he went into the outer shop, and returned with a volume of Bulwer's 'Ernest Maltravers'.

'What! are you a novel reader, Mr. Mackaye?'

'How do ye ken what I may ha' thocht gude to read in my time? Ye'll be pleased the noo to sit down an' begin at that page – an' read, mark, learn, an' inwardly digest, the history of Castruccio Cesarini* – an' the gude God gie ye grace to lay the same to heart.'

I read that fearful story; and my heart sunk, and my eyes were full of tears, long ere I had finished it. Suddenly I looked up at Mackaye, half angry at the pointed allusion to my own case.

The old man was watching me intently, with folded hands, and a smile of solemn interest and affection worthy of Socrates himself. He turned his head as I looked up, but his lips kept moving. I fancied, I know not why, that he was praying for me.

CHAPTER XXVI

THE TRIUMPHANT AUTHOR

So to the party I went, and had the delight of seeing and hearing the men with whose names I had been long acquainted, as the leaders of scientific discovery in this wondrous age; and more than one poet, too, over whose works I had gloated, whom

I had worshipped in secret. Intense was the pleasure of now realising to myself, as living men, wearing the same flesh and blood as myself, the names which had been to me mythic ideas. Lillian was there among them, more exquisite than ever; but even she at first attracted my eyes and thoughts less than did the truly great men around her. I hung on every word they spoke, I watched every gesture, as if they must have some deep significance; the very way in which they drank their coffee was a matter of interest to me. I was almost disappointed to see them eat and chat like common men. I expected that pearls and diamonds would drop from their lips, as they did from those of the girl in the fairy-tale,* every time they opened their mouths; and certainly the conversation that evening was a new world to me – though I could only, of course, be a listener. Indeed, I wished to be nothing more. I felt that I was taking my place there among the holy guild of authors – that I too, however humbly, had a thing to say, and had said it; and I was content to sit on the lowest step of the literary temple, without envy for those elder and more practised priests of wisdom, who had earned by long labour the freedom of the inner shrine. I should have been quite happy enough standing there, looking and listening – but I was at last forced to come forward. Lillian was busy chatting with grave, grey-headed men, who seemed as ready to flirt, and pet and admire the lovely little fairy, as if they had been as young and gay as herself. It was enough for me to see her appreciated and admired. I loved them for smiling on her, for handing her from her seat to the piano with reverent courtesy: gladly would I have taken their place: I was content, however, to be only a spectator; for it was not my rank, but my youth, I was glad to fancy, which denied me that blissful honour. But as she sang, I could not help stealing up to the piano; and, feasting my greedy eyes with every motion of those delicious lips, listen and listen, entranced, and living only in that melody.

Suddenly, after singing two or three songs, she began fingering the keys, and struck into an old air, wild and plaintive, rising and falling like the swell of an Æolian harp upon a distant breeze.

'Ah! now,' she said, 'if I could get words for that! What an exquisite lament somebody might write to it, if they could only thoroughly take in the feeling and meaning of it.'

'Perhaps,' I said, humbly, 'that is the only way to write songs – to let some air get possession of one's whole soul, and gradually inspire the words for itself; as the old Hebrew prophets had music played before them, to wake up the prophetic spirit within them.'

She looked up, just as if she had been unconscious of my presence till that moment.

'Ah! Mr. Locke! – well, if you understand my meaning so thoroughly, perhaps you will try and write some words for me.'

'I am afraid that I do not enter sufficiently into the meaning of the air.'

'Oh! then, listen while I play it over again. I am sure *you* ought to appreciate anything so sad and tender.'

And she did play it, to my delight, over again, even more gracefully and carefully than before – making the inarticulate sounds speak a mysterious train of thoughts and emotions. It is strange how little real intellect, in women especially, is required for an exquisite appreciation of the beauties of music – perhaps, because it appeals to the heart and not the head.

She rose and left the piano, saying, archly, 'Now, don't forget your promise;' and I, poor fool, my sunlight suddenly withdrawn, began torturing my brains on the instant to think of a subject.

As it happened, my attention was caught by hearing two gentlemen close to me discuss a beautiful sketch by Copley Fielding,* if I recollect rightly, which hung on the wall – a wild waste of tidal sands, with here and there a line of stake-nets fluttering in the wind – a grey shroud of rain sweeping up from the westward, through which low red cliffs glowed dimly in the rays of the setting sun – a train of horses and cattle splashing slowly through shallow desolate pools and creeks, their wet, red, and black hides glittering in one long line of level light.

They seemed thoroughly conversant with art; and as I listened to their criticisms, I learnt more in five minutes, about the characteristics of a really true and good picture, and about the perfection to which our unrivalled English landscape-painters have attained, than I ever did from all the books and criticisms which I had read. One of them had seen the spot represented, at the mouth of the Dee, and began telling wild stories of salmon-fishing, and wild-fowl shooting – and then a tale of a girl, who in bringing her father's cattle home across the sands, had been caught by a sudden flow of the tide, and found next day a corpse hanging among the stake-nets far below. The tragedy, the art of the picture, the simple, dreary grandeur of the scenery, took possession of me; and I stood gazing a long time, and fancying myself pacing the sands, and wondering whether there were shells upon it – I had often longed for once only in my life to pick up shells – when Lady Ellerton, whom I had not before noticed, woke me from my reverie.

I took the liberty of asking after Lord Ellerton.

'He is not in town – he has stayed behind for one day to attend a great meeting of his tenantry – you will see the account in the papers to-morrow morning – he comes to-morrow.' And as she spoke, her whole face and figure seemed to glow and heave, in spite of herself, with pride and affection.

'And now, come with me, Mr. Locke – the * * * ambassador* wishes to speak to you.'

'The * * * ambassador!' I said, startled; for let us be as democratic as we will, there is something in the name of great officers which awes, perhaps rightly, for the moment, and it requires a strong act of self-possession to recollect that 'a man's a man for a' that.' Besides, I knew enough of the great man in question to stand in awe of him for his own sake, having lately read a panegyric of him, which perfectly astounded me, by its description of his piety and virtue, his family affection, and patriarchal simplicity, the liberality and philanthropy of all his measures, and the enormous intellectual powers, and stores of learning, which enabled him, with the affairs of Europe on his shoulders, to write deeply and originally on the most abstruse question of theology, history, and science.

Lady Ellerton seemed to guess my thoughts. 'You need not be afraid of meeting an aristocrat, in the vulgar sense of the word. You will see one who, once perhaps as unknown as yourself, has risen by virtue and wisdom to guide the destinies of nations – and shall I tell you how? Not by fawning and yielding to the fancies of the great; not by compromising his own convictions to suit their prejudices'——

I felt the rebuke, but she went on—

'He owes his greatness to having dared, one evening, to contradict a crown-prince to his face, and fairly conquer him in argument, and thereby bind the truly royal heart to him for ever.'

'There are few scions of royalty to whose favour that would be a likely path.'

'True; and therefore the greater honour is due to the young student who could contradict, and the prince who could be contradicted.'

By this time we had arrived in the great man's presence; he was sitting with a little circle round him, in the further drawing-room, and certainly I never saw a nobler specimen of humanity. I felt myself at once before a hero – not of war and bloodshed, but of peace and civilisation; his portly and ample figure, fair hair and delicate complexion, and, above all, the benignant calm of his countenance, told of a character gentle and genial – at peace with himself and all the world; while the exquisite proportion of his chiselled and classic features, the lofty and ample brain, and the keen, thoughtful eye, bespoke, at the first glance, refinement and wisdom—

> The reason firm, the temperate will –
> Endurance, foresight, strength, and skill.*

I am not ashamed to say, Chartist as I am, that I felt inclined to fall upon my knees, and own a master of God's own making.

He received my beautiful guide with a look of chivalrous affection, which I observed that she returned with interest; and then spoke in a voice peculiarly bland and melodious.

'So, my dear lady, this is the *protégé* of whom you have so often spoken?'

So she had often spoken of me! Blind fool that I was, I only took it in as food for my own self-conceit, that my enemy (for so I actually fancied her) could not help praising me.

'I have read your little book, sir,' he said, in the same soft, benignant voice, 'with very great pleasure. It is another proof, if I required any, of the undercurrent of living and healthful thought which exists even in the less-known ranks of your great nation. I shall send it to some young friends of mine in Germany, to show them that Englishmen can feel acutely and speak boldly on the social evils of their country, without indulging in that frantic and bitter revolutionary spirit, which warps so many young minds among us. You understand the German language at all?'

I had not that honour.

'Well, you must learn it. We have much to teach you in the sphere of abstract thought, as you have much to teach us in those of the practical reason and the knowledge of mankind. I should be glad to see you some day in a German university. I am anxious to encourage a truly spiritual fraternization between the two great branches of the Teutonic stock, by welcoming all brave young English spirits to their ancient fatherland. Perhaps hereafter your kind friends here will be able to lend you to me. The means are easy, thank God! You will find in the Germans true brothers, in ways even more practical than sympathy and affection.'

I could not but thank the great man, with many blushes, and went home that night utterly '*tête montée*', as I believe the French phrase is – beside myself with gratified vanity and love; to lie sleepless under a severe fit of asthma – sent perhaps as a wholesome chastisement, to cool my excited spirits down to something like a rational pitch. As I lay castle-building, Lillian's wild air rang still in my ears, and combined itself somehow with that picture of the Cheshire Sands, and the story of the drowned girl, till it shaped itself into a song, which, as it is yet unpublished, and as I have hitherto obtruded little or nothing of my own composition on my readers, I may be excused for inserting here.

> O Mary, go and call the cattle home,
>   And call the cattle home,
>   And call the cattle home,
>   Across the sands o' Dee;
> That western wind was wild and dank wi' foam,
>   And all alone went she.

The creeping tide came up along the sand,
 And o'er and o'er the sand,
 And round and round the sand,
As far as eye could see;
The blinding mist came down and hid the land –
 And never home came she.

Oh, is it weed, or fish, or floating hair –
 A tress o' golden hair,
 O' drowned maiden's hair,
Above the nets at sea?
Was never salmon yet that shone so fair,
 Among the stakes on Dee.

They rowed her in across the rolling foam,
 The cruel crawling foam,
 The cruel hungry foam,
To her grave beside the sea:
But still the boatmen hear her call the cattle home
 Across the sands o' Dee.*

There – let it go! – it was meant as an offering for one whom it never reached.

About mid-day I took my way toward the dean's house, to thank him for his hospitality – and, I need not say, to present my offering at my idol's shrine; and as I went I conned over a dozen complimentary speeches about Lord Ellerton's wisdom, liberality, eloquence – but behold! the shutters of the house were closed. What could be the matter? It was full ten minutes before the door was opened; and then, at last, an old woman, her eyes red with weeping, made her appearance. My thoughts flew instantly to Lillian – something must have befallen her. I gasped out her name first, and then, recollecting myself, asked for the dean.

'They had all left town that morning.'

'Miss – Miss Winnstay – is she ill?'

'No.'

'Thank God!' I breathed freely again. What matter what happened to all the world beside?'

'Ay, thank God, indeed; but poor Lord Ellerton was thrown from his horse last night and brought home dead. A messenger came here by six this morning, and they're all gone off to * * *.

Her ladyship's raving mad. – And no wonder.' And she burst out crying afresh, and shut the door in my face.

Lord Ellerton dead! and Lillian gone too! Something whispered that I should have cause to remember that day. My heart sunk within me. When should I see her again?

That day was the 1st of June, 1845. On the 10th of April, 1848, I saw Lillian Winnstay again. Dare I write my history between those two points of time? Yes, even that must be done, for the sake of the rich who read, and the poor who suffer.

CHAPTER XXVII

THE PLUSH BREECHES TRAGEDY

My triumph had received a cruel check enough, when just at its height, and more were appointed to follow. Behold! some two days after, another – all the more bitter, because my conscience whispered that it was not altogether undeserved. The people's press had been hitherto praising and petting me lovingly enough. I had been classed (and Heaven knows that the comparison was dearer to me than all the applause of the wealthy) with the Corn-Law Rhymer,* and the author of the 'Purgatory of Suicides'.* My class had claimed my talents as their own – another 'voice fresh from the heart of Nature', another 'untutored songster of the wilderness', another 'prophet arisen among the suffering millions', – when, one day, behold in Mr. O'Flynn's paper a long and fierce attack* on me, my poems, my early history! How he could have got at some of the facts there mentioned, how he could have dared to inform his readers that I had broken my mother's heart by my misconduct, I cannot conceive; unless my worthy brother-in-law, the Baptist preacher, had been kind enough to furnish him with the materials. But however that may be, he showed me no mercy. I was suddenly discovered to be a time-server, a spy, a concealed aristocrat. Such paltry talent as I had, I had prostituted for the sake of fame. I had deserted The People's Cause for filthy lucre – an allurement which Mr. O'Flynn had always treated with withering scorn – *in print*.* Nay more, I would write, and notoriously did write, in any paper, Whig, Tory, or Radical, where I could earn a shilling by an enormous gooseberry,* or a scrap of private slander. And the working men were solemnly warned to beware of me and my writings, till the editor had further investigated certain ugly facts in my history, which he would in due time report to his patriotic and enlightened readers.

All this stung me in the most sensitive nerve of my whole heart, for I knew that I could not altogether exculpate myself; and to that miserable certainty was added the dread of some fresh exposure. Had he actually heard of the omissions in my poems? – and if he once touched on that subject, what could I answer? Oh! how bitterly now I felt the force of the critic's careless lash! – The awful responsibility of those written words, which we bandy about so thoughtlessly! How I recollected now, with shame and remorse, all the hasty and cruel utterances to which I, too, had given vent against those who had dared to differ from me; the harsh, one-sided judgments, the reckless imputations of motive, the bitter sneers, 'rejoicing in evil rather than in the truth.'* How I, too, had longed to prove my victims in the wrong, and turned away, not only lazily, but angrily, from many an exculpatory fact! And here was my Nemesis come at last. As I had done unto others, so it was done unto me!

It was right that it should be so. However indignant, mad, almost murderous, I felt at the time, I thank God for it now. It is good to be punished in kind. It is good to be made to feel what we have made others feel. It is good – anything is good, however bitter, which shows us that there is such a law as retribution; that we are not the sport of blind chance or a triumphant fiend, but that there is a God who judges the earth – righteous to repay every man according to his works.

But at the moment I had no such ray of comfort – and, full of rage and shame, I dashed the paper down before Mackaye. 'How shall I answer him? What shall I say?'

The old man read it all through with a grim saturnine smile.

'Hoolie,* hoolie, speech is o' silver – silence is o' gold, says Thomas Carlyle,* anent this an' ither matters. Wha 'd be fashed wi' sic blethers? Ye'll just abide patient, and haud still in the Lord, until this tyranny be owerpast. Commit your cause

to Him, said the auld Psalmist, an' he'll mak' your righteousness as clear as the light, an' your just dealing as the noonday.'*

'But I must explain; I owe it as a duty to myself; I must
refute these charges; I must justify myself to our friends.'

'Can ye do that same, laddie?' asked he, with one of his
quaint, searching looks. Somehow, I blushed, and could not
altogether meet his eye, while he went on, '——An' gin ye
could, whaur would ye do 't? I ken na periodical whar the
editor will gie ye a clear stage an' no favour to bang him ower
the lugs.'

'Then I will try some other paper.'

'An' what for then? They that read him, winna read the
ither; an' they that read the ither, winna read him. He has his
ain set o' dupes, like every ither editor; an' ye mun let him gang
his gate, an' feed his ain kye with his ain hay. He'll no change it
for your bidding.'

'What an abominable thing this whole business of the press
is, then, if each editor is to be allowed to humbug his readers
at his pleasure, without a possibility of exposing or contradicting
him!'

'An' ye've just spoken the truth, laddie. There's na mair
accursed inquisition, than this of thae self-elected popes, the
editors. That puir auld Roman ane, ye can bring him forat whan
ye list, bad as he is. "Fœnum habet in cornu";* his name's
ower his shop-door. But these anonymies – priests o' the order o'
Melchisedec by the deevil's side,* without father or mither
beginning o' years nor end o' days – without a local habitation
or a name* – as kittle to haud as a brock in a cairn——'*

'What do you mean, Mr. Mackaye?' asked I, for he was
getting altogether unintelligibly Scotch, as was his custom
when excited.

'Ou, I forgot; ye're a puir Southern body, an' no sensible
to the gran' metaphoric powers o' the true Dawric. But it's an
accursit state a'thegither, the noo, this o' the anonymous press –
oreeginally devised, ye ken, by Balaam the son o' Beor,* for
serving God wi'out the deevil's finding it out – an' noo, after
the way o' human institutions, translated ower to help folks to
serve the deevil without God's finding it out. I'm no astonished
at the puir expiring religious press for siccan a fa'; but for the

working men to be a' as bad – it's grewsome to behold. I'll tell
ye what, my bairn, there's na salvation for the workmen, while
they defile themselves this fashion, wi' a' the very idols o' their
ain tyrants – wi' salvation by act o' parliament – irresponsible
rights o' property – anonymous Balaamry – fechtin' that canny
auld farrant* fiend, Mammon, wi' his ain weapons – and then
a' fleyed,* because they get well beaten for their pains. I'm sair
forfaughten* this mony a year wi' watching the puir gowks,
trying to do God's wark wi' the deevil's tools. Tak' tent o' that.'

And I did 'tak' tent o' it'. Still there would have been as little
present consolation as usual in Mackaye's unwelcome truths,
even if the matter had stopped there. But, alas! it did not stop
there. O'Flynn seemed determined to 'run-a-muck' at me. Every
week some fresh attack appeared. The very passages about the
universities and church property, which had caused our quarrel,
were paraded against me, with free additions and comments;
and, at last, to my horror, out came the very story which I had
all along dreaded, about the expurgation of my poems, with the
coarsest allusions to petticoat influence – aristocratic kisses – and
the Duchess of Devonshire canvassing draymen for Fox,* &c.
&c. How he got a clue to the scandal I cannot conceive.
Mackaye and Crossthwaite, I had thought, were the only souls
to whom I had ever breathed the secret, and they denied
indignantly the having ever betrayed my weakness. How it
came out, I say again, I cannot conceive; except because it is a
great everlasting law, and sure to fulfil itself, sooner or later,
as we may see by the histories of every remarkable, and many
an unremarkable, man – 'There is nothing secret, but it shall be
made manifest; and whatsoever ye have spoken in the closet,
shall be proclaimed upon the house-tops.'*

For some time after that last exposure, I was thoroughly
crest-fallen – and not without reason. I had been giving a few
lectures among the working men, on various literary and social
subjects. I found my audience decrease – and those who
remained seemed more inclined to hiss than to applaud me.
In vain I ranted and quoted poetry, often more violently than
my own opinions justified. My words touched no responsive
chord in my hearers' hearts; they had lost faith in me.

At last, in the middle of a lecture on Shelley, I was indulging, and honestly too, in some very glowing and passionate praise of the true nobleness of a man, whom neither birth nor education could blind to the evils of society; who, for the sake of the suffering many could trample under foot his hereditary pride, and become an outcast for The People's Cause.

I heard a whisper close to me, from one whose opinion I valued, and value still – a scholar and a poet, one who had tasted poverty, and slander, and a prison, for The Good Cause:

'Fine talk; but it's "all in his day's work". Will he dare to say that to-morrow to the ladies at the West-end?'

No – I should not. I knew it; and at that instant I felt myself a liar, and stopped short – my tongue clove to the roof of my mouth. I fumbled at my papers – clutched the water-tumbler – tried to go on – stopped short again – caught up my hat, and rushed from the room, amid peals of astonished laughter.

It was some months after this that, fancying the storm blown over, I summoned up courage enough to attend a political meeting of our party; but even there my Nemesis met me full face. After some sanguinary speech, I really forget from whom, and, if I recollected, God forbid that I should tell now, I dared to controvert, mildly enough, Heaven knows, some especially frantic assertion or other. But before I could get out three sentences, O'Flynn flew at me with a coarse invective, hounded on, by-the-bye, by one who, calling himself a gentleman might have been expected to know better. But, indeed, he and O'Flynn had the same object in view, which was simply to sell their paper; and as a means to that great end, to pander to the fiercest passions of their readers, to bully and silence all moderate and rational Chartists, and pet and tar on* the physical-force men, till the poor fellows began to take them at their word. Then, when it came to deeds and not to talk, and people got frightened, and the sale of the paper decreased a little, a blessed change came over them – and they awoke one morning meeker than lambs; 'ulterior measures' had vanished back into the barbarous ages, pikes, vitriol-bottles, and all; and the public were entertained with nothing but homilies on patience and resignation, the 'triumphs of moral justice', the 'omnipotence of public opinion', and the 'gentle conquests of fraternal love' – till it was safe to talk treason and slaughter again.

But just then treason happened to be at a premium. Sedition, which had been floundering on in a confused, disconsolate, under-ground way ever since 1842, was supposed by the public to be dead; and for that very reason it was safe to talk it, or, at least, back up those who chose to do so. And so I got no quarter – though really, if the truth must be told, I had said nothing unreasonable.

Home I went disgusted, to toil on at my hack-writing, only praying that I might be let alone to scribble in peace, and often thinking, sadly, how little my friends in Harley-street could guess at the painful experience, the doubts, the struggles, the bitter cares, which went to the making of the poetry which they admired so much!

I was not, however, left alone to scribble in peace, either by O'Flynn or by his readers, who formed, alas! just then, only too large a portion of the thinking artisans; every day brought some fresh slight or annoyance with it, till I received one afternoon, by the Parcels Delivery Company, a large unpaid packet, containing, to my infinite disgust, an old pair of yellow plush breeches, with a recommendation to wear them, whose meaning could not be mistaken.*

Furious, I thrust the unoffending garment into the fire, and held it there with the tongs, regardless of the horrible smell which accompanied its martyrdom, till the lady-lodger on the first floor rushed down to inquire whether the house was on fire.

I answered her by hurling a book at her head, and brought down a volley of abuse, under which I sat in sulky patience, till Mackaye and Crossthwaite came in, and found her railing in the doorway, and me sitting over the fire, still intent on the frizzling remains of the breeches.

'Was this insult of your invention, Mr. Crossthwaite?' asked I, in a tone of lofty indignation, holding up the last scrap of unroasted plush.

Roars of laughter from both of them made me only more frantic, and I broke out so incoherently, that it was some time before the pair could make out the cause of my fury.

'Upon my honour, Locke,' quoth John, at last, holding his sides, 'I never sent them; though, on the whole – you've made my stomach ache so with laughing, I can't speak. But you must expect a joke or two, after your late fashionable connexions.'

I stood, still and white with rage.

'Really, my good fellow, how can you wonder if our friends suspect you? Can you deny that you've been off and on lately between flunkeydom and The Cause, like a donkey between two bottles of hay?* Have you not neglected our meetings? Have you not picked all the spice out of your poems? And can you expect to eat your cake and keep it too? You must be one thing or the other; and, though Sandy, here, is too kind-hearted to tell you, you have disappointed us both miserably – and there's the long and the short of it.'

I hid my face in my hands, and sat moodily over the fire; my conscience told me that I had nothing to answer.

'Whisht, Johnnie! Ye're ower sair on the lad. He's a' right at heart still, an' he'll do good service. But the deevil a'ways fechts hardest wi' them he's maist 'feard of. What's this anent agricultural distress ye had to tell me the noo?'

'There is a rising down in the country, a friend of mine writes me. The people are starving, not because bread is dear, but because it's cheap;* and, like sensible men, they're going to have a great meeting, to inquire the rights and wrong of all that. Now, I want to send a deputation down, to see how far they are inclined to go, and let them know we up in London are with them. And then we might get up a corresponding association, you know. It's a great opening for spreading the principles of the Charter.'

'I sair misdoubt, it's just bread they'll be wanting, they labourers, mair than liberty. Their God is their belly, I'm thinking, and a verra poor, empty idol he is the noo; sma' burnt-offerings, and fat o' rams he gets, to propitiate him. But ye might send down a canny body, just to spy out the nakedness o' the land.'

'I will go!' I said, starting up. 'They shall see that I do care for The Cause. If it's a dangerous mission, so much the better; it will prove my sincerity. Where is the place?'

'About ten miles from D * * *.'

'D * * *!' My heart sank – if it had been any other spot in England! But it was too late to retract. Sandy saw what was the matter, and tried to turn the subject; but I was peremptory, almost rude with him. I felt I must keep up my present excitement, or lose my heart, and my caste, for ever; and as the hour for the committee was at hand, I jumped up and set off thither with them, whether they would or not. I heard Sandy whisper to Crossthwaite, and turned quite fiercely on him.

'If you want to speak about me, speak out. If you fancy that I shall let my connexion with that place' (I could not bring myself to name it) 'stand in the way of my duty, you do not know me.'

I announced my intention at the meeting. It was at first received coldly; but I spoke energetically – perhaps, as some told me afterwards, actually eloquently. When I got heated, I alluded to my former stay at D*** and said (while my heart sunk at the bravado which I was uttering) that I should consider it a glory to retrieve my character with them, and devote myself to the cause of the oppressed, in the very locality whence had first arisen their unjust but pardonable suspicions. In short, generous, trusting hearts as they were, and always are, I talked them round; they shook me by the hand one by one, bade me God speed, told me that I stood higher than ever in their eyes, and then set to work to vote money from their funds for my travelling expenses, which I magnanimously refused, saying that I had a pound or two left from the sale of my poems, and that I must be allowed, as an act of repentance and restitution, to devote it to The Cause.

My triumph was complete. Even O'Flynn, who, like all Irishmen, had plenty of loose good-nature at bottom, and was as sudden and furious in his loves as in his hostilities, scrambled over the benches, regardless of patriots' toes, to shake me violently by the hand, and inform me that I was 'a broth of a boy', and that 'any little disagreements between us had vanished like a passing cloud from the sunshine of our fraternity' – when my eye was caught by a face which there was no mistaking – my cousin's!

Yes, there he was, watching me like a basilisk, with his dark, glittering, mesmeric eyes, out of a remote corner of the room – not in contempt or anger, but there was a quiet, assured, sardonic smile about his lips, which chilled me to the heart.

The meeting was sufficiently public to allow of his presence, but how had he found out its existence? Had he come there as a spy on me? Had he been in the room when my visit to D * * * was determined on? I trembled at the thought; and I trembled, too, lest he should be daring enough – and I knew he could dare anything – to claim acquaintance with me there and then. It would have ruined my new-restored reputation for ever. But he sat still and steady: and I had to go through the rest of the evening's business under the miserable, cramping knowledge that every word and gesture was being noted down by my most deadly enemy; trembling whenever I was addressed, lest some chance word of an acquaintance should implicate me still further – though, indeed, I was deep enough already. The meeting seemed interminable; and there I fidgeted, with my face scarlet – always seeing those basilisk eyes upon me – in fancy, for I dared not look again towards the corner where I knew they were.

At last it was over – the audience went out; and when I had courage to look round, my cousin had vanished among them. A load was taken off my breast, and I breathed freely again – for five minutes; – for I had not made ten steps up the street, when an arm was familiarly thrust through mine, and I found myself in the clutches of my evil genius.

'How are you, my dear fellow? Expected to meet you there. Why, what an orator you are! Really, I haven't heard more fluent or passionate English this month of Sundays. You must give me a lesson in sermon-preaching. I can tell you, we parsons want a hint or two in that line. So you're going down to D * * *, to see after theose poor starving labourers? 'Pon my honour, I've a great mind to go with you.'

So, then, he knew all! However, there was nothing for it but to brazen it out; and, besides, I was in his power, and however hateful to me his seeming cordiality might be, I dared not offend him at that moment.

'It would be well if you did. If you parsons would show yourselves at such places as these a little oftener, you would do more to make the people believe your mission real, than by all the tracts and sermons in the world.'

'But, my dear cousin' (and he began to snuffle and sink his

voice), 'there is so much sanguinary language, so much un-
sanctified impatience; you frighten away all the meek apostolic
men among the priesthood – the very ones who feel most for
the lost sheep of the flock.'

'Then the parsons are either great Pharisees or great cowards,
or both.'

'Very likely. I was in a precious fright myself, I know, when
I saw you recognised me. If I had not felt strengthened, you
know, as of course one ought to be in all trials, by the sense of
my holy calling, I think I should have bolted at once. However,
I took the precaution of bringing my Bowie* and revolver with
me, in case the worst came to the worst.'

'And a very needless precaution it was,' said I, half laughing
at the quaint incongruity of the priestly and the lay elements in
his speech. 'You don't seem to know much of working men's
meetings, or working men's morals. Why, that place was open
to all the world. The proceedings will be in the newspaper
to-morrow. The whole bench of bishops might have been there,
if they had chosen; and a great deal of good it would have done
them!'

'I fully agree with you, my dear fellow. No one hates the
bishops more than we true high-churchmen, I can tell you –
that's a great point of sympathy between us and the people.
But I must be off. By-the-bye, would you like me to tell our
friends at D * * *, that I met you? They often ask after you in
their letters, I assure you.'

This was a sting of complicated bitterness. I felt all that it
meant at once. So he was in constant correspondence with them,
while I——and that thought actually drove out of my head
the more pressing danger of his utterly ruining me in their
esteem, by telling them, as he had a very good right to do, that
I was going to preach Chartism to discontented mobs.

'Ah! well! perhaps you wouldn't wish it mentioned? As you
like, you know. Or, rather,' and he laid an iron grasp on my
arm, and dropped his voice – this time in earnest – 'as you
behave, my wise and loyal cousin! Good night.'

I went home – the excitement of self-applause, which the
meeting had called up, damped by a strange weight of fore-
boding. And yet I could not help laughing, when, just as I

was turning into bed, Crossthwaite knocked at my door, and, on being admitted, handed over to me a bundle wrapped up in paper.

'There's a pair of breeks for you – not plush ones, this time, old fellow – but you ought to look as smart as possible. There's so much in a man's looking dignified, and all that, when he's speechifying. So I've just brought you down my best black trousers to travel in. We're just of a size, you know; little and good, like a Welshman's cow. And if you tear them, why, we're not like poor, miserable, useless aristocrats; tailors and sailors can mend their own rents.' And he vanished, whistling the Marseillaise.

I went to bed and tossed about, fancying to myself my journey, my speech, the faces of the meeting, among which Lillian's would rise, in spite of all the sermons which I preached to myself on the impossibility of her being there, of my being known, of any harm happening from the movement; but I could not shake off the fear. If there were a riot, a rising! – If any harm were to happen to her! – If—— till, mobbed into fatigue by a rabble of such miserable hypothetic ghosts, I fell asleep, to dream that I was going to be hanged for sedition, and that the mob were all staring and hooting at me, and Lillian clapping her hands and setting them on; and I woke in an agony, to find Sandy Mackaye standing by my bedside with a light.

'Hoolie, laddie! ye need na jump up that way. I'm no gaun to burke* ye the nicht; but I canna sleep; I'm sair misdoubtful o' the thing. It seems a' richt, an' I've been praying for us, an' that's mickle for me, to be taught our way; but I dinna see aught for ye but to gang. If your heart is richt with God in this matter, then he's o' your side, an' I fear na what men may do to ye. An' yet, ye're my Joseph, as it were, the son o' my auld age, wi' a coat o' many colours,* plush breeks included; an' gin aught take ye, ye'll bring down my grey haffets wi' sorrow to the grave!'

The old man gazed at me as he spoke, with a deep, earnest affection I had never seen in him before; and the tears glistened in his eyes by the flaring candlelight, as he went on.

'I ha' been reading the Bible the nicht. It's strange how the words o't rise up, and open themselves, whiles, to puir distractit bodies; though, maybe, no always in just in the orthodox way. An' I fell on that, "Behold, I send ye forth as lambs in the midst of wolves. Be ye therefore wise as serpents an' harmless as doves";* an' that gave me comfort, laddie, for ye. Mind the warning; dinna gang wud, whatever ye may see an' hear; it's an ill way o' showing pity, to gang daft anent it. Dinna talk magniloquently; that's the workman's darling sin. An' mind ye dinna go too deep wi' them. Ye canna trust them to understand ye; they're puir foolish sheep that ha' no shepherd – swine that ha' no wash, rather. So cast na your pearls before swine, laddie, lest they trample them under their feet, an' turn again an' rend ye.'*

He went out, and I lay awake tossing till morning, making a thousand good resolutions – like the rest of mankind.

CHAPTER XXVIII

THE MEN WHO ARE EATEN

WITH many instructions from our friends, and warnings from Mackaye, I started next day on my journey. When I last caught sight of the old man, he was gazing fixedly after me, and using his pocket-handkerchief in a somewhat suspicious way. I had remarked how depressed he seemed, and my own spirits shared the depression. A presentiment of evil hung over me, which not even the excitement of the journey – to me a rare enjoyment – could dispel. I had no heart, somehow, to look at the country scenes around, which in general excited in me so much interest, and I tried to lose myself in summing up my stock of information on the question which I expected to hear discussed by the labourers. I found myself not altogether ignorant. The horrible disclosures of S.G.O.,* and the barbarous abominations of the Andover Workhouse,* then fresh in the public mind, had had their due effect on mine; and, like most thinking artisans, I had acquainted myself tolerably from books and newspapers with the general condition of the country labourers.

I arrived in the midst of a dreary, treeless country, whose broad brown and grey fields were only broken by an occasional line of dark doleful firs, at a knot of thatched hovels, all sinking and leaning every way but the right, the windows patched with paper, the doorways stopped with filth, which surrounded a beer-shop. That was my destination – unpromising enough for any one but an agitator. If discontent and misery are preparatives for liberty – and they are – so strange and unlike ours are the ways of God – I was likely enough to find them there.

I was welcomed by my intended host, a little pert snub-nosed shoemaker, who greeted me as his cousin from London – a relationship which it seemed prudent to accept.

He took me into his little cabin, and there, with the assistance of a shrewd good-natured wife, shared with me the best he had; and after supper commenced, mysteriously and in trembling, as if the very walls might have ears, a rambling bitter diatribe on the wrong and sufferings of the labourers; which went on till late in the night, and which I shall spare my readers: for if they have either brains or hearts, they ought to know more than I can tell them, from the public prints, and, indeed, from their own eyes – although , as a wise man says, there is nothing more difficult than to make people see first the facts which lie under their own nose.

Upon one point, however, which was new to me, he was very fierce – the custom of landlords letting the cottages with their farms, for the mere sake of saving themselves trouble; thus giving up all power of protecting the poor man, and delivering him over, bound hand and foot, even in the matter of his commonest home comforts, to farmers, too penurious, too ignorant, and often too poor, to keep the cottages in a state fit for the habitation of human beings. Thus the poor man's hovel, as well as his labour, became, he told me, a source of profit to the farmer, out of which he wrung the last drop of gain. The necessary repairs were always put off as long as possible – the labourers were robbed of their gardens – the slightest rebellion lost them not only work, but shelter from the elements; the slavery under which they groaned penetrated even to the fireside and to the bedroom.

'And who was the landlord of this parish?'

'Oh! he believed he was a very good sort of man, and uncommon kind to the people where he lived, but that was fifty miles away in another county; and he liked that estate better than this, and never came down here, except for the shooting.'

Full of many thoughts, and tired out with my journey, I went up to bed, in the same loft with the cobbler and his wife, and fell asleep, and dreamt of Lillian.

*

About eight o'clock the next morning, I started forth with my guide, the shoemaker, over as desolate a country as men can well conceive. Not a house was to be seen for miles, except the knot of hovels which we had left, and here and there a great dreary lump of farm-buildings, with its yard of yellow stacks. Beneath our feet the earth was iron, and the sky iron above our heads. Dark curdled clouds, 'which had built up everywhere an under-roof of doleful grey',* swept on before the bitter northern wind, which whistled through the low leafless hedges and rotting wattles, and crisped the dark sodden leaves of the scattered hollies, almost the only trees in sight.

We trudged on, over wide stubbles, thick with innumerable weeds; over wide fallows, in which the deserted ploughs stood frozen fast; then over clover and grass, burnt black with frost; then over a field of turnips, where we passed a large fold of hurdles, within which some hundred sheep stood, with their heads turned from the cutting blast. All was dreary, idle, silent; no sound or sign of human beings. One wondered where the people lived, who cultivated so vast a tract of civilised, over-peopled, nineteenth-century England. As we came up to the fold, two little boys hailed us from the inside – two little wretches with blue noses and white cheeks, scarecrows of rags and patches, their feet peeping through bursten shoes twice too big for them, who seemed to have shared between them a ragged pair of worsted gloves, and cowered among the sheep, under the shelter of a hurdle, crying and inarticulate with cold.

'What's the matter, boys?'

'Turmits is froze, and us can't turn the handle of the cutter. Do ye gie us a turn, please!'

We scrambled over the hurdles, and gave the miserable little creatures the benefit of ten minutes' labour. They seemed too small for such exertion: their little hands were purple with chilblains, and they were so sorefooted they could scarcely limp. I was surprised to find them at least three years older than their size and looks denoted, and still more surprised, too, to find that their salary for all this bitter exposure to the elements – such as I believe I could not have endured two days running – was the vast sum of one shilling a week each, Sundays included. 'They didn't never go to school, nor to church nether, except just now and then, sometimes – they had to mind the sheep.'

I went on, sickened with the contrast between the highly-bred, over-fed, fat, thick-woolled animals, with their troughs of turnips and malt-dust, and their racks of rich clover-hay, and their little pent-house of rock-salt, having nothing to do but to eat and sleep, and eat again, and the little half-starved shivering animals who were their slaves.* Man the master of the brutes? Bah! As society is now, the brutes are the masters – the horse, the sheep, the bullock, is the master, and the labourer is their slave. 'Oh! but the brutes are eaten!' Well; the horses at least are not eaten – they live, like landlords, till they die. And those who are eaten, are certainly not eaten by their human servants. The sheep they fat, another kills, to parody Shelley;* and, after all, is not the labourer, as well as the sheep, eaten by you, my dear Society? – devoured body and soul, not the less really because you are longer about the meal, there being an old prejudice against cannibalism, and also against murder – except after the Riot Act has been read.

'What!' shriek the insulted respectabilities, 'have we not paid him his wages weekly, and has he not lived upon them?' Yes; and have you not given your sheep and horses their daily wages, and have they not lived on them? You wanted to work them; and they could not work, you know, unless they were alive. But here lies your iniquity: you gave the labourer nothing but his daily food – not even his lodgings; the pigs were not stinted of their wash to pay for their stye-room, the man was; and his wages, thanks to your competitive system, were beaten down deliberately and conscientiously (for was it not according to political economy, and the laws thereof?)* to the minimum on which he could or would work, without the hope or the possibility of saving a farthing. You know how to invest your capital profitably, dear Society, and to save money over and above your income of daily comforts; but what has he saved? – what is he profited by all those years of labour? He has kept body and soul together – perhaps he could have done that without you or your help. But his wages are used up every Saturday night. When he stops working, you have in your pocket the whole real profits of his nearly fifty years' labour, and he has nothing. And then you say that you have not eaten him! You know, in your heart of hearts, that you have. Else, why in Heaven's name do you pay him poor's rates? If, as you say, he has been duly repaid in wages, what is the meaning of that half-a-crown a-week? – you owe him nothing. Oh! but the man would starve – common humanity forbids! What now, Society? Give him alms, if you will, on the score of humanity; but do not tax people for his support, whether they choose or not – that were a mere tyranny and robbery. If the landlord's feelings will not allow him to see the labourer starve, let him give, in God's name; but let him not cripple and drain, by compulsory poor-rates, the farmer who has paid him his 'just remuneration' of wages, and the parson who probably, out of his scanty income, gives away twice as much in alms as the landlord does out of his superfluous one. No, no; as long as you retain compulsory poor-laws, you confess that it is not merely humane, but just, to pay the labourer more than his wages. You confess yourself in debt to him, over and above, an uncertain sum, which it suits you not to define, because such an investigation would expose ugly gaps and patches in that same snug competitive and property world of yours; and, therefore, being the stronger party, you compel your debtor to give up the claim which you confess, for an annuity of half-a-crown a-week – that being the just-above-starving-point of the economic thermometer. And yet you say you have not eaten the labourer! You see, we workmen too have our thoughts about political economy, differing slightly from yours, truly – just as the man who is being hanged may take a somewhat different view of the process from the man who is hanging him. Which view is likely to be the more practical one?

With some such thoughts I walked across the open down,

toward a circular camp, the earthwork, probably, of some old British town. Inside it, some thousand or so of labouring people were swarming restlessly round a single large block of stone, some relic of Druid times, on which a tall man stood, his dark figure thrown out in bold relief against the dreary sky. As we pushed through the crowd, I was struck with the wan, haggard look of all faces; their lack-lustre eyes and drooping lips, stooping shoulders, heavy, dragging steps, gave them a crushed, dogged air, which was infinitely painful, and bespoke a grade of misery more habitual and degrading than that of the excitable and passionate artisan.

There were many women among them, talking shrilly, and looking even more pinched and wan than the men. I remarked, also, that many of the crowd carried heavy sticks, pitchforks, and other tools which might be used as fearful weapons – an ugly sign, which I ought to have heeded betimes.

They glared with sullen curiosity at me and my Londoner's clothes, as, with no small feeling of self-importance, I pushed my way to the foot of the stone. The man who stood on it seemed to have been speaking some time. His words, like all I heard that day, were utterly devoid of anything like eloquence or imagination – a dull string of somewhat incoherent complaints, which derived their force only from the intense earnestness, which attested their truthfulness. As far as I can recollect, I will give the substance of what I heard. But, indeed, I heard nothing but what has been bandied about from newspaper to newspaper for years – confessed by all parties, deplored by all parties, but never an attempt made to remedy it.

—'They farmers makes slaves on us. I can't hear no difference between a Christian and a nigger, except they flogs the niggers and starves the Christians; and I don't know which I'd choose. I served Farmer * * * seven year, off and on, and arter harvest he tells me he's no more work for me, nor my boy, nether, acause he's getting too big for him, so he gets a little 'un instead, and we does nothing; and my boy lies about, getting into bad ways, like hundreds more; and then we goes to board, and they bids us go and look for work; and we goes up next part to London. I couldn't get none; they'd enough to do, they said, to employ their own; and we begs our way home, and goes into the Union;* and they turns us out again in two or three days, and promises us work again, and gives us two days' gravel-pecking, and then says they has no more for us; and we was sore pinched, and laid a-bed all day; then next board-day we goes to 'em, and they gives us one day more – and that threw us off another week, and then next board-day we goes into the Union again for three days, and gets sent out again: and so I've been starving one-half of the time, and they putting us off and on o' purpose like that; and I'll bear it no longer, and that's what I says.'

He came down, and a tall, powerful, well-fed man, evidently in his Sunday smock-frock and clean yellow leggings, got up and began:

'I hav'n't no complaint to make about myself. I've a good master, and the parson's a right kind 'un, and that's more than all can say, and the squire's a real gentleman; and my master, he don't need to lower his wages. I gets my ten shillings a-week all the year round, and harvesting, and a pig, and a 'lotment – and that's just why I come here. If I can get it, why can't you?'

''Cause our masters bain't like yourn.'

'No, by George, there baint no money round here away like that, I can tell you.'

'And why ain't they?' continued the speaker. 'There's the shame on it. There's my master can grow five quarters where yourn only grows three; and so he can live and pay like a man; and so he say he don't care for free trade. You know, as well as I, that there's not half o' the land round here grows what it ought. They ain't no money to make it grow more, and besides, they won't employ no hands to keep it clean. I come across more weeds in one field here, than I've seen for nine year on our farm. Why arn't some o' you a-getting they weeds up? It 'ud pay 'em to farm better – and they knows that, but they 're too lazy; if they can just get a living off the land, they don't care; and they'd sooner save money out o' your wages, than save it by growing more corn – it's easier for 'em, it is. There's the work to be done, and they won't let you do it. There's you crying out for work, and work crying out for you – and nether of you can get to the other. I say that's a shame, I do. I say a poor man's a slave. He daren't leave his parish – nobody won't

employ him, as can employ his own folk. And if he stays in his
parish, it's just a chance whether he gets a good master or a bad
'un. He can't choose, and that's a shame, it is. Why should he
go starving because his master don't care to do the best by the
land? If they can't till the land, I say let them get out of it,
and let them work it as can. And I think as we ought all to sign
a petition to government, to tell 'em all about it; though I don't
see as how they could help us, unless they'd make a law to force
the squires to put in nobody to a farm as hadn't money to work
it fairly.'

'I says,' said the next speaker, a poor fellow whose sentences
were continually broken by a hacking cough, 'just what he said.
If they can't till the land, let them do it as can. But they won't;
they won't let us have a scrap on it, though we'd pay 'em more
for it nor ever they'd make for themselves. But they says it 'ud
make us too independent, if we had an acre or so o' land; and
so it 'ud, for they. And so I says as he did – they want to make
slaves on us altogether, just to get the flesh and bones off us at
their own price. Look you at this here down. – If I had an acre
on it, to make a garden on, I'd live well with my wages, off and
on. Why, if this here was in garden, it 'ud be worth twenty,
forty times, o' that it be now. And last spring I lays out o' work
from Christmas till barley-sowing, and I goes to the farmer and
axes for a bit o' land to dig and plant a few potatoes – and he
says, "You be d—d! If you're minding your garden after hours,
you'll not be fit to do a proper day's work for me in hours –
and I shall want you by-and-by, when the weather breaks" –
for it was frost most bitter, it was. "And if you gets potatoes
you'll be getting a pig – and then you'll want straw, and meal
to fat 'un – and then I'll not trust you in my barn, I can tell ye;"
and so there it was. And if I'd had only one half-acre of this
here very down as we stands on, as isn't worth five shilling a
year and I'd a given ten shilling for it – my belly wouldn't a'
been empty now. Oh, they be dogs in the manger, and the Lord
'll reward 'em therefor! First they says they can't afford to work
the land 'emselves, and then they wain't let us work it ether.
Then they says prices is so low they can't keep us on, and so
they lowers our wages; and then when prices goes up ever so
much, our wages don't go up with 'em. So, high prices or low

prices, it's all the same. With the one we can't buy bread, and with the other we can't get work. I don't mind free trade — not I: to be sure, if the loaf's cheap, we shall be ruined; but if the loaf's dear, we shall be starved — and for that, we is starved, now. Nobody don't care for us; for my part, I don't much care for myself. A man must die some time or other. Only I thinks if we could some time or other just see the Queen once, and tell her all about it, she'd take our part, and not see us put upon like that, I do.'

'Gentlemen!' cried my guide, the shoemaker, in a somewhat conceited and dictatorial tone, as he skipped up by the speaker's side, and gently shouldered him down, 'It an't like the ancient times as I've read of, when any poor man as had a petition could come promiscuously to the King's royal presence, and put it direct into his own hand, and be treated like a gentleman. Don't you know as how they locks up the Queen now-a-days, and never lets a poor soul come a-near her, lest she should hear the truth of all their iniquities? Why, they never lets her stir out without a lot o' dragoons with drawn swords, riding all around her; and if you dared to go up to her to ax mercy, whoot! they'd chop your head off before you could say "Please your Majesty." And then the hypocrites say as it's to keep her from being frightened — and that's true — for it's frightened she'd be, with a vengeance, if she knowed all that they grand folks make poor labourers suffer, to keep themselves in power and great glory. I tell ye, 'tarn't perpracticable, at all, to ax the Queen for anything; she's afeard of her life on 'em. You just take my advice, and sign a round-robin to the squires — you tell 'em as you're willing to till the land for 'em, if they'll let you. There's draining and digging enough to be done as 'ud keep ye all in work, arn't there?'

'Ay, ay; there's lots o' work to be done, if so be we could get at it. Everybody knows that.'

'Well, you tell 'em that. Tell 'em here's hundreds and hundreds of ye starving, and willing to work; and then tell 'em, if they won't find ye work, they shall find ye meat. There's lots o' victuals in their larders now; haven't you as good a right to it as their jackanapes o' footmen? The squires is at the bottom of it all. What do you stupid fellows go grumbling at the farmers for? Don't they squires tax the land twenty or thirty shillings an acre; and what do they do for that? The best of 'em, if he gets five thousand a-year out o' the land, don't give back five hundred in charity, or schools, or poor-rates – and what's that to speak of? And the main of 'em – curse 'em! – they drains the money out o' the land, and takes it up to London, or into foreign parts, to spend on fine clothes and fine dinners; or throws it away at elections, to make folks beastly drunk, and sell their souls for money – and we gets no good on it. I'll tell you what it's come to, my men – that we can't afford no more landlords. We can't afford 'em, and that's the truth of it!'

The crowd growled a dubious assent.

'Oh, yes, you can grumble at the farmers, acause you deals with them first-hand; but you be too stupid to do aught but hunt by sight. I be an old dog, and I hunts cunning. I sees farther than my nose, I does. I larnt politics to London when I was a prentice; and I ain't forgotten the plans of it. Look you here. The farmers, they say they can't live unless they can make four rents, one for labour, and one for stock, and one for rent, and one for themselves; ain't that about right? Very well; just now they can't make four rents – in course they can't. Now, who's to suffer for that – the farmer as works, or the labourer as works, or the landlord as does nothing? But he takes care on himself. He won't give up his rent – not he. Perhaps he might give back ten per cent., and what's that? – two shillings an acre, maybe. What's that, if corn falls two pound a load, and more? Then the farmer gets a stinting; and he can't stint hisself, he's bad enough off already; he's forty shillings out o' pocket on every load of wheat – that's eight shillings, maybe, on every acre of his land on a four-course shift – and where's the eight shillings to come from, for the landlord's only given him back two on it? He can't stint hisself, he daren't stint his stock, and so he stints the labourers; and so it's you as pays the landlord's rent – you, my boys, out o' your flesh and bones, you do – and you can't afford it any longer, by the look of you – so just tell 'em so!

This advice seemed to me as sadly unpractical as the rest. In short, there seemed to be no hope, no purpose, among them –

and they felt it; and I could hear, from the running comment of murmurs, that they were getting every moment more fierce and desperate at the contemplation of their own helplessness – a mood which the next speech was not likely to soften.

A pale, thin woman scrambled up on the stone, and stood there, her scanty and patched garments fluttering in the bitter breeze, as, with face sharpened with want, and eyes fierce with misery, she began, in a querulous, scornful falsetto:

'I am an honest woman. I brought up seven children decently, and never axed the parish for a farden, till my husband died. Then they tells me I can support myself and mine – and so I does. Early and late I hoed turmits, and early and late I rep, and left the children at home to mind each other; and one on 'em fell into the fire, and is gone to heaven, blessed angel! and two more it pleased the Lord to take in the fever; and the next, I hope, will soon be out o' this miserable sinful world. But look you here: three weeks agone, I goes to the board. I had no work. They say they could not relieve me for the first week, because I had money yet to take. – The hypocrites! they knowing as I couldn't but owe it all, and a lot more beside. Next week they sends the officer to inquire. That was ten days gone, and we starving. Then, on board-day, they gives me two loaves. Then, next week, they takes it off again. And when I goes over (five miles) to the board to ax why – they'd find me work – and they never did; so we goes on starving for another week – for no one wouldn't trust us; how could they, when we was in debt already a whole lot? – you're all in debt!'

'That we are.'

'There's some here as never made ten shillings a-week in their lives, as owes twenty pounds at the shop!'

'Ay, and more – and how's a man ever to pay that?'

'So this week, when I comes, they offers me the house. Would I go into the house? They'd be glad to have me, acause I'm strong and hearty and a good nurse. But would I, that am an honest woman, go to live with they offscourings – they' – (she used a strong word) – 'would I be parted from my children? Would I let them hear the talk, and keep the company as they will there, and learn all sorts o' sins that they never heard on, blessed be God! I'll starve first, and see them starve too –

though, Lord knows, it's hard. – Oh! it's hard,' she said, bursting into tears – 'to leave them as I did this morning, crying after their breakfasts, and I none to give 'em. I've got no bread – where should I? I've got no fire – how can I give one shilling and sixpence a hundred for coals? And if I did, who'd fetch 'em home? And if I dared break a hedge for a knitch o' wood, they'd put me in prison, they would, with the worst – what be I to do? What be you going to do? That's what I came here for. What be you going to do for us women – us that starve and stint, and wear our hands off for you men and your children, and get hard words, and hard blows from you? – Oh! If I was a man, I know what I'd do, I do! But I don't think you be men, three parts o' you, or you'd not see the widow and the orphan starve as you do, and sit quiet and grumble, as long as you can keep your own bodies and souls together. Eh! ye cowards!'

What more she would have said in her excitement, which had risen to an absolute scream, I cannot tell; but some prudent friend pulled her down off the stone, to be succeeded by a speaker more painful, if possible; an aged blind man, the worn-out melancholy of whose slow, feeble voice made my heart sink, and hushed the murmuring crowd into silent awe.

Slowly he turned his grey, sightless head from side to side, as if feeling for the faces below him – and then began:

'I heard you was all to be here – and I suppose you are; and I said I would come – though I suppose they'll take off my pay, if they hear of it. But I knows the reason of it, and the bad times and all. The Lord revealed it to me as clear as day, four year agone come Easter-tide. It's all along of our sins, and our wickedness – because we forgot Him – it is. I mind the old war times, what times they was, when there was smuggled brandy up and down in every public, and work more than hands could do. And then, how we all forgot the Lord, and went after our own lusts and pleasures – squires and parsons, and farmers and labouring folk, all alike. They oughted to ha' knowed better – and we oughted too. Many's the Sunday I spent in skittle-playing, and cock-fighting, and the pound I spent in beer as might ha' been keeping me now. We was an evil and perverse generation – and so one o' my sons went for a sodger, and was

shot at Waterloo, and the other fell into evil ways, and got sent
across seas – and I be left alone for my sins. But the Lord was
very gracious to me, and showed me how it was all a judgment
on my sins, He did. He has turned His face from us, and that's
why we're troubled. And so I don't see no use in this meeting.
It won't do no good; nothing won't do us no good, unless we
all repent of our wicked ways, our drinking, and our dirt, and
our love-children, and our picking and stealing, and gets the
Lord to turn our hearts, and to come back again, and have
mercy on us, and take us away speedily out of this wretched
world, where there's nothing but misery and sorrow, into His
everlasting glory, Amen! Folks say as the day of judgment's
a-coming soon – and I partly think so myself. I wish it was all
over, and we in heaven above; and that's all I have to say.'

It seemed a not unnatural revulsion, when a tall, fierce man,
with a forbidding squint, sprung jauntily on the stone, and
setting his arms a-kimbo, broke out:

'Here be I, Blinkey, and I has as good a right to speak as
ere a one. You're all blarned fools, you are. So's that old blind
buffer there. You sticks like pigs in a gate, hollering and
squeaking, and never helping yourselves. Why can't you do like
me? I never does no work – darned if I'll work to please the
farmers. The rich folks robs me, and I robs them, and that's
fair and equal. You only turn poachers – you only go stealing
turmits, and fire-ud, and all as you can find – and then you'll
not need to work. Arn't it yourn? The game's no one's, is it
now? – you know that. And if you takes turmits or corn, they're
yourn – you helped to grown 'em. And if you're put to prison,
I tell ye, it's a darned deal warmer, and better victuals too, than
ever a one of you gets at home, let alone the Union. Now I
knows the dodge. Whenever my wife's ready for her trouble,
I gets cotched; then I lives like a prince in gaol, and she goes
to the workus; and when it's all over, start fair again. Oh, you
blockheads! – to stand here shivering with empty bellies. – You
just go down to the farm and burn they stacks over the old
rascal's head; and then they that let you starve now, will be
forced to keep you then. If you can't get your share of the
poor-rates, try the county rates,* my bucks – you can get fat
on them at the Queen's expense – and that's more than you'll

do in ever a Union as I hear on. Who'll come down and pull the farm about the folks' ears. Warn't it he as turned five on yer off last week? and ain't he more corn there than 'ud feed you all round this day, and won't sell it, just because he's waiting till folks are starved enough, and prices rise? Curse the old villain! - who'll help to disappoint him o' that? Come along!'

A confused murmur arose, and a movement in the crowd. I felt that now or never was the time to speak. If once the spirit of mad aimless riot broke loose, I had not only no chance of a hearing, but every likelihood of being implicated in deeds which I abhorred; and I sprung on the stone and entreated a few minutes' attention, telling them that I was a deputation from one of the London Chartist committees. This seemed to turn the stream of their thoughts, and they gaped in stupid wonder at me, as I began hardly less excited than themselves.

I assured them of the sympathy of the London working men, made a comment on their own speeches – which the reader ought to be able to make for himself, and told them that I had come to entreat their assistance towards obtaining such a parliamentary representation as would secure them their rights. I explained the idea of the Charter, and begged for their help in carrying it out.

To all which they answered surlily, that they did not know anything about politics – that what they wanted was bread.

I went on, more vehement than ever, to show them how all their misery sprung (as I then fancied) from being un-represented – how the laws were made by the rich for the poor, and not by all for all – how the taxes bit deep into the necessaries of the labourer, and only nibbled at the luxuries of the rich – how the criminal-code exclusively attacked the crimes to which the poor were prone, while it dared not interfere with the subtler iniquities of the high-born and wealthy – how poor-rates, as I have just said, were a confession on the part of society that the labourer was not fully remunerated. I tried to make them see that their interest, as much as common justice, demanded that they should have a voice in the councils of the nation, such as would truly proclaim their wants, their rights, their wrongs; and I have seen no reason since then to unsay my words.

To all which they answered, that their stomachs were empty, and they wanted bread. 'And bread we will have!'

'Go, then,' I cried, losing my self-possession between disappointment and the maddening desire of influence – and, indeed, who could hear their story, or even look upon their faces, and not feel some indignation stir in him, unless self-interest had drugged his heart and conscience – 'go,' I cried, 'and get bread! After all, you have a right to it. No man is bound to starve. There are rights above all laws, and the right to live is one. Laws were made for man, not man for laws. If you had made the laws yourselves, they might bind you even in this extremity; but they were made in spite of you – against you. They rob you, crush you; even now they deny you bread. God has made the earth free to all, like the air and sunshine, and you are shut out from off it. The earth is yours, for you till it. Without you it would be a desert. Go and demand your share of that corn, the fruit of your own industry. What matter, if your tyrants imprison, murder you? – they can but kill your bodies at once, instead of killing them piecemeal, as they do now; and your blood will cry against them from the ground!! – Ay, Woe!' – I went on, carried away by feelings for which I shall make no apology; for, however confused, there was, and is, and ever will be, a God's truth in them, as this generation will find out at the moment when its own serene self-satisfaction crumbles underneath it – 'Woe unto those that grind the faces of the poor! Woe unto those who add house to house, and field to field, till they stand alone in the land, and there is no room left for the poor man! The wages of their reapers, which they have held back by fraud, cry out against them; and their cry has entered into the ears of the God of heaven——'

But I had no time to finish. The murmur swelled into a roar, for 'Bread! Bread!' My hearers had taken me at my word. I had raised the spirit; could I command him, now he was abroad?

'Go to Jennings's Farm!'

'No! he ain't no corn, he sold 'un all last week.'

'There's plenty at the Hall Farm! Rouse out the old steward!'

And, amid yells and execrations, the whole mass poured down the hill, sweeping me away with them. I was shocked

and terrified at their threats. I tried again and again to stop and
harangue them. I shouted myself hoarse about the duty of
honesty; warned them against pillage and violence; entreated
them to take nothing but the corn which they actually needed;
but my voice was drowned in the uproar. Still I felt myself in a
measure responsible for their conduct; I had helped to excite
them, and dare not, in honour, desert them; and, trembling,
I went on, prepared to see the worst; following, as a flag of
distress, a mouldy crust, brandished on the point of a pitchfork.

Bursting through the rotting and half-fallen palings, we
entered a wide, rushy, neglected park, and along an old gravel
road, now green with grass, we opened on a sheet of frozen
water, and, on the opposite bank, the huge square corpse of a
hall, the close-shuttered windows of which gave it a dead and
ghastly look, except where here and there a single open one
showed, as through a black empty eye-socket, the dark un-
furnished rooms within. On the right, beneath us, lay, amid
tall elms, a large mass of farm-buildings, into the yard of which
the whole mob rushed tumultuously – just in time to see an old
man on horseback dart out and gallop hatless up the park,
amid the yells of the mob.

'The old rascal's gone! and he'll call up the yeomanry.
We must be quick, boys!' shouted one; and the first signs of
plunder showed themselves in an indiscriminate chase after
various screaming geese and turkeys; while a few of the more
steady went up to the house-door, and, knocking, demanded
sternly the granary keys.

A fat virago planted herself in the doorway, and commenced
railing at them, with the cowardly courage which the fancied
immunity of their sex gives to coarse women; but she was
hastily shoved aside, and took shelter in an upper room, where
she stood screaming and cursing at the window.

The invaders returned, cramming their mouths with bread,
and chopping asunder flitches of bacon. The granary-doors were
broken open, and the contents scrambled for, amid immense
waste, by the starving wretches. It was a sad sight. Here was a
poor shivering woman, hiding scraps of food under her cloak,
and hurrying out of the yard to the children she had left at
home. There was a tall man, leaning against the palings,

gnawing ravenously at the same loaf with a little boy, who had scrambled up behind him. Then a huge blackguard came whistling up to me, with a can of ale. 'Drink, my beauty! you're dry with hollering by now!'

'The ale is neither yours nor mine; I won't touch it.'

'Darn your buttons! You said the wheat was ourn, acause we growed it – and thereby so's the beer – for we growed the barley too.'

And so thought the rest; for the yard was getting full of drunkards, a woman or two among them, reeling knee-deep in the loose straw among the pigs.

'Thresh out they ricks!' roared another.

'Get out the threshing-machine!'

'You harness the horses!'

'No! there bain't no time. Yeomanry 'll be here. You mun leave the ricks.'

'Darned if we do. Old Woods shan't get naught by they.'

'Fire 'em,* then, and go on to Slater's Farm!'

'As well be hung for a sheep as for a lamb,' hiccupped Blinkey, as he rushed through the yard with a lighted brand. I tried to stop him, but fell on my face in the deep straw, and got round the barns to the rick-yard, just in time to hear a crackle – there was no mistaking it; the windward stack was in a blaze of fire.

I stood awe-struck – I cannot tell how long – watching how the live flame-snakes crept and hissed, and leapt and roared, and rushed in long horizontal jets from stack to stack before the howling wind, and fastened their fiery talons on the barn-eaves, and swept over the peaked roofs, and hurled themselves in fiery flakes into the yard beyond – the food of man, the labour of years, devoured in aimless ruin! – Was it my doing? Was it not?

At last I recollected myself, and ran round again into the straw-yard, where the fire was now falling fast. The only thing which saved the house was the weltering mass of bullocks, pigs, and human beings drunk and sober, which trampled out unwittingly the flames as fast as they caught.

The fire had seized the roofs of the cart-stables, when a great lubberly boy blubbered out:

'Git my horses out! git my horses out o' the fire! I be so fond o' mun!'

'Well, they ain't done no harm, poor beasts!' and a dozen men ran in to save them; but the poor wretches, screaming with terror, refused to stir. I never knew what became of them – but their shrieks still haunt my dreams...

The yard now became a pandemonium. The more ruffianly part of the mob – and alas! there were but too many of them – hurled the furniture out of the windows, or ran off with anything that they could carry. In vain I expostulated, threatened; I was answered by laughter, curses, frantic dances, and brandished plunder. Then I first found out how large a portion of rascality shelters itself under the wing of every crowd; and at the moment, I almost excused the rich for over-looking the real sufferers, in indignation at the rascals. But even the really starving majority, whose faces proclaimed the grim fact of their misery, seemed gone mad for the moment. The old crust of sullen, dogged patience had broken up, and their whole souls had exploded into reckless fury and brutal revenge – and yet there was no hint of violence against the red fat woman, who, surrounded with her blubbering children, stood screaming and cursing at the first-floor window, getting redder and fatter at every scream. The worst personality she heard was a roar of laughter, in which, such is poor humanity, I could not but join, as her little starved drab of a maid-of-all-work ran out of the door, with a bundle of stolen finery under her arm, and high above the roaring of the flames, and the shouts of the rioters, rose her mistress's yell:

'Oh Betsey! Betsey! you little awdacious unremorseful hussey! – a-running away with my best bonnet and shawl!'

The laughter soon, however, subsided, when a man rushed into the yard, shouting, 'The yeomanry!'

At that sound, to my astonishment, a general panic ensued. The miserable wretches never stopped to inquire how many, or how far off, they were – but scrambled to every outlet of the yard, trampling each other down in their hurry. I leaped up on the wall, and saw, galloping down the park, a mighty armament of some fifteen men, with a tall officer at their head, mounted on a splendid horse.

'There they be! there they be! all the varmers, and young Squire Clayton wi' mun, on his grey hunter! O Lord! O Lord! and all their swords drawn!'

I thought of the old story in Herodotus – how the Scythian masters returned from war to the rebel slaves who had taken possession of their lands and wives, and brought them down on their knees with terror, at the mere sight of the old dreaded dog-whips.*

I did not care to run. I was utterly disgusted, disappointed with myself – the people. I longed, for the moment, to die and leave it all; and left almost alone, sat down on a stone, buried my head between my hands, and tried vainly to shut out from my ears the roaring of the fire.

At that moment 'Blinkey' staggered out past me and against me, a writing-desk in his hands, shouting, in his drunken glory, 'I've vound ut at last! I've got the old fellow's money! Hush! What a vule I be, hollering like that!' – And he was going to sneak off, with a face of drunken cunning, when I sprung up and seized him by the throat.

'Rascal! robber! lay that down! Have you not done mischief enough already?'

'I wain't have no sharing. What? Do you want un yourself, eh? Then we'll see who's the stronger!'

And in an instant he shook me from him, and dealt me a blow with the corner of the desk, that laid me on the ground...

I just recollect the tramp of the yeomanry horses, and the gleam and jingle of their arms, as they galloped into the yard. I caught a glimpse of the tall young officer, as his great grey horse swept through the air over the high yard-pales – a feat to me utterly astonishing. Half-a-dozen long strides – the wretched ruffian, staggering across the field with his booty, was caught up. – The clear blade gleamed in the air – and then a fearful yell – and after that I recollect nothing.

*

Slowly I recovered my consciousness. I was lying on a truckle-bed – stone walls and a grated window! A man stood over me with a large bunch of keys in his hand. He had been wrapping my head with wet towels. I knew, instinctively, where I was.

'Well, young man,' said he, in a not unkindly tone – 'and a nice job you've made of it! Do you know where you are?'

'Yes,' answered I, quietly; 'in D * * * gaol.'

'Exactly so!'

CHAPTER XXIX

THE TRIAL

THE day was come – quickly, thank Heaven; and I stood at the bar, with four or five miserable, haggard labourers, to take my trial for sedition, riot, and arson.*

I had passed the intervening weeks half stupified with the despair of utter disappointment: disappointment at myself and my own loss of self-possession, which had caused all my misfortune, – perhaps, too, and the thought was dreadful, that of my wretched fellow-sufferers, – disappointment with the labourers, with The Cause; and when the thought came over me, in addition, that I was irreparably disgraced in the eyes of my late patrons, parted for ever from Lillian by my own folly, I laid down my head, and longed to die.

Then, again, I would recover awhile, and pluck up heart. I would plead my cause myself – I would testify against the tyrants to their face – I would say no longer to their besotted slaves, but to the men themselves, 'Go to, ye rich men, weep and howl! The hire of your labourers who have reaped down your fields, which is by you kept back by fraud, crieth; and the cries of them that have reaped hath entered into the ears of the Lord God of Hosts.'* I would brave my fate – I would die protesting, and glory in my martyrdom. But——

'Martyrdom?' said Mackaye, who had come up to D * * *, and was busy night and day about my trial. 'Ye'll just leave alone the martyr dodge, my puir bairn. Ye're na martyr at a', ye'll understand, but a vara foolish callant, that lost his temper, an' cast his pearls before swine – an' very questionable pearls they, too, to judge by the price they fetch i' the market.'

And then my heart sank again. And a few days before the

trial a letter came, evidently in my cousin's handwriting, though only signed with his initials:

'SIR, – You are in a very great scrape – you will not deny that. How you will get out of it depends on your own common sense. You probably won't be hanged – for nobody believes that you had a hand in burning the farm; but, unless you take care, you will be transported. Call yourself John Nokes; entrust your case to a clever lawyer, and keep in the background. I warn you as a friend – if you try to speechify, and play the martyr, and let out who you are, the respectable people who have been patronising you will find it necessary for their own sakes to clap a stopper on you for good and all, to make you out an imposter and a swindler, and get you out of the way for life: – while, if you are quiet, it will suit them to be quiet too, and say nothing about you, if you say nothing about them; and then there will be a chance that they, as well as your own family, will do everything in their power to hush the matter up. So, again, don't let out your real name; and instruct your lawyers to know nothing about the W.'s; and then, perhaps, the Queen's counsel will know nothing about them either. Mind – you are warned, and woe to you if you are fool enough not to take the warning.
                                                                    G.L.'

Plead in a false name! Never, so help me Heaven! To go into court with a lie in my mouth – to make myself an impostor – probably a detected one – it seemed the most cunning scheme for ruining me, which my evil genius could have suggested, whether or not it might serve his own selfish ends. But as for the other hints, they seemed not unreasonable, and promised to save me trouble; while the continued pressure of anxiety and responsibility was getting intolerable to my over-wearied brain. So I showed the letter to Mackaye, who then told me that he had taken for granted that I should come to my right mind, and had therefore already engaged an old compatriot as attorney, and the best counsel which money could procure.

'But where did you get the money? You have not surely been spending your own savings on me?'

'I canna say that I wadna ha' so dune, in case o' need. But the men in town just subscribit; puir honest fellows.'

'What! is my folly to be the cause of robbing them of their slender earnings? Never, Mackaye! Besides, they cannot have subscribed enough to pay the barrister whom you just mentioned. Tell me the whole truth, or, positively, I will plead my cause myself.'

'Aweel, then, there was a bit bank-note or twa cam' to hand – I canna say whaur fra'. But thae that sent it direckit it to be expendit in the defence o' the sax prisoners – whereof ye make ane.'

Again a world of fruitless conjecture. It must be the same unknown friend who had paid my debt to my cousin – Lillian?

*

And so the day was come. I am not going to make a long picturesque description of my trial – trials have become lately quite hackneyed subjects, stock properties for the fiction-mongers* – neither indeed, could I do so, if I would. I recollect nothing of that day, but fragments – flashes of waking existence, scattered up and down in what seemed to me a whole life of heavy, confused, painful dreams, with the glare of all those faces concentrated on me – those countless eyes which I could not, could not meet – stony, careless, unsympathising – not even angry – only curious. If they had but frowned on me, gnashed their teeth on me, I could have glared back defiance; as it was, I stood cowed and stupified, a craven by the side of cravens.

Let me see – what can I recollect? Those faces – faces – everywhere faces – a faint, sickly smell of flowers – a perpetual whispering and rustling of dresses – and all through it, the voice of someone talking, talking – I seldom knew what, or whether it was counsel, witness, judge, or prisoner, that was speaking. I was like one asleep at a foolish lecture, who hears in dreams, and only wakes when the prosing stops. Was it not prosing? What was it to me what they said? They could not understand me – my motives – my excuses; the whole pleading on my side as well as the crown's, seemed one huge fallacy – beside the matter altogether – never touching the real point at issue, the eternal moral equity of my deeds or misdeeds. I had no doubt that it would all be conducted quite properly, and fairly, and according to the forms of law; but what was law to me? – I wanted justice. And so I let them go on their own way, conscious of but one thought – was Lillian in the court?

I dared not look and see. I dared not lift up my eyes toward the gaudy rows of ladies who had crowded to the 'interesting trial of the D * * * rioters'. The torture of anxiety was less than that of certainty might be, and I kept my eyes down, and wondered how on earth the attorneys had found in so simple a case enough to stuff those great blue bags.

When, however, anything did seem likely to touch on a reality, I woke up forthwith, in spite of myself. I recollect well, for instance, a squabble about challenging the jurymen; and my counsel's voice of pious indignation, as he asked, 'Do you call these agricultural gentlemen and farmers, however excellent and respectable – on which point Heaven forbid that I, &c. &c. – the prisoner's "pares", peers, equals, or likes? What single interest, opinion, or motive, have they in common, but the universal one of self-interest, which, in this case, happens to pull in exactly opposite directions? Your lordship has often animadverted fully and boldly on the practice of allowing a bench of squires to sit in judgment on a poacher; surely it is quite as unjust that agricultural rioters should be tried by a jury of the very class against whom they are accused of rebelling.'

'Perhaps my learned brother would like a jury of rioters?' suggested some Queen's counsel.

'Upon my word, then, it would be much the fairer plan.'

I wondered whether he would have dared to say as much in the street outside – and relapsed into indifference. I believe there was some long delay, and wrangling about law-quibbles, which seemed likely at one time to quash the whole prosecution; but I was rather glad than sorry to find that it had been over-ruled. It was all a play, a game of bowls – the bowls happening to be human heads – got up between the lawyers, for the edification of society; and it would have been a pity not to play it out, according to the rules and regulations thereof.

As for the evidence, its tenor may be easily supposed from my story. There were those who could swear to my language at the camp. I was seen accompanying the mob to the farm, and haranguing them. The noise was too great for the witnesses to hear all I said, but they were certain I talked about the sacred name of liberty. The farmer's wife had seen me run round to the stacks when they were fired – whether just before or just after, she never mentioned. She had seen me running up and down in front of the house, talking loudly, and gesticulating violently; she saw me, too, struggling with another rioter for her husband's desk; – and the rest of the witnesses, some of whom I am certain I had seen busy plundering, though they were ready to swear that they had been merely accidental passers-by, seemed to think that they proved their own innocence, and testified their pious indignation, by avoiding carefully any fact which could excuse me. But, somehow, my counsel thought differently; and cross-examined, and bullied, and tormented, and misstated – as he was bound to do; and so one witness after another, clumsy and cowardly enough already, was driven by his engines of torture, as if by a pitiless spell, to deny half that he had deposed truly, and confess a great deal that was utterly false – till confusion became worse confounded, and there seemed no truth anywhere, and no falsehood either, and 'naught was everything, and everything was naught';* till I began to have doubts whether the riot had ever occurred at all – and, indeed, doubts of my own identity also, when I had heard the counsel for the crown impute to me personally, as in duty bound, every seditious atrocity which had been committed either in England or France since 1793. To him, certainly, I did listen tolerably; it was 'as good as a play.' Atheism, blasphemy, vitriol-throwing, and community of women, were among my lighter offences – for had I not actually been engaged in a plot for the destruction of property? How did the court know that I had not spent the night before the riot, as 'the doctor' and his friends did before the riots of 1839,* in drawing lots for the estates of the surrounding gentlemen, with my deluded dupes and victims? – for of course I, and not want of work, had deluded them into rioting; at least, they never would have known that they were starving, if I had not stirred up their evil passions by daring to inform them of that otherwise impalpable fact. I, the only Chartist there? Might there not have been dozens of them ? – emissaries from London, dressed up as starving labourers, and rheumatic old women?* There were actually traces of a plan for seizing all the ladies in the country, and setting up a seraglio of them in D * * * Cathedral. How did the court know that there was not one?

Ay, how indeed? and how did I know either? I really began to question whether the man might not be right after all. The whole theory seemed so horribly coherent – possible – natural. I might have done it, under possession of the devil, and forgotten it in excitement – I might – perhaps I did. And if there, why not elsewhere? Perhaps I had helped Jourdan Coupe-tête at Lyons,* and been king of the Munster Anabaptists* – why not? What matter? When would this eternity of wigs, and bonnets, and glaring windows, and ear-grinding prate and jargon, as of a diabolic universe of street-organs, end – end – end – and I get quietly hanged, and done with it all for ever?

Oh, the horrible length of that day! It seemed to me as if I had been always on my trial, ever since I was born. I wondered at times how many years ago it had all begun. I felt what a far stronger and more single-hearted patriot than I, poor Somerville,* says of himself under the torture of the sergeant's cat, in a passage, whose horrible simplicity and unconscious pathos have haunted me ever since I read it; how, when only fifty out of his hundred lashes had fallen on the bleeding back, 'The time since they began was like a long period of life: I felt as if I had lived all the time of my real life in torture, and that the days when existence had a pleasure in it were a dream long, long gone by.'

The reader may begin to suspect that I was fast going mad; and I believe I was. If he has followed my story with a human heart, he may excuse me of any extreme weakness, if I did at moments totter on the verge of that abyss.

What saved me, I believe now, was the keen, bright look of love and confidence which flashed on me from Crossthwaite's glittering eyes, when he was called forward as a witness to my character. He spoke out like a man, I hear, that day. But the counsel for the crown tried to silence him triumphantly, by calling on him to confess himself a Chartist; as if a man must needs be a liar and a villain because he holds certain opinions about the franchise! However, that was, I heard, the general opinion of the court. And then Crossthwaite lost his temper, and called the Queen's counsel a hired bully, and so went down; having done, as I was told afterwards, no good to me.

And then there followed a passage of tongue-fence between Mackaye and some barrister, and great laughter at the barrister's expense; and then I heard the old man's voice rise thin and clear:

'Let him that is without sin amang ye, cast the first stane!'*

And as he went down he looked at me – a look full of despair. I never had had a ray of hope from the beginning; but now I began to think whether men suffered much when they were hung, and whether one woke at once into the next life, or had to wait till the body had returned to the dust, and watch the ugly process of one's own decay. I was not afraid of death – I never experienced that sensation. I am not physically brave. I am as thoroughly afraid of pain as any child can be; but that next world has never offered any prospect to me, save boundless food for my insatiable curiosity.

*

But at that moment my attorney thrust into my hand a little dirty scrap of paper. 'Do you know this man?'

I read it.

'SIR, – I wull tell all truthe. Mr. Lock is a murdered man if he be hanged. Lev me spek out, for love of the Lord.

J. DAVIS.'

No. I never had heard of him; and I let the paper fall.

A murdered man? I had known that all along. Had not the Queen's counsel been trying all day to murder me, as was their duty, seeing that they got their living thereby?

A few moments after a labouring man was in the witness-box; and, to my astonishment, telling the truth, the whole truth, and nothing but the truth.

I will not trouble the reader with his details, for they were simply and exactly what I have already stated. He was badgered, bullied, cross-examined, but nothing could shake him. With that dogged honesty and laconic dignity, which is the good side of the English peasant's character, he stood manfully to his assertion – that I had done everything that words or actions

could do to prevent violence, even to the danger of my own
personal safety. He swore to the words which I used when
trying to wrest the desk from the man who had stolen it; and
when the Queen's counsel asked him, tauntingly, who had set
him on bringing his new story there at the eleventh hour, he
answered, equally to the astonishment of his questioner and of
me,

'Muster Locke, hisself.'

'What! the prisoner?' almost screamed the counsellor, who
fancied, I suppose, that he had stumbled on a confession of
unblushing bribery.

'Yes, he; he there. As he went up over hill to meeting he
met my two boys a shep-minding; and, because the cutter was
froze, he stop and turn the handle for 'em for a matter of ten
minutes; and I was coming up over field, and says I, I'll hear
what that chap's got to say – there can't be no harm in going up
arter the likes of he; for, says I to myself, a man can't have got
any great wickedness a-plotting in he's head, when he'll stop a
ten minutes to help two boys as he never sot eyes on afore in his
life; and I think their honours 'll say the same.'

Whether my reader will agree or not with the worthy fellow,
my counsel, I need not say, did, and made full use of his hint.
All the previous evidence was now discovered to have corroborated the last witness, except where it had been notoriously
overthrown. I was extolled as a miracle of calm benevolence;
and black became grey, and grey became spotless white, and the
whole feeling of the court seemed changed in my favour; till
the little attorney popped up his head and whispered to me:

'By George! that last witness has saved your life.'

To which I answered 'Very well' – and turned stupidly back
upon that nightmare thought – was Lillian in the court?

*

At last a voice, the judge's, I believe, for it was grave, gentle,
almost compassionate, asked us one by one whether we had
anything to say in our own defence. I recollect an indistinct
murmur from one after another of the poor semi-brutes on my
left; and then my attorney, looking up to me, made me aware
that I was expected to speak. On the moment, somehow, my

whole courage returned to me. I felt that I must unburden my heart, now or never. With a sudden effort I roused myself, and looking fixedly and proudly at the reverend face opposite, began:

'The utmost offence which has been proved against me is a few bold words, producing consequences as unexpected as illogical. If the stupid ferocity with which my words were misunderstood, as by a horde of savages, rather than Englishmen; – if the moral and physical condition of these prisoners at my side; – of those witnesses who have borne testimony against me, miserable white slaves, miscalled free labourers; – ay, if a single walk through the farms and cottages on which this mischief was bred, affords no excuse for one indignant sentence——'

There she was! There she had been all the time – right opposite to me, close to the judge – cold, bright, curious – smiling! And as our eyes met, she turned away, and whispered gaily something to a young man who sat beside her.

Every drop of blood in my body rushed into my forehead; the court, the windows, and the faces, whirled round and round, and I fell senseless on the floor of the dock.

*

I next recollect some room or other in the gaol, Mackaye with both my hands in his; and the rough kindly voice of the gaoler congratulating me on having 'only got three years.'

'But you didn't show half a good pluck,' said some one. 'There's two on 'em transported, took it as bold as brass, and thanked the judge for getting 'em out o' this starving place "free gracious for nothing", says they.'

'Ah!' quoth the little attorney, rubbing his hands, 'you should have seen * * * and * * * after the row in '42!* They were the boys for the Bull Ring!* Gave a barrister as good as he brought, eh, Mr. Mackaye? My small services, you remember, were of no use – really no use at all – quite ashamed to send in my little account. Managed the case themselves, like two patriotic parties as they were, with a degree of forensic acuteness, inspired by the consciousness of a noble cause – Ahem! You remember, friend M.? Grand triumphs those, eh?'

'Ay,' said Sandy, 'I mind them unco weel – they cost me a' my few savings, mair by token; an' mony a braw fallow paid for ither folks' sins that tide. But my puir laddie here's no made o' that stuff. He's ower thin-skinned for a patriot.'

'Ah, well – this little taste of British justice will thicken his hide for him, eh?' and the attorney chuckled and winked. 'He'll come out again as tough as a bull-dog, and as surly too. Eh, Mr. Mackaye? eh?'

''Deed, then, I'm unco sair afeard that your opeenion is no a'thegither that improbable,' answered Sandy, with a drawl of unusual solemnity.

CHAPTER XXX

PRISON THOUGHTS

I was alone in my cell.

Three years' imprisonment! Thirty-six months! – one thousand and ninety-five days – and twenty-four whole hours in each of them! Well – I should sleep half the time: one-third at least. Perhaps I should not be able to sleep! To lie awake, and think – there! The thought was horrible – it was all horrible. To have three whole years cut out of my life, instead of having before me, as I had always as yet had, a mysterious Eldorado of new schemes and hopes, possible developments, possible triumphs, possible bliss – to have nothing, nothing before me but blank and stagnation, dead loss and waste: and then to go out again, and start once more where I had left off yesterday!

It should not be! I would not lose these years! I would show myself a man; they should feel my strength just when they fancied they had crushed me utterly! They might bury me, but I should rise again! – I should rise again more glorious, perhaps to be henceforth immortal, and live upon the lips of men. I would educate myself; I would read – what would I not read? These three years should be a time of sacred retirement and contemplation, as of Thebaid anchorite,* or Mahomet in his Arabian cave.* I would write pamphlets that should thunder through the land, and make tyrants tremble on their thrones! All England – at least all crushed and suffering hearts, should break forth at my fiery words into one roar of indignant sympathy. No – I would write a poem; I would concentrate all my experience, my aspirations, all the hopes and wrongs and sorrows of the poor, into one garland of thorns – one immortal epic of suffering. What should I call it? And I set to work deliberately – such a thing is man – to think of a title.

I looked up, and my eye caught the close bars of the little window; and then came over me, for the first time, the full meaning of that word – Prison; that word which the rich use so lightly, knowing well that there is no chance, in these days, of their ever finding themselves in one; for the higher classes never break the laws – seeing that they have made them to fit themselves. Ay, I was in prison. I could not go out or come in at will. I was watched, commanded at every turn. I was a brute animal, a puppet, a doll, that children put away in a cupboard, and there it lies. And yet my whole soul was as wide, fierce, roving, struggling, as ever. Horrible contradiction! The dreadful sense of helplessness, the crushing weight of necessity, seemed to choke me. The smooth white walls, the smooth white ceiling, seemed squeezing in closer and closer on me, and yet dilating into vast infinities, just as the merest knot of mould will transform itself, as one watches it, and nothing else, into enormous cliffs, long slopes of moor and spurs of mountain-range. Oh, those smooth white walls and ceiling! If there had but been a print – a stain of dirt – a cobweb, to fleck their unbroken ghastliness! They stared at me, like grim, impassive, featureless, formless fiends; all the more dreadful for their sleek hypocritic cleanliness – purity as of a saint-inquisitor watching with spotless conscience the victim on the rack. They choked me – I gasped for breath, stretched out my arms, rolled shrieking on the floor – the narrow chequered glimpse of free blue sky, seen through the window, seemed to fade dimmer and dimmer, farther and farther off. I sprang up, as if to follow it – rushed to the bars, shook and wrenched at them with my thin, puny arms – and stood spellbound, as I caught sight of the cathedral towers, standing out in grand repose against the horizontal fiery bars of sunset, like great angels at the gates of Paradise, watching in stately sorrow all the wailing and the wrong below. And beneath, beneath – the well-known roofs – Lillian's home, and all its proud and happy memories! It was but a corner of a gable, a scrap of garden, that I could see beyond intervening roofs and trees – but could I mistake them? There was the very cedar-tree; I knew its dark pyramid but too well! There I had walked by her; there, just behind that envious group of chestnuts, she was now. The light was fading; it must be six o'clock! she must be in her room now, dressing herself for dinner, looking so beautiful! And as I gazed, and gazed, all the intervening objects became transparent, and vanished before the intensity of my imagination. Were my poems in her room still? Perhaps she had thrown them away – the condemned rioter's poems! Was she thinking of me? Yes – with horror and contempt. Well, at least she was thinking of me. And she would understand me at last – she must. Some day she would know all I had borne for love of her – the depth, the might, the purity of my adoration. She would see the world honouring me, in the day of my triumph, when I was appreciated at last; – when I stood before the eyes of admiring men, a people's singer, a king of human spirits, great with the rank which genius gives, then she would find out what a man had loved her; then she would know the honour, the privilege of a poet's worship.

——But that trial scene!

Ay – that trial scene. That cold, unmoved smile! – when she knew me, must have known me, not to be the wretch which those hired slanderers had called me. If she had cared for me – if she had a woman's heart in her at all, any pity, any justice, would she not have spoken? Would she not have called on others to speak, and clear me of the calumny? Nonsense! Impossible! She – so frail, tender, retiring – how could she speak? How did I know that she had not felt for me? It was woman's nature – duty, to conceal her feelings; perhaps that after all was the true explanation of that smile. Perhaps, too, she might have spoken – might be even now pleading for me in secret; not that I wished to be pardoned – not I – but it would be so delicious to have her, her, pleading for me! Perhaps – perhaps I might hear of her – from her! Surely she could not leave me here so close, without some token! And I actually listened, I know not how long, expecting the door to open, and a message to arrive: till, with my eyes rivetted on that bit of gable, and my ears listening behind me like a hare's in her form, to catch every sound in the ward outside, I fell fast asleep, and forgot all in the heavy dreamless torpor of utter mental and bodily exhaustion.

I was awakened by the opening of my cell door, and the appearance of the turnkey.

'Well, young man, all right again? You've had a long nap; and no wonder, you've had a hard time of it lately; and a good lesson to you, too.'

'How long have I slept? I do not recollect going to bed. And how came I to lie down without undressing?'

'I found you, at lock-up hours, asleep there, kneeling on the chair, with your head on the window-sill; and a mercy you hadn't tumbled off and broke your back. Now, look here. – You seems a civil sort of chap; and civil gets as civil gives with me. Only don't you talk no politics. They aint no good to nobody, except the big 'uns, wot gets their living thereby; and I should think you'd had dose enough on 'em to last for a month of Sundays. So just get yourself tidy, there's a lad, and come along with me to chapel.'

I obeyed him, in that and other things; and I never received from him, or, indeed, from any one else there, aught but kindness. I have no complaint to make – but prison is prison. As for talking politics, I never, during those three years, exchanged as many sentences with any of my fellow-prisoners. What had I to say to them? Poachers and petty thieves – the scum of misery, ignorance, and rascality throughout the country. If my heart yearned toward them at times, it was generally shut close by the exclusive pride of superior intellect and knowledge. I considered it, as it was, a degradation to be classed with such; never asking myself how far I had brought that degradation on myself: and I loved to show my sense of injustice by walking, moody and silent, up and down a lonely corner of the yard; and at last contrived, under the plea of ill-health (and, truly, I never was ten minutes without coughing), to confine myself entirely to my cell, and escape altogether the company of a class whom I despised, almost hated, as my betrayers, before whom I had cast away my pearls – questionable though they were, according to Mackaye. Oh! there is, in the intellectual work-man's heart, as in all others, the root of Pharisaism – the lust after self-glorifying superiority, on the ground of 'genius'.

We too are men; frail, selfish, proud as others. The days are past, thank God, when the 'gentlemen button-makers' used to insist on a separate tap-room from the mere 'button-makers', on the ground of earning a few more shillings per week. But we are not yet thorough democrats, my brothers; we do not yet utterly believe our own loud doctrine of equality; nor shall we till – But I must not anticipate the stages of my own experience

*

I complain of no one, again I say – neither of judge, jury, gaolers, or chaplain. True, imprisonment was the worst possible remedy for my disease that could have been devised, if, as the new doctrine is, punishments are inflicted only to reform the criminal.* What could prison do for me, but embitter and confirm all my prejudices? But I do not see what else they could have done with me while law is what it is, and perhaps ever will be; dealing with the overt acts of the poor, and never touching the subtler and more spiritual iniquities of the rich respectable. When shall we see a nation ruled, not by the law, but by the Gospel; not in the letter which kills, but in the spirit which is love, forgiveness, life? When? God knows! And God does know.

*

But I did work, during those three years, for months at a time, steadily and severely; and, with little profit, alas! to my temper of mind. I gorged my intellect for I could do nothing else. The political questions which I longed to solve in some way or other, were tabooed by the well-meaning chaplain. He even forbid me a standard English work on political economy, which I had written to Mackaye to borrow for me; he was not so careful, it will be seen hereafter, with foreign books. He meant, of course, to keep my mind from what he considered at once useless and polluting; but the only effect of his method was, that all the doubts and questions remained, rankling and fierce, imperiously demanding my attention, and had to be solved by my own moody and soured meditations, warped and coloured by the strong sense of universal wrong.

Then he deluged me with tracts, weak and well-meaning, which informed me that 'Christians', being 'not of this world', had nothing to do with politics; and preached to me the divine right of kings, passive obedience to the powers – or impotences – that be, &c., &c., with such success as may be imagined. I opened them each, read a few sentences, and laid them by. They were written by good men, no doubt; but men who had an interest in keeping up the present system; at all events, by men who knew nothing of my temptations, my creed, my unbelief; who saw all heaven and earth from a station antipodal to my own: I had simply nothing to do with them.

And yet, excellent man! pious, benignant, compassionate! God forbid that I should, in writing these words, allow myself a desire so base as that of disparaging thee! However thy words failed of their purpose, that bright, gentle, earnest face never appeared without bringing balm to the wounded spirit. Hadst thou not recalled me to humanity, those three years would have made a savage and a madman of me. May God reward thee hereafter! Thou hast thy reward on earth in the gratitude of many a broken heart bound up, of drunkards sobered, thieves reclaimed, and outcasts taught to look for a paternal home denied them here on earth! While such thy deeds, what matter thine opinions?

But alas! (for the truth must be told, as a warning to those who have to face the educated working men), his opinions did matter to himself. The good man laboured under the delusion, common enough, of choosing his favourite weapons from his weakest faculty; and the very inferiority of his intellect prevented him from seeing where his true strength lay. He *would* argue; he would try and convert me from scepticism by what seemed to him reasoning, the common figure of which was, what logicians, I believe, call begging the question; and the common method what they call *ignoratio elenchi** – shooting at pigeons, while crows are the game desired. He always started by demanding my assent to the very question which lay at the bottom of my doubts. He would wrangle and wrestle blindly up and down, with tears of earnestness in his eyes, till he had lost his temper, as far as was possible for one so angel-guarded as he seemed to be; and then, when he found himself confused, contradicting his own words, making concessions at which he shuddered, for the sake of gaining from me assents which he found out the next moment I understood in quite a different sense from his, he would suddenly shift his ground, and try to knock me down authoritatively with a single text of Scripture; when all the while I wanted proof that Scripture had any authority at all.

He carefully confined himself, too, throughout, to the dogmatic phraseology of the pulpit; while I either did not understand, or required justification for, the strange, far-fetched, technical meanings, which he attached to his expressions. If he would only have talked English! – if clergymen would only preach in English! – and then they wonder that their sermons have no effect! Their notion seems to be, as my good chaplain's was, that the teacher is not to condescend to the scholar, much less to become all things to all men, if by any means he may save some; but that he has a right to demand that the scholar shall ascend to him before he is taught; that he shall raise himself up of his own strength into the teacher's region of thought as well as feeling; to do for himself, in short, under penalty of being called an unbeliever, just what the teacher professes to do for him.

At last, he seemed dimly to discover that I could not acquiesce in his conclusions, while I denied his premises; and so he lent me, in an ill-starred moment, 'Paley's Evidences',* and some tracts of the last generation against Deism. I read them, and remained, as hundreds more have done, just where I was before.

'Was Paley,' I asked, 'a really good and pious man?'

The really good and pious man hemmed and hawed.

'Because, if he was not, I can't trust a page of his special pleading, let it look as clever as the whole Old Bailey in one.'

Besides, I never denied the existence of Jesus of Nazareth, or his apostles. I doubted the myths and doctrines, which I believed to have been gradually built up round the true story. The fact was, he was, like most of his class, 'attacking extinct Satans',* fighting manfully against Voltaire, Volney, and Tom Paine;* while I was fighting for Strauss, Hennell,* and Emerson. And, at last, he gave me up for some weeks as a hopeless infidel, without ever having touched the points on which I disbelieved. He had never read Strauss – hardly even heard of him; and, till clergymen make up their minds to do that, and to answer

Strauss also, they will, as he did, leave the heretic artisan just where they found him.

The bad effect which all this had on my mind may easily be conceived. I felt myself his intellectual superior. I tripped him up, played with him, made him expose his weaknesses, till I really began to despise him. May Heaven forgive me for it! But it was not till long afterwards that I began, on looking back, to see how worthless was any superior cleverness of mine before his superior moral and spiritual excellence. That was just what he would not let me see at the time. I was worshipping intellect, mere intellect; and thence arose my doubts; and he tried to conquer them by exciting the very faculty which had begotten them. When will the clergy learn that their strength is in action, and not in argument? If they are to re-convert the masses, it must be by noble deeds, as Carlyle says; 'not by noisy theoretic laudation of *a* Church, but by silent practical demonstration of *the* Church.'*

*

But, the reader may ask, where was your Bible all this time?

Yes – there was a Bible in my cell – and the chaplain read to me, both privately and in chapel, such portions of it as he thought suited my case, or rather his utterly-mistaken view thereof. But to tell the truth, I cared not to read or listen. Was it not the book of the aristocrats – of kings and priests, passive obedience, and the slavery of the intellect? Had I been thrown under the influence of the more educated Independents in former years, I might have thought differently. They, at least, have contrived, with what logical consistence I know not, to reconcile orthodox Christianity with unflinching democratic opinions. But such was not my lot. My mother, as I said in my first chapter, had become a Baptist; because she believed that sect, and as I think rightly, to be the only one which logically and consistently carries out the Calvinistic theory; and now I looked back upon her delight in Gideon and Barak, Samson and Jehu,* only as the mystic application of rare exceptions to the fanaticism of a chosen few – the elect – the saints, who, as the fifth-monarchy men* held, were one day to rule the world with a rod of iron. And so I fell – willingly, alas! – into the vulgar belief about the politics of Scripture, common alike – strange unanimity! – to Infidel and Churchman. The great idea that the Bible is the history of mankind's deliverance from all tyranny, outward as well as inward; of the Jews, as the one free constitutional people among a world of slaves and tyrants; of their ruin, as the righteous fruit of a voluntary return to despotism; of the New Testament, as the good news that freedom, brotherhood, and equality, once confined only to Judæa and to Greece, and dimly seen even there, was henceforth to be the right of all mankind, the law of all society – who was there to tell me that? Who is there now to go forth and tell it to the millions who have suffered, and doubted, and despaired like me, and turn the hearts of the disobedient to the wisdom of the just, before the great and terrible day of the Lord come? Again I ask – who will go forth and preach that Gospel, and save his native land?

But, as I said before, I read, and steadily. In the first place, I, for the first time in my life, studied Shakspeare throughout; and found out now the treasure which I had overlooked. I assure my readers I am not going to give a lecture on him here, as I was minded to have done. Only, as I am asking questions, who will write us a 'People's Commentary on Shakspeare'?

Then I waded, making copious notes and extracts, through the whole of Hume, and Hallam's 'Middle Ages' and 'Constitutional History',* and found them barren to my soul. When (to ask a third and last question) will some man, of the spirit of Carlyle – one who is not ashamed to acknowledge the intervention of a God, a Providence, even of a devil, in the affairs of men – arise, and write a 'People's History of England'?

Then I laboured long months at learning French, for the mere purpose of reading French political economy after my liberation. But at last, in my impatience, I wrote to Sandy to send me Proudhon and Louis Blanc,* on the chance of their passing the good chaplain's censorship – and behold, they passed! He had never heard their names! He was, I suspect, utterly ignorant of French, and afraid of exposing his ignorance by venturing to criticise. As it was, I was allowed peaceable possession of them till within a few months of my liberation, with such consequences as may be imagined; and then, to his unfeigned terror and horror, he discovered, in some periodical, that he had been leaving in my hands books which advocated 'the destruction of property', and therefore, in his eyes, of all which is moral or sacred in earth and heaven! I gave them up without a struggle, so really painful was the good soul's concern, and the reproaches which he heaped, not on me – he never reproached me in his life – but on himself, for having so neglected his duty.

Then I read hard for a few months at physical science – at Zoology and Botany, and threw it aside again in bitterness of heart. It was too bitter to be tantalised with the description of Nature's wondrous forms, and I there a prisoner, between those four white walls!

Then I set to work to write an autobiography – at least to commit to paper in regular order the most striking incidents and conversations which I could recollect, and which I had noted down as they occurred in my diary. From that source I have drawn nearly the whole of my history up to this point. For the rest I must trust to memory – and, indeed, the strange deeds and sufferings, and the yet stranger revelations, of the last few months, have branded themselves deep enough upon my brain. I need not hope, or fear, that aught of them should slip my memory.

*

So went the weary time. Week after week, month after month, summer after summer, I scored the days off, like a lonely schoolboy, on the pages of a calendar; and day by day I went to my window, and knelt there, gazing at the gable and the cedar-tree. That was my only recreation. Sometimes, at first, my eyes used to wander over the wide prospect of rich lowlands, and farms, and hamlets, and I used to amuse myself with conjectures about the people who lived in them, and walked where they liked on God's earth: but soon I hated to look at the country; its perpetual change and progress mocked the dreary sameness of my dungeon. It was bitter, maddening, to see the grey boughs grow green with leaves, and the green fade to autumnal yellow, and the grey boughs reappear again, and I still there! The dark sleeping fallows bloomed with emerald blades of corn,

and then the corn grew deep and crisp, and blackened before
the summer breeze, in 'waves of shadow', as Mr. Tennyson
says in one of his most exquisite lyrics;* and then the fields
grew white to harvest day by day, and I saw the rows of sheaves
rise one by one, and the carts crawling homeward under their
load. I could almost hear the merry voices of the children round
them – children that could go into the woods, and pick wild
flowers, and I still there! No – I would look at nothing but the
gable, and the cedar-tree, and the tall cathedral towers; there
was no change in them – they did not laugh at me.

But she who lived beneath them? Months and seasons
crawled along, and yet no sign or hint of her! I was forgotten,
forsaken! And yet I gazed, and gazed. I could not forget her;
I could not forget what she had been to me. Eden was still
there, though I was shut out from it for ever: and so, like a
widower over the grave of her he loves, morning and evening
I watched the gable and the cedar-tree.

And my cousin? Ah, that was the thought, the only thought,
which made my life intolerable! What might he not be doing
in the mean time? I knew his purpose – I knew his power.
True, I had never seen a hint, a glance, which could have given
him hope; but he had three whole years to win her in – three
whole years, and I fettered, helpless, absent! 'Fool! could I have
won her if I had been free? At least, I would have tried:
we would have fought it fairly out, on even ground; we would
have seen which was the strongest, respectability and cunning,
or the simplicity of genius. But now!' – And I tore at the bars
of the window, and threw myself on the floor of my cell, and
longed to die.

CHAPTER XXXI

THE NEW CHURCH

IN a poor suburb of the city, which I could see well enough
from my little window, a new Gothic church was building.
When I first took up my abode in the cell, it was just begun –
the walls had hardly risen above the neighbouring sheds and

garden-fences. But month after month I had watched it grow-ing; I had seen one window after another filled with tracery, one buttress after another finished off with its carved pinnacle; then I had watched the skeleton of the roof gradually clothed in tiling; and then the glazing of the windows – some of them painted, I could see, from the iron network which was placed outside them the same day. Then the doors were put up – were they going to finish that handsome tower? No; it was left with its wooden cap, I supposed for further funds. But the nave, and the deep chancel behind it, were all finished, and sur-mounted by a cross, – and beautiful enough the little sanctuary looked, in the virgin-purity of its spotless freestone.* For eighteen months I watched it grow before my eyes – and I was still in my cell!

And then there was a grand procession of surplices and lawn sleeves; and among them I fancied I distinguished the old dean's stately figure, and turned my head away, and looked again, and fancied I distinguished another figure – it must have been mere imagination – the distance was far too great for me to identify any one; but I could not get out of my head the fancy – say rather, the instinct – that it was my cousin's; and that it was my cousin whom I saw daily after that, coming out and going in, when the bell rang to morning and evening prayers – for there were daily services there, and saints' day services, and Lent services, and three services on a Sunday, and six or seven on Good Friday and Easter-day. The little musical bell above the chancel-arch seemed always ringing; and still that figure haunted me like a nightmare, ever coming in and going out about its priestly calling – and I still in my cell! If it should be he! – so close to her! I shuddered at the thought; and, just because it was so intolerable, it clung to me, and tormented me, and kept me awake at nights, till I became utterly unable to study quietly, and spent hours at the narrow window, watching for the very figure which I loathed to see.

And then a Gothic school-house rose at the churchyard end, and troops of children poured in and out, and women came daily for alms; and when the frosts came on, every morning I saw a crowd, and soup carried away in pitchers, and clothes and blankets given away; the giving seemed endless, boundless;

and I thought of the times of the Roman Empire and the 'sportula',* when the poor had got to live upon the alms of the rich, more and more, year by year – till they devoured their own devourers, and the end came; and I shuddered. And yet it was a pleasant sight, as every new church is to the healthy-minded man, let his religious opinions be what they may. A fresh centre of civilisation, mercy, comfort for weary hearts, relief from frost and hunger; a fresh centre of instruction, humanising, disciplining, however meagre in my eyes, to hundreds of little savage spirits; altogether a pleasant sight, even to me there in my cell. And I used to wonder at the wasted power of the Church – her almost entire monopoly of the pulpits, the schools, the alms of England; and then thank Heaven, somewhat prematurely, that she knew and used so little her vast latent power for the destruction of liberty.

Or for its realisation?

Ay, that is the question! We shall not see it solved – at least, I never shall.

But still that figure haunted me; all through that winter I saw it, chatting with old women, patting children's heads, walking to the church with ladies; sometimes with a tiny, tripping figure. – I did not dare to let myself fancy who that might be.

*

December passed, and January came. I had now only two months more before my deliverance. One day I seemed to myself to have spent a whole life in that narrow room; and the next, the years and months seemed short and blank as a night's sleep on waking; and there was no salient point in all my memory, since that last sight of Lillian's smile, and the faces and the windows whirling round before me as I fell.

At last came a letter from Mackaye. 'Ye speired for news o' your cousin – an' I find he's a neebour o' yours; ca'd to a new kirk i' the city o' your captivity – an' na stickit* minister he makes, forbye he's ane o' these new Puseyite sectarians,* to judge by your uncle's report. I met the auld baillie-bodie on the street, an' I was gaun to pass him by, but he was sae fu' o' good news he could na but stop an' ha' a crack wi' me on politics;

for we ha' helpit thegither in certain municipal clanjamfries* o' late. An' he told me your cousin wins honour fast, an' mun surely die a bishop – puir bairn! An' besides that, he's gaun be married the spring. I dinna mind the leddy's name; but there's tocher* wi' lass o' his, I'll warrant. He's na laird o' Cockpen, for a penniless lass wi' a long pedigree.'*

As I sat meditating over this news – which made the torment of suspicion and suspense more intolerable than ever – behold a postscript, added some two days after.

'Oh! oh! Sic news! gran' news! news to make baith the ears o' him that heareth it to tingle. God is God, an' no the deevil after a'! Louis Philippe is doun!* – doun, doun, like a dog! an' the republic's proclaimed, an' the auld villain here in England, they say, a wanderer an' a beggar. I ha' sent ye the paper o' the day. PS. – 73, 37, 12. Oh, the Psalms are full o't! Never say the Bible's no true, mair. I've been unco faithless mysel, God forgive me! I got grieving to see the wicked in sic prosperity. I did na gang into the sanctuary eneugh, an' therefore I could na see the end of these men – how He does take them up suddenly after all, an' cast them doun; vanish they do, perish, an' come to a fearful end. Yea, like as a dream when one awaketh, so shalt thou make their image to vanish out of the city. Oh, but it's a day o' God! An' yet I'm sair afraid for they puir feckless French. I ha' na faith, ye ken, in the Celtic blude, an' its spirit o' lees. The Saxon spirit o' covetize is a grewsome house-fiend, and sae's our Norse's speerit o' shifts an' dodges; but the spirit of lees is warse. Puir lustful Reubens that they are! – unstable as water, they shall not excel.* Well, well – after all, there is a God that judgeth the earth; an' when a man kens that, he's learnt eneugh to last him till he dies.'

CHAPTER XXXII

THE TOWER OF BABEL

A glorious people vibrated again
   The lightning of the nations; Liberty
From heart to heart, from tower to tower, o'er France,
   Scattering contagious fire into the sky,
Gleamed. My soul spurned the chains of its dismay;
   And in the rapid plumes of song
   Clothed itself sublime and strong.*

SUBLIME and strong? Alas! not so. An outcast, heartless, faithless, and embittered, I went forth from my prison. – But yet Louis Philippe had fallen! And as I whirled back to Babylon and want, discontent and discord, my heart was light, my breath came thick and fierce. – The incubus of France had fallen! and from land to land, like the Beacon-fire which leapt from peak to peak proclaiming Troy's downfall, passed on the glare of burning idols, the crash of falling anarchies. Was I mad, sinful? Both – and yet neither. Was I mad and sinful, if on my return to my old haunts, amid the grasp of loving hands, and the caresses of those who called me in their honest flattery a martyr and a hero – what things, as Carlyle says, men will fall down and worship in their extreme need!* – was I mad and sinful, if daring hopes arose, and desperate words were spoken, and wild eyes read in wild eyes the thoughts they dare not utter? 'Liberty has risen from the dead, and we too will be free!'

Yes, mad and sinful; therefore are we as we are. Yet God has forgiven us – perhaps so have those men whose forgiveness is alone worth having.

Liberty? And is that word a dream, a lie, the watchword only of rebellious fiends, as bigots say even now? Our forefathers spoke not so—

   The shadow of her coming fell
   On Saxon Alfred's olive-tinctured brow.*

Had not freedom, progressive, expanding, descending, been the glory and the strength of England? Were Magna Charta and the Habeas Corpus Act, Hampden's resistance to ship-money, and the calm, righteous might of 1688* – were they all futilities and fallacies? Ever downwards, for seven hundred years, welling from the heaven-watered mountain peaks of wisdom, had spread the stream of liberty. The nobles had gained their charter from John; the middle classes from William of Orange: was not the time at hand, when from a Queen, more gentle, charitable, upright, spotless, than had ever sat on the throne of England, the working masses in their turn should gain their Charter?

If it was given, the gift was hers: if it was demanded to the uttermost, the demand would be made, not on her, but on those into whose hands her power had passed, the avowed representatives neither of the Crown nor of the people, but of the very commercial class which was devouring us.

Such was our dream. Insane and wicked were the passions which accompanied it; insane and wicked were the means we chose; and God in His mercy to us, rather than to Mammon, triumphant in his iniquity, fattening his heart even now for a spiritual day of slaughter more fearful than any physical slaughter which we in our folly had prepared for him – God frustrated them.

We confess our sins. Shall the Chartist alone be excluded from the promise, 'If we confess our sins, God is faithful and just to forgive us our sins, and cleanse us from all unrighteous-ness'?*

And yet, were there no excuses for us? I do not say for myself – and yet three years of prison might be some excuse for a soured and harshened spirit – but I will not avail myself of the excuse; for there were men, stancher Chartists than ever I had been – men who had suffered not only imprisonment, but loss of health and loss of fortune; men whose influence with the workmen was far wider than my own, and whose temptations were therefore all the greater, who manfully and righteously kept themselves aloof from all those frantic schemes, and now reap their reward, in being acknowledged as the true leaders of the artisans, while the mere preachers of sedition are scattered to the winds.*

But were there no excuses for the mass? Was there no excuse

in the spirit with which the English upper classes regarded the continental revolutions? No excuse in the undisguised dislike, fear, contempt, which they expressed for that very sacred name of Liberty, which had been for ages the pride of England and her laws—

> The old laws of England, they
> Whose reverend heads with age are grey –
> Children of a wiser day –
> And whose solemn voice must be
> Thine own echo, Liberty!*

for which, according to the latest improvements, is now substituted a bureaucracy of despotic commissions? Shame upon those who sneered at the very name of her to whom they owed the wealth they idolize! who cry down Liberty because God has given it to them in such priceless abundance, boundless as the sunshine and the air of heaven, that they are become unconscious of it as of the elements by which they live! Woe to those who despise the gift of God! Woe be those who have turned His grace into a cloak for tyranny; who, like the Jews of old, have trampled under foot His covenant at the very moment that they were asserting their exclusive right to it, and denying His all-embracing love!

And were there no excuses, too, in the very arguments which nineteen-twentieths of the public press used to deter us from following the example of the Continent? If there had been one word of sympathy with the deep wrongs of France, Germany, Italy, Hungary – one attempt to discriminate the righteous and God-inspired desire of freedom, from man's furious and self-willed perversion of it, we would have listened to them. But, instead, what was the first, last, cardinal, crowning argument? – 'The cost of sedition!' 'Revolutions interfered with trade!' and therefore they were damnable! Interfere with the food and labour of the millions? The millions would take the responsibility of that upon themselves. If the party of order cares so much for the millions, why had they left them what they are? No: it was with the profits of the few that revolutions interfered; with the Divine right, not so much of kings, but of money-making. They hampered Mammon, the very fiend who is devouring the masses. The one end and aim of existence was, the maintenance of order – of peace and room to make money in. And therefore Louis' spies might make France one great inquisition-hell; German princelets might sell their country piecemeal to French or Russian; the Hungarian constitution, almost the counterpart of our own, might be sacrificed at the will of an idiot or a villain; Papal misgovernment might continue to render Rome a worse den of thieves than even Papal superstitution could have made it without the addition of tyranny;* but Order must be maintained, for how else could the few make money out of the labour of the many? These were their own arguments. Whether they were likely to conciliate the workman to the powers that be, by informing him that those powers were avowedly the priests of the very system which was crushing him, let the reader judge.

The maintenance of order – of the order of disorder – that was to be the new God before whom the working classes were to bow in spell-bound awe: an idol more despicable and empty than even that old divine right of tyrants, newly applied by some well-meaning but illogical personages, not merely as of old to hereditary sovereigns, but to Louis Philippes, usurers, upstarts – why not hereafter to demagogues? Blindfold and desperate bigots! who would actually thus, in the imbecility of terror, deify that very right of the physically strongest and cunningest, which, if anything, is anti-christ itself. That argument against sedition, the workmen heard; and, recollecting 1688,* went on their way, such as it was, unheeding.

One word more, even at the risk of offending many whom I should be very sorry to offend, and I leave this hateful discussion. Let it ever be remembered that the working classes considered themselves deceived, cajoled, by the passers of the Reform Bill; that they cherished – whether rightly or wrongly it is now too late to ask – a deep-rooted grudge against those who had, as they thought, made their hopes and passions a stepping-stone towards their own selfish ends. They were told to support the Reform Bill, not only on account of its intrinsic righteousness – which God forbid that I should deny – but because it was the first of a glorious line of steps towards their enfranchisement; and now the very men who told them this, talked peremptorily of 'finality', showed themselves the most dogged and careless of conservatives, and pooh-poohed away every attempt at further enlargement of the suffrage.* They were told to support it as the remedy for their own social miseries; and behold, those miseries were year by year becoming deeper, more wide-spread, more hopeless; their entreaties for help and mercy, in 1842, and at other times, had been lazily laid by unanswered;* and almost the only practical efforts for their deliverance had been made by a Tory nobleman, the honoured and beloved Lord Ashley.* They found that they had, in helping to pass the Reform Bill, only helped to give power to the two very classes who crushed them – the great labour-kings, and the small shopkeepers; that they had blindly armed their oppressors with the additional weapon of an ever-increasing political majority. They had been told, too (let that never be forgotten), that in order to carry the Reform Bill, sedition itself was lawful;* they had seen the master-manufacturers themselves give the signal for the plug riots,* by stopping their mills. Their vanity, ferocity, sense of latent and fettered power, pride of numbers, and physical strength, had been flattered and pampered by those who now talked only of grape-shot and bayonets. They had heard the Reform Bill carried by the threats of men of rank and power, that 'Manchester should march upon London'.* Were their masters, then, to have a monopoly in sedition, as in everything else? What had been fair in order to compel the Reform Bill, must surely be fairer still to compel the fulfilment of Reform Bill pledges? And so, imitating the example of those whom they fancied had first used and then deserted them, they, in their madness, concocted a rebellion, not primarily against the laws and constitution of their land, but against Mammon – against that accursed system of competition, slavery of labour, absorption of the small capitalists by the large ones, and of the workmen by all, which is, and was, and ever will be, their internecine foe. Silly and sanguinary enough, were their schemes, God knows! and bootless enough had they suc-ceeded; for nothing flourishes in the revolutionary atmosphere but that lowest embodiment of Mammon, 'the black pool of Agio',* and its money-gamblers. But the battle remains still to be fought; the struggle is internecine; only no more with weapons of flesh and blood, but with a mightier weapon – with that association which is the true bane of Mammon – the embodiment of brotherhood and love.

We should have known that before the tenth of April? Most true, reader – but wrath is blindness. You too surely have read more wisdom than you have practised yet; seeing that you have your Bible, and perhaps, too, Mill's 'Political Economy'. Have you perused therein the priceless chapter 'On the probable Futurity of the Labouring Classes'? If not, let me give you the reference – vol. ii., p. 315, of the Second Edition.* Read it, thou self-satisfied Mammon, and perpend; for it is both a prophecy and a doom!

*

But, the reader may ask, how did you, with your experience of the reason, honesty, moderation, to be expected of mobs, join in a plan which, if it had succeeded, must have let loose on those 'who had' in London, the whole flood of those 'who had not'?

The reader shall hear. My story may be instructive, as a type of the feelings of thousands beside me.

It was the night after I had returned from D***; sitting in Crossthwaite's little room, I had heard with mingled anxiety and delight the plans of my friends. They were about to present a monster-petition in favour of the Charter; to accompany it *en masse* to the door of the House of Commons; and if it was refused admittance – why then, ulterior measures were the only hope. 'And they will refuse it!' said Crossthwaite; 'they're going, I hear, to revive some old law or other,* that forbids processions within such and such a distance of the House of Commons. Let them forbid! To carry arms, to go in public procession, to present petitions openly, instead of having them made a humbug of by being laid on the table unopened by some careless member – they're our rights, and we'll have them. There's no use mincing the matter: it's like the old fable of the farmer and his wheat – if we want it reaped, we must reap it ourselves. Public opinion, and the pressure from without, are the only things which have carried any measure in England for the last twenty years. Neither Whigs nor Tories deny it: the governed govern their governors — that's the "ordre du jour" just now — and we'll have our turn at it! We'll give those House of Commons oligarchs — those tools of the squires and the shop-keepers — we'll give them a taste of pressure from without, as shall make the bar of the house crack again.* And then to be under arms, day and night, till the Charter's granted!'

'And if it is refused?'

'Fight! that's the word, and no other. There's no other hope. No Charter, — No social reforms! We must give them ourselves, for no one else will. Look there, and judge for yourself!'

He pulled a letter out from among his papers, and threw it across to me.

'What's this?'

'That came while you were in gaol. There don't want many words about it. We sent up a memorial to government about the army and police clothing. We told 'em how it was the lowest, most tyrannous, most ill-paid of all the branches of slop-making; how men took to it only when they were starved out of everything else. We entreated them to have mercy on us — entreated them to interfere between the merciless contractors, and the poor wretches on whose flesh and blood contractors, sweaters, and colonels, were all fattening; and there's the answer we got.* Look at it; read it! Again and again I've been minded to placard it on the walls, that all the world might see the might and the mercies of the government. Read it! "Sorry to say that it is utterly out of the power of her Majesty's * * * s to interfere — as the question of wages rests entirely between the contractor and the workmen." '

'He lies!' I said. 'If it did, the workmen might put a pistol to the contractor's head, and say — "You shall not tempt the poor, needy, greedy, starving workers to their own destruction, and the destruction of their class; you shall not offer these murderous, poisonous prices. If we saw you offering our neigh-bour a glass of laudanum, we would stop you at all risks — and we will stop you now." No! no! John, the question don't lie between workman and contractor, but between workman and contractor-plus-grape-and-bayonets!'

'Look again. There's worse comes after that. "If government did interfere, it would not benefit the workman, as his rate of wages depends entirely on the amount of competition between the workmen themselves." Yes, my dear children, you must eat each other; we are far too fond parents to interfere with so delightful an amusement! Curse them – sleek, hard-hearted, impotent, do-nothings! They confess themselves powerless against competition – powerless against the very devil that is destroying us, faster and faster every year! They can't help us on a single point. They can't check population; and if they could, they can't get rid of the population which exists. They daren't give us a comprehensive emigration-scheme. They daren't lift a finger to prevent gluts in the labour-market. They daren't interfere between slave and slave, between slave and tyrant. They are cowards, and like cowards they shall fall!'

'Ay – like cowards they shall fall!' I answered; and from that moment I was a rebel and a conspirator.

'And will the country join us?'

'The cities will; never mind the country. They are too weak to resist their own tyrants – and they are too weak to resist us. The country's always drivelling in the background. A country-party's sure to be a party of imbecile bigots. Nobody minds them.'

I laughed. 'It always was so, John. When Christianity first spread, it was in the cities – till a pagan, a villager, got to mean a heathen for ever and ever.'

'And so it was in the French revolution; when Popery had died out of all the rest of France, the priests and the aristocrats still found their dupes in the remote provinces.'

'The sign of a dying system that, be sure. Woe to Toryism and the Church of England, and everything else, when it gets to boasting that its stronghold is still the hearts of the agricultural poor. It is the cities, John, the cities, where the light dawns first – where man meets man, and spirit quickens spirit, and intercourse breeds knowledge, and knowledge sympathy, and sympathy enthusiasm, combination, power irresistible; while the agriculturists remain ignorant, selfish, weak, because they are isolated from each other. Let the country go. The towns shall win the Charter for England! And then for social reform, sanitary reform, ædile reform, cheap food, interchange of free labour, liberty, equality, and brotherhood for ever!'

Such was our Babel-tower, whose top should reach to heaven.
To understand the maddening allurement of that dream, you
must have lain, like us, for years in darkness and the pit.
You must have struggled for bread, for lodging, for cleanliness,
for water, for education – for all that makes life worth living –
and found them becoming, year by year, more hopelessly impossible, if not to yourself, yet still to the millions less gifted
than yourself; you must have sat in darkness and the shadow of
death, till you are ready to welcome any ray of light, even
though it should be the glare of a volcano.

CHAPTER XXXIII

A PATRIOT'S REWARD

I NEVER shall forget one evening's walk, as Crossthwaite and
I strode back together from the Convention.* We had walked
on some way arm in arm in silence, under the crushing and
embittering sense of having something to conceal – something,
which if those who passed us so carelessly in the street had
known——! It makes a villain and a savage of a man, that
consciousness of a dark, hateful secret. And it was a hateful
one! – a dark and desperate necessity, which we tried to call by
noble names, that faltered on our lips as we pronounced them;
for the spirit of God was not in us; and instead of bright hope,
and the clear fixed lode-star of duty, weltered in our imaginations a wild possible future of tumult, and flame, and blood.

'It must be done! – it shall be done! – it will be done!'
burst out John, at last, in that positive, excited tone, which
indicated a half disbelief of his own words. 'I've been reading
Macerone on street-warfare;* and I see the way as clear as
day.'

I felt nothing but the dogged determination of despair.
'It must be tried, if the worst comes to the worst – but I have
no hope. I read Somerville's answer to that Colonel Macerone.*
Ten years ago he showed it was impossible. We cannot stand
against artillery; we have no arms.'

'I'll tell you where to buy plenty. There's a man, Power, or

Bower,* he's sold hundreds in the last few days; and he under-stands the matter. He tells us we're certain, safe. There are hundreds of young men in the government-offices ready to join, if we do but succeed at first. It all depends on that. The first hour settles the fate of a revolution.'

'If we succeed, yes – the cowardly world will always side with the conquering party; and we shall have every pickpocket and ruffian in our wake, plundering in the name of liberty and order.'

'Then we'll shoot them like dogs, as the French did! "Mort au voleurs"* shall be the word!'

'Unless they shoot us. The French had a national guard, who had property to lose, and took care of it. The shopkeepers here will be all against us; they'll all be sworn in special constables, to a man; and between them and the soldiers, we shall have three to one upon us.'

'Oh! that Power assures me the soldiers will fraternize. He says there are three regiments at least have promised solemnly to shoot their officers, and give up their arms to the mob.'

'Very important, if true – and very scoundrelly, too. I'd sooner be shot myself by fair fighting, than see officers shot by cowardly treason.'

'Well, it is ugly. I like fair play as well as any man. But it can't be done. There must be a surprise, a *coup de main*, as the French say' (poor Crossthwaite was always quoting French in those days). 'Once show our strength – burst upon the tyrants like a thunderclap; and then!—

> Men of England, he... . glory,
> Heroes of unwritten story,
> Rise, shake off the chains like dew
> Which in sleep have fallen on you!
> Ye are many, they are few!*

'That's just what I am afraid they are not. Let's go and find out this man Power, and hear his authority for the soldier-story. Who knows him?'

'Why, Mike Kelly and he have been a deal together of late. Kelly's a true heart, now – a true Irishman – ready for anything. Those Irish are the boys, after all – though I don't deny they do

bluster and have their way a little too much in the Convention.
But still Ireland's wrongs are England's. We have the same
oppressors. We must make common cause against the tyrants.'

'I wish to Heaven they would just have stayed at home, and
ranted on the other side of the water; they had their own way
there, and no Mammonite middle-class to keep them down;
and yet they never did an atom of good. Their eloquence is all
bombast, and what's more, Crossthwaite, though there are some
fine fellows among them, nine-tenths are liars – liars in grain,
and you know it——'

Crossthwaite turned angrily to me. 'Why, you are getting as
reactionary as old Mackaye himself!'

'I am not – and he is not. I am ready to die on a barricade
to-morrow, if it comes to that. I haven't six months' lease of
life – I am going into a consumption; and a bullet is as easy a
death as spitting up my lungs piecemeal. But I despise these
Irish, because I can't trust them – they can't trust each other –
they can't trust themselves. You know as well as I that you can't
get common justice done in Ireland, because you can depend
on no man's oath. You know as well as I, that in Parliament or
out, nine out of ten of them will stick at no lie, even if it has
been exposed and refuted fifty times over, provided it serves the
purpose of the moment; and I often think, that after all,
Mackaye's right, and what's the matter with Ireland is just that
and nothing else – that from the nobleman in his castle to
the beggar on his dunghill, they are a nation of liars, John
Crossthwaite!'

'Sandy's a prejudiced old Scotchman.'

'Sandy's a wiser man than you or I, and you know it.'

'Oh, I don't deny that; but he's getting old, and I think he
has been failing in his mind of late.'

'I'm afraid he's failing in his health; he has never been the
same man since they hooted him down in John-street.* But he
hasn't altered in his opinions one jot; and I'll tell you what –
I believe he's right. I'll die in this matter like a man, because
it's the cause of liberty; but I've fearful misgivings about it, just
because Irishmen are at the head of it.'

'Of course they are – they have the deepest wrongs; and that
makes them most earnest in the cause of right. The sympathy of

suffering, as they say themselves, has bound them to the English working man against the same oppressors.'

'Then let them fight those oppressors at home, and we'll do the same: that's the true way to show sympathy. Charity begins at home. They are always crying "Ireland for the Irish"; why can't they leave England for the English?'

'You're envious of O'Connor's power!'

'Say that again, John Crossthwaite, and we part for ever!' and I threw off his arm indignantly.

'No – but – don't let's quarrel, my dear old fellow – now, that perhaps, perhaps we may never meet again – but I can't bear to hear the Irish abused. They're noble, enthusiastic, generous fellows. If we English had half as warm hearts, we shouldn't be as we are now; and O'Connor's a glorious man, I tell you. Just think of him, the descendant of the ancient kings,* throwing away his rank, his name, all he had in the world, for the cause of the suffering millions!'

'That's a most aristocratic speech, John,' said I, smiling, in spite of my gloom. 'So you keep a leader because he's descended from ancient kings, do you? I should prefer him just because he was not – just because he was a working man, and come of workmen's blood. We shall see; we shall see whether he's stanch, after all. To my mind, little Cuffy's* worth a great deal more, as far as earnestness goes.'

'Oh! Cuffy's a low-bred, uneducated fellow!'

'Aristocrat again, John!' said I, as we went upstairs to Kelly's room; and Crossthwaite did not answer.

There was so great a hubbub inside Kelly's room, of English, French, and Irish, all talking at once, that we knocked at intervals for full five minutes, unheard by the noisy crew; and I, in despair, was trying the handle, which was fast, when, to my astonishment, a heavy blow was struck on the panel from the inside, and the point of a sharp instrument driven right through, close to my knees, with the exclamation—

'What do you think o' that, now, in a policeman's bread-basket?'

'I think,' answered I, as loud as I dare, and as near the dangerous door, 'if I intended really to use it, I wouldn't make such a fool's noise about it.'

There was a dead silence; the door was hastily opened, and Kelly's nose poked out; while we, in spite of the horribleness of the whole thing, could not help laughing at his face of terror. Seeing who we were, he welcomed us in at once, into a miserable apartment, full of pikes and daggers, brandished by some dozen miserable, ragged, half-starved artisans. Three-fourths, I saw at once, were slop-working tailors. There was a bloused and bearded Frenchman or two; but the majority were, as was to have been expected, the oppressed, the starved, the untaught, the despairing, the insane; 'the dangerous classes', which society creates, and then shrinks in horror, like Frankenstein, from the monster her own clumsy ambition has created. Thou Frankenstein Mammon! hast thou not had warnings enough, either to make thy machines like men, or stop thy bungling, and let God make them for Himself?

I will not repeat what I heard there. There is many a frantic ruffian of that night now sitting 'in his right mind' – though not yet 'clothed'* – waiting for God's deliverance, rather than his own.

We got Kelly out of the room into the street, and began inquiring of him the whereabouts of this said Bower, or Power. 'He didn't know,' – the feather-headed Irishman that he was! – 'Faix, by-the-bye, he'd forgotten – an' he went to look for him at the place he tould him, and they didn't know sich a one there——'

'Oh, ho! Mr. Power has an *alibi*, then? Perhaps an *alias* too?'

'He didn't know his name rightly. Some said it was Brown; but he was a broth of a boy – a thrue people's man. Bedad, he gov' away arms afthen and afthen to them that couldn't buy 'em. An' he's as free-spoken – och, but he's put me into the confidence! Come down the street a bit, and I'll tell yees. – I'll be Lord Lieutenant o' Dublin Castle meself, if it succades, as shure as there's no snakes in ould Ireland,* an' revenge her wrongs ankle deep in the bhlood o' the Saxon! Whirroo! for the marthyred memory o' the three hundred thousint vargens o' Wexford!'*

'Hold your tongue, you ass!' said Crossthwaite, as he clapped his hand over his mouth, expecting every moment to find us all three in the Rhadamanthine grasp* of a policeman; while I stood laughing, as people will, for mere disgust at the ridiculous which almost always intermingles with the horrible.

At last, out it came——

'Bedad! we're going to do it! London's to be set o' fire in seventeen places at the same moment, an' I'm to light two of them to me own self, and make a hollycrust – ay, that's the word – o' Ireland's scorpions, to sting themselves to death in circling flame——'

'You would not do such a villanous thing?' cried we, both at once.

'Bedad! but I won't harm a hair o' their heads! Shure, we'll save the women and childer alive, and run for the fire-ingins our blessed selves, and then out with the pikes, and seize the Bank and the Tower——

> An' av' I lives, I lives victhorious,
> An' av' I dies, my sowl in glory is;
> Love fa – a – are – well!'

I was getting desperate: the whole thing seemed at once so horrible and so impossible. There must be some villanous trap at the bottom of it.

'If you don't tell me more about this fellow Power, Mike,' said I, 'I'll blow your brains out on the spot: either you or he are villains.' And I valiantly pulled out my only weapon, the door-key, and put it to his head.

'Och! are ye mad, thin? He's a broth of a boy; and I'll tell ye. Shure he knows all about the red-coats, case he's an arthillery-man himself, and that's the way he's found out his gran' com-bustible.'

'An artillery-man?' said John. 'He told me he was a writer for the press!'

'Bedad, thin, he's mistaken himself intirely; for he tould me with his own mouth. And I'll show ye the thing he sowld me as is to do it. Shure, it'll set fire to the stones o' the street, av' ye pour a bit vitriol on it.'

'Set fire to stones? I must see that before I believe it.'

'Shure an' ye shall then. Where'll I buy a bit? Sorra a shop is there open this time o' night; an' troth I forgot the name o' it intirely! Poker o' Moses, but here's a bit in my pocket!'

And out of his tattered coat-tail he lugged a flask of powder and a lump of some cheap chemical salt, whose name I have, I am ashamed to say, forgotten.

'You're a pretty fellow to keep such things in the same pocket with gunpowder!'

'Come along to Mackaye's,' said Crossthwaite. 'I'll see to the bottom of this. Be hanged, but I think the fellow's a cursed *mouchard* – some government-spy!'

'Spy is he, thin? Och! the thief o' the world; I'll stab him! I'll murther him! an' burn the town aftherwards, all the same.'

'Unless,' said I, 'just as you've got your precious combustible to blaze off, up he comes from behind the corner and gives you in charge to a policeman. It's a villanous trap, you miserable fool, as sure as the moon's in heaven.'

'Upon my word, I am afraid it is – and I'm trapped too.'

'Blood and turf! thin, it's he that I'll trap, thin. There's two million free and inlightened Irishmen in London, to avenge my marthyrdom wi' pikes and baggonets like raving salviges, and blood for blood!'

'Like savages, indeed!' said I to Crossthwaite. 'And pretty savage company we are keeping. Liberty, like poverty, makes a man acquainted with strange companions!'

'And who's made 'em savages? Who has left them savages? That the greatest nation of the earth has had Ireland in her hands three hundred years – and her people still to be savages! – if that don't justify a revolution, what does? Why, it's just because these poor brutes are what they are, that rebellion becomes a sacred duty. It's for them – for such fools, brutes, as that there, and the millions more like him, and likely to remain like him, that I've made up my mind to do or die to-morrow!'

There was a grand half-truth, distorted, miscoloured in the words, that silenced me for the time.

We entered Mackaye's door; strangely enough at that time of night, it stood wide open. What could be the matter? I heard loud voices in the inner room, and ran forward calling his name, when, to my astonishment, out past me rushed a tall man, followed by a steaming kettle, which, missing him, took full effect on Kelly's chest as he stood in the entry, filling his shoes with boiling water, and producing a roar that might have been heard at Temple-bar.

'What's the matter?'

'Have I hit him?' said the old man, in a state of unusual excitement.

'Bedad! it was the man Power! the cursed spy! An' just as I was going to slate the villain nately, came the kittle, and kilt me all over!'

'Power? He's as many names as a pickpocket, and as many callings, too, I'll warrant. He came sneaking in to tell me the sogers were a' ready to gie up their arms if I'd come forward to them to-morrow. So I tauld him, sin' he was so sure o't, he'd better gang and tak the arms himsel; an' then he let out he'd been a policeman——'

'A policeman!' said both Crossthwaite and Kelly, with strong expletives.

'A policeman doon in Manchester; I thought I kenned his face fra the first. And when the rascal saw he'd let out too much, he wanted to make out that he'd been a' along a spy for the Chartists, while he was makin' believe to be a spy o' the goovernment's. Sae when he came that far, I just up wi' the het water, and bleezed awa' at him; an' noo I maun gang and het some mair, for my drap toddy.'

Sandy had a little vitriol in the house, so we took the combustible down into the cellar, and tried it. It blazed up; but burnt the stone as much as the reader may expect. We next tried it on a lump of wood. It just scorched the place where it lay, and then went out; leaving poor Kelly perfectly frantic with rage, terror, and disappointment. He dashed upstairs, and out into the street, on a wild-goose chase after the rascal, and we saw no more of him that night.

I relate a simple fact. I am afraid – perhaps, for the poor workmen's sake, I should say I am glad, that it was not an unique one. Villains of this kind, both in April and in June, mixed among the working men, excited their worst passions by bloodthirsty declamations and extravagant promises of success, sold them arms; and then; like the shameless wretch on whose evidence Cuffy and Jones* were principally convicted, bore witness against their own victims, unblushingly declaring themselves to have been all along the tools of the government. I entreat all those who disbelieve this apparently prodigious assertion, to read the evidence given on the trial of the John-street conspirators,* and judge for themselves.

*

'The petition's filling faster than ever!' said Crossthwaite, as that evening we returned to Mackaye's little back room.

'Dirt's plenty,' grumbled the old man, who had settled himself again to his pipe, with his feet on the fender, and his head half way up the chimney.

'Now, or never!' went on Crossthwaite, without minding him; 'Now, or never! The manufacturing districts seem more firm than ever.'

'An' words cheap,' commented Mackaye, *sotto voce*.

'Well,' I said, 'Heaven keep us from the necessity of ulterior measures! But what must be, must.'

'The government expect it, I can tell you. They're in a pitiable funk, I hear. One regiment's ordered to Uxbridge already, because they daren't trust it. They'll find soldiers are men, I do believe, after all.'

'Men they are,' said Sandy; 'an' therefore they'll no be fools eneugh to stan' by an' see ye pu' down a' that is, to build up ye yourselves dinna yet rightly ken what. Men? Ay, and wi' mair common sense in them than some that had mair opportunities.'

'I think I've settled everything,' went on Crossthwaite, who seemed not to have heard the last speech – 'settled everything – for poor Katie, I mean. If anything happens to me, she has friends at Cork – she thinks so at least – and they'd get her out to service somewhere – God knows!' And his face worked fearfully a minute.

'Dulce et decorum est pro patriâ mori!'* said I.

'There are twa methods o' fulfilling that saw, I'm thinkin'. Impreemis, to shoot your neebour; in secundis, to hang yersel.'

'What do you mean by grumbling at the whole thing in this way, Mr. Mackaye? Are you, too, going to shrink back from The Cause, now that liberty is at the very doors?'

'Ou, then, I'm stanch eneuch. I ha' laid in my ain stock o' wepons for the fecht at Armageddon.'

'You don't mean it? What have you got?'

'A braw new halter, an' a muckle nail. There's a gran' tough beam here ayont the ingle, will haud me a' crouse and cantie,* when the time comes.'

'What on earth do you mean?' asked we, both together.

'Ha' ye looked into the monster-petition?'

'Of course we have, and signed it too!'

'Monster? Ay, ferlie!* Monstrum horrendum, informe, ingens, cui lumen ademptum.* Desinit in piscem mulier formosa superne.* Leeberty, the bonnie lassie, wi' a sealgh's fud* to her! I'll no sign it. I dinna consort wi' shoplifters, an' idiots, an' suckin' bairns – wi' long nose an' short nose an' pug nose an' seventeen Deuks o' Wellington, let alone a baker's dizen o' Queens.* It's no company, that, for a puir auld patriot!'

'Why, my dear Mackaye,' said I, 'you know the Reform Bill petitions were just as bad.'

'And the Anti-Corn-law ones, too, for that matter,' said Crossthwaite. 'You know we can't help accidents; the petition will never be looked through.'

'It's always been the plan with Whigs and Tories, too!'

'I ken that better than ye, I guess.'

'And isn't everything fair in a good cause?' said Crossthwaite. 'Desperate men really can't be so dainty.'

'How lang ha' ye learnit that deil's lee, Johnnie? Ye were no o' that mind five year agone, lad. Ha' ye been to Exeter Ha' the while? A's fair in the cause o' Mammon; in the cause o' cheap bread, that means cheap wages; but in the cause o' God – wae's me, that ever I suld see this day ower again! ower again! Like the dog to his vomit – just as it was ten, twenty, fifty years agone! I'll just ha' a petition a' alane to mysel – I, an' a twa or three honest men. Besides, ye're just eight days ower time wi' it.

'What do you mean?'

'Suld ha' sent it in the 1st o' April, an' no the 10th; a' fools'-day wud ha' suited wi' it ferlie!'

'Mr. Mackaye,' said Crossthwaite, in a passion, 'I shall certainly inform the Convention of your extraordinary language!'

'Do, laddie! do, then! An' tell 'em this, too' – and, as he rose, his whole face and figure assumed a dignity, an awfulness, which I had never seen before in him – 'tell them that ha''

driven out * * * and * * *, an' every one that daur speak a word
o' common sense, or common humanity – them that stone the
prophets, an' quench the Spirit o' God, and love a lie, an' them
that mak' the same – them that think to bring about the reign
o' love an' britherhood wi' pikes an' vitriol-bottles, murther an'
blasphemy – tell 'em that ane o' fourscore years and mair – ane
that has grawn grey in the people's cause – that sat at the feet o'
Cartwright,* an' knelt by the death-bed o' Rabbie Burns – ane
that cheerit Burdett as he went to the Touer, an' spent his wee
earnings for Hunt an' Cobbett* – ane that beheld the shaking
o' the nations in the Ninety-three,* and heard the birth-shriek
o' a new-born world – ane that while he was yet a callant saw
Liberty afar off, an' seeing her was glad, as for a bonny bride,
an' followed her through the wilderness for threescore weary
waeful years – sends them the last message that e'er he'll send
on airth; tell 'em that they're the slaves o' warse than priests
and kings – the slaves o' their ain lusts an' passions – the slaves
o' every loud-tongued knave an' mountebank that 'll pamper
them in their self-conceit; and that the gude God 'll smite 'em
down, and bring 'em to nought, and scatter 'em abroad, till they
repent, an' get clean hearts an' a richt speerit within them, and
learn His lesson that He's been trying to teach 'em this threescore years – that the cause o' the people is the cause o' Him
that made the people; an' wae to them that tak' the deevil's
tools to do His wark wi'! Gude guide us! – What was yon,
Alton, laddie?'

'What?'

'But I saw a spunk* o' fire fa' into your bosom! I've na faith
in siccan heathen omens; but auld carlins* wud say it's a sign
o' death within the year – save ye from it, my puir misguidit
bairn! Aiblins a fire-flaught* o' my een, it might be – I've had
them unco often the day——'

And he stooped down to the fire, and began to light his pipe,
muttering to himself——

'Saxty years o' madness! saxty years o' madness! How lang,
O Lord, before thou bring these puir daft bodies to their richt
mind again?'

We stood watching him, and interchanging looks – expecting
something, we knew not what.

Suddenly he sank forward on his knees, with his hands on the bars of the grate; we rushed forward, and caught him up. He turned his eyes up to me, speechless, with a ghastly expression; one side of his face was all drawn aside – and helpless as a child, he let us lift him to his bed, and there he lay, staring at the ceiling.

*

Four weary days passed by – it was the night of the ninth of April. In the evening of that day his speech returned to him on a sudden – he seemed uneasy about something, and several times asked Katie the day of the month.

'Before the tenth – ay, we maun pray for that. I doubt but I'm ower hearty yet – I canna bide to see the shame o' that day——

*

Na – I'll tak' no potions nor pills – gin it were na for scruples o' conscience, I'd apocartereeze* a'thegither, after the manner o' the ancient philosophers. But it's no' lawful, I misdoubt, to starve onesel.'

'Here is the doctor,' said Katie.

'Doctor? Wha ca'd for doctors– Canst thou administer to a mind diseased?* Can ye tak' long nose, an' short nose, an' snub nose, an' seventeen Deuks o' Wellington out o' my puddins?* Will your castor-oil, an' your calomel, an' your croton, do that? D'ye ken a medicamentum that'll pit brains into workmen——? Non tribus Anticyris!* Tons o' hellebore – acres o' strait-waistcoats – a hall police-force o' head-doctors, winna do it. Juvat insanire* – this their way is their folly,* as auld Benjamin o' Tudela saith of the heathen.* Heigho! "Forty years lang was he greivit wi' this generation, an' swore in his wrath that they suldna enter into his rest."* Pulse? tongue? ay, shak' your lugs, an' tak' your fee, and dinna keep auld folk out o' their graves. Can ye sing?'

The doctor meekly confessed his inability.

That's pity – or I'd gar ye sing Auld-lang-syne,—

We twa hae paidlit in the burn –*

Aweel, aweel, aweel——'

*

Weary and solemn was that long night, as we sat there, with
the crushing weight of the morrow on our minds, watching by
that death-bed, listening hour after hour to the rambling
soliloquies of the old man, as 'he babbled of green fields';*
yet I verily believe that to all of us, especially to poor little Katie,
the active present interest of tending him, kept us from going
all but mad with anxiety and excitement. But it was weary
work: – and yet, too, strangely interesting, as at times there
came scraps of old Scotch love-poetry, contrasting sadly with
the grim withered lips that uttered them – hints to me of some
sorrow long since suffered, but never healed. I had never heard
him allude to such an event before but once, on the first day of
our acquaintance.

> I went to the kirk,
> My luve sat afore me;
> I trow my twa een
> Tauld him a sweet story.
> Aye wakin o' –
> Wakin aye and weary –
> I thocht a' the kirk
> Saw me an' my deary.*

"Aye wakin o"! – Do ye think, noo, we sall ha' knowledge in
the next warld, o' them we loved on eath? I askit that same o'
Rab Burns ance, sitting up a' canty at Tibbie Shiel's in Meggot
Vale, an' he said, puir chiel, he "didna ken ower well, we maun
bide and see"; – bide and see – that's the gran' philosophy o'
life, after a'. Aiblins folk 'll ken their true freens there; an'
there 'll be na mair luve coft* and sauld for siller—

> Gear and tocher is needit nane
> I'the countrie whaur my luve is gane.

                                  *

Gin I had a true freen the noo! to gang down the wynd,* an'
find if it war but an auld Abraham o' a blue-gown,* wi' a bit
crowd, or a fizzle-pipe,* to play me the Bush aboon Traquair!*
Na, na, na; it's singing the Lord's song in a strange land, that
wad be; an' I hope the application's no irreverent, for ane that
was rearit amang the hills o' God, an' the trees o' the forest
which He hath planted.

> Oh the broom, an the bonny yellow broom,
> The broom o' the Cowden-knowes!*

Hech, but she wud lilt that bonnily!

*

Did ye ever gang listering* saumons by nicht? Ou, but it's braw sport, wi' the scars an' the birks* a' glowering out blude-red i' the torch-light, and the bonnie hizzies skelping an' skirling* on the bank——

*

There was a gran' leddy, a bonny leddy, cam' in and talked like an angel o' God to puir auld Sandy, anent the salvation o' his soul. But I tauld her no to fash hersel. It's no my view o' human life, that a man's sent into the warld just to save his soul, an' creep out again. An' I said I wad leave the savin' o' my soul to Him that made my soul; it was in richt gude keepin' there, I'd warrant. An' then she was unco fleyed when she found I didna haud wi' the Athanasian creed. An' I tauld her, na'; if He that died on the cross was sic a ane as she and I teuk Him to be, there was na that pride nor spite in Him, be sure, to send a puir auld sinful, guideless body to eternal fire, because he didna a'thegither understand the honour due to His name.'*

'Who was this lady?'

He did not seem to know; and Katie had never heard of her before – 'some district visitor' or other?

*

'I sair misdoubt but the auld creeds are in the right anent Him, after a'. I'd gie muckle to think it – there's na comfort as it is. Aiblins there might be a wee comfort in that, for a poor auld worn-out patriot. But it's ower late to change. I tauld her that, too, ance. It's ower late to put new wine into auld bottles. I was unco drawn to the high doctrines ance, when I was a bit laddie, an' sat in the kirk by my minnie an' my daddie – a richt stern auld Cameronian sort o' body* he was, too; but as I grew, and grew, the bed was ower short for a man to stretch himsel thereon, an' the plaidie ower strait for a man to fauld himsel therein; and so I had to gang my gate a' naked in the matter o' formulæ, as Maister Tummas has it.'*

'Ah! do send for a priest, or a clergyman!' said Katie, who partly understood his meaning.

'Parson? He canna pit new skin on auld scars. Na bit stickit curate-laddie for me, to gang argumentin' wi' ane that's auld enough to be his gran'father. When the parsons will hear me anent God's people, then I'll hear them anent God.

> – Sae I'm wearing awa, Jean,
> To the land o' the leal –*

Gin I ever get thither. Katie, here, hauds wi' purgatory, ye ken; where souls are burnt clean again – like baccy-pipe—

> When Razor-brigg is ower and past,
>   Every night and alle;
> To Whinny Muir thou comest at last,
>   And God receive thy sawle.
>
> Gin hosen an' shoon thou gavest nane
>   Every night and alle;
> The whins shall pike thee intil the bane,
>   And God receive thy sawle.*

Amen. There's mair things aboon, as well as below, than are dreamt o' in our philosophy.* At least, where'er I go, I'll meet no long-nose, nor short-nose, nor snub-nose patriots there; nor puir gowks stealing the deil's tools to do God's wark wi'. Out among the eternities an' the realities – it's no that dreary outlook, after a', to find truth an' fact – naught but truth an' fact – e'en beside the worm that dieth not, and the fire that is not quenched!'*

'God forbid!' said Katie.

'God do whatsoever shall please Him, Katie – an' that's aye gude, like Himsel. Shall no the Judge of all the earth do right – right – right?'

And murmuring that word of words to himself, over and over, more and more faintly, he turned slowly over, and seemed to slumber——

Some half-hour passed before we tried to stir him. He was dead.

And the candles waned grey, and the great light streamed in

through every crack and cranny, and the sun had risen on the Tenth of April. What would be done before that sun had set?

What would be done? Just what we had the might to do; and therefore, according to the formula on which we were about to act, that mights are rights, just what we had the right to do – nothing. Futility, absurdity, vanity, and vexation of spirit. I shall make my next a short chapter. It is a day to be forgotten – and forgiven.

CHAPTER XXXIV

THE TENTH OF APRIL

AND he was gone at last! Kind women, whom his unknown charities had saved from shame, laid him out duly, and closed his eyes, and bound up that face that never would beam again with genial humour, those lips that would never again speak courage and counsel to the sinful, the oppressed, the forgotten. And there he lay, the old warrior dead upon his shield; worn out by long years of manful toil in The People's Cause; and, saddest thought of all, by disappointment in those for whom he spent his soul. True, he was aged; no one knew how old. He had said, more than eighty years; but we had shortened his life, and we knew it. He would never see that deliverance for which he had been toiling ever since the days when as a boy he had listened to Tooke and Cartwright,* and the patriarchs of the people's freedom. Bitter, bitter, were our thoughts, and bitter were our tears, as Crosswaite and I stood watching that beloved face, now in death refined to a grandeur, to a youthful simplicity and delicacy, which we had never seen on it before – calm and strong – the square jaws set firm even in death – the lower lip still clenched above the upper, as if in a divine indignation and everlasting protest, even in the grave, against the devourers of the earth. Yes, he was gone – the old lion, worn out with many wounds, dead in his cage. Where could we replace him? There were gallant men amongst us, eloquent, well-read, earnest – men whose names will ring through this land ere long – men who had been taught wisdom, even as he, by the sinfulness, the apathy, the ingratitude, as well as by the sufferings of their fellows. But where should we two find again the learning, the moderation, the long experience, above all the more than woman's tenderness of him whom we had lost? And at that time, too, of all others! Alas! we had despised his counsel; wayward and fierce, we would have none of his reproof; and now God had withdrawn him from us; the righteous was taken away from the evil to come. For we knew that evil was coming. We felt all along that we should *not* succeed. But we were desperate; and his death made us more desperate; still at the moment it drew us nearer to each other. Yes – we were rudderless upon a roaring sea, and all before us blank with lurid blinding mist; but still we were together, to live and die; and as we looked into each other's eyes, and clasped each other's hands above the dead man's face, we felt that there was love between us, as of Jonathan and David, passing the love of woman.*

Few words passed. Even our passionate artisan-nature, so sensitive and voluble in general, in comparison with the cold reserve of the field-labourer and the gentleman, was hushed in silent awe between the thought of the past and the thought of the future. We felt ourselves trembling between two worlds. We felt that to-morrow must decide our destiny – and we felt rightly, though little we guessed what that destiny would be!

But it was time to go. We had to prepare for the meeting. We must be at Kennington Common within three hours at furthest; and Crossthwaite hurried away, leaving Katie and me to watch the dead.

And then came across me the thought of another deathbed – my mother's – How she had lain and lain, while I was far away – And then I wondered whether she had suffered much, or faded away at last in a peaceful sleep, as he had – And then I wondered how her corpse had looked; and pictured it to myself, lying in the little old room, day after day, till they screwed the coffin down – before I came! – Cruel! Did she look as calm, as grand in death, as he who lay there? And as I watched the old man's features, I seemed to trace in them the strangest likeness to my mother's. The strangest likeness! I could not shake it off. It became intense – miraculous. Was it she, or was it he, who lay there? I shook myself and rose.

My loins ached, my limbs were heavy, my brain and eyes swam round. I must be over-fatigued by excitement and sleeplessness. I would go downstairs into the fresh air, and shake it off.

As I came down the passage, a woman, dressed in black, was standing at the door, speaking to one of the lodgers. 'And he is dead! Oh, if I had but known sooner that he was even ill!'

That voice – that figure – surely, I knew them! – them, at least, there was no mistaking! Or was it another phantom of my disordered brain? I pushed forward to the door, and as I did so she turned, and our eyes met full. It was she – Lady Ellerton! sad, worn, transformed by widow's weeds, but that face was like no other's still. Why did I drop my eyes and draw back at the first glance like a guilty coward? She beckoned me towards her, went out into the street, and herself began the conversation, from which I shrank, I know not why.

'When did he die?'

'Just at sunrise this morning. But how came you here to visit him? Were you the lady who, as he said, came to him a few days since?'

She did not answer my question. 'At sunrise this morning? – A fitting time for him to die, before he sees the ruin and disgrace of those for whom he laboured. And you, too, I hear, are taking your share in this projected madness and iniquity?'

'What right have you,' I asked, bristling up at a sudden suspicion that crossed me, 'to use such words about me?'

'Recollect,' she answered, mildly but firmly, 'your conduct, three years ago, at D * * *.'

'What,' I said, 'was it not proved upon my trial, that I exerted all my powers, endangered my very life to prevent outrage in that case?'

'It was proved upon your trial,' she replied, in a marked tone; 'but we were informed, and, alas! from authority only too good, namely, from that of an ear-witness, of the sanguinary and ferocious language which you were not afraid to use at the meeting in London, only two nights before the riot.'

I turned white with rage and indignation.

'Tell me,' I said – 'tell me, if you have any honour, who dared forge such an atrocious calumny! No! you need not tell me. I see well enough now. He should have told you that I exposed myself that night to insult, not by advocating, but by opposing violence, as I have always done – as I would now, were not I desperate – hopeless of any other path to liberty. And as for this coming struggle, have I not written to my cousin, humiliating as it was to me, to beg him to warn you all from me, lest——'

I could not finish the sentence.

'You wrote? He has warned us, but he never mentioned your name. He spoke of his knowledge as having been picked up by himself at personal risk to his clerical character.'

'The risk, I presume, of being known to have actually received a letter from a Chartist; but I wrote – on my honour I wrote – a week ago; and received no word of answer.'

'Is this true?' she asked.

'A man is not likely to deal in useless falsehoods, who knows not whether he shall live to see the set of sun!'

'Then you are implicated in this expected insurrection?'

'I am implicated,' I answered, 'with the people; what they do I shall do. Those who once called themselves the patrons of the tailor-poet, left the mistaken enthusiast to languish for three years in prison, without a sign, a hint of mercy, pity, remembrance. Society has cast me off; and, in casting me off, it has sent me off to my own people, where I should have stayed from the beginning. Now I am at my post, because I am among my class. If they triumph peacefully, I triumph with them. If they need blood to gain their rights, be it so. Let the blood be upon the head of those who refuse, not those who demand. At least, I shall be with my own people. And if I die, what better thing on earth can happen to me?'

'But the law?' she said.

'Do not talk to me of law! I know it too well in practice to be moved by any theories about it. Laws are no law, but tyranny, when the few make them, in order to oppress the many by them.'

'Oh!' she said, in a voice of passionate earnestness, which I had never heard from her before, 'stop – for God's sake, stop! You know not what you are saying – what you are doing. Oh! that I had met you before – that I had more time to speak to poor Mackaye! Oh! wait, wait – there is a deliverance for you!

but never in this path – never. And just while I, nobler far than I, are longing and struggling to find the means of telling you your deliverance, you, in the madness of your haste, are making it impossible!'

There was a wild sincerity in her words – an almost imploring tenderness in her tone.

'So young!' she said; 'so young to be lost thus!'

I was intensely moved. I felt, I knew, that she had a message for me. I felt that hers was the only intellect in the world to which I would have submitted mine; and, for one moment, all the angel and all the devil in me wrestled for the mastery. If I could but have trusted her one moment...No! all the pride, the spite, the suspicion, the prejudice of years, rolled back upon me. 'An aristocrat! and she, too, the one who has kept me from Lillian!' And in my bitterness, not daring to speak the real thought within me, I answered with a flippant sneer—

'Yes, madam! like Cordelia, so young, yet so untender!* – Thanks to the mercies of the upper classes!'

Did she turn away in indignation? No, by Heaven! there was nothing upon her face but the intensest yearning pity. If she had spoken again, she would have conquered; but before those perfect lips could open, the thought of thoughts flashed across me.

'Tell me one thing! Is my cousin George to be married to——' and I stopped.

'He is.'

'And yet,' I said, 'you wish to turn me back from dying on a barricade!' And without waiting for a reply, I hurried down the street in all the fury of despair.

*

I have promised to say little about the tenth of April, for indeed I have no heart to do so. Every one of Mackaye's predictions came true. We had arrayed against us, by our own folly, the very physical force to which we had appealed. The dread of general plunder and outrage by the savages of London, the national hatred of that French and Irish interference of which we had boasted, armed against us thousands of special constables,* who had in the abstract little or no objection to our political opinions. The practical common sense of England, whatever discontent it might feel with the existing system, refused to let it be hurled rudely down, on the mere chance of building up on its ruins something as yet untried, and even undefined. Above all, the people would not rise. Whatever sympathy they had with us, they did not care to show it. And then futility after futility exposed itself. The meeting which was to have been counted by hundreds of thousands, numbered hardly its tens of thousands;* and of them a frightful proportion were of those very rascal classes, against whom we ourselves had offered to be sworn in as special constables. O'Connor's courage failed him after all. He contrived to be called away, at the critical moment, by some problematical superintendent of police. Poor Cuffy, the honestest, if not the wisest, speaker there, leapt off the waggon, exclaiming that we were all 'humbugged and betrayed'; and the meeting broke up pitiably piecemeal, drenched and cowed, body and soul, by pouring rain on its way home – for the very heavens mercifully helped to quench our folly – while the monster-petition crawled ludicrously away in a hack cab, to be dragged to the floor of the House of Commons amid roars of laughter – 'inextinguishable laughter',* as of Tennyson's Epicurean Gods.

Careless of mankind.
For they lie beside their nectar, and their bolts are hurled
Far below them in the valleys, and the clouds are lightly curled
Round their golden houses, girdled with the gleaming world.
There they smile in secret, looking over wasted lands,
Blight and famine, plague and earthquake, roaring deeps and fiery sands,
Clanging fights, and flaming towns, and sinking ships, *and praying hands.*
But they smile, they find a music, centred in a doleful song,
Steaming up, a lamentation, and an ancient tale of wrong,
Like a tale of little meaning, though the words are strong;
Chanted by an ill-used race of men that cleave the soil,
Sow the seed and reap the harvest with enduring toil,
Storing little yearly dues of wheat, and wine, and oil;
Till they perish, and they suffer – some, 'tis whispered, down in hell
Suffer endless anguish! ——*

Truly – truly, great poets' words are vaster than the singers themselves suppose!

CHAPTER XXXV

THE LOWEST DEEP

SULLEN, disappointed, desperate, I strode along the streets that evening, careless whither I went. The people's cause was lost – the Charter a laughing-stock. That the party which monopolises wealth, rank, and, as it fancies, education and intelligence, should have been driven, degraded, to appeal to brute force for self-defence – that thought gave me a savage joy; but that it should have conquered by that last, lowest resource! – That the few should be still stronger than the many, or the many still too cold-hearted and coward to face the few – that sickened me. I hated the well-born young special constables whom I passed, because they would have fought. I hated the gent and shop-keeper special constables, because they would have run away. I hated my own party, because they had gone too far – because they had not gone far enough. I hated myself, because I had not produced some marvellous effect – though what that was to have been I could not tell – and hated myself all the more for that ignorance.

A group of effeminate shopkeepers passed me, shouting 'God save the Queen!' 'Hypocrites!' I cried in my heart – they mean 'God save our shops!' Liars! They keep up willingly the useful calumny, that their slaves and victims are disloyal as well as miserable!

I was utterly abased – no, not utterly; for my self-contempt still vented itself – not in forgiveness, but in universal hatred and defiance. Suddenly I perceived my cousin, laughing and jesting with a party of fashionable young specials: I shrank from him; and yet, I know not why, drew as near him as I could, unobserved – near enough to catch the words,

'Upon my honour, Locke, I believe you are a Chartist yourself at heart.'

'At least I am no Communist,' said he, in a significant tone.

'There is one little bit of real property which I have no intention of sharing with my neighbours.'

'What, the little beauty somewhere near Cavendish-square?'

'That's my business.'

'Whereby you mean that you are on your way to her now? Well, I am invited to the wedding, remember.'

He pushed on, laughingly, without answering. I followed him fast – 'near Cavendish-square!' – the very part of the town where Lillian lived! I had had, as yet, a horror of going near it; but now, an intolerable suspicion scourged me forward, and I dogged his steps, hiding behind pillars, and at the corners of streets, and then running on, till I got sight of him again. He went through Cavendish-square, up Harley-street – was it possible? I gnashed my teeth at the thought. But it must be so. He stopped at the dean's house, knocked, and entered, without parley.

In a minute I was breathless on the door-step, and knocked. I had no plan, no object, except the wild wish to see my own despair. I never thought of the chances of being recognised by the servants, or of anything else, except of Lillian by my cousin's side.

The footman came out smiling. 'What did I want?'

'I – I – Mr. Locke.'

'Well, you needn't be in such a hurry!' (with a significant grin). 'Mr. Locke's likely to be busy for a few minutes, yet, I expect!'

Evidently the man did not know me.

'Tell him that – that a person wishes to speak to him on particular business.' Though I had no more notion what that business was than the man himself.

'Sit down in the hall.'

And I heard the fellow, a moment afterwards, gossiping and laughing with the maids below about 'the young couple.'

To sit down was impossible; my only thought was – where was Lillian?

Voices in an adjoining room caught my ear. His! yes – and hers too – soft and low. What devil prompted me to turn eaves-dropper? to run headlong into temptation? I was close to the dining-room door, but they were not there – evidently they were in the back room, which, as I knew, opened into it with folding doors. I – I must confess all. – Noiselessly, with craft like a madman's, I turned the handle, slipped in as stealthily as a cat – the folding-doors were slightly open. – I had a view of all that passed within. A horrible fascination seemed to keep my eyes fixed on them, in spite of myself. Honour, shame, despair, bade me turn away, but in vain.

I saw them. – How can I write it? Yet I will. – I saw them sitting together on the sofa. Their arms were round each other. Her head lay upon his breast; he bent over her with an intense gaze, as of a basilisk, I thought; how do I know that it was not the fierceness of his love? Who could have helped loving her?

Suddenly she raised her head, and looked up in his face – her eyes brimming with tenderness, her cheeks burning with mingled delight and modesty – their lips met, and clung together. . . It seemed a life – an eternity – before they parted again. Then the spell was broken, and I rushed from the room.

Faint, giddy, and blind, I just recollect leaning against the wall of the staircase. He came hastily out, and started as he saw me. My face told all.

'What? Eavesdropping?' he said, in a tone of unutterable scorn. I answered nothing, but looked stupidly and fixedly in his face, while he glared at me with that keen, burning, intolerable eye. I longed to spring at his throat, but that eye held me as the snake's holds the deer. At last I found words.

'Traitor! everywhere – in everything – tricking me – supplanting me – in my friends – in my love!'

'Your love? Yours?' And the fixed eye still glared upon me. 'Listen, cousin Alton! The strong and the weak have been matched for the same prize: and what wonder, if the strong man conquers? Go and ask Lillian how she likes the thought of being a Communist's love!'

As when, in a nightmare, we try by a desperate effort to break the spell, I sprang forward, and struck at him; he put my hand by carelessly, and felled me bleeding to the ground. – I recollect hardly anything more, till I found myself thrust into the street by sneering footmen, and heard them call after me 'Chartist' and 'Communist' as I rushed along the pavement, careless where I went.

I strode and staggered on through street after street, running blindly against passengers, dashing under horses' heads, heedless of warnings and execrations, till I found myself, I know not how, on Waterloo Bridge. I had meant to go there when I left the door. – I knew that at least – and now I was there.

I buried myself in a recess of the bridge, and stared around and up and down.

I was alone – deserted even by myself. Mother, sister, friends, love, the idol of my life, were all gone. I could have borne that. But to be shamed, and know that I deserved it; to be deserted by my own honour, self-respect, strength of will – who can bear that?

I could have borne it, had one thing been left, – faith in my own destiny – the inner hope that God had called me to do a work for him.

'What drives the Frenchman to suicide?' I asked myself, arguing ever even in the face of death and hell – 'His faith in nothing but his own lusts and pleasures; and when they are gone, then comes the pan of charcoal* – and all is over. What drives the German? His faith in nothing but his own brain. He has fallen down and worshipped that miserable 'Ich' of his, and made that, and not God's will, the centre and root of his philosophy, his poetry, and his self-idolising æsthetics; and when it fails him, then for prussic acid, and nonentity. Those old Romans, too – why, they are the very experimentum crucis* of suicide! As long as they fancied that they had a calling to serve the state, they could live on and suffer. But when they found no more work left for them, then they could die – as Porcia died – as Cato* – as I ought. What is there left for me to do? outcast, disgraced, useless, decrepit——'

I looked out over the bridge into the desolate night. Below me the dark moaning river-eddies hurried downward. The wild west-wind howled past me, and leapt over the parapet downward. The huge reflection of Saint Paul's, the great tap-roots of light from lamp and window that shone upon the lurid stream, pointed down – down – down. A black wherry shot through the arch beneath me, still and smoothly downward. My brain began to whirl madly – I sprang upon the step. – A man rushed past me, clambered on the parapet, and threw up his arms wildly. – A moment more, and he would have leapt into the stream. The sight recalled me to my senses – say, rather, it re-awoke in me the spirit of mankind. I seized him by the arm, tore him down upon the pavement, and held him, in spite of his frantic struggles. It was Jemmy Downes! Gaunt, ragged, sodden, blear-eyed, drivelling, the worn-out gin-drinker stood, his momentary paroxysm of strength gone, trembling and staggering.

'Why won't you let a cove die? Why won't you let a cove die? They're all dead – drunk, and poisoned, and dead! What is there left?' – he burst out suddenly in his old ranting style – 'What is there left on earth to live for? The prayers of liberty are answered by the laughter of tyrants; her sun is sunk beneath the ocean wave, and her pipe put out by the raging billows of aristocracy! Those starving millions of Kennington Common – where are they? Where? I axes you,' he cried fiercely, raising his voice to a womanish scream – 'where are they?'

'Gone home to bed, like sensible people; and you had better go too.'

'Bed! I sold ours a month ago; but we'll go. Come along, and I'll show you my wife and family; and we'll have a tea-party – Jacob's Island tea.* Come along!

> Flea, flea, unfortunate flea!
> Bereft of his wife and his small family!'

He clutched my arm, and dragging me off towards the Surrey side, turned down Stamford-street.

I followed half perforce; and the man seemed quite demented – whether with gin or sorrow I could not tell. As he strode along the pavement, he kept continually looking back, with a perplexed terrified air, as if expecting some fearful object.

'The rats! – the rats!* don't you see 'em coming out of the gully holes, atween the area railings – dozens and dozens?'

'No; I saw none.'

'You lie; I hear their tails whisking; there's their shiny hats a-glistening, and every one on 'em with peelers' staves! Quick! quick! or they'll have me to the station-house.'

'Nonsense!' I said; 'we are free men! What are the policemen to us?'

'You lie!' cried he, with a fearful oath, and a wrench at my arm which almost threw me down. 'Do you call a sweater's man a free man?'

'You a sweater's man?'

'Ay!' with another oath. 'My men ran away – folks said I drank, too; but here I am; and I, that sweated others, I'm sweated myself – and I'm a slave! I'm a slave – a negro slave, I am, you aristocrat villain!'

'Mind me, Downes; if you will go quietly, I will go with you; but if you do not let go of my arm, I give you in charge to the first policeman I meet.'

'Oh, don't, don't!' whined the miserable wretch, as he almost fell on his knees, gin-drinkers' tears running down his face; 'or I shall be too late. – And then the rats 'll get in at the roof, and up through the floor, and eat 'em all up, and my work too – the grand new three-pound coat that I've been stitching at this ten days, for the sum of one half-crown sterling – and don't I wish I may see the money? Come on, quick; there are the rats, close behind!' And he dashed across the broad roaring thoroughfare of Bridge-street, and hurrying almost at a run down Tooley-street, plunged into the wildernesses of Bermondsey.

He stopped at the end of a miserable blind alley, where a dirty gas-lamp just served to make darkness visible, and show the patched windows and rickety doorways of the crazy houses, whose upper stories were lost in a brooding cloud of fog; and the pools of stagnant water at our feet; and the huge heap of cinders which filled up the waste end of the alley – a dreary, black, formless mound, on which two or three spectral dogs prowled up and down after the offal, appearing and vanishing like dark imps in and out of the black misty chaos beyond.

The neighbourhood was undergoing, as it seemed, 'improvements', of that peculiar metropolitan species which consists in pulling down the dwellings of the poor, and building up rich men's houses instead; and great buildings, within high temporary palings, had already eaten up half the little houses; as the great fish, and the great estates, and the great shopkeepers, eat up the little ones of their species – by the law of competition, lately discovered to be the true creator and pre-server of the universe.* There they loomed up, the tall bullies, against the dreary sky, looking down with their grim, proud, stony visages, on the misery which they were driving out of one corner, only to accumulate and intensify it in another.

The house at which we stopped was the last in the row; all its companions had been pulled down; and there it stood, leaning out with one naked ugly side into the gap, and stretching out long props, like feeble arms and crutches, to resist the work of demolition.

A group of slatternly people were in the entry, talking loudly, and as Downes pushed by them, a woman seized him by the arm.

'Oh! you unnatural villain! – To go away after your drink, and leave all them poor dear dead corpses locked up, without even letting a body go in to stretch them out!'

'And breeding the fever, too, to poison the whole house!' growled one.

'The relieving officer's been here, my cove,' said another; 'and he's gone for a peeler and a search warrant to break open the door, I can tell you!'

But Downes pushed past unheeding, unlocked a door at the end of the passage, thrust me in, locked it again, and then rushed across the room in chase of two or three rats, who vanished into cracks and holes.

And what a room! A low lean-to with wooden walls, without a single article of furniture; and through the broad chinks of the floor shone up as it were ugly glaring eyes, staring at us. – They were the reflections of the rushlight in the sewer below. The stench was frightful – the air heavy with pestilence. The first breath I drew made my heart sink, and my stomach turn. But I forgot everything in the object which lay before me, as Downes tore a half-finished coat off three corpses laid side by side on the bare floor.

There was his little Irish wife; – dead – and naked – the wasted white limbs gleamed in the lurid light; the unclosed eyes stared, as if reproachfully, at the husband whose drunkenness had brought her there to kill her with the pestilence; and on each side of her a little, shrivelled, impish, child-corpse – the wretched man had laid their arms round the dead mother's neck – and there they slept, their hungering and wailing over at last for ever: the rats had been busy already with them – but what matter to them now?

'Look!' he cried; 'I watched 'em dying! Day after day I saw the devils come up through the cracks, like little maggots and beetles, and all manner of ugly things, creeping down their throats; and I asked 'em, and they said they were the fever devils.'

It was too true; the poisonous exhalations had killed them. The wretched man's delirium tremens had given that horrible substantiality to the poisonous fever gases.

Suddenly Downes turned on me, almost menacingly. 'Money! money! I want some gin!'

I was thoroughly terrified – and there was no shame in feeling fear, locked up with a madman far my superior in size and strength, in so ghastly a place. But the shame, and the folly too, would have been in giving way to my fear; and with a boldness half assumed, half the real fruit of excitement and indignation at the horrors I beheld, I answered—

'If I had money, I would give you none. What do you want with gin? Look at the fruits of your accursed tippling. If you had taken my advice, my poor fellow,' I went on, gaining courage as I spoke, 'and become a water-drinker, like me——'

'Curse you and your water-drinking! If you had had no water to drink or wash with for two years but that – that,' pointing to the foul ditch below – 'If you had emptied the slops in there with one hand, and filled your kettle with the other——'

'Do you actually mean that that sewer is your only drinking water?'

'Where else can we get any? Everybody drinks it; and you shall, too – you shall!' he cried, with a fearful oath, 'and then see if you don't run off to the gin-shop, to take the taste of it out of your mouth. Drink? and who can help drinking, with his stomach turned with such hell-broth as that – or such a hell's blast as this air is here, ready to vomit from morning till night with the smells? I'll show you. You shall drink a bucket full of it, as sure as you live, you shall.'

And he ran out of the back door, upon a little balcony, which hung over the ditch.

I tried the door, but the key was gone, and the handle too. I beat furiously on it, and called for help. Two gruff authoritative voices were heard in the passage.

'Let us in; I'm the policeman!'

'Let me out, or mischief will happen!'

The policeman made a vigorous thrust at the crazy door; and just as it burst open, and the light of his lantern streamed into the horrible den, a heavy splash was heard outside.

'He has fallen into the ditch!'

'He'll be drowned, then, as sure as he's a born man,' shouted one of the crowd behind.

We rushed out on the balcony. The light of the policeman's lantern glared over the ghastly scene – along the double row of miserable house-backs, which lined the sides of the open tidal ditch – over strange rambling jetties, and balconies, and sleeping sheds, which hung on rotting piles over the black waters, with phosphorescent scraps of rotten fish gleaming and twinkling out of the dark hollows, like devilish grave-lights – over bubbles of poisonous gas, and bloated carcases of dogs, and lumps of offal, floating on the stagnant olive-green hell-broth – over the slow sullen rows of oily ripple which were dying away into the darkness far beyond, sending up, as they stirred, hot breaths of miasma – the only sign that a spark of humanity, after years of foul life, had quenched itself at last in that foul death. I almost fancied that I could see the haggard face staring up at me through the slimy water; but no – it was as opaque as stone.

I shuddered and went in again, to see slatternly gin-smelling women stripping off their clothes – true women even there – to cover the poor naked corpses; and pointing to the bruises which told a tale of long tyranny and cruelty; and mingling their lamentations with stories of shrieks and beating, and children locked up for hours to starve; and the men looked on sullenly, as if they too were guilty, or rushed out to relieve themselves by helping to find the drowned body. Ugh! it was the very mouth of hell, that room. And in the midst of all the rout, the relieving officer stood impassive, jotting down scraps of information, and warning us to appear the next day, to state

what we knew before the magistrates. Needless hypocrisy of
law! Too careless to save the woman and children from brutal
tyranny, nakedness, starvation! – Too superstitious to offend its
idol of vested interests, by protecting the poor man against his
tyrants, the house-owning shopkeepers under whose greed the
dwellings of the poor become nests of filth and pestilence,
drunkenness and degradation. Careless, superstitious, imbecile
law! – leaving the victims to die unhelped, and then, when the
fever and the tyranny has done its work, in thy sanctimonious
prudishness, drugging thy respectable conscience by a 'searching
inquiry' as to how it all happened – lest, forsooth, there should
have been 'foul play!' Is the knife or the bludgeon, then, the only
foul play, and not the cesspool and the curse of Rabshakeh?*
Go through Bermondsey or Spitalfields, St. Giles's or Lambeth,
and see if *there* is not foul play enough already – to be tried
hereafter at a more awful coroner's inquest than thou thinkest
of!

CHAPTER XXXVI

DREAM LAND

It must have been two o'clock in the morning before I reached
my lodgings. Too much exhausted to think, I hurried to my
bed. I remember now that I reeled strangely as I went upstairs.
I lay down, and was asleep in an instant.

How long I had slept I know not, when I awoke with a
strange confusion and whirling in my brain, and an intolerable
weight and pain about my back and loins. By the light of the
gas-lamp I saw a figure standing at the foot of my bed.
I could not discern the face, but I knew instinctively that it was
my mother. I called to her again and again, but she did not
answer. She moved slowly away, and passed out through the
wall of the room.

I tried to follow her, but could not. An enormous, unutterable
weight seemed to lie upon me. The bedclothes grew and grew
before me, and upon me, into a vast mountain, millions of miles
in height. Then it seemed all glowing red, like the cone of a

volcano. I heard the roaring of the fires within, the rattling of
the cinders down the heaving slope. A river ran from its
summit; and up that river-bed it seemed I was doomed to climb
and climb for ever, millions and millions of miles upwards,
against the rushing stream. The thought was intolerable, and
I shrieked aloud. A raging thirst had seized me. I tried to drink
the river-water, but it was boiling hot – sulphureous – reeking
of putrefaction. Suddenly I fancied that I could pass round the
foot of the mountain; and jumbling, as madmen will, the
sublime and the ridiculous, I sprang up to go round the foot of
my bed, which was the mountain.

I recollect lying on the floor. I recollect the people of the
house, who had been awoke by my shriek and my fall, rushing
in and calling to me. I could not rise or answer. I recollect a
doctor; and talk about brain fever and delirium. It was true.
I was in a raging fever. And my fancy, long pent-up and
crushed by circumstances, burst out in uncontrollable wildness,
and swept my other faculties with it helpless away over all
heaven and earth, presenting to me, as in a vast kaleidoscope,
fantastic symbols of all I had ever thought, or read, or felt.

That fancy of the mountain returned; but I had climbed it
now. I was wandering along the lower ridge of the Himalaya.
On my right the line of snow peaks showed like a rosy saw
against the clear blue morning sky. Raspberries and cyclamens
were peeping through the snow around me. As I looked down
the abysses, I could see far below, through the thin veils of blue
mist that wandered in the glens, the silver spires of giant
deodars, and huge rhododendrons that glowed like trees of
flame.* The longing of my life to behold that cradle of mankind
was satisfied. My eyes revelled in vastness, as they swept over
the broad flat jungle at the mountain foot, a desolate sheet of
dark gigantic grasses, furrowed with the paths of the buffalo
and rhinoceros, with barren sandy water-courses, desolate pools,
and here and there a single tree, stunted with malaria,* shattered
by mountain floods; and far beyond, the vast plains of
Hindoostan, enlaced with myriad silver rivers and canals, tanks
and rice-fields, cities with their mosques and minarets, gleaming
among the stately palm-groves along the boundless horizon.
Above me was a Hindoo temple, cut out of the yellow sand-

stone. I climbed up to the higher tier of pillars among monstrous shapes of gods and fiends, that mouthed and writhed and mocked at me, struggling to free themselves from their bed of rock. The bull Nundi* rose and tried to gore me; hundred-handed gods brandished quoits and sabres round my head; and Kali* dropped the skull from her gore-dripping jaws, to clutch me for her prey. Then my mother came, and seizing the pillars of the portico, bent them like reeds: an earthquake shook the hills – great sheets of woodland slid roaring and crashing into the valleys – a tornado swept through the temple halls, which rocked and tossed like a vessel in a storm: a crash – a cloud of yellow dust which filled the air – choked me – blinded me – buried me—

*

And Eleanor came by, and took my soul in the palm of her hand, as the angels did Faust's,* and carried it to a cavern by the sea-side, and dropped it in; and I fell and fell for ages. And all the velvet mosses, rock flowers, and sparkling spars and ores, fell with me, round me, in showers of diamonds, whirlwinds of emerald and ruby, and pattered into the sea that moaned below, and were quenched; and the light lessened above me to one small spark, and vanished; and I was in darkness, and turned again to my dust.

*

And I was at the lowest point of created life; a madrepore* rooted to the rock, fathoms below the tide-mark; and worst of all, my individuality was gone. I was not one thing, but many things – a crowd of innumerable polypi; and I grew and grew, and the more I grew the more I divided, and multiplied thousand and ten thousand-fold. If I could have thought, I should have gone mad at it; but I could only feel.

And I heard Eleanor and Lillian talking, as they floated past me through the deep, for they were two angels; and Lillian said, 'When will he be one again?'

And Eleanor said, 'He who falls from the golden ladder must climb through ages to its top. He who tears himself in pieces by his lusts, ages only can make him one again. The madrepore shall become a shell, and the shell a fish, and the fish a bird, and the bird a beast; and then he shall become a man again, and see the glory of the latter days.'

*

And I was a soft crab, under a stone on the seashore. With infinite starvation, and struggling, and kicking, I had got rid of my armour, shield by shield, and joint by joint, and cowered, naked and pitiable, in the dark, among dead shells and ooze. Suddenly the stone was turned up; and there was my cousin's hated face laughing at me, and pointing me out to Lillian. She laughed too, as I looked up, sneaking, ashamed, and defenceless, and squared up at him with my soft useless claws. Why should she not laugh? Are not crabs, and toads, and monkeys, and a hundred other strange forms of animal life, jests of nature – embodiments of a divine humour, at which men are meant to laugh and be merry? But alas! my cousin, as he turned away, thrust the stone back with his foot, and squelched me flat.

*

And I was a remora,* weak and helpless, till I could attach myself to some living thing; and then I had power to stop the largest ship. And Lillian was a flying-fish, and skimmed over the crests of the waves on gauzy wings. And my cousin was a huge shark, rushing after her, greedy and open-mouthed; and I saw her danger, and clung to him, and held him back; and just as I had stopped him, she turned and swam back into his open jaws.

*

Sand – sand – nothing but sand! The air was full of sand, drifting over granite temples, and painted kings and triumphs, and the skulls of a former world; and I was an ostrich, flying madly before the simoom wind,* and the giant sand pillars, which stalked across the plains, hunting me down. And Lillian was an Amazon queen, beautiful, and cold, and cruel; and she rode upon a charmed horse, and carried behind her on her saddle a spotted ounce,* which was my cousin; and, when I came near her, she made him leap down and course me. And we ran for miles and for days through the interminable sand, till he sprung on me, and dragged me down. And as I lay quivering and dying, she reined in her horse above me, and looked down at me with beautiful, pitiless eyes; and a wild Arab tore the plumes from my wings, and she took them and wreathed them in her golden hair. The broad and blood-red sun sank down beneath the sand, and the horse and the Amazon and the ostrich plumes shone blood-red in his lurid rays.

*

I was a mylodon* among South American forests – a vast sleepy mass, my elephantine limbs and yard-long talons contrasting strangely with the little meek rabbit's head, furnished with a poor dozen of clumsy grinders, and a very small kernel of brains, whose highest consciousness was the enjoyment of muscular strength. Where I had picked up the sensation which my dreams realized for me, I know not: my waking life, alas! had never given me experience of it. Has the mind power of creating sensations for itself? Surely it does so, in those delicious dreams about flying which haunt us poor wingless mortals, which would seem to give my namesake's philosophy the lie.* However that may be, intense and new was the animal delight, to plant my hinder claws at some tree-foot into the black rotting vegetable-mound which steamed rich gases up wherever it was pierced, and clasp my huge arms round the stem of some palm or tree-fern; and then slowly bring my enormous weight and muscle to bear upon it, till the stem bent like a withe, and the laced bark cracked, and the fibres groaned and shrieked, and the roots sprung up out of the soil; and then, with a slow circular wrench, the whole tree was twisted bodily out of the ground, and the maddening tension of my muscles suddenly relaxed, and I sank sleepily down upon the turf, to browse upon the crisp tart foliage, and fall asleep in the glare of sunshine which streamed through the new gap in the green forest roof. Much as I had envied the strong, I had never before suspected the delight of mere physical exertion. I now understood the wild gambols of the dog, and the madness which makes the horse gallop and strain onwards till he drops and dies. They fulfil their nature, as I was doing, and in that is always happiness.

But I did more – whether from mere animal destructiveness, or from the spark of humanity which was slowly rekindling in me, I began to delight in tearing up trees, for its own sake. I tried my strength daily on thicker and thicker boles. I crawled up to the high palm-tops, and bowed them down by my weight. My path through the forest was marked, like that of a tornado, by snapped and prostrate stems and withering branches. Had I been a few degrees more human, I might have expected a retribution for my sin. I had fractured my own skull three or four times already. I used often to pass the carcases of my race, killed, as geologists now find them, by the fall of the trees they had overthrown; but still I went on, more and more reckless, a slave, like many a so-called man, to the mere sense of power.

One day I wandered to the margin of the woods, and climbing a tree, surveyed a prospect new to me. For miles and miles, away to the white line of the smoking Cordillera,* stretched a low rolling plain; one vast thistle-bed, the down of which flew in grey gauzy clouds before a soft fitful breeze; innumerable finches fluttered and pecked above it, and bent the countless flower-heads. Far away, one tall tree rose above the level thistle-ocean. A strange longing seized me to go and tear it down. The forest-leaves seemed tasteless; my stomach sickened at them; nothing but that tree would satisfy me; and descending, I slowly brushed my way, with half-shut eyes, through the tall thistles which buried even my bulk.

At last, after days of painful crawling, I dragged my un-wieldiness to the tree-foot. Around it the plain was bare, and scored by burrows and heaps of earth, among which gold, some in dust, some in great knots and ingots, sparkled everywhere in the sun, in fearful contrast to the skulls and bones which lay bleaching round. Some were human, some were those of vast and monstrous beasts. I knew (one knows everything in dreams) that they had been slain by the winged ants, as large as panthers, who snuffed and watched around over the magic treasure. Of them I felt no fear; and they seemed not to perceive me, as I crawled, with greedy, hunger-sharpened eyes, up to the foot of the tree. It seemed miles in height. Its stem was bare and polished like a palm's, and above a vast feathery crown of dark green velvet slept in the still sunlight. But, wonders of wonders!

from among the branches hung great sea-green lilies, and, nestled in the heart of each of them, the bust of a beautiful girl. Their white bosoms and shoulders gleamed rosy-white against the emerald petals, like conch-shells half-hidden among sea-weeds, while their delicate waists melted mysteriously into the central sanctuary of the flower. Their long arms and golden tresses waved languishingly downward in the breeze; their eyes glittered like diamonds; their breaths perfumed the air.* A blind extacy seized me – I awoke again to humanity, and fiercely clasping the tree, shook and tore at it, in the blind hope of bringing nearer to me the magic beauties above: for I knew that I was in the famous land of Wak-Wak,* from which the Eastern merchants used to pluck those flower-born beauties, and bring them home to fill the harems of the Indian kings. Suddenly I heard a rustling in the thistles behind me, and looking round, saw again that dreaded face – my cousin!

He was dressed – strange jumble that dreams are! – like an American backwoodsman. He carried the same revolver and bowie-knive which he had showed me the fatal night that he intruded on the Chartist club. I shook with terror, but he, too, did not see me. He threw himself on his knees, and began fiercely digging and scraping for the gold.

The winged ants rushed on him, but he looked up, and 'held them with his glittering eye',* and they shrank back abashed into the thistle covert; while I strained and tugged on, and the faces of the dryads above grew sadder and older, and their tears fell on me like a fragrant rain.

Suddenly the tree-bole cracked – it was tottering. I looked round, and saw that my cousin knelt directly in the path of its fall. I tried to call to him to move; but how could a poor edentate* like myself articulate a word? I tried to catch his attention by signs – He would not see. I tried, convulsively, to hold the tree up, but it was too late; a sudden gust of air swept by, and down it rushed, with a roar like a whirlwind, and leaving my cousin untouched, struck me full across the loins, broke my backbone, and pinned me to the ground in mortal agony. I heard one wild shriek rise from the flower fairies, as they fell each from the lily cup, no longer of full human size, but withered, shrivelled, diminished a thousand-fold, and lay on the bare sand, like little rosy humming-birds' eggs, all crushed and dead.

The great blue heaven above me spoke, and cried, 'Selfish and sense-bound! thou hast murdered beauty!'

The sighing thistle-ocean answered, and murmured, 'Discontented! thou hast murdered beauty!'

One flower fairy alone lifted up her tiny cheek from the gold-strewn sand, and cried, 'Presumptuous! thou hast murdered beauty!'

It was Lillian's face – Lillian's voice! My cousin heard it too, and turned eagerly; and as my eyes closed in the last death-shiver, I saw him coolly pick up the little beautiful figure, which looked like a fragment of some exquisite cameo, and deliberately put it away in his cigar-case, as he said to himself, 'A charming tit-bit for me, when I return from the diggings!'

*

When I awoke again, I was a baby-ape in Borneon forests, perched among fragrant trailers and fantastic orchis flowers; and as I looked down, beneath the green roof, into the clear waters paved with unknown water-lilies on which the sun had never shone, I saw my face reflected in the pool – a melancholy, thoughtful countenance, with large projecting brow – it might have been a negro child's. And I felt stirring in me germs of a new and higher consciousness – yearnings of love towards the mother ape, who fed me and carried me from tree to tree. But I grew and grew; and then the weight of my destiny fell upon me. I saw year by year my brow recede, my neck enlarge, my jaw protrude; my teeth became tusks; skinny wattles grew from my cheeks – the animal faculties in me were swallowing up the intellectual. I watched in myself, with stupid self-disgust, the fearful degradation which goes on from youth to age in all the monkey race, especially in those which approach nearest to the human form. Long melancholy mopings, fruitless struggglings to think, were periodically succeeded by wild frenzies, agonies of lust and aimless ferocity. I flew upon my brother apes, and was driven off with wounds. I rushed howling down into the village gardens, destroying everything I met. I caught the birds and insects, and tore them to pieces with savage glee.

One day, as I sat among the boughs, I saw Lillian coming along
a flowery path – decked as Eve might have been, the day she
turned from Paradise. The skins of gorgeous birds were round
her waist; her hair was wreathed with fragrant tropic flowers.
On her bosom lay a baby – it was my cousin's. I knew her, and
hated her. The madness came upon me. I longed to leap from
the bough and tear her limb from limb; but brutal terror, the
dread of man which is the doom of beasts, kept me rooted to
my place. Then my cousin came – a hunter missionary; and
I heard him talk to her with pride of the new world of
civilisation and Christianity which he was organising in that
tropic wilderness. I listened with a dim jealous understanding –
not of the words, but of the facts. I saw them instinctively, as in
a dream. She pointed up to me in terror and disgust, as I sat
gnashing and gibbering overhead. He threw up the muzzle of
his rifle carelessly, and fired – I fell dead, but conscious still.
I knew that my carcase was carried to the settlement; and
I watched while a smirking, chuckling surgeon, dissected me,
bone by bone, and nerve by nerve. And as he was fingering at
my heart, and discoursing sneeringly about Van Helmont's
dreams of the Archæus,* and the animal spirit which dwells
within the solar plexus, Eleanor glided by again, like an angel,
and drew my soul out of the knot of nerves, with one velvet
finger-tip.

*

Child-dreams – more vague and fragmentary than my animal
ones; and yet more calm and simple, and gradually, as they led
me onward through a new life, ripening into detail, coherence,
and reflection. Dreams of a hut among the valleys of Thibet –
the young of forest animals, wild cats, and dogs, and fowls,
brought home to be my playmates, and grow up tame around
me. Snow-peaks which glittered white against the nightly sky,
barring in the horizon of the narrow valley, and yet seeming to
beckon upwards, outwards. Strange unspoken aspirations –
instincts which pointed to unfulfilled powers, a mighty destiny.
A sense, awful and yet cheering, of a wonder and a majesty, a
presence and a voice around, in the cliffs and the pine forests,
and the great blue rainless heaven. The music of loving voices,

the sacred names of child and father, mother, brother, sister, first of all inspirations. – Had we not an All-Father,* whose eyes looked down upon us from among those stars above; whose hand upheld the mountain roots below us? Did He not love us, too, even as we loved each other?

*

The noise of wheels crushing slowly through meadows of tall marigolds and asters, orchises and fragrant lilies. I lay, a child, upon a woman's bosom. Was she my mother, or Eleanor, or Lillian? Or was she neither, and yet all – some ideal of the great Arian tribe, containing in herself all future types of European women? So I slept and woke, and slept again, day after day, week after week, in the lazy bullock-waggon, among herds of grey cattle, guarded by huge lop-eared mastiffs; among shaggy white horses, heavy-horned sheep, and silky goats; among tall, bare-limbed men, with stone axes on their shoulders, and horn bows at their backs. Westward, through the boundless steppes, whither or why we knew not; but that the All-Father had sent us forth. And behind us the rosy snow-peaks died into ghastly grey, lower and lower as every evening came; and before us the plains spread infinite, with gleaming salt-lakes, and ever fresh tribes of gaudy flowers. Behind us dark lines of living beings streamed down the mountain slopes; around us dark lines crawled along the plains – all westward, westward ever – The tribes of the Holy Mountain* poured out like water to replenish the earth and subdue it – lava streams from the crater of that great soul-volcano – Titan babies, dumb angels of God, bearing with them in their unconscious pregnancy, the law, the freedom, the science, the poetry, the Christianity, of Europe and the world.

Westward ever – who could stand against us? We met the wild asses on the steppe, and tamed them, and made them our slaves. We slew the bison herds, and swam broad rivers on their skins. The Python snake lay across our path; the wolves and the wild dogs snarled at us out of their coverts; we slew them and went on. The forest rose in black tangled barriers; we hewed our way through them and went on. Strange giant tribes met us, and eagle-visaged hordes, fierce and foolish; we smote them hip and thigh, and went on, westward ever. Days and weeks and months rolled on, and our wheels rolled on with them. New alps rose up before us; we climbed and climbed them, till, in lonely glens, the mountain walls stood up, and barred our path.

Then one arose and said, 'Rocks are strong, but the All-Father is stronger. Let us pray to Him to send the earthquakes, and blast the mountains asunder.'

So we sat down and prayed, but the earthquake did not come.

Then another arose and said, 'Rocks are strong, but the All-Father is stronger. If we are the children of the All-Father, we, too, are stronger than the rocks. Let us portion out the valley, to every man an equal plot of ground; and bring out the sacred seeds, and sow, and build, and come up with me and bore the mountain.'

And all said, 'It is the voice of God. We will go up with thee, and bore the mountain; and thou shalt be our king, for thou art wisest, and the spirit of the All-Father is on thee; and whosoever will not go up with thee shall die as a coward and an idler.'

So we went up; and in the morning we bored the mountain, and at night we came down and tilled the ground, and sowed wheat and barley, and planted orchards. And in the upper glens, we met the mining dwarfs, and saw their tools of iron and copper, and their rock-houses and forges, and envied them. But they would give us none of them: then our king said—

'The All-Father has given all things and all wisdom. Woe to him who keeps them to himself: we will teach you to sow the sacred seeds; and do you teach us your smith-work, or you die.'

Then the dwarfs taught us smith-work; and we loved them, for they were wise; and they married our sons and daughters; and we went on boring the mountain.

Then some of us arose and said, 'We are stronger than our brethren, and can till more ground than they. Give us a greater portion of land, to each according to his power.'

But the king said, 'Wherefore? that ye may eat and drink more than your brethren? Have you larger stomachs, as well as stronger arms? As much as a man needs for himself, that he may do for himself. The rest is the gift of the All-Father, and we must do his work therewith. For the sake of the women and children, for the sake of the sick and the aged, let him that is stronger go up and work the harder at the mountain.' And all men said, 'It is well spoken.'

So we were all equal – for none took more than he needed; and we were all free, because we loved to obey the king by whom the spirit spoke; and we were all brothers, because we had one work, and one hope, and one All-Father.

But I grew up to be a man; and twenty years were past, and the mountain was not bored through; and the king grew old, and men began to love their flocks and herds better than quarrying, and they gave up boring through the mountain. And the strong and the cunning said, 'What can we do with all this might of ours?' So, because they had no other way of employing it, they turned it against each other, and swallowed up the heritage of the weak: and a few grew rich, and many poor; and the valley was filled with sorrow, for the land became too narrow for them.

Then I arose and said, 'How is this?' And they said, 'We must make provision for our children.'

And I answered, 'The All-Father meant neither you nor your children to devour your brethren. Why do you not break up more waste ground? Why do you not try to grow more corn in your fields?'

And they answered, 'We till the ground as our forefathers did: we will keep to the old traditions.'

And I answered, 'Oh ye hypocrites! have ye not forgotten the old traditions, that each man should have his equal share of ground, and that we should go on working at the mountain, for the sake of the weak and the children, the fatherless and the widow?'

And they answered nought for a while.

Then one said, 'Are we not better off as we are? We buy the poor man's ground for a price, and we pay him his wages for tilling it for us – and we know better how to manage it than he.'

And I said, 'Oh ye hypocrites! See how your lie works! Those who were free are now slaves. Those who had peace of mind are now anxious from day to day for their daily bread.

And the multitude gets poorer and poorer, while ye grow fatter and fatter. If ye had gone on boring the mountain, ye would have had no time to eat up your brethren.'

Then they laughed and said, 'Thou art a singer of songs, and a dreamer of dreams. Let those who want to get through the mountain go up and bore it; we are well enough here. Come now, sing us pleasant songs, and talk no more foolish dreams, and we will reward thee.'

Then they brought out a veiled maiden, and said, 'Look! her feet are like ivory, and her hair like threads of gold; and she is the sweetest singer in the whole valley. And she shall be thine, if thou wilt be like other people, and prophesy smooth things unto us, and torment us no more with talk about liberty, equality, and brotherhood; for they never were, and never will be, on this earth. Living is too hard work to give in to such fancies.'

And when the maiden's veil was lifted, it was Lillian. And she clasped me round the neck, and cried, 'Come! I will be your bride, and you shall be rich and powerful; and all men shall speak well of you, and you shall write songs, and we will sing them together, and feast and play from dawn to dawn.'

And I wept; and turned me about, and cried, 'Wife and child, song and wealth, are pleasant; but blessed is the work which the All-Father has given the people to do. Let the maimed and the halt and the blind, the needy and the fatherless, come up after me, and we will bore the mountain.'

But the rich drove me out, and drove back those who would have followed me. So I went up by myself, and bored the mountain seven years, weeping; and every year Lillian came to me, and said, 'Come, and be my husband, for my beauty is fading, and youth passes fast away.' But I set my heart steadfastly to the work.

And when seven years were over, the poor were so multiplied, that the rich had not wherewith to pay their labour. And there came a famine in the land, and many of the poor died. Then the rich said, 'If we let these men starve, they will turn on us, and kill us, for hunger has no conscience, and they are all but like the beasts that perish.' So they all brought, one a bullock, another a sack of meal, each according to his substance, and fed the poor therewith; and said to them, 'Behold our love and mercy towards you!' But the more they gave, the less they had wherewithal to pay their labourers; and the more they gave, the less the poor liked to work; so that at last they had not wherewithal to pay for tilling the ground, and each man had to go and till his own, and knew not how; so the land lay waste, and there was great perplexity.

Then I went down to them and said, 'If you had hearkened to me, and not robbed your brethren of their land, you would never had come into this strait; for by this time the mountain would have been bored through.'

Then they cursed the mountain, and me, and Him who made them, and came down to my cottage at night, and cried, 'One-sided and left-handed! father of confusion, and disciple of dead donkeys, see to what thou hast brought the land, with thy blasphemous doctrines! Here we are starving, and not only we, but the poor misguided victims of thy abominable notions!'

'You have become wondrous pitiful to the poor,' said I, 'since you found that they would not starve that you might wanton.'

Then once more Lillian came to me, thin and pale and worn. 'See, I, too, am starving! and you have been the cause of it; but I will forgive all if you will help us but this once.'

'How shall I help you?'

'You are a poet and an orator, and win over all hearts with your talk and your songs. Go down to the tribes of the plain, and persuade them to send us up warriors, that we may put down these riotous and idle wretches; and you shall be king of all the land, and I will be your slave, by day and night.'

But I went out, and quarried steadfastly at the mountain.

And when I came back the next morning, the poor had risen against the rich, one and all, crying, 'As you have done to us, so will we do to you'; and they hunted them down like wild beasts, and slew many of them, and threw their carcases on the dunghill, and took possession of their land and houses, and cried, 'We will be all free and equal as our forefathers were, and live here, and eat and drink, and take our pleasure.'

Then I ran out, and cried to them, 'Fools! will you do as these rich did, and neglect the work of God! If you do to them as they have done to you, you will sin as they sinned, and devour each other at the last, as they devoured you. The old paths are best. Let each man, rich or poor, have his equal share of the land, as it was at first, and go up and dig through the mountain, and possess the good land beyond, where no man need jostle his neighbour, or rob him, when the land becomes too small for you. Were the rich only in fault? Did not you, too, neglect the work which the All-Father had given you, and run every man after his own comfort? So you entered into a lie, and by your own sin raised up the rich men to be your punishment. For the last time, who will go up with me to the mountain?'

Then they all cried with one voice, 'We have sinned! We will go up and pierce the mountain, and fulfil the work which God set to our forefathers.'

We went up, and the first stroke that I struck, a crag fell out; and behold, the light of day! and far below us the good land and large, stretching away boundless towards the western sun.

*

I sat by the cave's mouth at the dawning of the day. Past me the tribe poured down, young and old, with their waggons, and their cattle, their seeds, and their arms, as of old – yet not as of old – wiser and stronger, taught by long labour and sore affliction. Downward they streamed from the cave's mouth into the glens, following the guidance of the silver water-courses; and as they passed me, each kissed my hands and feet, and cried, 'Thou hast saved us – thou hast given up all for us. Come and be our king!'

'Nay,' I said, 'I have been your king this many a year; for I have been the servant of you all.'

I went down with them into the plain, and called them round me. Many times they besought me to go with them and lead them.

'No,' I said; 'I am old and grey-headed, and I am not as I have been. Choose out the wisest and most righteous among you, and let him lead you. But bind him to yourselves with an oath, that whenever he shall say to you, "Stay here, and let us sit down and build, and dwell here for ever", you shall cast him out of his office, and make him a hewer of wood and a drawer of water, and choose one who will lead you forwards in the spirit of God.'

The crowd opened, and a woman came forward into the circle. Her face was veiled, but we all knew her for a prophetess. Slowly she stepped into the midst, chanting a mystic song. Whether it spoke of past, present, or future, we knew not; but it sank deep into all our hearts.

> True freedom stands in meekness —
> True strength in utter weakness —
> Justice in forgiveness lies —
> Riches in self-sacrifice —
> Own no rank but God's own spirit —
> Wisdom rule! — and worth inherit!
> Work for all, and all employ —
> Share with all, and all enjoy —
> God alike to all has given,
> Heaven as Earth, and Earth as Heaven,
> When the land shall find her king again,
> And the reign of God is come.

We all listened awe-struck. She turned to us and continued, 'Hearken to me, children of Japhet,* the unresting!

'On the holy mountain of Paradise,* in the Asgard of the Hindoo-Koh,* in the cup of the four rivers,* in the womb of the mother of nations, in brotherhood, equality, and freedom, the sons of men were begotten, at the wedding of the heaven and the earth. Mighty infants, you did the right you knew not of, and sinned not, because there was no temptation. By selfishness you fell, and became beasts of prey. Each man coveted the universe for his own lusts, and not that he might fulfil in it God's command to people and subdue it. Long have you wandered — and long will you wander still. For here you have no abiding city. You shall build cities, and they shall crumble; you shall invent forms of society and religion, and they shall fail in the hour of need. You shall call the lands by your own names, and fresh waves of men shall sweep you forth, westward, westward ever, till you have travelled round the path of the sun, to the place from whence you came. For out of Paradise you went, and unto Paradise you shall return; you shall become once more as little children, and renew your youth like the eagle's. Feature by feature, and limb by limb ye shall renew it; age after age, gradually and painfully, by hunger and pestilence, by superstitions and tyrannies, by need and blank despair, shall you be driven back to the All-Father's home, till you become as you were before you fell, and left the likeness of your father for the likeness of the beasts. Out of Paradise you came, from liberty, equality, and brotherhood, and unto them you shall return again. You went forth in unconscious infancy – you shall return in thoughtful manhood. You went forth in ignorance and need – you shall return in science and wealth, philosophy and art. You went forth with the world a wilderness before you – you shall return when it is a garden behind you. You went forth selfish savages – you shall return as the brothers of the Son of God.

'And for you,' she said, looking on me, 'your penance is accomplished. You have learned what it is to be a man. You have lost your life and saved it. He that gives up house, or land, or wife, or child, for God's sake, it shall be repaid him an hundred-fold. Awake!'

Surely I knew that voice! She lifted her veil. The face was Lillian's? No! – Eleanor's!

Gently she touched my hand – I sank down into soft, weary, happy sleep.

The spell was snapped. My fever and my dreams faded away together, and I woke to the twittering of the sparrows, and the scent of the poplar leaves, and the sights and sounds of my childhood, and found Eleanor and her uncle sitting by my bed, and with them Crossthwaite's little wife.

I would have spoken, but Eleanor laid her finger on her lips, and taking her uncle's arm, glided from the room. Katie kept stubbornly a smiling silence, and I was fain to obey my new-found guardian angels.

What need of many words? Slowly, and with relapses into insensibility, I passed, like one who recovers from drowning, through the painful gate of birth into another life. The fury of passion had been replaced by a delicious weakness. The thunder-clouds had passed roaring down the wind, and the calm bright holy evening was come. My heart, like a fretful child, had stamped and wept itself to sleep. I was past even gratitude;

infinite submission and humility, feelings too long forgotten, absorbed my whole being. Only, I never dared meet Eleanor's eye. Her voice was like an angel's when she spoke to me – friend, mother, sister, all in one. But I had a dim recollection of being unjust to her – of some bar between us.

Katie and Crossthwaite, as they sat by me, tender and careful nurses both, told me, in time, that to Eleanor I owed all my comforts. I could not thank her – the debt was infinite, inexplicable. I felt as if I must speak all my heart or none; and I watched her lavish kindness with a sort of sleepy, passive wonder, like a new-born babe.

At last, one day, my kind nurses allowed me to speak a little. I broached to Crossthwaite the subject which filled my thoughts. 'How came I here? How came you here? and Lady Ellerton? What is the meaning of it all?'

'The meaning is, that Lady Ellerton, as they call her, is an angel out of heaven. Ah, Alton! she was your true friend, after all, if you had but known it, and not that other one at all.'

I turned my head away.

'Whisht – howld then, Johnny darlint! and don't go tormenting the poor dear sowl, just when he's comin' round again.'

'No, no! tell me all. I must – I ought – I deserve to bear it. How did she come here?'

'Why then, it's my belief, she had her eye on you ever since you came out of that Bastille, and before that, too; and she found you out at Mackaye's, and me with you, for I was there looking after you. If it hadn't been for your illness, I'd have been in Texas now, with our friends, for all's up with the Charter, and the country's too hot, at least for me. I'm sick of the whole thing together, patriots, aristocrats, and every body else, except this blessed angel. And I've got a couple of hundred to emigrate with; and what's more, so have you.'

'How's that?'

'Why, when poor dear old Mackaye's will was read, and you raving mad in the next room, he had left all his stock-in-trade, that was, the books, to some of our friends, to form a workmen's library with, and £400 he'd saved, to be parted between you and me, on condition that we'd G.T.T.,* and cool down across the Atlantic, for seven years come the tenth of April.'

So then, by the lasting love of my adopted father, I was at present at least out of the reach of want! My heart was ready to overflow at my eyes; but I could not rest till I had heard more of Lady Ellerton. What brought her here, to nurse me as if she had been a sister?

'Why, then, she lives not far off by. When her husband died, his cousin got the estate and title, and so she came, Katie tells me, and lived for one year down somewhere in the East-end among the needlewomen; and spent her whole fortune on the poor, and never kept a servant, so they say, but made her own bed and cooked her own dinner, and got her bread with her own needle, to see what it was really like. And she learnt a lesson there, I can tell you, and God bless her for it. For now she's got a large house hereby, with fifty or more in it, all at work together, sharing the earnings among themselves, and putting into their own pockets the profits which would have gone to their tyrants; and she keeps the accounts for them, and gets the goods sold, and manages everything, and reads to them while they work, and teaches them every day.'

'And takes her victuals with them,' said Katie, 'share and share alike. She that was so grand a lady, to demane herself to the poor unfortunate young things! She's as blessed a saint as any a one in the Calendar, if they'll forgive me for saying so.'

'Ay! demeaning, indeed! for the best of it is, they're not the respectable ones only, though she spends hundreds on them——'

'And sure, haven't I seen it with my own eyes, when I've been there charing?'

'Ay, but those she lives with are the fallen and the lost ones – those that the rich would not set up in business, or help them to emigrate, or lift them out of the gutter with a pair of tongs, for fear they should stain their own whitewash in handling them.'

'And sure they're as dacent as meself now, the poor darlints! It was misery druv 'em to it, every one; perhaps it might hav' druv me the same way if I'd a lot o' childer, and Johnny gone to glory – and the blessed saints save him from that same at all at all!'

'What! from going to glory?' said John.

'Och, thin, and wouldn't I just go mad if ever such ill luck happened to yees as to be taken to heaven in the prime of your days, asthore?'

And she began sobbing, and hugging and kissing the little man; and then suddenly recollecting herself, scolded him heartily for making such a 'whillybaloo', and thrust him out of my room, to re-commence kissing him in the next, leaving me to many meditations.

CHAPTER XXXVII

THE TRUE DEMAGOGUE

I USED to try to arrange my thoughts, but could not; the past seemed swept away and buried, like the wreck of some drowned land after a flood. Ploughed by affliction to the core, my heart lay fallow for every seed that fell. Eleanor understood me, and gently and gradually, beneath her skilful hand, the chaos began again to bloom with verdure. She and Crossthwaite used to sit and read to me – from the Bible, from poets, from every book which could suggest soothing, graceful, or hopeful fancies. Now, out of the stillness of the darkened chamber, one or two priceless sentences of à Kempis,* or a spirit-stirring Hebrew psalm, would fall upon my ear: and then there was silence again; and I was left to brood over the words in vacancy, till they became a fibre of my own soul's core. Again and again the stories of Lazarus and the Magdalene alternated with Milton's Penseroso, or with Wordsworth's tenderest and most solemn strains. Exquisite prints from the history of our Lord's life and death were hung one by one, each for a few days, opposite my bed, where they might catch my eye the moment that I woke, the moment before I fell asleep. I heard one day the good dean remonstrating with her on the 'sentimentalism' of her mode of treatment.

'Poor drowned butterfly!' she answered, smiling, 'he must be fed with honey-dew. Have I not surely had practice enough already?'

'Yes, angel that you are!' answered the old man. 'You have

indeed had practice enough!' and lifting her hand reverentially to his lips, he turned and left the room.

She sat down by me as I lay, and began to read from Tennyson's Lotus-Eaters. But it was not reading – it was rather a soft dreamy chant, which rose and fell like the waves of sound on an Æolian harp.

> There is sweet music here that softer falls
> Than petals from blown roses on the grass,
> Or night dews on still waters between walls
> Of shadowy granite, in a gleaming pass;
> Music that gentlier on the spirit lies
> Than tired eye-lids upon tired eyes;
> Music that brings sweet sleep down from the blissful skies.
> Here are cool mosses deep,
> And through the moss the ivies creep,
> And in the stream the long-leaved flowers weep,
> And from the craggy ledge the poppy hangs in sleep.
>
> Why are we weigh'd upon with heaviness,
> And utterly consumed with sharp distress,
> While all things else have rest from weariness?
> All things have rest: why should we toil alone?
> We only toil, who are the first of things,
> And make perpetual moan,
> Still from one sorrow to another thrown:
> Nor ever fold our wings,
> And cease from wanderings;
> Nor steep our brows in slumber's holy balm;
> Nor hearken what the inner spirit sings,
> 'There is no joy but calm!'
> Why should we only toil, the roof and crown of things?

She paused—

> My soul was an enchanted boat
> Which, like a sleeping swan, did float
> Upon the silver waves of her sweet singing.*

Half unconscious, I looked up. Before me hung a copy of Raffaelle's cartoon of the Miraculous Draught of Fishes. As my eye wandered over it, it seemed to blend into harmony with the feelings which the poem had stirred. I seemed to float upon the glassy lake. I watched the vista of the waters and mountains, receding into the dreamy infinite of the still summer sky. Softly from distant shores came the hum of eager multitudes; towers and palaces slept quietly beneath the eastern sun. In front, fantastic fishes, and the birds of the mountain and the lake, confessed His power, who sat there in His calm godlike beauty, His eye ranging over all that still infinity of His own works, over all that wondrous line of figures, which seemed to express every gradation of spiritual consciousness, from the dark self-condemned dislike of Judas's averted and wily face, through mere animal greediness to the first dawnings of surprise, and on to the manly awe and gratitude of Andrew's majestic figure, and the self-abhorrent humility of Peter, as he shrank down into the bottom of the skiff, and with convulsive palms and bursting brow, seemed to press out from his inmost heart the words, 'Depart from me, for I am a sinful man, O Lord!'* Truly, pictures are the books of the unlearned, and of the mis-learned too. Glorious Raffaelle! Shakspeare of the south! Mighty preacher, to whose blessed intuition it was given to know all human hearts, to embody in form and colour all spiritual truths, common alike to Protestant and Papist, to workman and to sage – oh that I may meet thee before the throne of God, if it be but to thank thee for that one picture, in which thou didst reveal to me, in a single glance, every step of my own spiritual history!

She seemed to follow my eyes, and guess from them the workings of my heart; for now, in a low half-abstracted voice, as Diotima may have talked of old,* she began to speak of rest and labour, of death and life; of a labour which is perfect rest – of a daily death, which is but daily birth – of weakness, which is the strength of God; and so she wandered on in her speech to Him who died for us. And gradually she turned to me. She laid one finger solemnly on my listless palm, as her words and voice became more intense, more personal. She talked of Him, as Mary may have talked just risen from His feet. She spoke of Him as I had never heard Him spoken of before – with a tender passionate loyalty, kept down and softened by the deepest awe. The sense of her intense belief, shining out in every lineament of her face, carried conviction to my heart more than ten thousand arguments could do. It must be true! – Was not the power of it around her like a glory? She spoke of Him as near us – watching us – in words of such vivid eloquence that I turned half-startled to her, as if I expected to see Him standing by her side.

She spoke of Him as the great Reformer; and yet as the true conservative; the inspirer of all new truths, revealing in His Bible to every age abysses of new wisdom, as the times require; and yet the vindicator of all which is ancient and eternal – the justifier of His own dealings with man from the beginning. She spoke of Him as the true demagogue – the champion of the poor; and yet as the true King, above and below all earthly rank; on whose will alone all real superiority of man to man, all the time-justified and time-honoured usages of the family, the society, the nation, stand and shall stand for ever.

*

And then she changed her tone; and in a voice of infinite tenderness, she spoke of Him as the Creator, the Word, the Inspirer, the only perfect Artist, the Fountain of all Genius.

She made me feel – would that His ministers had made me feel it before, since they say that they believe it – that He had passed victorious through my vilest temptations, that He sympathised with my every struggle.

She told me how He, in the first dawn of manhood, full of the dim consciousness of His own power, full of strange yearning presentiments about His own sad and glorious destiny, went up into the wilderness, as every youth, above all every genius, must, there to be tempted of the devil. She told how alone with the wild beasts, and the brute powers of nature, He saw into the open secret – the mystery of man's twofold life, His kingship over earth, His sonship under God: and conquered in the might of His knowledge. How He was tempted, like every genius, to use His creative powers for selfish ends – to yield to the lust of display and singularity, and break through those laws which He came to reveal and to fulfil – to do one little act of evil, that He might secure thereby the harvest of good which was the object of His life: and how He had conquered in the faith that He was the son of God. She told me how He had borne the sorrows of genius; how the slightest pang that I had ever felt was but a dim faint pattern of His; how He, above all men, had felt the agony of calumny, misconception, misinterpretation; how He had fought with bigotry and stupidity, casting His pearls before swine, knowing full well what it was to speak to the deaf and the blind; how He had wept over Jerusalem, in the bitterness of disappointed patriotism, when He had tried in vain to awaken within a nation of slavish and yet rebellious bigots, the consciousness of their glorious calling. . . .

It was too much – I hid my face in the coverlet, and burst out into a long, low, and yet most happy weeping. She rose and went to the window and beckoned Katie from the room within.

'I am afraid,' she said, 'my conversation has been too much for him.'

'Showers sweeten the air,' said Katie; and truly enough, as my own lightened brain told me.

Eleanor – for so I must call her now – stood watching me for a few minutes, and then glided back to the bed-side, and sat down again.

'You find the room quiet?'

'Wonderfully quiet. The roar of the city outside is almost soothing, and the noise of every carriage seems to cease suddenly, just as it becomes painfully near.'

'We have had straw laid down,' she answered, 'all along this part of the street.'

This last drop of kindness filled the cup to overflowing: a veil fell from before my eyes – it was she who had been my friend, my guardian angel, from the beginning!

'You – you – idiot that I have been! I see it all now. It was you who laid that paper to catch my eye on that first evening at D***! – you paid my debt to my cousin! – you visited Mackaye in his last illness!'

She made a sign of assent.

'You saw from the beginning my danger, my weakness! – you tried to turn me from my frantic and fruitless passion! – you tried to save me from the very gulf into which I forced myself! – and I – I have hated you in return – cherished suspicions too ridiculous to confess, only equalled by the absurdity of that other dream!'

'Would that other dream have ever given you peace, even if it had ever become reality?'

She spoke gently, slowly, seriously; waiting between each question for the answer which I dared not give.

'What was it that you adored? a soul, or a face? The inward reality, or the outward symbol, which is only valuable as a sacrament of the loveliness within?'

'Ay!' thought I, 'and was that loveliness within? What was that beauty but a hollow mask?' How barren, borrowed, trivial, every thought and word of hers seemed now as I looked back upon them, in comparison with the rich luxuriance, the startling originality, of thought and deed and sympathy, in her who now sat by me, wan and faded, beautiful no more as men call beauty, but with the spirit of an archangel gazing from those clear fiery eyes! And as I looked at her, an emotion utterly new to me arose; utter trust, delight, submission, gratitude, awe – if it was love, it was love as of a dog towards his master. . . .

'Ay,' I murmured, half unconscious that I spoke aloud, 'her I loved, and love no longer; but you, you, I worship, and for ever!'

'Worship God!' she answered. 'If it shall please you hereafter to call me friend, I shall refuse neither the name nor its duties. But remember always, that whatsoever interest I feel in you, and, indeed, have felt from the first time I saw your poems, I cannot give or accept friendship upon any ground so shallow and changeable as personal preference. The time was, when I thought it a mark of superior intellect and refinement to be as exclusive in my friendships as in my theories. Now I have learnt that that is most spiritual and noble which is also most universal. If we are to call each other friends, it must be for a reason which equally includes the outcast and the profligate, the felon and the slave.'

'What do you mean?' I asked, half disappointed.

'Only for the sake of Him who died for all alike.'

Why did she rise and call Crossthwaite from the next room where he was writing? Was it from the womanly tact and delicacy which feared lest my excited feelings might lead me on to some too daring expression, and give me the pain of a rebuff, however gentle; or was it that she wished him, as well as me, to hear the memorable words which followed, to which she seemed to have been all along alluring me, and calling up in my mind, one by one, the very questions to which she had prepared the answers?

'That name!' I answered. 'Alas! has it not been in every age the watchword, not of an all-embracing charity, but of self-conceit and bigotry, excommunication and persecution?'

'That is what men have made it; not God, or He who bears it, the Son of God. Yes, men have separated from each other, slandered each other, murdered each other in that name; and blasphemed it by that very act. But when did they unite in any name but that? Look all history through – from the early churches, unconscious and infantile ideas of God's kingdom, as Eden was of the human race, when love alone was law, and none said that aught that he possessed was his own, but they had all things in common – Whose name was the bond of unity for that brotherhood, such as the earth had never seen – when the Roman lady and the Negro slave partook together at the table of the same bread and wine, and sat together at the feet of the Syrian tent-maker?* – "One is our Master, even Christ, who sits at the right hand of God, and in Him we are all brothers."* Not self-chosen preference for His precepts, but the over-whelming faith in His presence, His rule, His love, bound those rich hearts together. Look onward, too, at the first followers of St. Bennet and St. Francis, at the Cameronians* among their Scottish hills, or the little persecuted flock who in a dark and godless time gathered around John Wesley by pit-mouths and on Cornish cliffs – Look, too, at the great societies of our own days, which, however imperfectly, still lovingly and earnestly do their measure of God's work at home and abroad; and say, when was there ever real union, co-operation, philanthropy, equality, brotherhood, among men, save in loyalty to Him – Jesus, who died upon the cross?'

And she bowed her head reverently before that unseen Majesty; and then looked up at us again – Those eyes, now brimming full of earnest tears, would have melted stonier hearts than ours that day.

'Do you not believe me? Then I must quote against you one of your own prophets – a ruined angel – even as you might have been.

'When Camille Desmoulins, the revolutionary, about to die, as is the fate of such, by the hands of revolutionaries, was asked his age, he answered, they say, that it was the same as that of the "bon sans-culotte Jesus."* I do not blame those who shrink from that speech as blasphemous. I, too, have spoken hasty words and hard, and prided myself on breaking the bruised reed, and quenching the smoking flax.* Time was, when I should have been the loudest in denouncing poor Camille; but I have long since seemed to see in those words the distortion of an almighty truth – a truth that shall shake thrones and principalities and powers, and fill the earth with its sound, as with the trump of God; a prophecy like Balaam's of old – "I shall see Him, but not nigh; I shall behold Him, but not near."* . . . Take all the heroes, prophets, poets, philosophers – where will you find the true demagogue – the speaker to man simply as man – the friend of publicans and sinners, the stern foe of the scribe and the Pharisee – with whom was no respect of persons – where is he? Socrates and Plato were noble; Zerdusht and Confutzee, for aught we know, were nobler still;* but what were they but the exclusive mystagogues* of an enlightened few, like our own Emersons and Strausses,* to compare great with small? What gospel have they, or Strauss, or Emerson, for the poor, the suffering, the oppressed? The People's Friend? Where will you find him, but in Jesus of Nazareth?'

'We feel that; I assure you, we feel that,' said Crossthwaite. 'There are thousands of us who delight in His moral teaching, as the perfection of human excellence.'

'And what gospel is there in a moral teaching? What good news is it to the savage of St. Giles's, to the artisan, crushed by the competition of others and his own evil habits, to tell him that he can be free – if he can make himself free? That all men are his equals – if he can rise to their level, or pull them down to his? – All men his brothers – if he can only stop them from devouring him, or making it necessary for him to devour them? Liberty, equality, and brotherhood? Let the history of every nation, of every revolution – let your own sad experience, speak – have they been aught as yet but delusive phantoms – angels that turned to fiends the moment you seemed about to clasp them? Remember the tenth of April, and the plots thereof, and answer your own hearts!'

Crossthwaite buried his face in his hands.

'What!' I answered passionately, 'will you rob us poor creatures of our only faith, our only hope, on earth? Let us be deceived, and deceived again; yet we will believe! We will hope on in spite of hope. We may die, but the idea lives for ever. Liberty, equality, and fraternity must come. We know, we know, that they must come; and woe to those who seek to rob us of our faith!'

'Keep, keep your faith,' she cried; 'for it is not yours, but God's, who gave it! But do not seek to realise that idea for yourselves.'

'Why, then, in the name of reason and mercy?'

'Because it is realised already for you. You are free; God has made you free. You are equals – you are brothers; for He is your king, who is no respecter of persons. He is your king, who has bought for you the rights of sons of God. He is your king, to whom all power is given in heaven and earth; who reigns, and will reign, till He has put all enemies under His feet. That was Luther's charter – with that alone he freed half Europe.* That is your charter, and mine; the everlasting ground of our rights, our mights, our duties, of ever-gathering storm for the oppressor, of ever-brightening sunshine for the oppressed. Own no other. Claim your investiture as free men from none but God. His will, His love, is a stronger ground, surely, than abstract rights and ethnological opinions. Abstract rights? What ground, what root have they, but the ever-changing opinions of men, how anew and dying anew with each fresh generation? – while the word of God stands sure – "You are mine, and I am yours, bound to you in an everlasting covenant."*

'Abstract rights? They are sure to end, in practice, only in the tyranny of their father – opinion. In favoured England here, the notions of abstract right among the many are not so incorrect, thanks to three centuries of Protestant civilisation; but only because the right notions suit the many at this moment.

But in America, even now, the same ideas of abstract right do not interfere with the tyranny of the white man over the black. Why should they? The white man is handsomer, stronger, cunninger, worthier than the black. The black is more like an ape than the white man – he is – the fact is there; and no notions of an abstract right will put that down: nothing but another fact – a mightier, more universal fact – Jesus of Nazareth died for the negro as well as for the white. Looked at apart from Him, each race, each individual of mankind, stands separate and alone, owing no more brotherhood to each other than wolf to wolf, or pike to pike – himself a mightier beast of prey – even as he has proved himself in every age. Looked at as he is, as joined into one family in Christ, his archetype and head, even the most frantic declamations of the French democrat, about the majesty of the people, the divinity of mankind, become rational, reverent, and literal. God's grace outrivals all man's boasting – "I have said, ye are gods, and ye are all the children of the Most Highest";* – "children of God, members of Christ, of His body, of His flesh, and of His bones",* – "kings and priests to God",* – free inheritors of the spirit of wisdom and understanding, the spirit of prudence and courage, of reverence and love, the spirit of Him who has said, "Behold, the days come, when I will pour out my spirit upon all flesh, and no one shall teach his brother, saying, Know the Lord, for all shall know Him, from the least even unto the greatest. Ay, even on the slaves and on the handmaidens in those days will I pour out of my spirit, saith the Lord!" '*

'And that is really in the Bible?' asked Crossthwaite.

'Ay' – she went on, her figure dilating, and her eyes flashing, like an inspired prophetess – 'that is in the Bible! What would you more than that? That is your charter; the only ground of all charters. You, like all mankind, have had dim inspirations, confused yearnings after your future destiny, and, like all the world from the beginning, you have tried to realise, by self-willed methods of your own, what you can only do by God's inspiration, by God's method. Like the builders of Babel in old time, you have said, "Go to, let us build us a city and a tower, whose top shall reach to heaven"* – And God has confounded you as He did them. By mistrust, division, passion, and folly, you are scattered abroad. Even in these last few days, the last dregs of your late plot have exploded miserably and ludicrously – your late companions are in prison, and the name of Chartist is a laughing-stock as well as an abomination.'

'Good Heavens! Is this true?' asked I, looking at Crossthwaite for confirmation.

'Too true, dear boy, too true; and if it had not been for these two angels here, I should have been in Newgate now!'

'Yes,' she went on. 'The Charter seems dead, and liberty further off than ever.'

'That seems true enough, indeed,' said I, bitterly.

'Yes. But it is because Liberty is God's beloved child, that He will not have her purity sullied by the touch of the profane. Because He loves the people, He will allow none but Himself to lead the people. Because He loves the people, He will teach the people by afflictions. And even now, while all this madness has been destroying itself, He has been hiding you in His secret place from the strife of tongues, that you may have to look for a state founded on better things than acts of parliament, social contracts, and abstract rights – a city whose foundations are in the eternal promises, whose builder and maker is God.'

She paused. – 'Go on, go on,' cried Crossthwaite and I in the same breath.

'That state, that city, Jesus said, was come – was now within us, had we eyes to see. And it is come. Call it the church, the gospel, civilisation, freedom, democracy, association, what you will – I shall call it by the name by which my Master spoke of it – the name which includes all these, and more than these – the kingdom of God. "Without observation'', as He promised,* secretly, but mightily, it has been growing, spreading, since that first Whitsuntide; civilising, humanising, uniting this distracted earth. Men have fancied they found it in this system or in that, and in them only. They have cursed it in its own name, when they found it too wide for their own narrow notions. They have cried, "Lo here!" and "Lo there!"* "To this communion!" or "To that set of opinions!" But it has gone its way – the way of Him who made all things, and redeemed all things to Himself. In every age it has been a gospel to the poor. In every age it has, sooner or later, claimed the steps of civilisation, the discoveries of science, as God's inspirations, not man's inventions. In every age, it has taught men to do that by God which they had failed in doing without Him. It is now ready, if we may judge by the signs of the times, once again to penetrate, to convert, to re-organise, the political and social life of England, perhaps of the world; to vindicate democracy as the will and gift of God. Take it for the ground of your rights. If, henceforth, you claim political enfranchisement, claim it not as mere men, who may be villains, savages, animals, slaves of their own prejudices and passions; but as members of Christ, children of God, inheritors of the kingdom of heaven, and therefore bound to realise it on earth. All other rights are mere mights – mere selfish demands to become tyrants in your turn. If you wish to justify your Charter, do it on that ground. Claim your share in national life, only because the nation is a spiritual body, whose king is the Son of God; whose work, whose national character and powers, are allotted to it by the Spirit of Christ. Claim universal suffrage, only on the ground of the universal redemption of mankind – the universal priesthood of Christians. That argument will conquer, when all have failed; for God will make it conquer. Claim the disenfranchisement of every man, rich or poor, who breaks the laws of God and man, not merely because he is an obstacle to you, but because he is a traitor to your common King in heaven, and to the spiritual kingdom of which he is a citizen. Denounce the effete idol of property qualification, not because it happens to strengthen class interests against you, but because, as your mystic dream reminded you, and, therefore, as you knew long ago, there is no real rank, no real power, but worth; and worth consists not in property, but in the grace of God. Claim, if you will, annual parliaments, as a means of enforcing the responsibility of rulers to the Christian community, of which they are to be, not the lords, but the ministers – the servants of all. But claim these, and all else for which you long, not from man, but from God, the King of men. And therefore, before you attempt to obtain them, make yourselves worthy of them – perhaps by that process you will find some of them have become less needful. At all events, do not ask, do not hope, that He will give them to you, before you are able to profit by them. Believe that He has kept them from you hitherto, because they would have been curses, and not blessings. Oh! look back, look back, at the history of English Radicalism for the last half century, and judge by your own deeds, your own words; were you fit for those privileges which you so frantically demanded? Do not answer me, that those who had them were equally unfit; but thank God, if the case be indeed so, that your incapacity was not added to theirs, to make confusion worse confounded! Learn a new lesson. Believe at last that you are in Christ, and become new creatures. With those miserable, awful, farce-tragedies of April and June,* let old things pass away, and all things become new. Believe that your kingdom is not of this world, but of One whose servants must not fight. He that believeth, as the prophet says, will not make haste.* Beloved suffering brothers! – are not your times in the hand of One who loved you to the death, who conquered, as you must do, not by wrath, but by martyrdom? Try no more to meet Mammon with his own weapons, but commit your cause to Him who judges righteously, who is even now coming out of His place to judge the earth, and to help the fatherless and poor unto their right, that the man of the world may be no more exalted against them – the poor man of Nazareth, crucified for you!'

She ceased, and there was silence for a few moments, as if angels were waiting, hushed, to carry our repentance to the throne of Him we had forgotten.

Crossthwaite had kept his face fast buried in his hands; now he looked up with brimming eyes—

'I see it – I see it all now. Oh, my God! my God! What infidels we have been!'

CHAPTER XXXVIII

MIRACLES AND SCIENCE

SUNRISE, they say, often at first draws up and deepens the very mists which it is about to scatter: and even so, as the excitement of my first coviction cooled, dark doubts arose to dim the new-born light of hope and trust within me. The question of miracles had been ever since I had read Strauss* my greatest stumbling-block – perhaps not unwillingly, for my doubts pampered my sense of intellectual acuteness and scientific knowledge; and 'a little knowledge is a dangerous thing.' But now that they interfered with nobler, more important, more immediately practical ideas, I longed to have them removed – I longed even to swallow them down on trust – to take the miracles 'into the bargain' as it were, for the sake of that mighty gospel of deliverance for the people, which accompanied them. Mean subterfuge! which would not, could not, satisfy me. The thing was too precious, too all-important, to take one tittle of it on trust. I could not bear the consciousness of one hollow spot – the nether fires of doubt glaring through, even at one little crevice. I took my doubts to Lady Ellerton – Eleanor, as I must now call her, for she never allowed herself to be addressed by her title – and she referred me to her uncle—

'I could say somewhat on that point myself. But since your doubts are scientific ones, I had rather that you should discuss them with one whose knowledge of such subjects you, and all England with you, must revere.'

'Ah, but – pardon me; he is a clergyman.'

'And therefore bound to prove, whether he believes in his own proof or not. Unworthy suspicion!' she cried, with a touch of her old manner. 'If you had known that man's literary history for the last thirty years, you would not suspect him, at least, of sacrificing truth and conscience to interest, or to fear of the world's insults.'

I was rebuked; and not without hope and confidence, I broached the question to the good dean when he came in – as he happened to do that very day.

'I hardly like to state my difficulties,' I began – 'for I am afraid that I must hurt myself in your eyes by offending your – prejudices, if you will pardon so plain-spoken an expression.'

'If', he replied, in his bland courtly way, 'I am so unfortunate as to have any prejudices left, you cannot do me a greater kindness than by offending them – or by any other means, however severe – to make me conscious of the locality of such a secret canker.'

'But I am afraid that your own teaching has created, or at least corroborated, these doubts of mine.'

'How so?'

'You first taught me to revere science. You first taught me to admire and trust the immutable order, the perfect harmony of the laws of Nature.'

'Ah! I comprehend now!' he answered, in a somewhat mournful tone – 'How much we have to answer for! How often, in our carelessness, we offend those little ones, whose souls are precious in the sight of God! I have thought long and earnestly on the very subject which now distresses you; perhaps every doubt which has passed through your mind, has exercised my own; and, strange to say, you first set me on that new path of thought. A conversation which passed between us years ago at D * * * on the antithesis of natural and revealed religion – perhaps you recollect it?'

Yes, I recollected it better than he fancied, and recollected too – I thrust the thought behind me – it was even yet intolerable.

'That conversation first awoke in me the sense of an hitherto unconscious inconsistency – a desire to reconcile two lines of thought – which I had hitherto considered as parallel, and impossible to unite. To you, and to my beloved niece here, I owe gratitude for that evening's talk; and you are freely welcome to all my conclusions, for you have been, indirectly, the originator of them all.'

'Then, I must confess, that miracles seem to me impossible, just because they break the laws of Nature. Pardon me – but there seems something blasphemous in supposing that God can mar His own order: His power I do not call in question, but the very thought of His so doing is abhorrent to me.'

'It is as abhorrent to me as it can be to you, to Goethe, or to Strauss; and yet I believe firmly in our Lord's miracles.'

'How so, if they break the laws of Nature?'

'Who told you, my dear young friend, that to break the customs of Nature, is to break her laws? A phenomenon, an appearance, whether it be a miracle or a comet, need not contradict them because it is rare, because it is as yet not referable to them. Nature's deepest laws, her only true laws, are her invisible ones. All analyses (I think you know enough to understand my terms) whether of appearances, of causes, or of elements, only lead us down to fresh appearances – we cannot see a law, let the power of our lens be ever so immense. The true causes remain just as impalpable, as unfathomable as ever, eluding equally our microscope and our induction – ever tending towards some great primal law, as Mr. Grove has well shown lately in his most valuable pamphlet* – some great primal law, I say, manifesting itself, according to circumstances, in countless diverse and unexpected forms – till all that the philosopher as well as the divine can say, is – The Spirit of Life, impalpable, transcendental, direct from God, is the only real cause. It "bloweth where it listeth, and thou hearest the sound thereof, but canst not tell whence it cometh, or whither it goeth.* What, if miracles should be the orderly results of some such deep, most orderly, and yet most spiritual law?'

'I feel the force of your argument, but——'

'But you will confess, at least, that you, after the fashion of the crowd, have begun your argument by begging the very question in dispute, and may have, after all, created the very difficulty which torments you.'

'I confess it; but I cannot see how the miracles of Jesus – of our Lord – have anything of order in them.'

'Tell me, then – to try the Socratic method – is disease, or health, the order and law of Nature?'

'Health, surely; we all confess that by calling diseases disorders.'

'Then, would one who healed diseases be a restorer, or a breaker of order?'

'A restorer, doubtless; but——'

'Like a patient scholar, and a scholarly patient, allow me to "exhibit" my own medicines according to my own notion of the various crises of your distemper. I assure you I will not play you false, or entrap you by quips and special pleading. You are aware that our Lord's miracles were almost exclusively miracles of healing – restorations of that order of health which disease was breaking – that when the Scribes and Pharisees, superstitious and sense-bound, asked Him for a sign from heaven, a contra-natural prodigy, He refused them as peremptorily as He did the fiend's "Command these stones that they be made bread."* You will quote against me the water turned into wine, as an exception to this rule. St. Augustine answered that objection centuries ago,* by the same argument as I am now using. Allow Jesus to have been the Lord of Creation, and what was He doing then, but what He does in the maturing of every grape – transformed from air and water even as that wine in Cana? Goethe himself, unwittingly, has made Mephistopheles even see as much as that—

> Wine is sap, and grapes are wood,
> The wooden board yields wine as good.'*

'But the time? – so infinitely shorter than that which Nature usually occupies in the process!'

'Time and space are no Gods, as a wise German says;* and as the electric telegraph ought already to have taught you. They are customs, but who has proved them to be laws, of Nature? No; analyse these miracles one by one, fairly, carefully, scientifically, and you will find that if you want prodigies really blasphemous and absurd, infractions of the laws of Nature, amputated limbs growing again, and dead men walking away with their heads under their arms, you must go to the Popish legends,* but not to the miracles of the Gospels. And now for your "but"——'

'The raising of the dead to life? Surely death is the appointed end of every animal – ay, of every species, and of man among the rest.'

'Who denies it? But is premature death? – the death of Jairus's daughter, of the widow's son at Nain,* the death of Jesus himself, in the prime of youth and vigour – or rather that gradual decay of ripe old age, through which I now, thank God, so fast am travelling? What nobler restoration of order, what clearer vindication of the laws of Nature from the disorder of diseases, than to recal the dead to their natural and normal period of life?'

I was silent a few moments, having nothing to answer; then—

'After all, these may have been restorations of the law of Nature. But why was the law broken in order to restore it? The Tenth of April has taught me, at least, that disorder cannot cast disorder out.'

'Again, I ask, why do you assume the very point in question? Again I ask, who knows what really are the laws of Nature?

You have heard Bacon's golden rule – "Nature is conquered by obeying her"?'*

'I have.'

'Then who more likely, who more certain, to fulfil that law to hitherto unattained perfection, than He who came to obey, not outward nature merely, but, as Bacon meant, the inner ideas, the spirit of Nature, which is the will of God? – He who came to do utterly, not His own will, but the will of the Father who sent Him? Who is so presumptuous as to limit the future triumphs of science? Surely no one who has watched her giant strides during the last century. Shall Stephenson and Faraday, and the inventors of the calculating machine, and the electric telegraph,* have fulfilled such wonders by their weak and partial obedience to the "Will of God expressed in things" – and He who obeyed, even unto the death, have possessed no higher power than theirs?'

'Indeed,' I said, 'your words stagger me. But there is another old objection which they have re-awakened in my mind. You will say I am shifting my ground sadly. But you must pardon me.'

'Let us hear. They need not be irrelevant. The unconscious logic of association is often deeper and truer than any syllogism.'

'These modern discoveries in medicine seem to show that Christ's miracles may be attributed to natural causes.'

'And thereby justify them. For what else have I been arguing. The difficulty lies only in the rationalist's shallow and sensuous view of Nature, and in his ambiguous slip-slop trick of using the word natural to mean, in one sentence, "material", and in the next, as I use it, only "normal and orderly." Every new wonder in medicine which this great age discovers – what does it prove, but that Christ need have broken no natural laws to do that of old, which can be done now without breaking them – if you will but believe that these gifts of healing are all inspired and revealed by Him who is the Great Physician, the Life, the Lord of that vital energy by whom all cures are wrought.

'The surgeons of St. George's* make the boy walk who has been lame from his mother's womb. But have they given life to a single bone or muscle of his limbs? They have only put them into that position – those circumstances, in which the God-given life in them can have its free and normal play, and produce the cure which they only assist. I claim that miracle of science, as I do all future ones, as the inspiration of Him who made the lame to walk in Judea, not by producing new organs, but by His creative will – quickening and liberating those which already existed.

'The mesmerist, again, says that he can cure a spirit of infirmity, an hysteric or paralytic patient,* by shedding forth on them his own vital energy; and, therefore he will have it, that Christ's miracles were but mesmeric feats. I grant, for the sake of argument, that he possesses the power which he claims; though I may think his facts too new, too undigested, often too exaggerated, to claim my certain assent. But, I say, I take you on your own ground; and, indeed, if man be the image of God, his vital energy may, for aught I know, be able, like God's, to communicate some spark of life – But then, what must have been the vital energy of Him, who was the life itself; who was filled without measure with the spirit, not only of humanity, but with that of God the Lord and Giver of life? Do but let the Bible tell its own story; grant, for the sake of argument, the truth of the dogmas which it asserts throughout, and it becomes a consistent whole. When a man begins, as Strauss does, by assuming the falsity of its conclusions, no wonder if he finds its premises a fragmentary chaos of contradictions.'

'And what else,' asked Eleanor, passionately, 'what else is the meaning of that highest human honour, the Sacrament of the Lord's Supper, but a perennial token that the same life-giving spirit is the free right of all?'

And thereon followed happy, peaceful, hopeful words, which the reader, if he call himself a Christian, ought to be able to imagine for himself. I am afraid that writing from memory, I should do as little justice to them as I have to the dean's arguments in this chapter. Of the consequences which they produced in me, I will speak anon.

CHAPTER XXXIX

NEMESIS

It was a month or more before I summoned courage to ask after my cousin.

Eleanor looked solemnly at me.

'Did you not know it? He is dead.'

'Dead!' I was almost stunned by the announcement.

'Of typhus fever. He died three weeks ago; and not only he, but the servant who brushed his clothes, and the shopman, who had, a few days before, brought him a new coat home.'

'How did you learn all this?'

'From Mr. Crossthwaite. But the strangest part of the sad story is to come. Crossthwaite's suspicions were aroused by some incidental circumstances, and knowing of Downes' death, and the fact that you most probably caught your fever in that miserable being's house, he made such inquiries as satisfied him that it was no other than your cousin's coat.'

'Which covered the corpses in that fearful chamber?'

'It was indeed.'

'Just, awful God! And this was the consistent Nemesis of all poor George's thrift and cunning, of his determination to carry the buy-cheap-and-sell-dear commercialism, in which he had been brought up, into every act of life! Did I rejoice? No; all revenge, all spite had been scourged out of me. I mourned for him as for a brother, till the thought flashed across me – Lillian was free! Half unconscious, I stammered her name inquiringly.

'Judge for yourself,' answered Eleanor, mildly, yet with a deep severe meaning in her tone.

I was silent.

*

The tempest in my heart was ready to burst forth again; but she, my guardian-angel, soothed it for me.

'She is much changed; sorrow and sickness – for she, too, has had the fever, – and, alas! less resignation or peace within, than those who love her would have wished to see, have worn her down. Little remains now of that loveliness.'

'Which I idolized in my folly!'

'Thank God, thank God! that you see that at last: I knew it all along. I knew that there was nothing there for your heart to rest upon – nothing to satisfy your intellect – and, therefore, I tried to turn you from your dream. I did it harshly, angrily, too sharply, yet not explicitly enough. I ought to have made allowances for you. I should have known how enchanting, intoxicating, mere outward perfection must have been to one of your perceptions, shut out so long as you had been from the beautiful in art and nature. But I was cruel. Alas! I had not then learnt to sympathise; and I have often since felt with terror, that I, too, may have many of your sins to answer for; that I, even I, helped to drive you on to bitterness and despair.'

'Oh, do not say so! You have done to me, meant to me, nothing but good.'

'Be not too sure of that. You little know me. You little know the pride which I have fostered – even the mean anger against you, for being the protegé of any one but myself. That exclusiveness, and shyness, and proud reserve, is the bane of our English character – it has been the bane of mine – daily I strive to root it out. Come – I will do so now. You wonder why I am here. You shall hear somewhat of my story; and do not fancy that I am showing you a peculiar mark of honour or confidence. If the history of my life can be of use to the meanest, they are welcome to the secrets of my inmost heart.

'I was my parents' only child, an heiress, highly born, and highly educated. Every circumstance of humanity which could pamper pride was mine, and I battened on the poison. I painted, I sang, I wrote in prose and verse – they told me, not without success. Men said that I was beautiful – I knew that myself, and revelled and gloried in the thought. Accustomed to see myself the centre of all my parents' hopes and fears, to be surrounded by flatterers, to indulge in secret the still more fatal triumph of contempt for those I thought less gifted than myself, self became the centre of my thoughts. Pleasure was all I thought of. But not what the vulgar call pleasure. That I disdained, while like you, I worshipped all that was pleasurable to the intellect and the taste. The beautiful was my God. I lived, in deliberate intoxication, on poetry, music, painting, and every antitype of them which I could find in the world around. At last I met with – one whom you once saw. He first awoke in me the sense of the vast duties and responsibilities of my station – his example first taught me to care for the many rather than for the few. It was a blessed lesson: yet even that I turned to poison, by making self, still self, the object of my very benevolence. To be a philanthropist, a philosopher, a feudal queen, amid the blessings and the praise of dependent hundreds – that was my new ideal; for that I turned the whole force of my intellect to the study of history, of social and economic questions. From Bentham and Malthus to Fourier and Proudhon,* I read them all. I made them all fit into that idol-temple of self which I was rearing, and fancied that I did my duty, by becoming one of the great ones of the earth. My ideal was not the crucified Nazarene, but some Hairoun Alraschid,* in luxurious splendour, pampering his pride by bestowing as a favour those mercies which God commands as the right of all. I thought to serve God, forsooth, by serving Mammon and myself. Fool that I was! I could not see God's handwriting on the wall against me. "How hardly shall they that have riches enter into the kingdom of heaven"!*...

'You gave me, unintentionally, a warning hint. The capabilities which I saw in you made me suspect that those below might be more nearly my equals than I had yet fancied. Your vivid descriptions of the misery among whole classes of workmen – misery caused and ever increased by the very system of society itself – gave a momentary shock to my fairy palace. They drove me back upon the simple old question, which has been asked by every honest heart, age after age, "What right have I to revel in luxury, while thousands are starving? Why do I pride myself on doling out to them small fractions of that wealth, which, if sacrificed utterly and at once, might help to raise hundreds to a civilisation as high as my own?" I could not face the thought; and angry with you for having awakened it, however unintentionally, I shrank back behind the pitiable worn-out fallacy, that luxury was necessary to give employment. I knew that it was a fallacy; I knew that the labour spent in producing unnecessary things for one rich man, may just as well have gone in producing necessaries for a hundred poor, or employ the architect and the painter for public bodies as well as private individuals. That even for the production of luxuries, the monopolising demand of the rich was not required – that the appliances of real civilisation, the landscapes, gardens, stately rooms, baths, books, pictures, works of art, collections of curiosities, which now went to pamper me alone – me, one single human soul – might be helping, in an associate society, to civilise a hundred families, now debarred from them by isolated poverty, without robbing me of an atom of the real enjoyment or benefit of them. I knew it, I say, to be a fallacy, and yet I hid behind it from the eye of God. Besides, "it always had been so – the few rich, and the many poor. I was but one more among millions." '

She paused a moment, as if to gather strength, and then continued:

'The blow came. My idol – for he, too, was an idol – To please him I had begun – To please myself in pleasing him, I was trying to become great – and with him went from me that sphere of labour which was to witness the triumph of my pride. I saw the estate pass into other hands; a mighty change passed over me, as impossible, perhaps, as unfitting, for me to analyse. I was considered mad. Perhaps I was so: there is a Divine insanity, a celestial folly, which conquers worlds. At least, when that period was past, I had done and suffered so strangely, that nothing henceforth could seem strange to me. I had broken the yoke of custom and opinion. My only ground was now the bare realities of human life and duty. In poverty and loneliness I thought out the problems of society, and seemed to myself to have found the one solution – self-sacrifice. Following my first impulse, I had given largely to every charitable institution I could hear of – God forbid that I should regret those gifts – yet the money, I soon found, might have been better spent. One by one, every institution disappointed me; they seemed, after all, only means for keeping the poor in their degradation, by making it just not intolerable to them – means for enabling Mammon to draw fresh victims into his den, by taking off his hands those whom he had already worn out into uselessness. Then I tried association among my own sex* – among the most miserable and degraded of them.

I simply tried to put them into a position in which they might work for each other, and not for a single tyrant; in which that tyrant's profits might be divided among the slaves themselves. Experienced men warned me that I should fail; that such a plan would be destroyed by the innate selfishness and rivalry of human nature; that it demanded what was impossible to find, good faith, fraternal love, overruling moral influence. I answered, that I knew that already; that nothing but Christianity alone could supply that want, but that it could and should apply it; that I would teach them to live as sisters, by living with them as their sister myself. To become the teacher, the minister, the slave of those whom I was trying to rescue, was now my one idea; to lead them on, not by machinery, but by precept, by example, by the influence of every gift and talent which God had bestowed upon me; to devote to them my enthusiasm, my eloquence, my poetry, my art, my science; to tell them who had bestowed these gifts on me, and would bestow, to each according to her measure, the same on them; to make my workrooms, in one word, not a machinery, but a family. And I have succeeded – as others will succeed, long after my name, my small endeavours, are forgotten amid the great new world – new Church I should have said – of enfranchised and fraternal labour.'

And this was the suspected aristocrat! Oh, my brothers, my brothers! little you know how many a noble soul, among those ranks which you consider only as your foes, is yearning to love, to help, to live and die for you, did they but know the way! Is it their fault, if God has placed them where they are? Is it their fault, if they refuse to part with their wealth, before they are sure that such a sacrifice would really be a mercy to you? Show yourselves worthy of association. Show that you can do justly, love mercy, and walk humbly with your God, as brothers before one Father, subjects of one crucified King – and see then whether the spirit of self-sacrifice is dead among the rich! See whether there are not left in England yet seven thousand who have not bowed the knee to Mammon, who will not fear to 'give their substance to the free', if they find that the Son has made you free – free from your own sins, as well as from the sins of others!

CHAPTER XL

PRIESTS AND PEOPLE

'BUT after all,' I said one day, 'the great practical objection still remains unanswered – the clergy? Are we to throw ourselves into their hands after all? Are we, who have been declaiming all our lives against priestcraft, voluntarily to forge again the chains of our slavery to a class whom we neither trust nor honour?'

She smiled. 'If you will examine the Prayer-Book, you will not find, as far as I am aware, anything which binds a man to become the slave of the priesthood, voluntarily or otherwise. Whether the people become priest-ridden or not, hereafter, will depend, as it always has done, utterly on themselves. As long as the people act upon their spiritual liberty, and live with eyes undimmed by superstitious fear, fixed in loving boldness on their Father in heaven, and their King, the first-born among many brethren, the priesthood will remain, as God intended them, only the interpreters and witnesses of His will and His kingdom. But let them turn their eyes from Him to aught in earth or heaven beside, and there will be no lack of priestcraft, of veils to hide Him from them, tyrants to keep them from Him, idols to ape His likeness. A sinful people will be sure to be a priest-ridden people; in reality, though not in name; by journalists and demagogues, if not by class-leaders and popes: and of the two, I confess I should prefer a Hildebrand* to an O'Flynn.'

'But,' I replied, 'we do not love, we do not trust, we do not respect the clergy. Has their conduct to the masses for the last century deserved that we should do so? Will you ask us to obey the men whom we despise?'

'God forbid!' she answered. 'But you must surely be aware of the miraculous, ever-increasing improvement in the clergy.'

'In morals,' I said, 'and in industry, doubtless; but not upon those points which are to us just now dearer than their morals or their industry, because they involve the very existence of our own industry and our own morals – I mean, social and political subjects. On them the clergy seem to me as ignorant, as bigoted, as aristocratic as ever.'

'But, suppose that there were a rapidly-increasing class among the clergy, who were willing to help you to the uttermost – and you must feel that their help would be worth having – towards the attainment of social reform, if you would waive for a time merely political reform?'

'What!' I said, 'give up the very ideas for which we have struggled, and sinned, and all but died? and will struggle, and, if need be, die for still, or confess ourselves traitors to the common weal?'

'The Charter, like its supporters, must die to itself before it lives to God. Is it not even now further off than ever?'

'It seems so indeed – but what do you mean?'

'You regarded the Charter as an absolute end. You made a selfish and a self-willed idol of it. And therefore God's blessing did not rest on it or you.'

'We want it as a means as well as an end – as a means for the highest and widest social reform, as well as a right dependent on eternal justice.'

'Let the working classes prove that, then,' she replied, 'in their actions now. If it be true, as I would fain believe it to be, let them show that they are willing to give up their will to God's will; to compass those social reforms by the means which God puts in their way, and wait for His own good time to give them, or not to give them, those means which they in their own minds prefer. This is what I meant by saying that Chartism must die to itself before it has a chance of living to God. You must feel, too, that Chartism has sinned – has defiled itself in the eyes of the wise, the good, the gentle. Your only way now to soften the prejudice against it is to show that you can live like men and brothers and Christians without it. You cannot wonder if the clergy shall object awhile to help you towards that Charter, which the majority of you demanded for the express purpose of destroying the creed which the clergy do believe, however badly they may have acted upon it.'

'It is all true enough – bitterly true. But yet, why do we need the help of the clergy?'

'Because you need the help of the whole nation; because

there are other classes to be considered beside yourselves; because the nation is neither the few nor the many, but the all; because it is only by the co-operation of all the members of a body, that any one member can fulfil its calling in health and freedom; because, as long as you stand aloof from the clergy, or from any other class, through pride, self-interest, or wilful ignorance, you are keeping up those very class distinctions of which you and I too complain, as "hateful equally to God and to his enemies"; and, finally, because the clergy are the class which God has appointed to unite all others; which, in as far as it fulfils its calling, and is indeed a priesthood, is above and below all rank, and knows no man after the flesh, but only on the ground of his spiritual worth, and his birthright in that kingdom which is the heritage of all.'

'Truly,' I answered, 'the idea is a noble one – But look at the reality! Has not priestly pandering to tyrants made the Church, in every age, a scoff and a byword among free men?'

'May it ever do so,' she replied, 'whenever such a sin exists! But yet, look at the other side of the picture. Did not the priesthood, in the first ages, glory not in the name, but, what is better, in the office, of democrats? Did not the Roman tyrants hunt them down as wild beasts, because they were democrats, proclaiming to the slave and to the barbarian a spiritual freedom and a heavenly citizenship, before which the Roman well knew his power must vanish into nought? Who, during the invasion of the barbarians, protected the poor against their conquerors? Who, in the middle age, stood between the baron and his serfs? Who, in their monasteries, realised spiritual democracy, – the nothingness of rank and wealth, the practical might of co-operation and self-sacrifice? Who delivered England from the Pope? Who spread throughout every cottage in the land the Bible and Protestantism, the book and the religion which declares that a man's soul is free in the sight of God? Who, at the martyr's stake in Oxford, "lighted the candle in England that shall never be put out"?* Who, by suffering, and not by re-bellion, drove the last perjured Stuart from his throne, and united every sect and class in one of the noblest steps in England's progress?* You will say these are the exceptions; I say nay; they are rather a few great and striking manifestations of an influence which has been, unseen though not unfelt, at work for ages, converting, consecrating, organising, every fresh invention of mankind, and which is now on the eve of christianising democracy, as it did Mediæval Feudalism, Tudor Nationalism, Whig Constitutionalism; and which will succeed in christianising it, and so alone making it rational, human, possible; because the priesthood alone, of all human institutions, testifies of Christ the King of men, the Lord of all things, the inspirer of all discoveries; who reigns, and will reign, till He has put all things under His feet, and the kingdoms of the world have become the kingdoms of God and of His Christ. Be sure, as it always has been, so will it be now. Without the priesthood there is no freedom for the people. Statesmen know it; and, therefore, those who would keep the people fettered, find it necessary to keep the priesthood fettered also. The people never can be themselves without co-operation with the priesthood; and the priesthood never can be themselves without co-operation with the people. They may help to make a sect-Church for the rich, as they have been doing, or a sect-Church for paupers (which is also the most subtle form of a sect-Church for the rich), as a party in England are trying now to do – as I once gladly would have done myself: but if they would be truly priests of God, and priests of the Universal Church, they must be priests of the people, priests of the masses, priests after the likeness of Him who died on the cross.'

'And are there any men,' I said, 'who believe this? and, what is more, have courage to act upon it, now in the very hour of Mammon's triumph?'

'There are those who are willing, who are determined, whatever it may cost them, to fraternise with those whom they take shame to themselves for having neglected; to preach and to organise, in concert with them, a Holy War against the social abuses which are England's shame; and, first and foremost, against the fiend of competition. They do not want to be dictators to the working men. They know that they have a message to the artisan, but they know, too, that the artisan has a message to them; and they are not afraid to hear it. They do not wish to make him a puppet for any system of their own; they only are willing, if he will take the hand they offer him, to devote themselves, body and soul, to the great end of enabling the artisan to govern himself; to produce in the capacity of a free man, and not of a slave; to eat the food he earns, and wear the clothes he makes. Will your working brothers co-operate with these men? Are they, do you think, such bigots as to let political differences stand between them and those who fain would treat them as their brothers; or will they fight manfully side by side with them in the battle against Mammon, trusting to God, that if in anything they are otherwise minded, He will, in His own good time, reveal even that unto them? Do you think, to take one instance, the men of your own trade would heartily join a handful of these men in an experiment of associate labour, even though there should be a clergyman or two among them?'

'Join them?' I said. 'Can you ask the question? I, for one, would devote myself, body and soul, to any enterprise so noble. Crossthwaite would ask for nothing higher, than to be a hewer of wood and a drawer of water to an establishment of associate workmen. But, alas! his fate is fixed for the New World; and mine, I verily believe, for sickness and the grave. And yet I will answer for it, that, in the hopes of helping such a project, he would give up Mackaye's bequest, for the mere sake of remaining in England: and for me, if I have but a month of life, it is at the service of such men as you describe.'

'Ah!' she said, musingly, 'if poor Mackaye had but had somewhat more faith in the future, that fatal condition would perhaps never have been attached to his bequest. And yet, perhaps, it is better as it is. Crossthwaite's mind may want quite as much as yours does, a few years of a simpler and brighter atmosphere to soften and refresh it again. Besides, your health it too weak, your life, I know, too valuable to your class, for us to trust you on such a voyage alone. He must go with you.'

'With me?' I said. 'You must be misinformed; I have no thought of leaving England.'

'You know the opinion of the physicians?'

'I know that my life is not likely to be a long one; that immediate removal to a southern, if possible to a tropical, climate, is considered the only means of preserving it. For the former, I care little; *non est tanti vivere.** And, indeed, the latter, even if it would succeed, is impossible. Crossthwaite will live and thrive by the labour of his hands; while, for such a helpless invalid as I to travel, would be to dissipate the little capital which poor Mackaye has left me.'

'The day will come, when society will find it profitable, as well as just, to put the means of preserving life by travel within the reach of the poorest. But individuals must always begin by setting the examples, which the state too slowly, though surely (for the world is God's world after all) will learn to copy. All is arranged for you. Crossthwaite, you know, would have sailed ere now, had it not been for your fever. Next week you start with him for Texas. No; make no objections. All expenses are defrayed – no matter by whom.'

'By you! by you! Who else?'

'Do you think that I monopolise the generosity of England? Do you think warm hearts beat only in the breasts of working men? But, if it were I, would not that be only another reason for submitting? You must go. You will have, for the next three years, such an allowance as will support you in comfort, whether you choose to remain stationary, or, as I hope, to travel southward into Mexico. Your passage-money is already paid.'

Why should I attempt to describe my feelings? I gasped for breath, and looked stupidly at her for a minute or two. – The second darling hope of my life within my reach, just as the first had been snatched from me! At last I found words.

'No, no, noble lady! Do not tempt me! Who am I, the slave of impulse, useless, worn out in mind and body, that you should waste such generosity upon me? I do not refuse from the honest pride of independence; I have not man enough left in me even for that. But will you, of all people, ask me to desert the starving suffering thousands, to whom my heart, my honour are engaged; to give up the purpose of my life, and pamper my fancy in a luxurious paradise, while they are slaving here?'

'What? Cannot God find champions for them when you are gone? Has He not found them already? Believe me, that Tenth of April, which you fancied the death-day of liberty, has awakened a spirit in high as well as in low life, which children yet unborn will bless.'

'Oh, do not mistake me! Have I not confessed my own weakness? But if I have one healthy nerve left in me, soul or body, it will retain its strength only as long as it thrills with devotion to the people's cause. If I live, I must live among them, for them. If I die, I must die at my post. I could not rest, except in labour. I dare not fly, like Jonah, from the call of God.* In the deepest shade of the virgin forests, on the loneliest peak of the Cordilleras,* He would find me out; and I should hear His still small voice reproving me, as it reproved the fugitive patriot-seer of old – What doest thou here, Elijah?'*

I was excited, and spoke, I am afraid, after my custom, somewhat too magniloquently. But she answered only with a quiet smile:

'So you are a Chartist still?'

'If by a Chartist you mean one who fancies that a change in mere political circumstances will bring about a millenium, I am no longer one. That dream is gone – with others. But if to be a Chartist is to love my brothers with every faculty of my soul – to wish to live and die struggling for their rights, endeavouring to make them, not electors merely, but fit to be electors, senators, kings and priests to God and to His Christ – if that be the Chartism of the future, then am I seven-fold a Chartist, and ready to confess it before men, though I were thrust forth from every door in England.'

She was silent a moment.

' "The stone which the builders rejected is become the head-stone of the corner."* Surely the old English spirit has cast its madness, and begins to speak once more as it spoke in Naseby fights and Smithfield fires!'*

'And yet you would quench it in me amid the enervating climate of the Tropics?'

'Need it be quenched there? Was it quenched in Drake, in Hawkins, and the conquerors of Hindostan?* Weakness, like strength, is from within, of the spirit, and not of the sunshine. I would send you thither, that you may gain new strength, new knowledge to carry out your dream and mine. Do not refuse me the honour of preserving you. Do not forbid me to employ my wealth in the only way which reconciles my conscience to the possession of it. I have saved many a woman already; and this one thing remained – the highest of all my hopes and longings – that God would allow me, ere I died, to save a man. I have longed to find some noble soul, as Carlyle says, fallen down by the wayside,* and lift it up, and heal its wounds, and teach it the secret of its heavenly birthright, and consecrate it to its King in heaven. I have longed to find a man of the people, whom I could train to be the poet of the people.'

'Me, at least, you have saved, have taught, have trained! Oh that your care had been bestowed on some more worthy object!'

'Let me at least, then, perfect my own work. You do not – it is a sign of your humility that you do not – appreciate the value of this rest. You underrate at once your own powers, and the shock which they have received.'

'If I must go, then, why so far? Why put you to so great expense? If you must be generous, send me to some place nearer home – to Italy, to the coast of Devon, or the Isle of Wight, where invalids like me are said to find all the advantages which are so often, perhaps too hastily, sought in foreign lands.'

'No,' she said, smiling; 'you are my servant now, by the laws of chivalry, and you must fulfil my quest. I have long hoped for a Tropic poet; one who should leave the routine imagery of European civilisation, its meagre scenery, and physically decrepit races, for the grandeur, the luxuriance, the infinite and strongly-marked variety of Tropic nature, the paradisaic beauty and simplicity of Tropic humanity. I am tired of the old images; of the barren alternation between Italy and the Highlands. I had once dreamt of going to the Tropics myself; but my work lay elsewhere. Go for me, and for the people. See if you cannot help to infuse some new blood into the aged veins of English literature; see if you cannot, by observing man in his mere simple and primeval state, bring home fresh conceptions of beauty, fresh spiritual and physical laws of his existence, that you may realise them here at home – (how, I see as yet but dimly; but He who teaches the facts will surely teach their application) – in the cottages, in the play-grounds, the reading-rooms, the churches of working men.'

'But I know so little – I have seen so little!'

'That very fact, I flatter myself, gives you an especial

vocation for my scheme. Your ignorance of cultivated English scenery, and of Italian art, will enable you to approach with a more reverend, simple, and unprejudiced, eye, the primeval forms of beauty – God's work, not man's. Sin you will see there, and anarchy, and tyranny: but I do not send you to look for a society, but for nature. I do not send you to become a barbarian settler, but to bring home to the realms of civilisation those ideas of physical perfection, which as yet, alas! barbarism, rather than civilisation, has preserved. Do not despise your old love for the beautiful. Do not fancy that because you have let it become an idol and a tyrant, it was not therefore the gift of God. Cherish it, develop it to the last; steep your whole soul in beauty; watch it in its most vast and complex harmonies, and not less in its most faint and fragmentary traces. Only, hitherto you have blindly worshipped it; now you must learn to comprehend, to master, to embody it; to show it forth to men as the sacrament of Heaven, the finger-mark of God!'

Who could resist such pleading from those lips? I at least could not.

CHAPTER XLI

FREEDOM, EQUALITY, AND BROTHERHOOD

BEFORE the same Father, the same King, crucified for all alike, we had partaken of the same bread and wine, we had prayed for the same spirit. Side by side, around the chair on which I lay propped up with pillows, coughing my span of life away, had knelt the high-born countess, the cultivated philosopher, the repentant rebel, the wild Irish girl, her slavish and exclusive creed exchanged for one more free and all-embracing; and that no extremest type of human condition might be wanting, the reclaimed Magdalene* was there – two pale worn girls from Eleanor's asylum, in whom I recognised the needlewomen to whom Mackaye had taken me, on a memorable night seven years before. Thus – and how better? – had God rewarded their loving care of that poor dying fellow-slave.

Yes – we had knelt together: and I had felt that we were

one – that there was a bond between us, real, eternal, independent of ourselves, knit not by man, but God; and the peace of God, which passes understanding, came over me like the clear sunshine after weary rain.

One by one they shook me by the hand, and quitted the room; and Eleanor and I were left alone.

'See!' she said, 'Freedom, Equality, and Brotherhood are come; but not as you expected.'

Blissful, repentant tears blinded my eyes, as I replied, not to her, but Him who spoke by her—

'Lord! not as I will, but as thou wilt!'*

'Yes,' she continued, 'Freedom, Equality, and Brotherhood are here. Realise them in thine own self, and so alone thou helpest to make them realities for all. Not from without, from Charters and Republics, but from within, from the Spirit working in each; not by wrath and haste, but by patience made perfect through suffering, canst thou proclaim their good news to the groaning masses, and deliver them, as thy Master did before thee, by the cross, and not the sword. Divine paradox! – Folly to the rich and mighty – the watchword of the weak, in whose weakness is God's strength made perfect. "In your patience possess ye your souls, for the coming of the Lord draweth nigh."* Yes – He came then, and the Babel-tyranny of Rome fell, even as the more fearful, more subtle, and more diabolic tyranny of Mammon shall fall ere long – suicidal, even now crumbling by its innate decay. Yes – Babylon the Great – the commercial world of selfish competition, drunken with the blood of God's people, whose merchandise is the bodies and souls of men – her doom is gone forth. And then – then – when they, the tyrants of the earth, who lived delicately with her rejoicing in her sins, the plutocrats and bureaucrats, the money-changers and devourers of labour, are crying to the rocks to hide them, and to the hills to cover them, from the wrath of Him that sitteth on the throne – then labour shall be free at last, and the poor shall eat and be satisfied, with things that eye hath not seen nor ear heard, nor hath it entered into the heart of man to conceive, but which God has prepared for those who love Him. Then the earth shall be full of the knowledge of the Lord, as the waters cover the sea, and mankind at last shall own their

King — Him in whom they are all redeemed into the glorious liberty of the Sons of God, and He shall reign indeed on earth, and none but His saints shall rule beside Him. And then shall this sacrament be an everlasting sign to all the nations of the world, as it has been to you this day, of freedom, equality, brotherhood, of glory to God in the highest, and on earth peace, good-will toward men. Do you believe?'

Again I answered, not her, but Him who sent her—

'Lord, I believe! Help thou mine unbelief!'*

'And now, farewell. I shall not see you again before you start – and ere you return – My health has been fast declining lately.'

I started – I had not dared to confess to myself how thin her features had become of late. I had tried not to hear the dry and hectic cough, or see the burning spot on either cheek – but it was too true; and with a broken voice, I cried:

'Oh that I might die, and join you!'

'Not so – I trust that you have still a work to do. But if not, promise me that, whatever be the event of your voyage, you will publish, in good time, an honest history of your life; extenuating nothing, exaggerating nothing, ashamed to confess or to proclaim nothing. It may perhaps awaken some rich man to look down and take pity on the brains and hearts more noble than his own, which lie struggling in poverty and misguidance, among these foul sties, which civilisation rears – and calls them cities. Now, once again, farewell!'

She held out her hand – I would have fallen at her feet, but the thought of that common sacrament withheld me. I seized her hand, covered it with adoring kisses – Slowly she withdrew it, and glided from the room——

What need of more words? I obeyed her – sailed – and here I am.

*

Yes! I have seen the land! Like a purple fringe upon the golden water, 'while the parting day dies like the dolphin',* there it lay upon the far horizon – the great young free New World! – and every tree and flower and insect on it new! – a wonder and a joy – which I shall never see...

No, – I shall never reach the land. I felt it all along. Weaker and weaker, day by day, with bleeding lungs and failing limbs, I have travelled the ocean-paths. The iron has entered too deeply into my soul*...

Hark! Merry voices on deck are welcoming their future home. Laugh on, happy ones! – come out of Egypt and the house of bondage, and the waste and howling wilderness of slavery and competition, workhouses and prisons, into a good land and large, a land flowing with milk and honey,* where you will sit every one under his own vine and his own fig-tree, and look into the faces of your rosy children – and see in them a blessing and not a curse! Oh, England! stern mother-land, when wilt thou renew thy youth? – Thou wilderness of man's making, not God's!... Is it not written, that the days shall come when the forest shall break forth into singing, and the wilderness shall blossom like the rose?*

Hark! again, sweet and clear, across the still night sea, ring out the notes of Crossthwaite's bugle – the first luxury, poor fellow, he ever allowed himself; and yet not a selfish one, for music, like mercy, is twice blessed—

It blesseth him that gives and him that takes.*

There is the spirit-stirring marching air of the German workmen students:

Thou, thou, thou, and thou,
Sir Master, fare thee well. –

Perhaps a half reproachful hint to the poor old England he is leaving. What a glorious metre! warming one's whole heart into life and energy! If I could but write in such a metre one true people's song, that should embody all my sorrow, indignation, hope – fitting last words for a poet of the people – for they will be my last words—— Well – thank God! at least I shall not be buried in a London churchyard! It may be a foolish fancy – but I have made them promise to lay me up among the virgin woods, where, if the soul ever visits the place of its body's rest, I may snatch glimpses of that natural beauty from which I was barred out in life, and watch the gorgeous flowers that bloom above my dust, and hear the forest birds sing around the Poet's grave.

Hark to the grand lilt of the 'Good Time Coming'!* – Song which has cheered ten thousand hearts, which has already taken root that it may live and grow for ever – fitting melody to soothe my dying ears! – Ah! how should there not be A Good Time Coming? – Hope, and trust, and infinite deliverance! – a time such as eye hath not seen nor ear heard, nor hath it entered into the heart of man to conceive! – coming surely, soon or late, to those for whom a God did not disdain to die!

*

Our only remaining duty is to give an extract from a letter written by John Crossthwaite, and dated—

Galveston, Texas, Oct., 1848.

'I am happy. Katie is happy. There is peace among us here, like "the clear down-shining after rain."* But I thirst and long already for the expiration of my seven years' exile, wholesome as I believe it to be. My only wish is to return and assist in the Emancipation of Labour, and give my small aid in that fraternal union of all classes which I hear is surely, though slowly, spreading in my mother-land.

'And now for my poor friend, whose papers, according to my promise to him, I transmit to you. On the very night on which he seems to have concluded them – an hour after we had made the land – we found him in his cabin, dead, his head resting on the table as peacefully as if he had slumbered. On a sheet of paper by him were written the following verses; the ink was not yet dry:

MY LAST WORDS.

I

Weep, weep, weep, and weep,
For pauper, dolt, and slave;
Hark! from wasted moor and fen,
Feverous alley, workhouse den,
Swells the wail of Englishmen;
'Work! or the grave!'

II

Down, down, down, and down,
With idler, knave, and tyrant;
Why for sluggards stint and moil?
He that will not live by toil
Has no right on English soil;
God's word's our warrant!

III

Up, up, up, and up,
Face your game, and play it!
The night is past – behold the sun! –
The cup is full, the web is spun,
The Judge is set, the doom begun;
Who shall stay it?*

THE END

EXPLANATORY NOTES

THE following abbreviations are used:

Cooper: Thomas Cooper, *The Life of Thomas Cooper*, 2nd edn., Hodder & Stoughton, London, 1872.

Gammage: R. G. Gammage, *History of the Chartist Movement, 1837–1854*, 2nd edn., Browne & Browne, Newcastle-on-Tyne, 1894.

Letters and Memories: Frances E. Kingsley, *Charles Kingsley. His Letters and Memories of his Life*, ed. by his wife. 2 vols., C. Kegan Paul, London, 1877.

Works of Carlyle: Thomas Carlyle, *The Works of Thomas Carlyle*, ed. H. D. Traill. 30 vols., Chapman & Hall, London, 1896–9.

5 *'the eye only sees...the power of seeing'*. Compare 'for indeed it is well said, "in every object there is inexhaustible meaning: the eye sees in it what the eye brings means of seeing".' *The French Revolution, Works of Carlyle*, II, p. 5.

7 *Independent*. Congregationalist. They were called Independents because they had no synod or council governing them.

Baptist. The Baptists are a Nonconformist sect who object to the baptism of infants, and baptise adults by immersion. 'Particular Baptists' seceded from the Independents in 1633.

a presumptuous fiction...and call it 'charity'. Kingsley is referring here to the problems raised by the doctrine of 'election', by which only a chosen few were declared to have received redemption, yet the baptism of infants was common, and is referred to in *The Book of Common Prayer* as 'this charitable work'.

Star-Chamber butchers. Under James and Charles I, the Star Chamber dispensed with a jury and became an instrument of royal tyranny. Though not strictly empowered to try ecclesiastical matters, its concern with fraud, libel and conspiracy led to savage punishments being inflicted on men for their religious views. These involved, as well as imprisonment, mutilation.

battle-fields of Naseby and Sedgemoor. Naseby, 14 June 1645, was a Royalist defeat; Sedgemoor, 6 July 1685, ended Monmouth's rebellion against James II.

stories of Gideon and Barak, and Samson and Jephthah. All were warriors and judges who freed Israel from the power of oppressors (Judg. 4–8; 9–16).

'the sword of the Lord and of Gideon'. Judg. 7: 20.

8 *'children of wrath and of the devil'*. Acts 13: 10.

9 *phrenologist*. Phrenology was the pseudo-scientific theory of F. J. Gall (1758–1828), that the moral and intellectual qualities of a person could be judged by feeling the surface of the bony development of the skull.

Battersea-fields. The present Battersea Park. The area at that time contained market gardens.

10 *Vedas*. The books containing the sacred writings of Hinduism.

11 *'a mother in Israel'*. Judg. 5: 7; 2 Sam. 20: 19. The phrase is used to describe women of great faith and wisdom.

'vital Christianity'. Christianity which makes central the ideas of original sin, justification by faith, and eternal salvation.

12 *Unitarianism*. Unitarians believe in the single being of God and consequently deny the divinity of Christ. They attracted the attention of working men, founding early mechanics' institutes and lecturing widely throughout the country.

13 *they were my heroes, my models*. Jehu, as the agent of God, killed all the royal house of Ahab of Israel, and many of that of Ahaziah of Judah (2 Kgs. 9–11). Nabal was an

immensely wealthy landowner who refused hospitality to David's men (2 Sam. 25).

Reformation-martyrs, Cromwell and Hampden, Sidney and Monmouth. Protestants, who were burned at the stake during the Catholic persecution of Mary Tudor. John Hampden twice refused to pay taxes or forced loans levied by Charles I. Algernon Sidney was a strong advocate of republican government, convicted of high treason and executed under Charles II; on the accession of the Catholic James II, James Scott, Duke of Monmouth, attempted to seize the throne, but failed and was executed.

proofs of the divine right of kings, the eternal necessity of slavery!. Compare Deut. 17: 14 and 1 Sam. 9: 17; Lev. 25: 44–6 and Exod. 21: 20–1.

Salamis and Marathon. Victories of the Greeks over the Persians, described by Herodotus and others.

14 *'laid up all these things, and treasured them in her heart'*. Luke 2: 19.

15 *antinomian*. Antinomians held that moral rules were not binding, because if each person were predestined to be saved or to be damned, it was not really important what anyone did.

17 *'The heart of man...at enmity with God'*. Eccles. 8: 11.

18 *'no part nor lot'*. Acts 8: 21.

Jesus, He loves one and all...So——. Printed in Kingsley's *Poems* as 'Child Ballad', and dated 1845.

Apollyons. Devils (Rev. 9: 11).

'an infant Timothy!'. Timothy, though young, was advised by Paul to set an example in faith and purity and not to neglect his gifts (2 Tim. 1: 5–6; Phil, 2: 19–22).

19 *'die and give no sign'*. Misquoted from 2 *Henry VI*, III. iii. 29.

20 *You sit in a cloud...is built*. From Kingsley's *The Saint's Tragedy*, Act II, sc. iv.

21 *money...'makes the man'*. Greek saying, ascribed by Pindar to Aristodemus.

'*Behold I send you forth . . . as doves.*'. Matt. 10: 16.

fighting more or less extinct Satans, as Mr. Carlyle says. Compare 'and looking discover, almost in contact with him, what the *real* Satanas, and soul-devouring, world-devouring *Devil*, now is! Original Sin and suchlike are bad enough, I doubt not: but distilled Gin, dark Ignorance, Stupidity, dark Corn-Law, Bastille and Company, what are they! *Will* he discover our new real Satan, whom he has to fight; or go on droning through his old nose-spectacles about old extinct Satans.' *Past and Present, Works of Carlyle*, X, p. 243.

22 *the great King Laissez-faire.* Kingsley's dislike of *laissez-faire*, the doctrine that government interference in individual action should be kept to a minimum, stems in part from Carlyle: see, for example, 'Chartism' in *Critical and Miscellaneous Essays, Works of Carlyle*, VI, pp. 155ff.

Thomas Cooper. Thomas Cooper (1805–92), a Leicester shoe-maker, Chartist, lecturer and author of a poem 'The Purgatory of Suicides' (1845). In the Advertisement to his poem he describes himself in words echoed here as 'an individual who bent over the last and wielded the awl till three and twenty'.

23 bleu foncé. Navy-blue hempen, linen or woollen cloth.

24 *tin.* Money.

footing. Money paid to one's fellow workers on beginning a job.

stumpy. Money; *tizzy.* Sixpence.

half-and-half. Ale and beer, or ale and porter, in equal quantities.

Father Mathy. Theobald Mathew, a Franciscan friar, known as 'The Apostle of Temperance'. He led a widely successful temperance crusade in Ireland in 1838.

blunt: Ready money.

Don't his mother know he's out?. A popular catch phrase.

Half-price at the Victory. The Royal Victoria (later the Old Vic) was a popular mid-nineteenth century theatre, producing melodramas, farces and burlesques. Its chiefly working-class patrons were allowed in for half-price if they arrived after 8.30 p.m.

25 *The ministers talk...of his beer*. From a popular ballad, 'I likes a drop of Good Beer'.

cockloft. Garret.

kivarten. Farthing.

26 *Die, die, die...the sky!*. A misquotation of Pyramus's dying speech from *A Midsummer Night's Dream*, V. i. 292–5.

heavy. A drink of porter and stout.

flams. Tricks.

27 *'their brothers' keepers'*. Gen. 4: 9.

iniquitous and destructive alterations in the system of employment. A reference to the rapidly growing practice of contracting work out.

Peterloo. A word coined to denote an occasion, seen by some at the time as a grim parody of Waterloo, when a mass meeting in support of parliamentary reform at St. Peter's Field, Manchester, on 16 August 1819, was broken up by cavalry and yeomanry.

29 *'I looked to the right hand and to the left, and no man cared for my soul'*. An approximate quotation of Ps. 142: 4.

The fiery soul which, working out its way...tenement of clay. Compare Dryden's *Absalom and Achitophel*, I, ll. 156–8.

30 *'By the law was the knowledge of sin'*. Rom. 3: 20.

31 *'The Life and Poems of J. Bethune'*. John Bethune was a self-taught Scots poet who worked as a cowherd, stone-breaker and weaver. He died in 1839, aged twenty-seven, and an edition of his poems was published posthumously by his brother.

32 *'bating not a jot of heart or hope'*. Milton, 'Sonnet to Mr. Cyriack Skinner, upon his Blindness.'

33 *Mr. Deville.* J. De Ville was the author of a popular manual of phrenology, *Outlines of Phrenology, as an accompaniment to the phrenological bust* (1824).

34 *to teach the young idea how to shoot.* James Thomson, *The Seasons,* 'Spring', l. 1150.

soul-destroying trash. Compare 'Close thy *Byron;* open thy *Goethe.' Sartor Resartus, Works of Carlyle,* I, p. 153.

warren. (Scots) permission; *scunnered.* sickened.

Hornitos of Jorullo. small conical smoking mounds thrown up when the volcano erupted in 1759. They were described by Alexander von Humboldt, who visited Jorullo in the course of extensive travels in Mexico and South America between 1799 and 1804.

Attic bee. Sophocles.

35 *Dawric Scotch.* Broad Scots.

Hamilton's literal translation between the lines. James Hamilton (1769–1829) advocated the use of interlinear translation when teaching classical and modern languages.

37 *There is a race of mortals...middle age.* Byron, *Manfred,* III. i. 138–40.

38 *Deist.* One who believes in the existence of a god without accepting revelation.

one of those who creep into widows' houses...long prayers. Mark 12: 40.

39 *Howe and Baxter, Owen.* Three eminent Nonconformist divines: John Howe (1630–1705) is best known for *The Living Temple of God* (c. 1675); Richard Baxter (1615–91) wrote *The Saints' Everlasting Rest* (1650), and numerous hymns; John Owen (1616–83) gained a reputation for vast knowledge of Calvinist theology.

40 **The portraits...scandalised by them. – ED.* The note was added in response to criticism by Daniel Macmillan, who saw the work in manuscript. He had strong Baptist connections. Andrew Fuller (1754–1815) was the first secretary of the Baptist Missionary Society; Robert Hall (1764–1831) was famous for his pulpit oratory; Dr.

William Carey (1761–1834) was an early Baptist mission-ary to India. Swift's 'Essay on the Fates of Clergymen' was originally published in *The Intelligencer*, no. 5, 1728, as 'A Description of what the world calls Discretion'.

41 *'The deil's amang the tailors'...as the sang says*. 'The Devil Among the Taylors' is an old Scottish dance tune.

stickit. (Scots) stabbed, murdered.

Hech! sic a parish...drucken the bell. A topographical booklet, *Dunkeld: Its Straths and Glens* (1879), quotes a version of these lines and suggests they may have their origin in the invasion of Robert Macdonnachie, during the time of Bishop Bruce.

42 *'Fox's Martyrs'*. John Foxe's *Actes and Monuments of these latter perilous times touching matters of the Church* (1563) was popularly known as the 'Book of Martyrs'.

44 *huge mustachoed war-machines*. Compare *Past and Present*, *Works of Carlyle*, X, p. 261, where the soldier is referred to as 'the human battle-engine'.

'A soldier, after all...kill me'. Compare Carlyle, loc. cit.

46 *fire-arms would be the end of all your old knights*. After describing the combat between knight Bradamant and a giant, Ariosto laments in an aside the passing of the spirit of chivalry which the invention of gunpowder and use of fire-arms had brought about:

> How could'st thou, curst invention, ever find
> Reception in the brave, the generous mind!
> By thee the glorious war is turn'd to shame,
> By thee the trade of arms has lost its fame...

Orlando Furioso, J. Hoole's translation, 1799, XI, ll. 174–7.

48 *Mr. O'Flynn*. A portrait of Feargus O'Connor, the main Chartist leader in the 1840s. See note for p. 189, below.

The Irish Æschines. Aeschines was an Athenian orator, famous for his opposition to Demosthenes. He is supposed to have had a fine appearance and voice, and a vehement style, and was considered at the time an inept and vain opportunist.

Conciliation Hall. The headquarters in Dublin of the Royal Association of Ireland, which advocated repeal of the Act of Union of Great Britain with Ireland. O'Connor supported the movement for repeal.

'*Dei voluntatem in rebus revelatam*'. i.e. the will of God revealed in things. This was a favourite quotation of Kingsley's, and is elsewhere ascribed by him to Bacon. O'Flynn prefers to ascribe it to a countryman: compare the Rev. Panurgus O'Blareaway in *Yeast*, who 'used to attribute all quotations whatsoever to Irish geniuses'.

undeveloped Aspasias. Aspasia was a courtesan from Miletus who became the mistress of the Athenian general and statesman Pericles. She is said by Plutarch to have instigated the war with Samos which took place in 440 and 439 BC.

Gracchi. Tiberius Gracchus (d. 133 BC) and Gaius Gracchus (d. 121 BC) were two brothers who both held the office of tribune and introduced laws of an egalitarian tendency. Their activities used to be referred to as 'the sedition of the Gracchi'.

50 *Sufficent for* [*unto*] *the day is the evil thereof*. See Matt. 6: 34.

51 '*till their torments do, by length of time, become their elements*'. From Mammon's speech, *Paradise Lost*, II, ll. 274–5.

our part of the press. Popular journals played an important part in the Chartist movement. Chief amongst these was the *Northern Star* (1838–52), owned by O'Connor, which was estimated to have a weekly circulation of 48,000 in 1839.

52 *Pisgah*. Deut. 34: 1–4. From here Moses beheld the Promised Land.

'*the good time coming*'. The Good Time Coming' was a popular Chartist song of the period, written by Charles Mackay.

Moloch-Mammon. Moloch: the chief god of the Ammon-
ites, to whom children were sacrificed; Mammon: wealth.

little ones in mines and factories. The plight of such
children had been brought before the public in various
Blue Books, e.g. 1831–2 Report of the Select Committee
on Factories; 1833 Report of the Commissioners on the
Employment of Children in Factories; 1842 Report of the
Commission on the Labour of Women and Children in
Mines, and also in Mayhew's articles on 'Labour and the
Poor' in the *Morning Chronicle* (Oct. 1849–Dec. 1850).

Tooting pandemoniums. Poor law schools like Drouet's in
Tooting where 180 children died in 1849 from an out-
break of cholera. Dickens wrote four articles on the disaster
in the *Examiner*, concluding 'The cholera (or some unusually malignant form of typhus) broke out in M.
Drouet's farm for children, because it was brutally conducted, vilely kept, preposterously inspected, dishonestly
defended, a disgrace to a Christian community, and a stain
upon a civilized land.'

arise, and go over Jordan. Josh. 3–4.

54 *my eye fell upon the chapter . . . was subject unto them.*
Luke 2: 41–52.

But on reading further . . . rebuff. Compare Matt. 12: 46–
50; Mark 3: 31–5; Luke 8: 19–21.

55 *What right have you . . . my father's works?* Compare
Luke 2: 49.

58 *A demp unpleasant body.* After a phrase by Mr. Mantalini
in Dickens, *Nicholas Nickleby* (ch. 34): 'me – who for her
sake will become a demd, damp, moist, unpleasant body!'

59 *Memorialise the Health of Towns Commission.* Petition
the Commission for Enquiring into the State of Large
Towns and Populous Districts.

blister. A plaster which raised blisters, formerly used in
medicine.

*Rj. Aquae pumpis purae quantum suff. Applicatur extero
pro re nata.* Rj. originally an abbreviation for 'recipe',

often headed prescriptions. 'Take a sufficient quantity of pure pump water. It is applied externally as needed.'

Tip us your daddle. Give me your hand.

Brandy hot with. Brandy with hot water and sugar.

the Leander. The oldest English open rowing club, dating from early in the nineteenth century. Before it was reorganized in 1862, it was a club of London oarsmen.

60 *like Doll Tearsheet's abuse...a solemn 'Very well'.* 2 *Henry IV*, V. iv. 31.

having been a guardian myself, and knowing the hact... out of his mother. Under the provisions of the Poor Law Amendment Act, 1834, the giving of poor relief was normally ordered by the board of guardians, an annually elected body of ordinary citizens. Sections 56 and 57 made parents chargeable for relief given to a child under sixteen.

61 *comato-crapulose.* i.e. drunkenly lethargic.

St. George's. St. George's Hospital, then at Hyde Park Corner.

62 *in these days of Dutch painting and Boz.* A tribute to Dickens's descriptive skill in such works as *Sketches by Boz* (1836–7), his attention to detail being considered to be like the realistic interiors and portraits of the Dutch school of painters: Vermeer, Rembrandt, Pieter de Hooch, and others.

63 *the magic seal of Solomon.* The seal holds down the evil efreet in 'The History of the Fisherman', *The Arabian Nights' Entertainments*.

Athol brose. (Scots) a mixture of whisky and meal, or whisky and honey.

64 *gang preaching the virtues o' evil-savoured smoke "ad daemones abigendos".* James I wrote *A Counterblaste to Tobacco* (1604), and he also wrote *Daemonologie* (1599), where he praises the excellence of foul smoke for driving away devils.

Benthamite. Reflecting the utilitarian views of Jeremy Bentham and his followers.

Icon Basilike. Εἰκὼν Βασιλική, The Pourtraicture of His Sacred Majestie in his Solitudes and Sufferings, a book published shortly after the execution of Charles I in 1649, and containing explanations, meditations and prayers apparently composed by him. It was widely accepted as genuine, but had in fact been written by a royalist supporter, John Gauden.

Michael Angelo's well known skinless model. A figure such as Kingsley describes seems earlier to have been called an 'anatomy': see the *OED*. Ercole Bottari in his eighteenth-century life of Michelangelo mentions a wax anatomical model owned by the Florentine academicians of his time and called the anatomy of Michelangelo; so Michelangèlo may himself have had some such figure.

65 *'Harrington's Oceana'.* James Harrington's *The Commonwealth of Oceana*, a work on government in which the establishing of an ideal republic in an imaginary country representing England is described. It was published during the Protectorate of Cromwell, and dedicated to him.

66 *baillie body.* (Scots) an authoritative sort of man.

Ye're an unaccreedited hero, the noo, as Thomas Carlyle has it. Compare 'As we said of the Valet, so of the Sceptic: He does not know a Hero when he sees him!...It is, at bottom, the same thing that both the Valet and he expect: the garnitures of some *acknowledged* royalty, which *then* they will acknowledge!' *On Heroes, Works of Carlyle*, V, p. 208.

"But gin ye do weel by yoursel...ye'll find a' men speak well o' ye". Ps. 49: 18.

67 *old Sawney.* A derisive nickname for a Scotsman, derived from 'Alexander'.

The children of this world...children of light. Luke 16: 8.

68 *in his smart Rochester.* Presumably a style of greatcoat or morning coat like the Chesterfield, the Byron or the Albert.

much better ones at Dulwich. i.e. in the Dulwich College picture gallery.

69 *Anathema Maranatha*. 1 Cor. 16: 22 reads in the Author-
ized Version 'If any man love not the Lord Jesus Christ,
let him be Anathema Maranatha', where the final words
apparently refer to an especially severe form of anathema-
tization. This interpretation of the Greek text is not
accepted today.

*with sneers at the fellows of the college...government
commission*. The affairs of Dulwich College were first
investigated by the Charity Commissioners in 1834, but
the allegations of excessive wealth of the master and
fellows and abuse of the founder's intentions in the
instruction of the scholars were dismissed when the matter
came to court. Two petitions were presented to the Archbishop of Canterbury as Visitor in 1848 and 1849, the
second being heard in the Court of Arches in April 1850.
The Archbishop decreed reforms, with costs against the
College; but comprehensive reform required a new legal
foundation, which was supplied by an Act of Parliament
in 1857.

70 *'the man and his wife were both naked, and not ashamed'.*
Gen. 2: 25.

Guido's St. Sebastian. Guido Reni (1575–1642) was one
of the greatest painters of the Bolognese school. Some early
depictions of the saint show an elderly man, but in Renais-
sance paintings of his martyrdom, he is young and pierced
by arrows. The picture in the Dulwich gallery is actually a
copy of the original at Bologna.

'O Lord how long?'. Rev. 6: 10.

71 *excited, as the Venus of Praxiteles...and death*. Kingsley
had reviewed Mrs. Jameson's *Sacred and Legendary Art*
(1848), and will have read there of instances where Italian
women had been moved by representations of St. Sebastian
to 'passion, madness, and death' (II, p. 23). Pliny, *Natural
History*, xxxvi, 20 ff., tells how the Venus of Cnidus
excited the passion of a Greek youth.

the spirit of that true St. Margaret...leaping waves.
The incident took place during the persecution of the

Covenanters in the Restoration period. Margaret Wilson, an eighteen-year-old girl, and an older woman were executed by the method described on the sands of Solway Firth, for refusing to take the Abjuration Oath. The deaths were popularly blamed on John Graham of Claverhouse, a Royalist officer involved in the persecution.

masque. i.e. face.

Praxiteles. Greek sculptor of the fourth century BC.

privet-flowers, Horace and Ariosto would have said, more true to Nature. Horace is not cited as having used the phrase. Kingsley was perhaps thinking of Virgil's comparison of the passing beauty of a youth to privet-flowers, in the second Eclogue. In his description of Alcina, the ideal of female beauty, in *Orlando Furioso*, Ariosto compares her skin to privet-flowers (can. VII, st. xi ff.)

72 *'where no air of heaven could visit her cheek too roughly'*. Compare *Hamlet*, I. ii. 140–2.

73 *Venus Victrix*. i.e. conquering Venus. Pompey dedicated the temple in his theatre to Venus Victrix (55 BC).

those daughters of Moab. Num. 25: 1.

74 *as Sam Slick says*. The humorous sayings of Sam Slick became catch-phrases on both sides of the Atlantic. He was a Yankee clockmaker in the works of T. C. Haliburton (1796–1865).

Carus's tea-parties. William Carus was Dean of Trinity, 1832–50.

76 *King Cophetua*. A legendary king in Africa, who loved and married a beggar-maid. The story is told in Tennyson's poem 'The Beggar Maid'.

the Burton Arch. The façade and arch at Hyde Park Corner, designed by Decimus Burton (1800–81).

hope deferred, making [maketh] the heart sick. See Prov. 13: 12.

78 *ye'll ha' a chance o' finding yersel a lion, and a flunkey*. Collections of verse by working men had something of a vogue in the early nineteenth century, and the effects

of often short-lived patronage could be disastrous. See Southey's 'Introductory Essay' to *The Lives and Works of Our Uneducated Poets* (1831).

gauge whusky like Burns. Burns at one time worked as an excise man and gauged ale-barrels.

leave ye to die in a ditch as they did wi' puir Thom. William Thom (*c.* 1798–1848), author of *Rhymes and Recollections of a Handloom Weaver* (1844), was 'lionized' for a short period by society but returned to his family in Dundee to die in poverty.

78–9 *"a universal liars-rock substrawtum", as Mr. Carlyle says*. Compare 'Dig down where you will, through the Parliament-floor or elsewhere, how infallibly do you, at spade's depth below the service [sic], come upon this universal *Liars*-rock substratum!' *Past and Present, Works of Carlyle*, X, p. 254.

79 *tak the cauld-water-cure off Waterloo Bridge*. The bridge was noted for suicides. Compare Thomas Hood's poem 'The Bridge of Sighs'.

the Humane Society. i.e. the Royal Humane Society, founded in 1774, 'for affording immediate relief to persons apparently dead from drowning'.

thae French indoctrinating pedants. Presumably Saint-Simon, Fourier, Compte, and their followers.

the Roman History. That of Livy, which covered the whole period from 753 BC, when Rome was supposed to have been founded, to 9 BC.

the legends of Brutus, and Cocles, and Scaevola, and the retreat to the Mons Sacer, and the Gladiator's war. See Livy i–ii; xcv; and Plutarch's 'Life of Crassus'.

80 *the corsair*. Of Byron's poem of that name.

Leonidas. King of Sparta (491–480 BC) and the hero of the defence of the pass of Thermopylae in 480 BC against the invading Persian army.

the Maccabee who stabbed the Sultan's elephant. Eleazar Savaran, who killed the elephant of Antiochus Eupator of

Syria during a battle against him in 163 BC (1 Macc. 6: 43–6).

82 *Oxford has seen...as wild Icarias...fathered by a red Republic.* A reference to the Oxford Movement, 1833–45, led by John Henry Newman, Edward Pusey and John Keble, and centred at Oxford, which aimed to restore the High Church ideals of the seventeenth century. Gradually there arose a group, followers of Newman, who tended more towards submission to Rome. Kingsley here compares them to Icarius, a mythical Greek, who was taught the cultivation of the vine by the god Dionysus. He was killed by the friends of some peasants who had become intoxicated with wine he had given them.

John Bethune. See note for p. 31 above.

83 *'Purgatory of Suicides'. The Purgatory of Suicides: a Prison Rhyme in Ten Books* (1845). The circumstances of its composition are described in Cooper's autobiography. See also note for p. 22, above.

Prince. John Critchley Prince (1808–66), known as 'The Reed-maker Poet'. His best-known collection was *Hours with the Muses* (1841). In the Sketch of the Author's Life, appended to the third edition, Prince is said to have revelled in *Robinson Crusoe*, and 'the horrible and mysterious grandeur of Ann Radcliffe and "Monk Lewis"', but no mention is made of the books Kingsley cites.

ye education-pedants, who fancy you can teach the masses ...every soul alike. This description, and the later words 'not in miseducating the poor', were perhaps aimed at the supporters of the innovations in elementary education made when Sir J. R. Kay-Shuttleworth was Secretary to the Committee of Education of the Privy Council. Compare the opening of Dickens's *Hard Times* (1854).

'the swinish multitude.'. 'Learning will be cast into the mire, and trodden down under the hoofs of a swinish multitude.' Burke, *Reflections on the Revolution in France.* Compare Matt. 7: 6.

406 EXPLANATORY NOTES

ashamed to show foreheads. Another reference to phrenology. See note for p. 9, above.

84 *I met with Mr. Tennyson's poems; . . . women that I found there*. In a review of *In Memoriam* and other works by Tennyson in *Fraser's Magazine* (Sept. 1850), Kingsley referred to 'such subtle subjective pictures of womanhood as Adeline, Isabel, and Eleanor': see 'Isabel' and 'Adeline' in *Poems, chiefly Lyrical* (1830), and 'Eleänore' in *Poems* (1833). The review is reprinted in *Literary and General Lectures and Essays*.

85 *Wallis, or Cook*. Samuel Wallis (1728–95), sailed round the Horn through Polynesia and back by the Cape in 1766–8; James Cook (1728–79) explored parts of Australia and New Zealand and in the course of his third voyage first landed at Hawaii in the Sandwich Islands, April 1769. See Cook's *A Voyage to the Pacific Ocean* (1784), and Wallis's *An Account of a Voyage round the World* (1773) The incident of the naked island beauties is reported as occurring when The Resolution landed at Tahiti in August 1773, on Cook's second voyage.

86 *lift*. (Scots) sky.

lintie. (Scots) linnet.

as fusionless as a docken. (Scots) as worthless as a dock.

87 *through Clare Market to St. Giles's*. Two districts in London noted for poverty and vice.

the library which God has given thee. The British Museum library.

88 *a mair damnable man-devouring idol than ony red-hot statue o' Moloch, or wicker Gogmagog, wherein thae auld Britons burnt their prisoners*. Victims were sacrificed to Moloch in a ceremony involving fire. 2 Kgs. 23: 10. Gogmagog is the chief of the giants of Ancient Britain in Geoffrey of Monmouth's history. In *De Bello Gallico*, Caesar relates how the Druids 'use figures of immense size, whose limbs, woven out of twigs, they fill with living

men and set on fire, and the men perish in a sheet of flame'.

to buy beer poisoned wi' grains o' paradise...saut. The adulteration of beer with these substances was common. 'Guinea-grains' or 'grains of paradise' was a seed, cardamon, added to beer and spirits for its pungent taste. 'Cocculus indicus' or picro-toxin was an intoxicant, producing muscular contractions, followed by narcosis and coma.

92 *to send us out to the colonies.* Emigration as a solution to the problems of the working-class came to be seriously considered as a practical measure after Lord Ashley and Mr. Sidney Herbert proposed a plan for it at a public meeting on 3 December 1849. This later became known as 'Mr. Sidney Herbert's Emigration Plan' and was hailed as wise and philanthropic, especially by the *Morning Chronicle*, though there was opposition to it in some quarters.

93 *stitch, stitch, stitch...a song about that.* Thomas Hood's 'The Song of the Shirt'.

With hues as when some mighty painter...eclipse. A version of two lines in Shelley's *The Revolt of Islam* (cant. V, st. xxiii).

95 *'Werterism'.* Commenting on the influence of Goethe's *The Sorrows of Young Werther* (1774), Carlyle wrote of how '*Werter*, infusing itself into the core and whole spirit of Literature, gave birth to a race of Sentimentalists, who have raged and wailed in every part of the world.' *Critical and Miscellaneous Essays, Works of Carlyle*, XXVI, p. 218. In his later writings, he frequently referred to 'Werterism' in this sense.

the Jew of old. Jeremiah. Compare Jer. 13: 27 and 9: 1.

'Cholera Chaunt'. The actual title of the poem, which was written in 1848, is 'The Mowers; an anticipation of the Cholera'. The first and last stanzas are quoted here, with slight differences from the original. See *The Poetical Works of Charles Mackay* (1868), p. 244.

96 *hunger is...a better sauce than any Ude invents.* A

variant of the proverbial, 'The best sauce in the world is hunger.' Ude, chef to Louis XVI, was said to have been the most able and learned of cooks.

how I thanked Creswick...sapphire. Thomas Creswick (1811–69), an English landscape painter of chiefly rural scenery; Anthony Vandyke Copley Fielding (1787–1855), a watercolour artist, noted for marines and landscape; Thomas Sidney Cooper (1803–1902), a painter chiefly of landscapes and animals: he painted Queen Victoria's prize cattle; Clarkson Stanfield (1793–1867), a painter of marine subjects who showed great technical knowledge of shipping.

97 *to see in history...obey and justify.* Kingsley's wife records that *The French Revolution* 'had had a remarkable effect on his mind...in establishing and intensifying his belief in God's righteous government of the world.' *Letters and Memories,* I, p. 53.

Brought up...in a part of England. Somersby, Lincolnshire.

Mariana's moat. Tennyson's 'The Dying Swan', st. iii, and 'Mariana', st. iv.

98 *Landseer and his dogs.* Sir Edwin Landseer's paintings of domestic animals, often in settings with some human interest, were immensely popular. He drew Sir Walter Scott's dogs at Abbotsford, and Queen Victoria's pets.

Fielding and his downs. See note for p. 96, above.

'whereby men live, and in all which is the life of the spirit'. Isa. 38: 16.

99 *barnacles.* (Scots) spectacles.

Tom Sheridan's answer to his father.

> 'Come, come,' said Tom's father, 'at your time of life,
> There's no longer excuse for thus playing the rake –
> It is time you should think, boy of taking a wife' –
> 'Why, so it is, father – whose wife shall I take?'

'A Joke Versified', *The Poetical Works of Thomas Moore* (1844), p. 486.

lallans. (Scots) lowlands Scots speech.

kye are laired. (Scots) cattle are stuck in the mud.

aestro percitus. Inspired in a frenzied way.

100 Author's note** *a series of noble letters on 'Labour and the Poor'.* This series appeared 19 Oct. 1849 to 12 Dec. 1850, the articles on London being contributed by Henry Mayhew. Those on tailors were in the issues of 11, 14 and 18 Dec. 1849.

'That will be better for them', as Mahomet...used to say. Mahomet often stressed the importance of good deeds, as being prudent as well as righteous. For example: 'So render to the kinsman his due, and to the needy and to the wayfarer. That is best for those who seek the pleasure of Allah.' *The Quran* (tr. M.Z. Khan), xxx, 36–41.

101 *the fast decreasing honourable trade.* Traditional bespoke tailoring, with the work done on the premises at a price negotiated directly between master and man.

determined, like Rehoboam of old, to go a-head with the times. 1 Kgs. 12: 6–14.

The government knew none such. Government contract work was described by Mayhew as 'the worse of all, and the starved-out and sweated-out tailor's last resource'. *Morning Chronicle*, 18 Dec. 1849.

sweaters. Grinding employers of underpaid labour; often in tailoring, a middle-man was known as a sweater.

102 *the registered guanaco vest, and the patent elastic omni-seasonum paletot.* Guanaco, a reddish-brown wool from the South American llama, was made into cloth popular for waistcoats. Paletots, or short overcoats, were made of a cloth resembling Melton, known as 'black elastic'. After 1848, they might be waterproofed.

103 *"One and all", as the Cornishmen say.* This is the motto of the County of Cornwall.

King of the Cannibal Islands. A popular pantomime figure in *Harlequin and Poonoowingkeewangflibeedeeflobeedee-*

buskeebang. King of the Cannibal Islands, first performed in December 1845.

We shall become the slaves…of Jews, middlemen, and sweaters. In *Cheap Clothes and Nasty* Kingsley gives a graphic account of the working conditions of men boarded with sweaters, sleeping six or seven to a small room and living on a starvation diet.

104 *a deputation…to a member of parliament*. In *Sybil, or The Two Nations* (1854) (Bk. IV, ch. 5) Disraeli describes a similarly discouraging reception suffered by a deputation of Chartists when they call on a succession of seven members of parliament.

choking and strangling…in the black hole of Calcutta. Some very exaggerated stories were circulated in the eighteenth century by people who claimed to be survivors of the Black Hole of Calcutta – the punishment cell of the barracks in Fort William, Calcutta, where 146 Europeans were said to have been shut in for a night in 1756, only twenty-three of whom survived till morning.

105 *I will sweep a crossing – I will turn cress-gatherer, ragpicker*. All near-begging occupations, described by Mayhew in his *Morning Chronicle* articles.

106 *Oh! for six hundred men like Barbaroux's Marseillois… die!*. Charles Jean Marie Barbaroux was a Girondist who led the Marseilles contingent of insurrectionists in the attack on the Tuileries on 10 August 1792. For an account of this attack, and the source of the quotation, see Carlyle's *The French Revolution*, *Works of Carlyle*, III, p. 258, pp. 292 ff.

Why, it's a fact, that the colonels of the regiments… make their own vile profit out of us tailors. Mayhew had drawn attention to this abuse in his letter of 9 November 1849 in the *Morning Chronicle*, quoting a passage from a report made in 1833 by the Select Committee on Army and Navy Appointments: 'We have 105 battalions of infantry; the clothing of these costs 255,000 [pounds] a-year by the arms estimates, of which 63,000 [pounds] a-year go to the colonels as their emoluments.'

107 *the six points*. See Introduction.

ulterior measures. These were violent measures. See also Introduction.

108 *just half-price time*. 8.30 p.m. See note for p. 24 above.

109 *the Bill of Rights*. This was enacted under William and Mary in 1689, and confirmed various basic rights of parliament which had been disregarded by the Stuart kings.

"Talismanic Palladium". i.e. magically effective support. In Virgil and other ancient authors, the 'palladium' is a statue of the goddess Pallas, thought to secure the safety of Troy.

110 *"the possession of one-tenthousandth part of a talker in the national palaver"*. Past and Present, Works of Carlyle, X, p. 219.

Lord Ashley. Anthony Ashley Cooper, later seventh Earl of Shaftesbury (1801–85), philanthropist and politician, active in many nineteenth-century reform movements.

One set informs the world that it is to be regenerated by cheap bread. Kingsley has in mind the political party known as the Manchester School, whose leaders were Richard Cobden and John Bright. It was thought to represent the interests of manufacturers, especially in the North, and supported free trade and *laissez-faire* principles. See *Letters and Memories*, I, p. 314.

'freedom of industry'. In *The Wealth of Nations*, IV, iii, Adam Smith argues, in answer to those who fear that free trade will cause heavy unemployment, that it will encourage 'the free exercise of industry'.

Another party's nostrum is more churches, more schools, more clergymen. This is a reference to the Evangelical group in the Church of England who were concerned to increase the number of churches and the provision of clergy, particularly in large towns. In the first half of the nineteenth century, voluntary societies of the Church provided large sums for this purpose. See K. S. Inglis,

Churches and the Working Classes in Victorian England (1963), pp. 6ff.

111 *'Morison's-Pill-remedies'*, as Thomas Carlyle calls them. See *Past and Present, Works of Carlyle*, X, p. 23: 'I am sorry I have got no Morrison's Pill for curing the maladies of Society. It were infinitely handier if we had a Morrison's Pill, Act of Parliament, or remedial measure, which men could swallow, one good time, and then go on in their old courses, cleared from all miseries and mischiefs!' James Morison, Hygeist, produced 'universal medicines' and pills, which were widely advertised during the early Victorian period.

carbuncle. A precious stone of a red colour, but also a mythical gem, said to emit light in the dark.

we had, de facto, *like Coriolanus banished the Romans, turned our master off.* When the Roman people declared Coriolanus banished, he replied, '*I banish you*,' and left the city. *Coriolanus*, III, iii, 121.

112 Facilis descensus Averni. i.e. the descent to Hell is easy. Virgil, *Aeneid*, VI, l. 126.

Malthusian doctrines. i.e. that population would increase beyond the means of subsistence but for the positive checks of famine, war and disease, and the preventive check of restraint in marriage. T. R. Malthus, *An Essay on the Principle of Population...with an inquiry into...the future removal or mitigation of the evils which it occasions*, 2nd edn., London, 1803.

like Miss Martineau. In Harriet Martineau's *Illustrations of Political Economy* (1832–4), certain of the stories are intended to illustrate the Malthusian principles.

113 *as St. Paul said.* 1 Cor. 7: 29.

To every man...but once a life –. T. B. Macaulay, *Lays of Ancient Rome* (1842), 'Horatius' st. xxvii, ll. 3–4.

   'To every man upon this earth
   Death cometh soon or late.'

the widow o' Zareptha. 1 Kgs. 17: 8–16.

115 *The El Dorado of Raleigh's Guiana settlers.* The story of the existence of El Dorado, a fabulously wealthy city in the S. American interior, seems to have been fabricated by Juan Martin de Albujar, a Spanish settler who had lived among the Indians. Captives made on Spanish expeditions to the interior used to admit under torture to knowledge of it, but always said it was further off than their tribe. See the Introduction to T. Harlow's edition (1928) of *The Discoverie of the large rich and bewtiful empyre of Guiana*, by Sir Walter Raleigh.

Red House. A well-known inn in Battersea Fields, which was a favourite haunt of sportsmen.

116 *The world was all before me, where to choose.* Milton, *Paradise Lost*, XII, l. 646, adapted to the context.

117 *men whose class no dirt or rags could hide, any more than they could Ulysses!* When Ulysses returned home after long wanderings, disguised as a beggar, he was recognized by his nurse and his dog.

118 'the yard where the gentlemen live when they go out of town'. Very similar to the replies of London street children, recorded by Mayhew in his *Morning Chronicle* 'Letters'.

121 *getting 'em to put into clubs, and such like.* Compare *Letters and Memories*, I. p. 123: 'New clubs for the poor, shoe club, coal club, maternal society, a loan fund and lending library, were established one after another.'

122 *some sort o' papishes.* Tractarians, or High-Churchmen.

123 *so sure as a man got a fresh child, he went and got another loaf...Christian.* The system which this labourer describes, by which relief was paid according to the number of children in a family, was much practised before 1834. It was known as the Allowance System.

125 *They'd riot...as they did five-and-twenty year agone.* The fluctuation in the price of corn during 1815–16 led to widespread disturbance in Cambridgeshire. Agricultural labourers, armed with pikes and guns, established a reign of terror in some localities.

Oliver Cromwell, as dug Botsham lode, to the head of us. A 'lode' is a ditch for carrying off water from a fen; Bottisham is a village about six miles north-east of Cambridge. Cromwell was a gentleman-farmer in the fen area in his early period, and one of the main organizers and commanders of the eastern Parliamentary forces.

Metholl. Methwold, W. Norfolk.

patten. (Fens) skate.

from Whit'sea Mere to Denver Sluice. Whittlesey is in Cambridgeshire, about five miles from Peterborough; Denver is in W. Norfolk.

129 *Trinity.* Since the speaker is an undergraduate of Trinity College, he is presumably referring to Trinity Hall, the older foundation.

as well gruelled as so many posters. (Cambridge University slang) i.e. as exhausted as post-horses.

'*a fancy waterman*'. A 'fancy waterman's' costume would have been a well-cut coat, trimmed and lined in a bright colour, breeches and a cap.

130 *gyp.* (Cambridge University slang) a college servant.

132 *the stuff which has held Gibraltar.* Gibraltar was held against the Spaniards for nearly three years (1779–81) by General Elliott.

snob. Here probably used to mean 'townsman', rather than 'low-bred fellow'.

135 *the farce of swearing to the Thirty-Nine Articles.* At Cambridge the obligation of subscription to the Thirty-Nine Articles had been abolished for undergraduates in 1775, though all recipients of degrees had to declare themselves members of the Church of England. Undergraduates at Oxford, however, had, when they matriculated, to subscribe to the Thirty-Nine Articles.

136 *the Simeonite party.* The Cambridge Evangelicals. The name derives from Charles Simeon (1759–1836), vicar of Holy Trinity and a much respected preacher.

Peter Priggins. The pseudonym of Joseph Thomas Hewlett, author of *Peter Priggins, the College Scout* (1841), and *College Life; or the Proctor's Note-Book* (1843).

the Irish scribblers. Writers such as Charles James Lever, whose racy novels of Irish life were popular in the 1840s and '50s.

137 *You refuse to admit any who are not members of the Church of England.* There were Roman Catholic, Jewish and Mohammedan students at Cambridge in the mid-nineteenth century, but most students were at least nominal Anglicans. See also note for p. 135, above.

139 *'storied windows richly dight'.* Milton 'Il Penseroso', l. 159.

140 *my Ulysses polumechane, polutrope, panurge.* i.e. my resourceful, wily, unscrupulous friend. The adjectives are transliterations of Greek ones, the first two of which are epithets applied to Ulysses in the *Odyssey.*

play Panurge to your lordship's Pantagruel. Panurge was the drunken and roguish friend and follower of Pantagruel, Gargantua's son in Rabelais' *Gargantua and Pantagruel* (1532–4).

loaded with hemp. Pantagruel loaded some of the ships of his fleet with the herb Pantagruellion (ibid., III, xlix).

graeculus esuriens. Hungry Greek. Compare Juvenal, *Satires,* III, l. 78: 'Tell a hungry Greek to go to heaven – he'll attempt it.'

142 *like the Delphic Pythoness upon the sacred tripod.* The priestess of Delphi, called the Pythia, seated herself upon a tripod before prophesying.

a certain epigram of that old turkey-cock's. The epigram is supposed to have been written by Goethe to express his own relationship to a lesser author called Pustkucher. See 'Goethe' in *Critical and Miscellaneous Essays, Works of Carlyle,* XXVI.

143 *He intends to come the Mirabeau...nobleman's hat.* Sir Samuel Romilly, who knew Mirabeau personally, wrote

of him: 'it was his furious resentment of the restraint and punishment consequent on his irregularities, and the extravagant excess of vanity, and *not* any really noble sentiment or exalted views of benefit to his fellow-creatures, that made him a reformer.' *Quarterly Review*, June–Sept. 1840, LXVI, pp. 590ff.

a little Gil Blas morality. Gil Blas' adventurous career was furthered by his cheerfully acknowledged obsequiousness and cunning. Alain René le Sage, *Histoire de Gil Blas de Santillane* (1715–35).

don't go into King Cambyses' vein, or Queen Hecuba's tears, either. i.e. don't be pompous, and don't start weeping. Compare *1 Henry IV*, II, iv and *Hamlet*, II, ii.

Griffin's Optics. William Nathaniel Griffin's *A Treatise on Optics* (1838), for many years a standard work.

144 *post obits*. A 'post obit' is a bond securing repayment of a sum of money on the death of the person from whom the borrower expects to inherit.

145 fera naturae. Living in the wild state.

Roberts's Eastern sketches. After a visit to the East, David Roberts brought out a five-volume series of sketches: *The Holy Land, Egypt, Arabia, and Syria* (1842–9).

146 *'Notes in Egypt'*. Probably Sir Frederick Henniker's *Notes during a Visit to Egypt* (1823).

'Goethe's Walverwandschaften'. The novel, *Die Wahlverwandtschaften* (1809), or *Elective Affinities*.

Murray's hand-books. John Murray published a series of guidebooks for travellers, from 1820 onwards.

Bell's Life in London...*the* Ecclesiologist...*'McCulloch on Taxation'*. The first was a sporting and the second a theological journal. They had 'got down' J. R. McCulloch's *A Treatise on the Principles and practical influence of Taxation and the Funding System* (1845).

The blood of Odin...the tanner's of Falaise!. William the Conqueror is supposed to have been the illegitimate son of Robert, duke of Normandy, and Arlette, daughter of a Falaise tanner. Odin was the chief Norse god; for the background to the idea of William's descent from him, see *On Heroes, Works of Carlyle*, V, Lecture 1.

150 *Underneath her petticoat...peeped in and out.* Sir John Suckling, *A Ballad upon a Wedding*, st. viii:

> Her feet beneath her petticoat
> Like little mice, stole in and out.

macte virtute puer. Livy *Historia* VII, xxxvi. It could be rendered 'Well done, boy' or 'Keep improving'.

151 *St. Mark's.* St. Mark's Training College, Chelsea, founded in 1841 by the National Society.

153 "*speech is silver...while silence is golden*". Compare *Sartor Resartus, Works of Carlyle*, I, p. 174.

154 *Mr. Carlyle's dictum about the valet species.* On Heroes, *Works of Carlyle*, V, p. 208.

155 *Tractarians.* Sympathisers with the Oxford Movement, and the *Tracts for the Times* (1833–41), issued by Pusey, Newman, Keble, R. H. Froude, and others.

Socrates when he saved Alcibiades at Delium. The story is told in Plutarch's 'Life of Alcibiades', but the incident was at Potidaea, not Delium. At Delium, Alcibiades saved Socrates.

157 *the tall rape.* This is probably the plant Brassica napus, grown for sheep fodder, though the rape is also an old name for the turnip.

158 *a really pious and universally respected archbishop... family.* William Howley, Archbishop of Canterbury 1828–48, was the son of a minister and of no private fortune, and yet 'lived in considerable state at Lambeth Palace' and left £120,000 to his wife. Greville in his *Memoirs* called him a 'very ordinary man'.

159 '*speaking evil of dignities*'. 2 Pet. 2: 10.

'*the swinish multitude*'. See note for p. 83, above.

161 *asked me if I understood Browning's Sordello.* The poem, published in 1840, was notoriously difficult to understand.

Jane Welsh Carlyle said that she read it through and did not know whether Sordello was a man, a city, or a book.

162 *Mr. Hullah.* John Pyke Hullah, composer and organist, was one of the first to teach choral singing in England by the tonic sol-fa method. He wrote several manuals popularizing his theories, including *Wilhem's Method of Teaching Singing* (1841), and *Systems and Singing Masters* (1842). He and Kingsley became friends and Hullah set to music a number of Kingsley's poems, including 'The Sands of Dee': see Chapter XXVI.

163 *Her voice is hovering...consuming ecstasies.* Shelley 'To Constantia, singing', *Posthumous Poems* (1824), st. iii.

164 *Like the Quakers...paroxysmic.* Worship by the Quakers, or Society of Friends, began with silence, all waiting for a person to be inspired by the Holy Spirit to speak.

165 *Watts' 'Logic', and Locke 'On the Use of the Understanding'.* Isaac Watts, *Logic* (1725); John Locke *Of the Conduct of the Understanding* (1706) (posthumous).

'Aristotle', 'Ritter on Induction', and Kant's 'Prolegomena' and 'Logic'. Aristotle is supposed to have created logic, or the science of reasoning; his system is contained in the six treatises which make up the *Organon*. August Heinrich Ritter *Einleitung in die Logik* (1823) – probably an English translation of this work. Kant's *Prolegomena to any future Metaphysics* (1783) was intended as an introduction to the *Critique of Pure Reason* (1781). His *Logic* was published in 1800.

Whately. Richard Whately, *Elements of Logic* (1826). *'Fiat experimentum in corpore vili'.* 'Let the experiment be made upon some common body.'

166 *Bingley, Bewick...and Saturday Magazines, &c., &c.* William Bingley, *Memoirs of British Quadrupeds* (1809), *Animated Nature* (1814) and *A Practical Introduction to Botany* (1817); Thomas Bewick, *A General History of Quadrupeds* (1790), *History of British Birds* (1797–1804); Baron Alexander von Humboldt, *Voyage aux régions equinoxials du nouveau continent* (1814–27). Charles

Darwin published in 1839 the narrative of the cruise of the *Beagle*, which extended from Brazil to the west coast of S. America, and then through the Pacific. *The Penny Magazine* (1832–46) was a popular weekly issued by the Society for the Diffusion of Useful Knowledge; quite a lot of space was devoted to natural science. *The Saturday Magazine* (1832–44) was another similar penny magazine, published at first by the Society for Promoting Christian Knowledge.

longing to find his real lords...*execrate his sham ones*. Compare *Past and Present*, *Works of Carlyle*, X, p. 123: 'Have true reverence, and what indeed is inseparable therefrom, reverence the right man, all is well; have sham-reverence, and what also follows, greet with it the wrong man, then all is ill, and there is nothing well.'

167 *Geryon Trifurcifer*. Geryon: a mythical monster slain by Hercules in one of his labours. Also, however, in Dante's *Inferno*, a monster symbolising Fraud, which had a kind and gracious face, but a serpent's body with a forked tail and a sting. It is *Inferno* Kingsley clearly had in mind. Trifurcifer: 'altogether base'.

link between the Chelonia...connects both with the Herbivorous Cetacea. Chelonia: subdivision of the reptile class, to which turtles and tortoises belong. Perenni branchiate Batrachians: the Batrachia include frogs, toads and newts. Herbivorous Cetacea: almost extinct herbivorous mammals which include the manatees and dugongs.

Cuvier's 'Animal Kingdom'. The translation by Edward Griffith of *La Règne Animal*, Paris 1817, was for a long time the standard work on zoology.

170 *it is our duty to believe that they are reconcilable by fuller knowledge*. Kingsley always urged clergy to face the great scientific developments of the time and not to fear or disregard them when they appeared to go against theology. 'If it be said that the doctrine of evolution, by doing away with the theory of creation, does away with that of final causes – let us answer boldly, Not in the least. We might

accept what Mr. Darwin and Professor Huxley have written on physical science, and yet preserve our natural theology. . .That we should have to develop it, I do not deny. That we should have to relinquish it, I do.' *Letters and Memories*, II, p. 347.

a Deist. See note for p. 38, above.

171 *They complain. . .the laws of Nature*. Writing to Thomas Cooper on this matter, Kingsley says, 'I will just say, that I believe as devoutly as you, Goethe, or Strauss, that God never does – if one dare use the word, never *can* – break the Laws of Nature. . .but that Christ's Miracles (not Popish ones) seem to me the highest realizations of those very laws.' *Letters nad Memories*, I, p. 377.

172 *the artful dodger*. After the character in Dickens's *Oliver Twist*, first published in *Bentley's Miscellany* (1837–8). Compare the Dodger's remarks when telling Oliver for the first time about Fagin: 'And don't he know me? Oh no! Not in the least! By no means. Certainly not!'

172 *with as little reverence as Voltaire himself could have desired*. Voltaire consistently attacked the Church and its priests in his writings.

174 *Cobbett can tell you that*. In his 'Letter to Parson Malthus, on the Rights of the Poor. . .', *Political Register*, May 1819, Cobbett wrote of 'the church, from which the poor had a *right* to demand a maintenance, and from which they received it, too, until the *robbery of the poor* (which had been called a *robbery of the church*) took place, in the reign of King Henry the Eighth'.

175 *frothy, insincere, official rant, as Mr. Carlyle would call it*. Compare *Past and Present, Works of Carlyle*, X, p. 223, where Sir Jabesh Windbag, MP, 'strong only in the faith that Paragraphs and Plausibilities bring votes; that Force of Public Opinion. . .is the primal Necessity' goes forward on 'yeasty insane Froth-Oceans'.

179 *"Oh, that I had wings like a dove. . .at rest"*! Ps. 55: 6.

180 *as that most noble and excellent man, Dr. Arnold, did, by interfering in politics*. Compare A. P. Stanley, *The Life*

and Correspondence of Thomas Arnold (1844), pp. 151, 217ff., 264ff. Writing of the publication of *Principles of Church Reform* in 1833, Stanley says 'The storm, which had thus been gathering for some time past, now burst upon [Arnold] – beginning in theological and political opposition, but gradually including within its sweep every topic, personal or professional, which could expose him to obloquy.'

"all was vanity...the earth abideth for ever." Ecc. 1: 2–4.

181 *from the cedar of Lebanon to the hyssop that groweth on the wall.* 1 Kgs. 4: 33.

"These rocks, at least, tell me no lies, as men do." See Carlyle's translation of Goethe's *Wilhelm Meister's Travels, Works of Carlyle*, XXIV, p. 223, p. 229. Wilhelm comes across Jarno, wandering in the Alps, and when asked why he has chosen to cut himself off from the society of men, who, in Wilhelm's opinion, are more entertaining than rocks, he replies: 'Not they! for my rocks are at least incomprehensible.' He then sets off alone – 'now I will dive into the chasms of rocks, and with them begin a mute unfathomable conversation.' This appears to be the passage Kingsley has in mind.

Owens. Sir Richard Owen (1804–92) was an eminent comparative anatomist and palaeontologist.

182 *Poor dear Southey was a great verse-maker...imitation in any class.* Southey was an ardent republican in his early years, and became an equally ardent Tory later. Shelley's writings show his Radical sympathies, e.g. *The Masque of Anarchy* (1819), an indictment of Castlereagh's administration, and a protest at 'Peterloo'. Burns wrote a number of poems in favour of the French Revolution and the principles behind it.

183 *Gowk, Telemachus, hearken!* Gowk: fool; Telemachus was the son of Ulysses and Penelope, and left his mother to journey abroad (*Odyssey*, II).

the Circean cup. Circe, 'of the braided tresses', offered

some of Ulysses' men a magic cup: they drank, and were turned into swine.

cuif-Mentor. Cuif (Scots) fool. Mentor, or rather the goddess Athene in disguise, advised Telemachus, in fatherly fashion, before and during his travels.

towmond. (Scots) twelve-month.

184 *O'Flynn's* Weekly Warwhoop. See note for p. 189, below.

"*to be put into ane o' the priest's offices, that ye may eat a piece o' bread.*" 1 Sam. 2: 36.

gowd shoulder-knot. An ornamental knot of ribbon or metal lace worn on the shoulder by gentlemen's servants; the mark of a livery servant.

186 fraus pia. A deceit thought excusable to bring about some good end, especially the advancement of religion.

Elia and his Bridget. Charles Lamb in 1796 undertook the charge of his sister who, in a temporary fit of insanity, had killed their mother.

187 *sowing the east wind.* i.e. advancing antisocial and harmful doctrines (Gen. 41: 6, 23–7 and Hos. 8: 7).

188 *the* furor scribendi. The madness of writing.

'*My mouth craved it of me*', *as Solomon says*. Prov. 16: 26.

the honourable trade. See note for p. 101, above.

the goose. The tailor's smoothing-iron.

189 *Mr. O'Flynn.* The portrait of O'Flynn which follows is clearly based on the Chartist leader, Feargus O'Connor (1794–1855), though O'Connor is also referred to by name when Kingsley describes the events of 10 April 1848. He entered Parliament in 1832 as repeal Member for County Cork, and subsequently lived mainly in England. He was proprietor of the *Northern Star*, by far the most successful Chartist newspaper. See further, D. Read and E. Glasgow, *Feargus O'Connor, Irishman and Chartist* (1961).

The Commonwealth, *and* Standard of Freedom, *the* Plain Speaker. The *Commonwealth*, May 1848 – only two

numbers were issued; *Standard of Freedom*, July 1848–
Oct. 1851; Thomas Cooper edited the *Plain Speaker*,
Jan.–Aug. 1849.

190 *Exeter Hall*. A large public hall in the Strand, where
religious and philanthropic meetings were held. The name
here means 'the Evangelicals'.

'*Peace! peace!...in an instant.*' Compare Ezek. 13: 10–16
and Isa. 30: 13.

'*unsophisticated'...the cat no perfume*'. Compare *King
Lear*, III. iv. 102–3.

191 *the Birmingham Bullring*. A triangular space in the centre
of the city, often used for Chartist meetings.

*decamped in the disguise of sailors, old women, and
dissenting preachers*. See note for p. 277, below.

priest of the blue-bag. i.e. a barrister. In Common-law
courts barristers' bags are red or dark blue, the red being
reserved for queen's counsels and serjeants.

poor misguided Mitchell. John Mitchel (1815–75), Irish
nationalist and member of the Young Ireland party. In
May 1848 he was tried for treasonable felony and transported for fourteen years, after publishing an open letter
inciting his countrymen to rebel. Some sections of the
press were distinctly sympathetic, especially as all Catholic
jurors were excluded at the trial. The *Daily News*, 29 May
1848, wrote of 'the severity of the punishment thus
awarded and the courage with which he met his doom'.

192 '*their twenty-thousandth part of a talker in the national
palaver*'. See note for p. 110, above.

'*The world was all before me, where to choose*'. See note
for p. 116, above.

193 *He could say, with the old Moslem...who hath resisted
his will?*' In his lecture on 'The Hero as Prophet' Carlyle
wrote: '"*Allah, akbar,* God is great." Understand that His
will is the best for you; that howsoever sore to flesh-and-
blood, you will find it the wisest, best.' *Works of Carlyle*,
V, p. 63.

To read the Dispatch, *is to be excommunicated.* Probably the *Weekly Dispatch*, 27 Sept. 1801 to 24 June 1928, is intended. It has been described as 'Radical, Anti-Poor-Law, and Anti-Episcopal – *The Dispatch* addressed itself chiefly to the operatives and artizans'. C. Mitchell, *The Newspaper Press Directory*, 3rd edn., 1851, p. 97.

194 *Mr. Horsman.* Edward Horsman (1807–76), a Liberal politician, criticized the ecclesiastical policy of the government in 1847, and moved a vote of censure of the Ecclesiastical Commissioners. In April 1850, he attacked the church establishment during a debate on the Ecclesiastical Commission Bill. He published *Five Speeches on Ecclesiastical Affairs delivered in the House of Commons 1847, 1848, and 1849.*

Dr. Arnold. See also note for p. 180, above.

living either by the accursed system of pew rents...price of corn. The practice of allowing worshippers to rent and appropriate pews in church came under attack from the middle of the century, especially by those who felt it created social distinctions among churchgoers and discouraged the working-classes from attending. Another source of clerical income, tithes, was commuted to a rent-charge on land, depending on the price of corn, by the Tithes Commutation Act of 1836.

196 *Lane's 'Arabian Nights'.* Edward Lane's translation of *The Arabian Nights' Entertainments* (1839–41).

chironomic signs. Gesticulations.
a huge corpulent Egyptian Memnon. A colossal statue near Egyptian Thebes, erroneously supposed to represent Memnon, a personage in the Trojan war.

punctum indifferens. The point between, as with two magnetic poles where there is no force. Compare Carlyle's use of the idea in *Sartor Resartus*, *Works of Carlyle*, I, p. 146.

197 *strick a perpendicular.* An act of geomancy, for which see the note below.

efreets. Evil spirits or monsters of Mohammedan mythology, which occur frequently in *The Arabian Nights' Entertainments*.

Salverte. Anne Joseph Eusèbe Bacconière-Salverte, the English translation of a work by whom appeared in 1846 with the title *The Philosophy of Magic, Prodigies and apparent Miracles*. The main contentions were that many of the fabulous happenings of the past could be explained naturally, and that the level of scientific knowledge existing in earlier times had been underestimated. Biblical revelations were treated in this way, and so the book became controversial.

Mesmerism. F. A. Mesmer (1734–1815), an Austrian doctor, induced states of hypnosis in patients by the power of his eyes.

benj and opium. Indian hemp and opium were two of the substances discussed by Salverte as causes of many of the 'miracles' and prodigies he investigated.

aiblins. (Scots) perhaps.

198 *geomancy, nor coskinomancy*. Geomancy: divination by means of signs derived from the earth, as by throwing a handful of earth down at random and studying the resulting formation; also divination by studying lines drawn from dots made at random. Coskinomancy: divination by the turning of a sieve held on the point of a pair of shears or scissors.

cave o' Trophawnius. The cave of Trophonius was a famous oracle at Lebadeia in Boeotia.

200 *caulker*. A small draught of spirits.

202 *an old Jew, of a most un-'Caucasian' cast of features, however 'high-nosed', as Mr. Disraeli has it*. In his novel *Coningsby* (1844), where the Jewish financier Sidonia believes the Jews 'a pure race of the Caucasian organization'; in *Henrietta Temple* (1837), where Sir Frederick Armine has a 'high and aquiline' nose; and in *Tancred* (1847), where Tancred has a 'slightly elevated' nose.

203 *in a scientific attitude*. With his fists up and chin lowered, like a boxer.

a complete nineteenth-century St. Michael. The saint is customarily shown standing with his foot on Lucifer's head.

205 *The auld Romans made slaves o' their debitors.* In primitive Rome insolvent debtors might be sold into foreign slavery by their creditors. The practice was forbidden by the fourth century BC.

good Major Cartwright. John Cartwright (1740–1824), political reformer and author of *The English Constitution produced and illustrated* (1823), and many other works.

Riot Acts. Such as the Six Acts of 1819, which infringed what are usually considered to be ordinary English rights.

206 *as Bunyan has it.* When Pliable departs, leaving Christian in the Slough of Despond, Bunyan writes, 'so away he went, and Christian saw him no more' (*The Pilgrim's Progress*).

Owenite 'it's-nobody's-fault' harangues. In *A New View of Society: or Essay on the Principle of the Formation of Human Character* (1813), Robert Owen says 'the character of man is, without a single exception, always formed for him... Man, therefore, never did, nor is it possible that he ever can, form his own character.'

the dishonourable trade. i.e. discreditable branch of tailoring, by which work was contracted out to middle-men, who employed labour at very low wages. See also note for p. 101, above.

a very Leonidas. Leonidas of Tarentum, a Greek epigrammatist of the third century BC, who wrote much about drunkenness and the vices attendant upon poverty.

Et propter veetam veevendi perdere causas!. 'For the sake of keeping alive, to lose the reasons for living.'

207 *your rights were just equivalent to your mights.* Compare the various discussions of mights and rights in Carlyle's works, for example: 'All fighting... is the dusty conflict of strengths, each thinking itself the strongest, or in other words, the justest; – of Mights which do in the long-run

...mean Rights.' *Past and Present, Works of Carlyle*, X, p. 190; also *Chartism*, XXIX.

goose. See note for p. 188, above.

there's a command in Deuteronomy. Deut. 24: 6.

in the 'Arabian Nights'. See 'Abd Allah of the Land and Abd Allah of the Sea'.

For a' that...for a' that. The last four lines of the song by Burns.

208 *Mr. Windrush*. A portrait of Ralph Waldo Emerson, who had given a number of lectures in London in 1848. Kingsley's *Phaethon* (1852) is an anti-Emerson work, and *Hypatia* (1853) is also partly aimed at him. Kingsley's strong opposition to Emerson is made clear in an unpublished letter to Daniel Macmillan, 2 August 1852, where he says he is 'determined...to fight Emerson & Co. as long as I can hold my hands up – as the great false prophets of the day.'

Clavers. John Graham of Claverhouse, Viscount Dundee, a Royalist officer concerned in the persecution of the Scottish Covenanters during the reigns of Charles II and James II.

209 *They made puir Rabbie Burns an anything-arian*. Kingsley ascribed Burns's partial loss of faith to the repugnance for the kirk shown in a number of his poems. He did write some verses celebrating 'New Light' Calvinism, and so was claimed by its leaders as a supporter.

putting down my hurdies on...a haspit pew! i.e. sitting down in a latched pew. See also the note for p. 194, above.

His style, which was altogether Emersonian. Compare Emerson's *Essays*.

As for the devil, Novalis...a necessary illusion. 'Novalis' was the pseudonym of Friedrich von Hardenberg (1772–1801). Carlyle had quoted this idea of his in a review of his works included in *Critical and Miscellaneous Essays*.

210 *muscanonge*. A variety of large pike.

wi' the Pharisee. Luke 18: 11.

211 *Theodore of Mopsuestia*. Theodore, bishop of Mopsuestia in Cilicia (*c.* 340–428). He held that Christ was a man, whose identity with God consisted only in a 'loving accord' between his will and the divine will.

212 *the soul-saving business is...as Master Tummas says somewhere*. Compare 'Man has lost the *soul* out of him ...There is no religion; there is no God; man has lost his soul and vainly seeks antiseptic salt.' *Past and Present, Works of Carlyle*, X, p. 137.

213 *carbonari, illuminati, vehmgericht, samothracian*. All secret and extremist sects.

214 *that much misunderstood politeecian, Mr. John Cade... Hoose o' Commons*. Sir James Graham, in 1844, criticized Charles Buller, and others opposed to the Hours of Labour in Factories Bill, for advocating 'Jack Cade legislation', and Buller replied that 'If those were the principles of Mr. Cade...then he must say, that of all the politicians of this country, Mr. Cade had been the most grossly misrepresented.'

When pleasant Spring...surprised them a'. A stanza of Burns's version of the old song *John Barleycorn*, with the first line slightly altered to suit the context.

216 *the true 'purple locks' which Homer so often talks of*. Homer refers to the dark locks of Hector (*Iliad*, XXII, l. 401) and Poseidon (*Odyssey*, IX, l. 536), and Poseidon is also often called dark-haired. The Greek word here translated 'dark' can also mean 'dark blue', whence Kingsley's 'purple locks'.

Eastern Zubeydehs and Nourmahals. Zubeydeh was the wife of the caliph of Baghdad, Haroon Er-Rasheed and Nourmahal was wife of the Mogul emperor, Jahangir.

'herself the fairest far'. Compare Spenser's *The Faerie Queene*, Bk. VI, can. x, st. xii–xiv, xxv–xxvi.

217 *to bind up the broken-hearted...the captives*. Isa. 61: 1.

Elizabeth Fry. Elizabeth Fry (1780–1845) was born into a wealthy Quaker banking family and devoted a large part of her life to philanthropy, especially prison reform.

219 *Pater Priggins – or Laver.* See notes for p. 136, above.

Barnwell. An estate, originally that of an Augustinian priory, on the outskirts of Cambridge. It was frequented by prostitutes.

spalpeen. (Irish) youngster or contemptible person.

Eugène Sue. Marie-Joseph Eugène Sue wrote serial romances containing scenes of horror similar to Mrs. Radcliffe's work.

Holloway's ointment, and Parr's life pills. Advertisements for these proprietary medicines appeared regularly in the *Northern Star.* The issue for 3 March 1849, for example, advertises Holloway's ointment and pills under the slogan 'Try ere you despair', claiming that they cured almost anything; and the same issue also advertises Parr's pills, which were rejuvenators, said to derive from Thomas Parr (1483–1635).

Moses & Son's doggrel. E. Moses & Son, Merchants, Tailors, Clothiers, Hatters, had three large London establishments. Their catalogues were sprinkled with doggerel verses. They were engaged in the 'dishonourable' trade, hence the reference to slavery of labour to capital.

220 *doited.* (Scots) foolish, childish.

the Howitt and Eliza Cook school. Howitt's *Journal of Literature and Popular Progress* (1847–49), and *Eliza Cook's Journal* (1849–51), were popular weekly journals.

224 *the Wesleys, and Whitfields.* Charles and John Wesley, and George Whitfield (1714–70) were the main founders of the Methodist Church. They were all originally members of the Church of England who sought reform rather than schism.

you rich, who used to be told, in St. James's time, to weep and howl. James 5: 1.

225 *"This people, these masses, who know not the Gospel, are accursed".* John 7: 49.

"how hardly shall they who have",...kingdom of heaven". Mark 10: 23.

Mr. Bye-Ends. 'A very arch Fellow, a downright Hypocrite; one that would be Religious, which way ever the World went, but so cunning, that he would be sure never to lose, nor suffer for it.'

228 *goading me onward, as the gadfly did Io.* Io was changed to a heifer to conceal her from Hera's jealousy when Zeus fell in love with her; Hara then sent a gadfly to persecute her and goad her to long wanderings.

'*Oh, that I had wings as a dove...rest!*' Ps. 55: 6.

229 '*a double-minded man, unstable in all his ways.*' James 1: 8.

231 *the precious balms that break the head.* Compare Ps. 141: 5.
Bedlam. St. Mary of Bethlehem Hospital, the famous asylum. It was situated at that time in Lambeth.

232 *the* Spectator. The journal had been started in 1828 as an organ of 'educated Radicalism'. It had a reputation for serious, high-minded comment.

233 '*till he stood alone in the land, and there was no place left*'. Isa. 49: 20.

234 *like the man's in the 'Arabian Nights'.* In 'The Barber's Story of his Fifth Brother' the man, like Alton, is indulging in a reverie of future prosperity and happiness while sitting behind a tray displaying the glass he hopes to sell at a handsome profit. He is just imagining spurning a beautiful woman with his foot, when he finds he has overturned the tray.

236 *the history of Castruccio Cesarini.* Cesarini, a character in Bulwer Lytton's *Ernest Maltravers* (1837), is a poet, restlessly seeking fame. His first book of poems is a failure, and he becomes bitter, but is soon lionized by the fashionable world. He pretends he is wealthy and gambles until 'in the high road to destruction'. Finally he turns against his former friend Maltravers, and loses his reason.

237 *the girl in the fairy-tale.* 'Toads and Diamonds'; see for example Andrew Lang's *The Blue Fairy Book* (1889).

238 *Copley Fielding.* See note for p. 96, above.

239 *the *** ambassador.* The sketch which follows is based on Baron Christian Bunsen, who was Prussian ambassador to London 1842–54, and a member of the Maurice circle. He was a theologian and scholar, as well as a career diplomat. Frederick William III and the crown prince are supposed to have valued his candour and 'his demeanour, which is that of a man who crouches before no one'.

240 *The reason firm...and skill.* From Wordsworth's 'She was a Phantom of Delight'.

241–2 *O Mary, go and call the cattle home...sands o' Dee.* Included in Kingsley's *Poems* as 'The Sands of Dee'.

243 *the Corn-Law Rhymer.* Ebenezer Elliott, a Sheffield working-class poet, so called from the title of a collection of his poems, *Corn-Law Rhymes* (1828).

the author of the 'Purgatory of Suicides'. Thomas Cooper. See also notes for pp. 22, 83, above.

in Mr. O'Flynn's paper a long and fierce attack. O'Connor attacked Cooper in the *Northern Star*, 25 July 1845.

filthy lucre...which Mr. O'Flynn had always treated with withering scorn – in print. It is estimated that the *Northern Star*, at the height of its success in 1839, was worth £13,000 per annum, most of it clear profit for O'Connor.

244 *an enormous gooseberry.* A sensational, but trivial, piece of news.

'rejoicing in evil rather than in the truth'. 1 Cor. 13: 6.

Hoolie. (Scots) Softly, carefully.

speech is o' silver – silence is o' gold, says Thomas Carlyle. See note for p. 153, above.

245 *Commit your cause...dealing as the noonday.* Ps. 37: 5–6.

'Fœnum habet in cornu'. 'He has hay on his horns.' Horace, *Satires*, I. iv. 34. It was a Roman practice to fasten hay to the horns of wild oxen.

priests o' the order o' Melchisedec by the deevil's side. i.e. in the devil's service instead of Christ's. Heb. 6: 20 and 7: 1–3.

without a local habitation or a name. Compare *A Midsummer Night's Dream*, V. i. 17.

as kittle to haud as a brock in a cairn. (Scots) i.e. as difficult to get hold of as a badger in a pile of stones.

by Balaam the son o' Beor. Num. 22: 37, 24: 3–4, 10.

246 *farrant.* (Scots) cunning.

fleyed. (Scots) frightened.

forfaughten. (Scots) tired.

the Duchess of Devonshire canvassing draymen for Fox. Fox's success in the 1784 election was said to have been due to the support of Whig ladies, and especially to the canvassing of the Duchess of Devonshire. The beautiful Duchess was reputed to have conversed with a cobbler, and even kissed a butcher.

'*There is nothing secret...the house-tops*'. Luke 12: 2–3.

247 *pet and tar on.* Incite (archaic).

248 *an old pair of yellow plush breeches...whose meaning could not be mistaken.* They were, of course, the garment of a servant. Mr. Charles J. Yellowplush in Thackeray's *The Yellowplush Correspondence* (1837–8), is a footman.

249 *like a donkey between two bottles of hay.* Proverbial. A 'bottle' of hay is a bundle.

The people are starving, not because bread is dear, but because it's cheap. The removal of the duty on imported corn in 1846–9 led to a massive increase in the amount of corn and flour imported. Home production was consequently depressed, and many farm-workers were laid off.

252 *Bowie.* A long knife with the blade double-edged at the point, invented by Colonel James Bowie and used as a weapon in the south and south-west of the United States.

253 *burke.* i.e. murder.

ye're my Joseph...wi' a coat o' many colours. Gen. 37: 3, 34-5.

254 *"Behold, I send ye forth...as doves".* See note for p. 21, above.

cast na your pearls before swine...rend ye. Matt. 7: 6.

the horrible disclosures of S.G.O. Lord Sidney Godolphin Osborne, a Dorset rector and a brother-in-law of Kingsley's, wrote a series of letters on matters of public concern to *The Times* from 1844 to 1888; they were signed S.G.O. The early letters probably did much to make conditions of life of farm-workers generally known.

the barbarous abominations of the Andover Workhouse. In 1845 *The Times* published a series of letters by S.G.O. as an enquiry into the affairs of the Andover Union, where the Master was charged with immorality, drunkenness and abuse of stores.

256 *'which had built up everywhere an under-roof of doleful grey'.* Tennyson's 'The Dying Swan'.

257 *the contrast between the highly-bred...animals...and the little half-starved shivering animals who were their slaves.* Carlyle makes a similar contrast in *Past and Present, Works of Carlyle,* X, p. 22: 'Why, the four-footed worker has already *got* all that this two-handed one is clamouring for!...There is not a horse in England, able and willing to work, but *has* due food and lodging; and goes about sleek-coated, satisfied in heart.'

The sheep they fat, another kills, to parody Shelley. 'Song to the Men of England', st. v:

> The seed ye sow, another reaps;
> The wealth ye find, another keeps.

for was it not according to political economy, and the laws thereof? The theory is that of Ricardo, in *The Principles of Political Economy and Taxation* (1817). Kingsley perhaps knew the summary in J. S. Mill's *Principles of Political Economy* (1848), Bk. II, ch. xi, 2.

260 *goes into the Union.* i.e. the workhouse, so called after the

practice by which two or more parishes were consolidated for the administration of the poor laws, and jointly erected a workhouse.

266 *If you can't get your share of the poor-rates, try the county rates*. Rates levied on the whole county for the purpose of maintaining bridges, roads, asylums and prisons. It is, of course, the last of these that Blinkey has in mind.

270 *Fire 'em*. Incendiarism was a popular form of protest in southern England in the 1830s and '40s. During 1844-5 the *Northern Star* reported three or four such cases a week.

272 *the old story in Herodotus...dog-whips*. On their return after an absence of twenty-eight years fighting the Medes, the Scythian lords found their wives had borne children to their slaves. Disdaining to use swords, as with equals, the lords took out horse-whips, and their opponents fled (Herodotus, Bk. IV, 1-4).

273 *to take my trial for sedition, riot, and arson*. Thomas Cooper was tried at the Spring Assizes at Stafford in 1843 for sedition, conspiracy and arson.

'*Go to, ye rich men...Lord God of Hosts*'. James 5: 1, 4.

275 *trials...quite hackneyed subjects, stock properties for the fiction-mongers*. Perhaps a reference to the popularity of the 'Newgate' novel, so called because of its concern with criminals. Bulwer's *Pelham* (1828), *Paul Clifford* (1830), *Eugene Aram* (1832), Dickens's *Oliver Twist* (1837-8), and Ainsworth's *Jack Shepherd* (1839), all featured an account of a trial.

277 '*naught was everything, and everything was naught*'. James and Horatio Smith, *Rejected Addresses*, no. viii, 'Cui bono?'.

as 'the doctor' and his friends did before the riots of 1839. Doctor Peter Murray McDouall was tried for sedition and attending unlawful meetings following the Birmingham riots in 1839. He was sentenced to twelve months' imprisonment. Such rumours as this about the Chartists' attitude to property were widespread. See Gammage, pp. 157-8.

dressed up as starving labourers, and rheumatic old women. Thomas Cooper posed on one occasion as a commercial traveller. McDouall is said to have stayed in Leeds disguised as a working man after a proclamation offering fifty pounds for his capture. See Cooper, pp. 195–6, 201–2; Gammage, pp. 163, 228–9.

278 *Jourdan Coupe-tête at Lyons*. General Mathieu Jouve Jourdan, responsible for a horrible massacre at Avignon in 1791, was notorious for his cruelty, as his nickname suggests.

king of the Munster Anabaptists. The Anabaptists, an extreme religious sect, captured the city of Munster in 1532, and are supposed to have tried to establish a holy kingdom there.

poor Somerville. Alexander Somerville; the quotation is from his *The Autobiography of a Working Man* by One Who has Whistled at the Plough (1848).

279 *'Let him that is without sin amang ye, cast the first stane!'* John 8: 7.

281 *you should have seen *** and *** after the row in '42*. In 1842 the Chartists tried to organize a general strike, to continue until the provisions of the Charter were enacted by Parliament. After riots in the Potteries, Thomas Cooper and John Richards conducted their own defence at Stafford Assizes, and subsequently at the court of the Queen's Bench in London. See Cooper, pp. 217–18, 229–36; *Letters and Memories*, I, p. 221.

the Bull Ring. See above, note for p. 191.

282 *Thebaid anchorite*. i.e. an early Christian hermit in the Thebaid (upper Egypt). Compare Kingsley's *The Hermits*.

Mahomet in his Arabian cave. Before he began his ministry, Mahomet used to retire to meditate to a cave in Mt. Hira, near Mecca.

286 *if . . . punishments are inflicted only to reform the criminal*. Carlyle describes a visit to a model prison, and attacks the new humanitarian attitude to prisoners in *Latter Day*

Pamphlets (1850), *Works of Carlyle*, XX, p. 73: 'Indeed, it is wonderful to hear what account we at present give ourselves of the punishment of criminals; No "revenge" – O Heavens, no;...It is for the purpose of improving the poor criminal himself.'

287   ignoratio elenchi. An argument that appears to refute an opponent while actually disproving something not advanced by him.

288   '*Paley's Evidences*'. William Paley, *A View of the Evidences of Christianity* (1794), a work arguing the genuineness of the Christian revelation.

'*attacking extinct Satans*'. See note for p. 21, above.

Volney, and Tom Paine. The Comte de Volney (1757–1820), author of a well-known work of a radical and atheistic tendency, called *Les Ruines, ou Méditations sur les Revolutions des Empires*; Thomas Paine (1737–1809), author of *The Rights of Man*, a defence of the French Revolution.

Strauss, Hennell. D. F. Strauss, who in *Das Leben Jesu* (1835) attempted to show that the gospel narrative was mainly a collection of myths. George Eliot published a translation of the fourth edition in 1846. Charles Christian Hennell wrote *Inquiry concerning the Origin of Christianity* (1838), and *Christian Theism* (1839).

289   *as Carlyle says; 'not by noisy theoretic laudation... demonstration of* the *Church*'. 'That certain human souls, living on this practical Earth, should think to save themselves and a ruined world by noisy theoretic demonstrations and laudations of *the* Church, instead of sane, unnoisy, unconscious, but *practical*, total, heart-and-soul demonstration of *a* Church...this also was a thing we were to see'. *Past and Present, Works of Carlyle*, X, p. 117.

I looked back upon her delight in Gideon and Barak, Samson and Jehu. See note for p. 7, above.

the fifth-monarchy men. These were English fanatics of the seventeenth century, who believed that the second coming of Christ was imminent, and Christians must seek to establish the kingdom of God by force. The name comes from Dan. 2: 36–44.

290 *the whole of Hume, and Hallam's 'Middle Ages' and 'Constitutional History'.* David Hume's *History of Great Britain* (1754–61); Henry Hallam's *A View of the State of Europe during the Middle Ages* (1818) and *The Constitutional History of England* (1827).

to send me Proudhon and Louis Blanc. Apparently Proudhon's *Qu'est-ce que la propriété* (1840) and *Avertissement aux propriétaires* (1842), and Louis Blanc's *L'Organisation du travail* (1839). Louis Blanc (1811–82) was a socialist politician and historian.

292 *as Mr. Tennyson says in one of his most exquisite lyrics.* 'The Poet's Song.'

293 *freestone.* fine-grained sandstone or limestone.

294 *'sportula'.* A gift or fee given by patricians. It might be a small basket of food, whence the name, which means 'little basket'.

stickit. (Scots) merely short-lived.

Puseyite sectarians. Ultra High Church supporters of E. B. Pusey.

295 *clanjamfries.* (Scots) affairs.

tocher. (Scots) dowry.

He's na laird o' Cockpen, for a penniless lass wi' a long pedigree. In the anonymous poem 'The Laird o'Cockpen', the laird seeks in marriage a lady so described.

Louis Philippe is doun! Louis Philippe of France abdicated on 24 February 1848, and went into exile in England. He was popularly rumoured to have arrived with only a few possessions: 'The whole of the luggage which the party brought was a small portmanteau about a foot long.' *The Daily News*, 4 March 1848. In fact, he seems to have been unofficially assisted in exile by the British government. He died here two years later.

Puir lustful Reubens that they are!...not excel. Gen. 49: 3–4.

296 *A glorious people vibrated again...sublime and strong.*
The opening of Shelley's 'Ode to Liberty', adapted to the
context.

*what things, as Carlyle says, men will fall down and
worship in their extreme need!* Compare 'Under baleful
Atheisms, Mammonisms, Joe-Manton Dilettantisms, with
their appropriate Cants and Idolisms, and whatsoever
scandalous rubbish obscures and all but extinguishes the
soul of man, – religion now is.' *Past and Present, Works of
Carlyle*, X, p. 230.

The shadow...olive-tinctured brow. Shelley's 'Ode to
Liberty', st. ix.

296–7 *Were Magna Charta...the calm, righteous might of
1688.* All four were milestones in the rights of the common people. Hampden: see note for p. 13, above. In 1688
Parliament deposed James II for attempting to subvert the
constitution, violating the fundamental laws, and with-
drawing from the kingdom.

'If we confess our sins...all unrighteousness'. 1 John 1: 9.

*for there were men, stancher Chartists...scattered to the
winds.* The description fits pretty well the famous 'moral
force' Chartist leader, William Lovett.

298 *The old laws of England...Liberty!* Shelley's 'The Mask
of Anarchy', st. lxxxii.

299 *Louis' spies...addition of tyranny.* Left-wing political
societies and public political meetings were illegal in
France in 1848. German activists sought the unification of
Germany, and it was feared the rulers of the states might
retain power by alliances with France and Russia. Hungary
was ruled by the Habsburg Emperors of Austria, who were
thought to disregard the provisions of the constitution in
the Austrian interest.

recollecting 1688. See note for p. 296, above.

299–300 *the very few men who told them this...the suffrage.*
When Thomas Workley, Radical MP, proposed an extension of the franchise in the House of Commons on 20

Nov. 1837, Lord John Russell, referring to the Reform Act of 1832, said that they had planned 'an extensive measure'; 'in bringing forward the extensive measure we might be assured that we were bringing forward one which might have a prospect of being a final measure.' In all, only twenty-two members of the newly elected House had been in favour of further reform.

300 *their entreaties...laid by unanswered.* When the second Chartist National Petition was presented to the House of Commons in May 1842, it was moved that the petitioners should be heard at the bar of the House through their agents. The motion was defeated after a debate.

Lord Ashley. See note for p. 110, above.

They had been told...that in order to carry the Reform Bill, sedition itself was lawful. The Radical press advised: 'To those excluded from the Bill – Assist the Bill-men in the cause; but should you take arms in defence of Reform, do business on your own account. Defend the good cause, and claim equal rights.' J. R. M. Butler, *The Passing of the Great Reform Bill*, 1964 edn., p. 382.

the plug riots. The Plug Plot in Lancashire and elsewhere in 1842 was so called because striking workers drew the plugs from the boilers, so that no steam could be raised. It was rumoured that manufacturers who belonged to the Anti-Corn Law League had planned to provoke strikes by wage reductions and lock-outs.

'Manchester should march upon London'. Molesworth, the nineteenth-century historian, declared that Manchester was the centre of 'a lawless turbulence which embarrassed the Government...and dismayed the inhabitants of more favourable parts of the kingdom'. It was often believed that 'if England was to have a revolution on the French model...it would begin in Manchester'. Ed. A. Briggs, *Chartist Studies*, 1959, p. 29.

'the black pool of Agio'. 'Agio' then meant the percentage difference of value between standard money and a depressed and fluctuating ordinary currency. The whole

phrase clearly indicates a money market such as, for example, the Paris bourse.

301 *vol. ii, p. 315, of the Second Edition.* The chapter in Mill referred to foresees a growing independence of working men through better education, more political and civil rights for both sexes, and eventually efforts at cooperative industry, in which the workers not only share in the profits but may become masters themselves.

they're going…to revive some old law or other. The Chartists intended in 1848 to carry the third National Petition to the House of Commons in a great procession, but on 7 April it was proclaimed that such a procession would be opposed by armed force. The banning was justified by reference to a seventeenth-century statute, which however had been disregarded when the second petition was presented.

302 *make the bar of the house crack again.* The Bar consists of two rods which can be drawn across the ends of the benches to form the boundary of the House. Crossthwaite is perhaps alluding to the famous occasion on 20 April 1653, when Cromwell and thirty soldiers hoped to bring about the dissolution of Parliament if the House of Commons rejected their petition.

there's the answer we got. Compare *Cheap Clothes and Nasty*, where a similar reply from the Admiralty is reproduced in full.

304 *the Convention.* The Chartist National Convention assembled in the John Street Institution on 4 April 1848.

Macerone on street-warfare. Francis Maceroni, *Defensive Instructions for the People: containing the new and improved combinations of arms, called Foot Lancers, miscellaneous instructions on the subject of small arms and ammunitions, street and house fighting, and field fortifications* (1832).

I read Somerville's answer to that Colonel Macerone. Alexander Somerville, *Warnings to the People on Street Welfare, Letter I*, May 1839, in which he systematically refutes Maceroni's arguments. The latter's book contained ludicrous and dangerously misleading statements. Somerville quotes some of them: 'Those who rush upon the cannon's mouth are far less liable to be injured by it than they who hesitate, or flee', and 'Any regular troops must be instantly destroyed if you can but once close upon them with your lances.'

304–5 *There's a man, Power, or Bower.* The story of the *agent provocateur* which follows is based on incidents involving Thomas Cooper, who probably described them to Kingsley himself. See Cooper, pp. 303–8. But Power also resembles a police agent called Powell who gave evidence at the trials of certain Chartists in the summer of 1848. He admitted: 'I encouraged and stimulated these men, in order to inform against them. I gave the men some bullets.' Gammage, pp. 338–40.

305 *"Mort au voleurs".* Compare *The French Revolution, Works of Carlyle,* III, p. 118, where there is a description of the citizens sacking the Castries Hotel and destroying its contents; 'amid steady popular cheers, absolutely without theft: for there goes a cry, "He shall be hanged that steals a nail".'

Men of England...they are few. A merging of two stanzas (xxxvii–viii) of Shelley's 'The Mask of Anarchy' (1832), written on the occasion of the 'Peterloo' massacre at Manchester.

306 *in John-street.* i.e. in the Literary and Scientific Institution, John Street. It was a building leased to Owenite Socialists, where lectures and meetings were held.

307 *the descendant of the ancient kings.* O'Connor is said to have believed his family to be descended from Roderick O'Connor, one time high king of Ireland.

little Cuffy. William Cuffy (1787–1870), a London East End tailor and Chartist. He was transported for life in the summer of 1848, and did not return to England.

308 *'in his right mind' – though not yet 'clothed'.* Mark 5: 15.

as shure as there's no snakes in ould Ireland. According to legend, St. Patrick drove all snakes out of Ireland.

the three hundred thousint vargens o' Wexford. Kelly invents female casualties and exaggerates the number slain at this Irish town, stormed by Cromwell in 1649. According to Carlyle, Cromwell reported the casualties in his despatches as being two thousand armed men.

Rhadamanthine grasp. Rhadamanthus compelled the dead in hell to confess their crimes, and punished them.

311 *Jones.* Ernest Jones (1819–68), a writer and barrister who became the main Chartist leader in the Movement's last phase. He gave up the editorship of the *Northern Star* in May 1848 to serve as a member of the National Assembly (see following note), and in July was sentenced to two years' imprisonment for sedition. See further John Saville, *Ernest Jones: Chartist* (1952).

312 *the John-street conspirators.* After the failure of the third Chartist National Petition, a National Assembly was elected. It met in the John Street Institution from 1 to 13 May 1848. There followed further political activity in London, including revolutionary plotting; and later in the summer five men were transported for life, and twenty-six sentenced to terms of imprisonment.

Dulce et decorum est pro patriâ mori. Horace, *Odes*, III, ii.

313 *a' crouse and cantie.* (Scots) all comfortable and snug.

ferlie. (Scots) wonderfully.

Monstrum horrendum . . . ademptum. 'A monster horrible, misshapen, huge, deprived of sight.' *Aeneid*, III, l. 658.

Desinit in piscem mulier formosa superne. 'There ends in a fish a woman lovely above.' Horace, *Ars Poetica*, l. 4.

sealgh's fud. Seal's tail.

long nose . . . dizen o' Queens. The 1848 Petition contained the names of Pug Nose and Flat Nose, and also Victoria Rex and Duke of Wellington.

314 *Cartwright.* See above, note for p. 205.

that cheerit Burdett . . . Cobbett. Sir Francis Burdett, the

Member for Westminster, was sent to the Tower in 1810 for questioning Parliament's right to imprison a man for libelling its members; Henry Hunt (1773–1835), the radical politician known as Orator Hunt, who was one of the main leaders of the reform agitation before 1820; William Cobbett was imprisoned in 1810 and heavily fined for his outspoken comments in his *Political Register*.

the Ninety-three. The French Revolution.

spunk. (Scots) spark.

carlins. (Scots) women.

fire-flaught. (Scots) flash of light.

315 *I'd apocartereeze*. I'd starve myself.

Canst thou administer to a mind diseased? Compare *Macbeth*, V. iii.

puddins. (Scots) intestines.

Non tribus Anticyris! 'Not by three Anticyras.' Horace, *Ars Poetica*, l. 300. The Aegean island of Anticyra was famous for the growing of black hellebore, a plant used to treat madness.

Juvat insanire. 'It is pleasant to be mad.' Horace, *Odes*, III, xix.

this their way is their folly. Ps. 49: 13.

as auld Benjamin o' Tudela saith of the heathen. Compare Thomas Wright (ed.), *The Travels of Rabbi Benjamin of Tudela* (1848), p. 80. Rabbi Benjamin was a Jewish traveller who died in 1173.

"Forty years lang...his rest." Ps. 95: 10, 11.

We twa hae paidlit in the burn. Compare Burns's version of the song.

316 *'he babbled of green fields'*. *Henry V*. II. iii. Said of the dying Falstaff.

I went to the kirk...my deary. Compare Burns's song 'Ay waukin, O.'

coft. (Scots) bought.

wynd. (Scots) lane.

Abraham o' a blue-gown: Inmates of Bedlam who were not dangerous were kept in Abraham Ward and allowed out in distinctive dress. Hence harmless lunatics generally, and beggars pretending to be mad, were called Abraham Men.

a bit crowd, or *a fizzle-pipe.* A rude fiddle, or a whistle.

the Bush aboon Traquair. An old Scots song, possibly composed by Robert Crawford.

317 *Oh the broom...Cowden-knowes!* The first two lines of the refrain of 'The Broom of Cowdenknowe', an old Scots song. Knowe: small hill.

listering. (Scots) spearing.

birks. (Scots) trees.

skelping an' skirling. (Scots) skipping and shrieking.

because he didna a'thegither understand the honour due to His name. After lengthy and obscure pronouncements about the Trinity and the Incarnation, the Athanasian creed says 'This is the Catholick Faith: which except a man believe faithfully, he cannot be saved.'

Cameronian sort o' body. i.e. strict Presbyterian and Scots separatist. The Cameronians, named after the Revd. Richard Cameron, were a sect of strict Presbyterians who fanatically opposed the Act of Union of England and Scotland passed in 1707.

318 *a' naked in the matter o' formulae, as Maister Tummas has it. Past and Present, Works of Carlyle*, X, p. 127.

Sae I'm wearing awa...leal. From 'The Land o' the Leal', by Caroline Nairne. Leal: loyal.

When Razor-brigg...thy sawle. A version of the second and third stanzas of the northern chant 'A Lyke Wake Dirge'. Brigg: bridge. Whinny Muir: Furze Heath. Pike thee intil the bane: pick you to the bone. Lyke: corpse. Wake: watching.

There's mair things...our philosophy. Compare *Hamlet*, I. v.

the worm that dieth not, and the fire that is not quenched. Isa. 66: 24.

319 *Tooke and Cartwright.* John Horne Tooke (1736–1812) the radical politician and philologist; Major John Cartwright, 'the Father of Reform' (see note for p. 205). There was a considerable reform campaign about 1780, which led to the founding of the Society for Promoting Constitutional Information, and the introduction of two unsuccessful Parliamentary bills by the younger Pitt in 1882 and 1885. Cartwright stimulated the founding of the Society, and Horne Tooke was a prominent member.

320 *there was love...woman.* 2 Sam. 1: 26.

323 *so young, yet so untender!* King Lear, I. i.

thousands of special constables. 120,000, according to the estimate in *The Annual Register*, 1848.

324 *The meeting...numbered hardly its tens of thousands.* The number present was estimated by *The Times* to be 20,000, including bystanders. The official estimates were similar.

'inextinguishable laughter'. Shelley, *Prometheus Unbound*, Act IV, l. 334.

Careless of mankind...endless anguish! Part of the Choric Song in Tennyson's 'The Lotus Eaters', slightly altered. 'And praying hands' is italicized because a petition in due form to the House of Commons includes a 'prayer' expressing its object.

328 *the pan of charcoal.* i.e. committing suicide by inhaling fumes from burning charcoal.

they are the very experimentum crucis. i.e. they are absolutely the crucial test.

as Porcia died – as Cato. Porcia, the wife of Marcus Brutus, is said to have resolutely killed herself after her husband's defeat and death. Her father Cato, 'the conscience of Rome', had earlier killed himself to avoid capture by Julius Caesar.

329 *Jacob's Island tea.* Jacob's Island was a slum area south of

the river, and immediately to the east of St. Saviour's Dock. It was surrounded by a broad ditch, connected to the Thames, which served both as a sewer and a water supply. Mayhew drew attention to the conditions there in an article 'The Cholera Districts of Bermondsey' in the *Morning Chronicle*, 24 September 1849; and Kingsley, after a visit, promoted a campaign for proper sanitation. 'As we passed along the reeking banks of the sewer the sun shone upon a narrow lip of water. In the bright light it appeared the colour of strong green tea.' Mayhew, op. cit.

The rats – the rats! The latter part of this chapter is reminiscent of the pursuit and death of Bill Sykes in *Oliver Twist* (1837–8). He too has a terrifying vision, is sought by the police in Jacob's Island, and meets his death at Folly Ditch, as it was called.

330–1 *by the law of competition...true creator and preserver of the universe.* Compare Mill's *Principles of Political Economy*, Bk. II, ch. iv, § 1 and Bk. IV, ch. vii, § 7.

334 *the curse of Rabshakeh.* i.e. having to consume one's own excreta. 2 Kgs. 18: 27.

335 *giant deodars...trees of flame.* Compare A. von Humboldt's *Cosmos*, (London, 1848–9), I. p. 9. Deodar: a species of cedar.

malaria. i.e. bad air, due to the swampy ground.

336 *Nundi.* The bull on which, in Hindu mythology, the god Siva rides.

Kali. A goddess who is Siva's wife, who also however has other forms. She is represented as a woman with long hair and four arms, who wears a necklace of human skulls. She beheaded a giant, and drank his blood.

as the angels did Faust's. Compare the conclusion of Goethe's *Faust*, Pt. II.

madrepore. An organism which produces branching coral.

337 *remora.* The sucking-fish, so called on account of a suction disc on its head. It was an ancient belief that it could stop a ship to which it attached itself.

simoom wind. A hot, dust-laden wind which sweeps in a narrow path across deserts.

spotted ounce. A cat of the leopard family. It was formerly supposed to be used for hunting in Persia, but this was by confusion with the cheetah.

338 *mylodon*. An extinct genus of gigantic sloth.

give my namesake's philosophy the lie. See John Locke's *Essay Concerning Human Understanding* (1690).

339 *Cordillera*. A name for the mountains of the Andes.

339-40 *But, wonders of wonders!...perfumed the air*. Compare Lane's *The Arabian Nights' Entertainments*, III, p. 523; Ovid's *Metamorphoses*, Bk. IX, 'The Fable of Dryope'; Bk. X, 'Hyacinthus Transformed into a Flower'.

340 *the famous land of Wak-Wak*. Seven islands in 'The Story of Hasan of El-Basrah' in *The Arabian Nights*.

'*held them with his glittering eye*'. Compare Coleridge, 'The Rime of the Ancient Mariner', Pt. I.

edentate. An animal without incisor and canine teeth. The mylodon had a few cylindrical teeth.

342 *Van Helmont's dreams of the Archæus*. Jan Baptista van Helmont, a seventeenth-century Flemish doctor and chemist, developed following Paracelsus a theory of the Archæus, a vital principle supposed to be present in living things. He is said to have thought that in humans it was situated in the stomach.

343 *All-Father*. A title of Odin, the chief Scandinavian god, in the Icelandic *Eddas*.
the Holy Mountain. See note for p. 349, below.

349 *children of Japhet*. See Gen. 10.

the holy mountain of Paradise. This seems to be a mountain in the Pamirs area, north-west of Kashmir, which Kingsley identifies with Mount Meru, the Hindu home of the gods. Mount Meru is north of the Himalayas, and associated with four rivers. It is immediately south of the Land of the Blessed, and is the centre of the world.

the Asgard of the Hindoo-Koh. Asgard: home of the gods in Scandinavian mythology. The Hindu-Koh: the 'Indian Caucasus', the great mountain complex of the Hindu Kush, the Pamirs and the Himalayas.

the cup of the four rivers. The mountain knot of the Pamirs, the four rivers being the Indus, Oxus, Jaxartes and Tarim.

351 *G. T. T.* i.e. 'Gone to Texas'. Absconding gentry used to mark 'G.T.T.' on the doors of their abandoned dwellings, for the information of enquiring creditors.

353 *à Kempis*. i.e. the fifteenth-century devotional work *Of the Imitation of Christ*, attributed to Thomas à Kempis.

354 *My soul...sweet singing*. Shelley, *Prometheus Unbound*, II. v. 72–4, slightly altered to suit the context.

355 *'Depart from me, for I am a sinful man, O Lord!* Luke, 5: 8.

as Diotima may have talked of old. In Plato's *Symposium*, Socrates relates how Diotima of Mantineia explained to him the nature of love.

359 *when the Roman lady...tent-maker*. Acts 16: 14–17. St. Paul was a tent-maker. Acts 18: 1–3.

"One is our Master, even Christ...all brothers." Matt. 23: 8.

Cameronians. See note for p. 317, above.

360 *When Camille Desmoulins..."bon sans-culotte Jesus"*. Compare *The French Revolution, Works of Carlyle*, IV, p. 257. Camille Desmoulins was a supporter of Danton, and was executed with him in April 1794.

breaking the bruised reed, and quenching the smoking flax. Isa. 42: 3.

"I shall see Him, but not nigh; I shall behold Him, but not near". Num. 24: 17.

Zerdusht and Confutzee, for aught we know, were nobler still. Little is in fact known about the life of Zoroaster (Zerdusht); he seems to have lived about 600 BC, and the tradition is that he was a priest. Little too is known for certain about the life of Confucius (Kung Fu tse). He was born in Shantung, about the same time.

mystagogues. i.e. teacher of mystical doctrines.

Emersons and Strausses. See notes for pp. 208, 288, above.

361 *with that alone he freed half Europe.* Freed it, that is, from the authority of the Roman Catholic priesthood.

"*You are mine...in an everlasting covenant.*" Jer. 32: 38–40.

362 "*I have said, ye are gods...children of the Most Highest*". Gal. 3: 26–30.

"*children of God...and of His bones*". 1 Cor. 12: 12–27, Eph. 5: 30.

"*kings and priests to God*". Rev. 1: 6.

"*Behold, the days come...saith the Lord!*" Joel 2: 28–29, Jer. 31: 34.

"*Go to, let us build us a city...reach to heaven*". Gen. 11: 4.

363 "*Without observation,*" *as He promised.* Luke 17: 20.

They have cried "*Lo here!*" *and* "*Lo there!*" Luke 17: 21.

365 *those miserable, awful, farce-tragedies of April and June.* The two occasions in 1848 when the London Chartists planned an insurrection, with unsuccessful result.

Believe that your kingdom...will not make haste. John 18: 36, Isa. 28: 16.

Strauss. See note for p. 288, above.

368 *as Mr. Grove has well shown...pamphlet.* W. R. Grove's *On the Correlation of Physical Forces* (1846), which became well-known and was reprinted a number of times. He discussed the conversion of forces of different kinds into one another, anticipating perhaps the later idea of the conservation of energy.

It "*bloweth where it listeth...it goeth*". John 3: 8.

when the Scribes and Pharisees...be made bread." Matt. 4: 3; 12: 38–9.

368-9 *St. Augustine answered that objection centuries ago.* In *De Trinitate*, Bk. III, v, pp. 8ff., where he writes: 'Who draws up the sap through the root of the vine to the bunch of grapes, and makes the wine, except God…But when, at the command of the Lord, the water was turned into wine with an extraordinary quickness, the divine power was made manifest.'

369 *Wine is sap…wine as good.* Mephistopheles performs his own 'miracle' in the cellar in Leipzig in a scene of Goethe's *Faust*, when he bores a hole in the table before each drinker and each is provided with his choice of wine. *Faust*, Pt. I, ll. 762-3.

Time and space are no Gods, as a wise German says. Compare Carlyle, *Sartor Resartus*, Bk. III, ch. viii: 'Time and Space are not God, but the creations of God.'

you must go to the Popish legends. The lives of the saints described many such miracles. Eleven were said to have carried away their heads after decapitation.

the death of Jairus's daughter, of the widow's son at Nain. Mark 6: 22-43; Luke 7: 11-16.

370 *Bacon's golden rule – "Nature is conquered by obeying her".* Compare *Novum Organon*, Bk. I, Aphorism cxxix: 'Nor the empire of man over things is founded on the arts and sciences alone, for Nature is only to be commanded by obeying her.'

the inventors of the calculating machine, and the electric telegraph. These are usually supposed to be Charles Babbage and Samuel Morse.

the surgeons of St. George's. See note for p. 61, above. The eminent surgeon Sir Benjamin Collins Brodie (1783-1862) worked at St. George's, and was President of the Royal College of Surgeons in 1844. He had published a treatise *On the Pathology and Surgery of Diseases of the Joints* in 1819.

371 *The mesmerist…can cure a spirit of infirmity, an hysteric or paralytic patient.* Harriet Martineau believed herself to have been cured of a five years' illness by

mesmerism. In *Letters on Mesmerism* (1845) she writes, 'I felt as if my life were fed from day to day. The vital force infused or induced was as clear and certain as the strength given by food.' See note for p. 197, above.

374 *From Bentham and Malthus to Fourier and Proudhon.* For Malthus and Proudhon, see the notes for pp. 112 and 290, above. François Marie Charles Fourier (1772–1837) was a French social philosopher who much influenced some of the Christian Socialists. He devised a system in which the population was divided into phalanxes, or small communist groups.

Hairoun Alraschid. Caliph of Bagdad 784–809 and well-known from *The Arabian Nights' Entertainments*, where he is described as a benevolent man, living in great splendour.

"How hardly shall they that have riches enter into the kingdom of heaven". Mark 10: 23.

375 *I tried association among my own sex.* See Introduction.

377 *Hildebrand.* Gregory VII, an eleventh-century Pope who engaged much in secular politics.

379 *"lighted the candle in England that shall never be put out".* Hugh Latimer, sometime Bishop of Worcester, is said to have said as the flame was applied to the pyre on which he was burned alive with Ridley: 'Be of good comfort, Master Ridley, and play the man; we shall this day light such a candle, by God's grace, in England, as I trust shall never be put out.'

Who, by suffering, and not by rebellion, drove the last perjured Stuart from his throne…progress. This refers to the trial of seven bishops in 1688 for seditiously libelling King James II. They were acquitted, but the disaffection of the Anglican clergy must have been increased, and may have contributed to the deposition of the king the following year.

381 *non est tanti vivere.* 'Living is not worthwhile.'

383 *I dare not fly, like Jonah, from the call of God.* Jonah 1: 3. *the Cordilleras.* The Andes.

His still small voice reproving me...What doest thou here, Elijah? 1 Kgs. 19: 12–13.

"*The stone which the builders rejected is become the head-stone of the corner*". Ps. 118: 22.

Naseby fights and Smithfield fires. See notes for pp. 7 and 13, above. Martyrs were burned at the stake at Smithfield during the persecution under Queen Mary.

the conquerors of Hindostan. Kingsley probably means Robert Clive, Warren Hastings and Lord Wellesley.

384 *I have longed to find some noble soul, as Carlyle says, fallen down by the wayside.* Compare *The Life of Schiller, Works of Carlyle*, XXV, p. 43: 'Many are the noble souls that have perished bitterly, with their tasks unfinished, under these corroding woes!'

385 *the reclaimed Magdalene.* Luke 7: 37–50.

386 *Lord! not as I will, but as thou wilt!* Matt. 26: 39.

"*In your patience possess ye your souls, for the coming of the Lord draweth nigh*". Luke 21: 19; James 5: 8.

387 *Lord, I believe! Help thou mine unbelief!* Mark 9: 24.

'*while the parting day dies like the dolphin*'. Byron's *Childe Harold's Pilgrimage*, can. iv, st. 29.

388 *The iron has entered too deeply into my soul.* Compare the translation of Psalm 105 in *The Book of Common Prayer*.

a good land and large...flowing with milk and honey. Ex. 3: 8.

the forest shall break forth...blossom like the rose. Isa. 35: 1; 55: 12.

It blesseth him that gives and him that takes. The Merchant of Venice, IV. i.

389 '*Good Time Coming*'. See note for p. 52, above.

"*the clear down-shining after rain*". 2 Sam. 23:4.

389–90 *Weep, weep, weep...stay it?* Included revised in Kingsley's *Poems*, under the title 'Alton Locke's Song'.